THE BLACK PRINCE

ALSO BY MICHAEL JONES

Bosworth 1485

THE
BLACK PRINCE

England's Greatest Medieval Warrior

MICHAEL JONES

PEGASUS BOOKS
NEW YORK LONDON

THE BLACK PRINCE

Pegasus Books, Ltd.
148 West 37th Street, 13th Floor
New York, NY 10018

First Pegasus Books paperback edition September 2019
First Pegasus Books hardcover edition May 2018

ISBN: 978-1-64313-229-7

10 9 8 7 6 5 4 3 2

Printed in the United States of America
Distributed by Simon & Schuster
www.pegasusbooks.com

CONTENTS

A NOTE ON NOMENCLATURE, CURRENCY AND SOURCES

Nomenclature

Following usual convention, I have anglicized the names of the kings of France and members of the House of Valois, and also the dukes of Brittany and Burgundy. Medieval noblemen are usually referred to by their aristocratic title. However, when that title frequently changes, I have followed the convention of using their place of birth, for example in the case of Henry of Grosmont, who was successively earl of Derby, then earl and duke of Lancaster; and for John of Gaunt, who succeeded to the duchy of Lancaster after Grosmont's death. For clarity I have anglicized the Christian name of Peter IV of Aragon, but not his contemporary Pedro of Castile. To avoid confusion between the subject of this book, Edward of Woodstock, and his father, Edward III, I have for the former frequently used the appellation 'the Black Prince' or 'the Prince' (capitalizing to distinguish him from his younger brothers), even though it is a later term.

Measurements

Heights and dimensions are given using the metric system, with the imperial equivalent in brackets, and distances using the imperial system, with the metric equivalent in brackets.

Currency

In the fourteenth century England used a silver standard of currency. The unit of account was the pound sterling (£) which was equal to one and a half marks of silver. The pound was divided into twenty shillings (s), each of twelve pence (d). There was also, from 1344, a gold coinage based on the noble, which was conventionally worth 6s 8d, but was rarely used. It would, however, be significant in the calculation of the ransom of King John II and also in the introduction of gold coinage into Gascony and then the principality of Aquitaine by the Black Prince.

France also used a silver standard. The units of account were the *livre tournois*, the pound of Tours, and the *livre bordelaise*, the pound of Bordeaux, which was used in the duchy of Gascony, and would also be the currency for the principality of Aquitaine. These were also divided into twenty shillings (*sous*) and twelve pence (*deniers*). The pound sterling was worth five *livres tournois* and five *livres bordelaises*. The French gold coin, the *écu d'or* (so named because the king was shown on the obverse side holding a heraldic shield (*écu*) but also referred to as a crown, was minted between 1337 and 1355. It was initially worth about 4s sterling, but by the time of the Black Prince's raid in 1355 the quality had been reduced and its value had fallen to slightly less than 3s. In the ransom negotiations with John II the rate of the *écu* was fixed at half a noble, that is 3s 4d. One of the many achievements of Charles V would be to mint a coinage that kept a stable value.

The gold florin of Florence circulated in both countries and was the nearest thing to an international standard of value in fourteenth-century Europe. It was worth slightly less than 3s. The Black Prince's campaign in Spain in 1367 also gave rise to a number of transactions in the Castilian gold coin the *dobla*, which was struck in quantity from the reign of Alfonso XI and was worth a little less than 4s.

On his arrival in Bordeaux in September 1355 the Black Prince introduced a gold coin, the *léopard*, into Gascon currency (on 29 September), as an equivalent to the English noble (6s 8d), although its real value in the late 1350s was actually a little over six shillings sterling. On the creation of the principality of Aquitaine in July 1362 he was granted the right to strike gold and silver coin in his own name and image. The two most interesting gold coins are the *pavillon d'or* (struck in 1364, and described in the text, in Chapter Seven), and the *hardi d'or*, struck in the summer of 1368. Again, both were equivalents of the English noble.

The *hardi d'or* was the result of negotiations with the estates of Aquitaine at Angoulême in January 1368 where, in return for the right to levy the *fouage*, the Prince promised to keep currency values stable (the gold content of the *pavillon* had dropped, reducing its value to around 5s 6d sterling). Its design suggests an intimation of the troubles ahead. It features a prominent display of the Prince's sword, held aloft with the militant reverse legend 'My strength comes from the Lord', as if already anticipating a French attack. But within months of it being minted, the Black Prince was confined to his bed with illness.

Sources

The unfolding narrative of the Black Prince's life draws on a wide variety of sources, primary and secondary, which are listed in the Bibliography and referred to in the Notes. Some brief comments should be made about one particular source, the life of the Prince composed (around 1385) by the Chandos Herald. We do not know this Herald's name, but he probably came from Hainault and he and the chronicler Jean Froissart seem to have known each other (Froissart uses his work, particularly for the Prince's expedition to Spain in 1367). The Herald was in the Black Prince's service in Aquitaine in the 1360s and it is his account of the Nájera campaign, of which he was an eye-witness, that is of particular interest.

Extracts from the Chandos Herald are rendered in prose, although in its original form it was a French poem of some 4,000 words. Its modern title of convenience, 'The Life of the Black Prince', would have probably bewildered its medieval author, whose intention was to describe the 'feats of arms', the chivalric credentials, of his hero 'the most noble Prince of Wales and Aquitaine'. The poem exists in two manuscripts: one held at Worcester College, Oxford, the other at Senate House Library, University of London (Mildred Pope and Eleanor Lodge made a reliable prose translation from the former in 1910; Diana Tyson compared both texts in 1975). It is laudatory and uncritical and – like all primary source material – needs to be used with care. And yet the sense of drama that unfolds within its pages, as the Prince's army crosses the Pyrenees by the pass of Roncesvalles in atrocious winter weather, and camps out before the battle of Nájera (fought on 'a fair and beautiful plain, where there was neither bush nor tree') in an orchard, under the olive trees, reminds us that at heart the Black Prince's life is a powerful human story – and one of both triumph and tragedy.

IMAGE CREDITS

Chapter openers
Images from 'William Bruges's Garter Book', 1430–40, a pictorial book of arms of the Order of the Garter; British Library.

1. Edward III; 2. Edward, Prince of Wales; 3. Sir John Chandos; 4. Sir James Audley; 5. Jean de Grailly, Captal de Buch; 6. Thomas, earl of Warwick; 7. Henry of Grosmont; 8. Sir Nigel Loring; 9. Sir Bartholomew Burghersh; 10. Sir Thomas Holland; 11. William, earl of Salisbury.

Plate section
Images 1, 2, 3, 10, 11, 12, 19 reproduced courtesy of the Dean and Chapter of Canterbury; 4 Robert Stainforth, wikimedia commons; 5 Sir Phillip Preston; 6 Chensiyuan, wikimedia commons; 7 anonymous, Louvre Museum; 8 Jean Froissart, *Chroniques*, Volume i; 9 Pinpin, wikimedia commons; 13 British Library; 14 Patrick Janiek; 15 British Museum; 16 Archaeological Museum of Spain; 17 Mary-Theresa Madill; 18 Louvre Museum.

LIST OF MAPS

1. The Black Prince's campaigns: 1346, 1355, 1356, 1359-60 and 1367.
2. The extent of the duchy of Gascony in 1355 and the principality of Aquitaine in 1363.
3. The Battle of Crécy, 26 August 1346.
4. The Battle of Poitiers, 19 September 1356.
5. The Battle of Nájera, 3 April 1367.

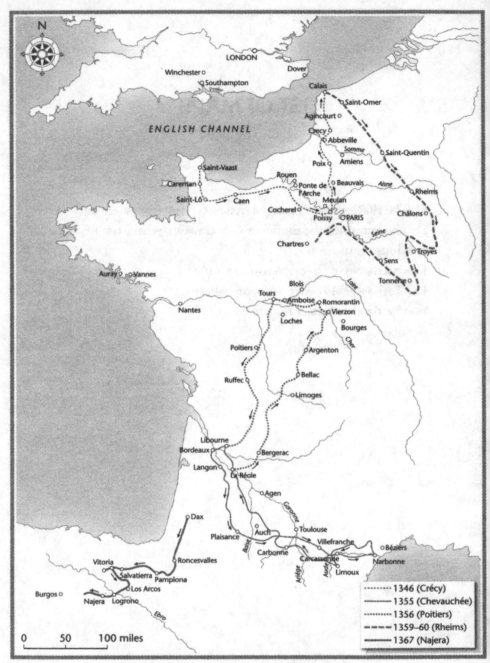

The Black Prince's Military Campaigns

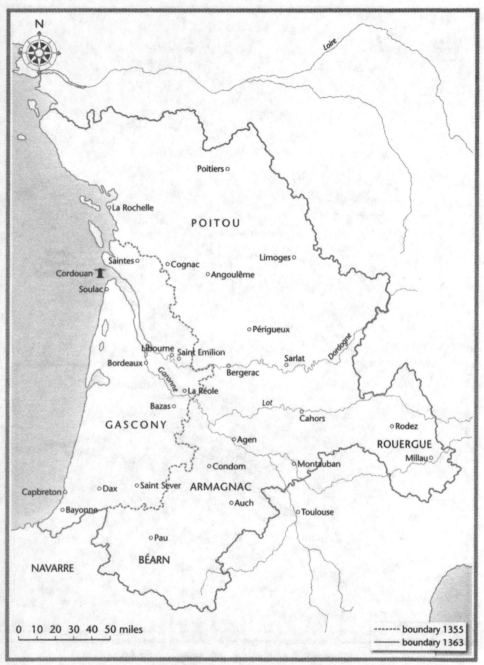

N

Loire

Poitiers

La Rochelle

POITOU

Saintes

Cordouan

Soulac

Cognac

Limoges

Angoulême

Périgueux

Dordogne

Libourne

Saint Emilion

Bordeaux

Garonne

Sarlat

Bergerac

La Réole

Bazas

GASCONY

Lot

Cahors

Rodez

Agen

ROUERGUE

Condom

Montauban

Millau

Capbreton

Dax

Saint Sever

ARMAGNAC

Auch

Bayonne

Toulouse

Pau

NAVARRE

BÉARN

0 10 20 30 40 50 miles

------- boundary 1355
———— boundary 1363

Aquitaine: 1355 and 1363

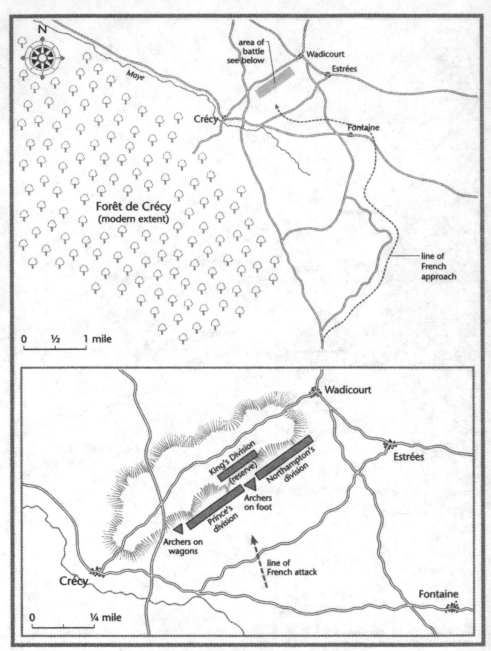

The Battle of Crécy, 26 August 1346
Dispositions at the start of the battle

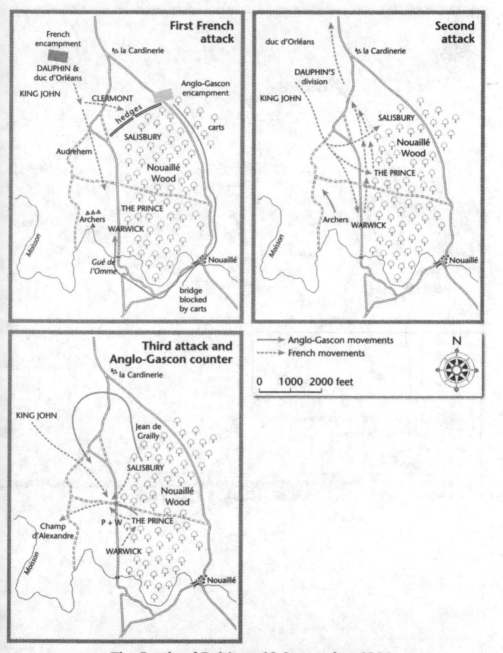

The Battle of Poitiers, 19 September 1356
(Based on Le Baker and the Anonimalle Chronicle)

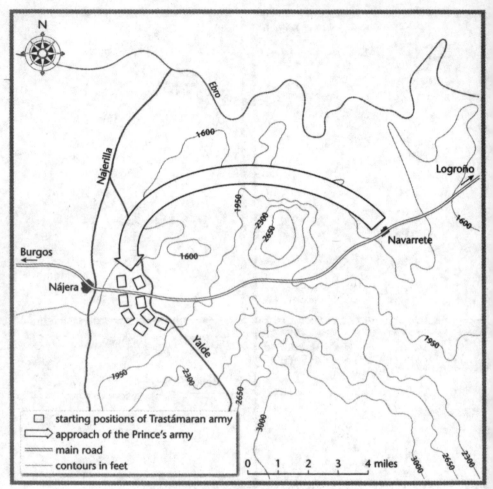

The Battle of Nájera, 3 April 1367

TIMELINE

15 JUNE 1330	Birth of Edward, eldest son of King Edward III and Queen Philippa of Hainault at Woodstock Palace, Oxfordshire; he is known to posterity as the Black Prince.
19 OCTOBER 1330	In a coup organized by Edward III and some of his closest supporters, Roger Mortimer, earl of March, the favourite of Queen Mother Isabella, is seized at Nottingham castle; the seventeen-year-old monarch now takes effective control over his kingdom.
29 NOVEMBER 1330	After a three-day trial Mortimer is executed for treason — one of the charges being the murder of the king's father, Edward II — and Isabella is effectively exiled from government and the court; she is placed in seclusion at Castle Rising in Norfolk.
16 JUNE 1332	Birth of the Prince's sister Isabella.
18 MARCH 1333	The Black Prince is created earl of Chester.
19 JULY 1333	Defeat of the Scots at Halidon Hill; Edward III avenges his father's defeat at Bannockburn.
c. FEBRUARY 1334	Birth of the Prince's sister Joan.
9 FEBRUARY 1337	The Black Prince is created duke of Cornwall.
16 JULY 1338– 21 FEBRUARY 1340	The Prince is appointed 'guardian of England' by his father, Edward, during the latter's absence on campaign. The Prince will also fill this role between 22 June and 30 November 1340, and between 5 October 1342 and 2 March 1343.
27 NOVEMBER 1338	Birth of the Prince's brother Lionel of Antwerp.
6 MARCH 1340	Birth of the Prince's brother John of Gaunt.

24 JUNE 1340	Edward III defeats French fleet in Battle of Sluys.
5 JUNE 1341	Birth of the Prince's brother Edmund of Langley.
28 APRIL 1343	The Black Prince is created Prince of Wales.
19–22 JANUARY 1344	A great tournament is held at Windsor, which culminates in Edward III's creation of the Order of the Round Table.
10 OCTOBER 1344	Birth of the Prince's sister Mary.
3 JULY 1345	The Black Prince and his father sail to Sluys for three weeks of negotiations concerning the future of the county of Flanders.
12 JULY 1346	Edward III and the Prince land at Saint-Vaast-la-Hogue in the Cotentin with an invading army.
20 JULY 1346	Birth of the Black Prince's sister Margaret.
26 AUGUST 1346	The Battle of Crécy: a decisive victory over the French army of King Philip VI, where the Prince, fighting with considerable valour in the English vanguard, 'wins his spurs'.
2 SEPTEMBER 1348	Death from plague of the Prince's sister, Joan (on her way to marry Pedro, the son and heir of Alfonso XI of Castile), near Bordeaux.
23 APRIL 1349	First meeting of the newly formed Order of the Garter at Windsor, on St George's Day.
1 JANUARY 1350	Edward III and the Black Prince repulse a French attempt to capture Calais.
29 AUGUST 1350	Sea battle off Winchelsea; defeat of a combined Castilian and Genoese fleet.
7 JANUARY 1355	Birth of the Prince's brother Thomas of Woodstock.
10 JULY 1355	The Black Prince is appointed king's lieutenant in Gascony.
16 SEPTEMBER 1355	The Prince arrives in Bordeaux with his army.
5 OCTOBER 1355	The beginning of the Black Prince's 'great raid' across southern France
28 OCTOBER 1355	The Prince and his army make a surprise crossing of the Garonne south of Toulouse, outwitting the count of Armagnac's forces.

8 NOVEMBER 1355	The Black Prince's army reaches its most easterly point of march, at Narbonne.
28 NOVEMBER 1355	The Prince's force returns to Gascony.
2 DECEMBER 1355	His Anglo-Gascon army formally disbands at La Réole.
25 JUNE 1356	The Prince leaves Bordeaux for the mustering-point of La Réole, where he will gather a fresh Anglo-Gascon force
6 JULY 1356	The Black Prince leaves La Réole for his second great raid into French territory.
4 AUGUST 1356	After a delay of several weeks at Bergerac, caused by Jean, count of Armagnac's decision to invade Gascony, the Prince decides to split his forces and marches north with a reduced army.
30 AUGUST	The Black Prince besieges Romorantin.
4 SEPTEMBER 1356– 8 SEPTEMBER 1356	The main French force leaves Chartres, now intent on confronting and destroying the Prince's army.
19 SEPTEMBER 1356	The Black Prince and his Anglo-Gascon army defeat the French at the Battle of Poitiers and capture King John II.
5 OCTOBER 1356	The Prince returns in triumph to Bordeaux.
3 MAY 1357	The Black Prince and King John arrive at Plymouth.
24 MAY 1357	A glorious reception is held for the Prince and John II of France in London.
28 OCTOBER 1359	Edward III, the Black Prince and an English army disembark at Calais to undertake the Rheims campaign.
10 MARCH 1360	The high point of the campaign is an agreement between Edward III and the advisers of the thirteen-year-old Philip de Rouvres, duke of Burgundy, indicating that Edward's coronation at Rheims – as king of England and France – is now a real possibility. But the English army is growing increasingly exhausted and is unable to draw the French into battle.
13 APRIL 1360	'Black Monday': the English army, marching close to Paris, is hit by a freak storm in the Beauce, losing men, horses and provisions. This startling misfortune is

seen as a divine warning, and both sides return to peace negotiations.

8 MAY 1360	The peace treaty of Brétigny is sealed.
8 JULY 1360	With negotiations between England and France complete, and a ransom agreement for the French king in place, the Black Prince escorts John II from London (pausing to make an offering at Canterbury Cathedral) and bids him farewell at Dover.
24 OCTOBER 1360	The treaty of Brétigny is ratified at Calais.
10 OCTOBER 1361	The marriage of the Black Prince and Joan of Kent is celebrated at Windsor, with the king, queen and archbishop of Canterbury in attendance.
19 JULY 1362	The Black Prince is created prince of Aquitaine.
29 JUNE 1363	The Prince, Joan of Kent, their household and a substantial retinue headed by the earl of Warwick arrive in Bordeaux.
9 JULY 1363	The Prince begins taking homage from the Gascon nobility at the cathedral of St André.
4 AUGUST 1363	The Prince arrives at Bergerac to take further homage and commences a tour of Aquitaine.
18 AUGUST 1363	After a five-day stay at Périgueux, the Prince moves to the castle of Angoulême, which will become one of his favourite residences.
23 AUGUST 1363	The Black Prince arrives at Cognac.
12 JANUARY 1364	After staying at La Rochelle and Poitiers through the autumn of 1363, the Prince moves south to Agen and spends Christmas there. He receives homage from Gaston Fébus, count of Foix, for all his lands except the vicomté of Béarn.
8 APRIL 1364	After returning to England as surety for the remainder of his ransom, King John II of France falls ill and dies at the Savoy Palace in London.
29 SEPTEMBER 1364	The Battle of Auray, a decisive clash in the War of the Breton Succession. The Black Prince's friend, John de Montfort, supported by a contingent of English

troops under Sir John Chandos, defeats and kills his rival Charles of Blois. John becomes duke of Brittany the following year.

27 JANUARY 1365   Birth of the Prince's first son, Edward of Angoulême.

2 APRIL 1365   Jean, count of Armagnac, comes to render homage to the Black Prince at Angoulême, but insists that the Prince's coat of arms, put up by his seneschal Sir Thomas Wettenhall, is removed from Rodez. The act of homage is postponed.

27 APRIL 1365   A magnificent tournament is held to celebrate the christening of the Prince's son.

12 JULY 1365   The count of Armagnac meets with the Prince at Bordeaux; after an awkward stand-off, his homage is finally given and accepted.

7 SEPTEMBER 1365   A treaty of mutual assistance is signed between John de Montfort, duke of Brittany, and the Black Prince.

c. 22 MARCH 1366   The marriage of John duke of Brittany and the Prince's stepdaughter Joan Holland is held at Nantes.

1 AUGUST 1366   The Black Prince meets the exiled Pedro, king of Castile, at Bayonne.

23 SEPTEMBER 1366   After a tense period of negotiation, a treaty between the Prince and Pedro of Castile is signed at Libourne.

6 JANUARY 1367   The birth of the Black Prince's second son, Richard of Bordeaux (the future Richard II).

13 JANUARY 1367   The Anglo-Gascon army at Dax is joined by reinforcements under John of Gaunt.

20 FEBRUARY 1367   The main body of the Black Prince's army crosses the Pyrenees at Roncesvalles in terrible winter weather.

28 FEBRUARY 1367   A letter of challenge is dispatched to the Prince by Enrique of Trastamara, Pedro's illegitimate brother, who has seized the throne of Castile.

11 MARCH 1367   Charles of Navarre arranges to be 'captured' by Olivier de Mauny, a partisan of du Guesclin. The Black Prince, fearing treachery, leaves the kingdom of Navarre and takes the westward route to Burgos.

19 MARCH 1367	The Black Prince finds his passage blocked by a Castilian and French army under Enrique and du Guesclin near Vitoria.
25 MARCH 1367	Enrique's brother Tello and the Marshal d'Audrehem make a surprise night attack on the English camp and wipe out a reconnaissance force under Sir William Felton.
1 APRIL 1367	The Black Prince changes his line of approach to Burgos, retraces his steps and crosses the River Ebro at Logrono, then advances to Navarrete. Enrique of Trastamara marches south to block his route, taking up a strong defensive position on the River Najarilla at Nájera.
3 APRIL 1367	The Black Prince wins a victory at Nájera that restores Pedro of Castile to the throne. However, Enrique escapes from the battlefield.
2 AND 6 MAY 1367	The treaty of Libourne is renegotiated at Burgos; Pedro is forced to pay a much larger sum of money.
13 AUGUST 1367	Treaty of Aigues-Mortes between Enrique of Trastamara and Louis duke of Anjou.
27 DECEMBER 1367	A ransom agreement between the Black Prince and his captive from Nájera, Bertrand du Guesclin, is finalized.
17 JANUARY 1368	The Black Prince releases du Guesclin from captivity.
18 JANUARY 1368	The general assembly of Aquitaine – the Estates – meets at Angoulême to discuss the levying of a *fouage* (a property tax).
26 JANUARY 1368	After a week of negotiation, and a series of concessions by the Prince, the *fouage* is approved by the assembly, at a rate of 10 sous (Gascon shillings) for each household in the principality, to run for five years. A small group of noblemen refuses to accept it.
30 JUNE 1368	An agreement of mutual assistance is made between Charles V of France and the chief appellants, the count of Armagnac and the lord of Albret.
7 OCTOBER 1368	Death of the Black Prince's brother (Edward III's second surviving son) Lionel, duke of Clarence.

18 NOVEMBER 1368	First signs of a serious deterioration in the Prince's health. He is confined to his bed, and cared for by one of the leading physicians of Bordeaux, Pierre de Manhi.
23 NOVEMBER 1368	Charles V summons the Black Prince to the Paris Parlement.
27 JANUARY 1369	The Prince writes to all the lords, bishops and towns of Aquitaine concerning the rebellion of the count of Armagnac.
10 FEBRUARY 1369	Guillaume Hamon, an experienced surgeon with twenty years of service to Edward III's family, is sent to the Prince.
28 FEBRUARY 1369	Charles V writes to Armagnac warning him not to take up arms against the Black Prince until the legal appeals process is completed.
23 MARCH 1369	Pedro I is murdered at Montiel by Enrique of Trastamara, who once more becomes king of Castile.
3 JUNE 1369	Resumption of war between England and France.
15 AUGUST 1369	Death of Queen Philippa, the Prince's mother.
23 AUGUST 1369	Death of Sir James Audley of sickness – possibly plague – at Fontenay-le-Comte (Vendée), shortly after the successful recapture of La Roche-sur-Yon.
1 JANUARY 1370	Death of Sir John Chandos at Lussac.
19 SEPTEMBER 1370	The Black Prince recaptures Limoges.
c. 29 SEPTEMBER 1370	Death of the Prince's elder son, Edward of Angoulême.
2 OCTOBER 1370	Charles V appoints Bertrand du Guesclin constable of France.
11 OCTOBER 1370	The Black Prince appoints his brother John of Gaunt as his lieutenant in Aquitaine.
5 NOVEMBER 1370	Edward III revokes the fouage.
2 DECEMBER 1370	A draft treaty is drawn up between King Edward and Charles of Navarre, but the Prince refuses to give his assent to it.
4 DECEMBER 1370	Bertrand du Guesclin defeats part of Sir Robert Knolles's army – commanded by Walter Lord

FitzWalter — at Pontvallain (in Maine), shattering the legend of English invincibility in battle.

EARLY JANUARY 1371   The Black Prince, his wife and surviving son leave Bordeaux for England.

23 JUNE 1372   An expedition to Gascony under the earl of Pembroke is annihilated by the Castilian fleet in a sea battle off La Rochelle.

23 AUGUST 1372   Jean de Grailly, Captal de Buch, is captured by the French at Soubise.

8 SEPTEMBER 1372   La Rochelle surrenders to a French army commanded by the constable du Guesclin.

5 NOVEMBER 1372   The Prince formally surrenders all his rights in Aquitaine to Edward III.

21 MARCH 1373   Du Guesclin's victory at Chizé leads to a rapid reconquest of Poitou by the forces of Charles V.

1 JULY 1373   John of Gaunt's army lands at Calais. This great raid crosses much of France — arriving at Bordeaux on 24 December, some six months later — but achieves little.

25 SEPTEMBER 1374   An inquisition is held in Flint to identify likely supporters of Owain Lawgoch, a Welsh soldier and descendant of the House of Llywelyn, who Charles V is encouraging to claim the principality of Wales.

28 APRIL 1376   Opening of the 'Good Parliament'. Neither Edward III nor the Black Prince is well enough to attend.

1 JUNE 1376   The Prince's condition worsens and his father has him moved to the palace of Westminster.

8 JUNE 1376   Death of the Black Prince.

29 SEPTEMBER 1376   Burial of the Prince in Canterbury Cathedral.

21 JUNE 1377   Death of Edward III.

5 JULY 1377   Burial of Edward III in Westminster Abbey.

16 JULY 1377   The coronation of the Black Prince's son, Richard II.

PROLOGUE

I walk into Canterbury Cathedral, a place of pilgrimage, whose soaring Gothic architecture surrounds the remains of its martyred twelfth-century archbishop. I am searching for a magnificent tomb, close to the shrine of Thomas à Becket. However, it is not a medieval prelate I am seeking but a warrior prince, one of the greatest war leaders England was ever to know. Born at Woodstock in 1330 and christened Edward after his father, his life was spent in the pursuit of a chivalric ideal, whether fighting in battles or jousting at tournaments, or courting the affections of the beautiful Joan of Kent, who would become his wife.

The tomb itself is of latten, a copper alloy that radiates a glowing, golden hue. Edward of Woodstock lies to the side of the cathedral choir in full plate and mail armour, displaying the leopards and the lilies, the coats of arms of England and France. His father, King Edward III, had claimed the throne of France in right of his mother, Isabella (the Prince's grandmother), and his son would uphold that right on the battlefield. His face displays remarkable strength and assurance. By his side is a burnished sword. He is of medium build, and every inch a warrior.

For many years his gauntlets, shield, helmet and crest, scabbard and jupon (a padded tunic worn over armour) hung above his tomb. They were the 'achievements' of a knight of renown, brought into the cathedral during his funeral service and then displayed for the admiration of posterity. More recently, they were moved under glass casing for better protection, and are shortly to undergo a period of conservation assessment before being restored to public view. In the interim, I have been offered a unique chance to inspect them.

After donning gloves, I lift one of the gauntlets and admire its workmanship. It is made of copper-gilt, and closely resembles the one on the Prince's effigy. It is narrow at the wrist and widens at the cuff, in an hourglass shape, allowing freedom of movement. Some of its finger plates still survive, as does one of the knuckle spikes, known as 'gadlings', in the shape of a tiny leopard. It is a high-quality artefact of war, forged with terrible yet beautiful artistry.

The great iron helm, with its riveted plates, is still imposing. It combines protection and decoration, its pierced breathing holes formed into the shape of a crown. Above it is a 'cap of maintenance' — a high-fitting velvet cap worn as a sign of nobility or special honour — and a magnificent heraldic crest. It is in the shape of a leopard with a long, swinging tail, made from moulded leather and covered with gilt. Its mouth is wide open, as if it is about to roar.

The shield is surprisingly light, made of poplar and covered with layers of leather and canvas, and is a decorative piece, showing the leopards and lilies (fleurs de lys). Its lack of strapping suggests it was made for the funeral. And then there is the jupon, in red and blue silk velvet, again displaying the arms of England and France, the lilies and leopards, and embroidered in gilt thread. It is padded, stuffed with wool and lined with satin, and to be worn over armour for additional protection. It laces up at the front. I am struck by its length — 1 metre (3 ft 4 in) from shoulder to lower hem. It suggests the Prince was at most around 1.67 metres (5 ft 6 in) tall. His power as a fighter came from more than his build.

The documents kept in the cathedral archive reveal a warrior of keen intellect and unusual piety. The Prince's ordinances for the foundation of his chantry, in 1363, in honour of the Holy Trinity, gave specific instructions for the types of service to be conducted and the prayers to be recited. His grasp of detail extended to the chaplains' clothing and personal allowances, and the location of their living quarters; his tone is brisk and businesslike.

The archives show us a man who could cut to the heart of an issue. A letter to his steward of Wallingford of 17 February 1359 pointed out that insufficient information had been provided, and gave instruction on what was to be remedied and finished: 'All this is to be given to the king's council in London by 8 May, so that the matter can quickly be concluded.' Here was a prince who surrounded himself with talented subordinates and had a firm grasp of his rights and sources of revenue. And yet, he was always struggling to meet the costs of his chivalric lifestyle.

The Prince's martial exploits were the stuff of legend even in his own lifetime. On 26 August 1346, at the age of sixteen, he fought heroically with his father in an army that crushed the French at Crécy. Ten years later, on 19 September 1356, by now a commander in his own right, he turned the tables on his numerically superior opponent, capturing King John II of France in battle at Poitiers, one of the great English victories of the Hundred Years War. In 1362, he became prince of Aquitaine, holding a magnificent court at Bordeaux that mesmerized the brave but unruly Gascon nobility and drew them like moths to the flame of his cause.

Five years later, he led a great Anglo-Gascon army across the Pyrenees into Spain (crossing by the mountain pass at Roncesvalles, where Count Roland had fought a valiant rearguard action to save Charlemagne's army seven centuries earlier), winning a stunning victory against the odds at Nájera that restored to the throne King Pedro of Castile, who had been ousted by his bastard half-brother. Edward's meteoric military rise captured the imagination of Europe. The chronicler Jean Froissart saw him — at the outset of his career at least — as a model of chivalric virtue.

Edward became known to posterity as the 'Black Prince', a soubriquet that was not in existence when the Chandos Herald wrote a long poem (*circa* 1385) on *La Vie et Faites d'Armes d'une tres noble*

Prince de Wales et Aquitaine (The Life and Feats of Arms of the most noble Prince of Wales and Aquitaine), a tribute to a man seen as a paragon of chivalry, and in fact was used only from the sixteenth century. It is found in notes of the antiquary John Leland in the early 1540s and first appeared in print in Richard Grafton's *Chronicle* in 1569. More than twenty years later, in William Shakespeare's *Henry V* (Act 2, Scene 4) the French ruler Charles VI says that his countrymen fear King Henry because of his ancestry, his 'heroical seed':

> He is bred out of that bloody strain
> That haunted us in our familiar paths.
> Witness our too much memorable shame,
> When Cressy battle fatally was struck,
> And all our princes captured by the hand
> Of that black name, Edward, Black Prince of Wales.

That 'black name' is now the standard way of describing the man. Some have suggested that the 'Black' is an allusion to the black armour that he wore at his first battle (although the evidence for this is scanty); others, that it is derived from the cruel way he waged war in France. When I inspect the tomb itself, I notice that the heraldic backdrop to his tournament badges is black – the colour forms part of a show of jousting prowess. Whatever the explanation for this knightly soubriquet, it was synonymous with a single-minded dedication to the warrior ethos, and the fighting fraternity of Europe's elite.

In 1688 the antiquary Joshua Barnes wrote a historical biography of Edward III and his son, the Black Prince, praising the prince's feats-of-arms; some seventy years later David Hume, in his *History of England,* also extolled his martial virtues. Indeed, in the eighteenth and nineteenth centuries this 'Black Prince' was seen in straightforward, heroic terms. On 16 September 1903 a mounted statue of the Prince was unveiled in City Square, Leeds, proclaiming him as 'the flower of England's chivalry'. However, modern scholarship has been more critical of him, criticizing his lack of administrative

ability and also his failures of political judgement. He is seen as
fixated on his military career, inflexible in his approach to government and limited in his broader abilities. As I gaze on the tomb,
I wonder if French manuscript collections, many of them under-
exploited, can cast fresh light on this fascinating figure.

The chronicler of the abbey of Moissac, Aymeric de Peyrac, for
example, showed that the Prince could be engaging, humorous and
pleasingly direct. He recalled the Prince asking one of the monks,
who was famed for his melodious singing voice, to take Mass. At
its end, the Prince greeted the man, thanked him and said: 'I am
sorry so much misfortune has befallen you – and that your good
friends are no longer with you.' The monk looked a little surprised
and asked him why he had said that. 'Well,' the Prince replied, 'I
noticed that in the service you rushed through the Office for the
Living but seemed to spend an eternity on the Office for the Dead.'
The monk looked at the Prince for a while, smiled, and then said:
'I feel that the living can more easily look after themselves; it is
those souls trapped in purgatory who really need my assistance.'
This was an age of violence and frequent visitations of the plague, a
horror that struck communities rapidly and without warning; an
age that demanded the warrior should prepare to face death, at any
time or place. For a moment the Black Prince seemed lost in his
own thoughts. Then he smiled back, and thanked the monk for his
answer. The two men became friends.

The last years of the Prince's life were blighted by sickness and
he was only able to attend his final military engagement, the siege
of Limoges, in 1370, carried on a stretcher. According to the chronicler Jean Froissart, the Black Prince – increasingly frustrated by
his own debilitating sickness and the deteriorating war situation –
sacked the town and put its civilian population to the sword. This
striking image of a chivalric hero falling below the standards that
had made him admired throughout Europe has lodged itself in the
popular imagination, but I find myself wondering whether it really
happened in the way that Froissart described it.

Whatever the truth of Limoges, there was now a cloud hanging over English fortunes. The Prince relinquished his duchy of Aquitaine due to ill health and spent his last years confined to his sickbed. He died on 8 June 1376, aged only forty-five. Nine years later the Black Prince's magnificent tomb was completed by his son, now ruling the kingdom as Richard II. There was no more appetite for foreign war; the realm was divided by internal dissension and unrest. The Prince's memorial at Canterbury became a memorial to a bygone era.

And yet, what an era it was. As I look at the magnificent tomb, I am conscious that the burial arrangements set out in the Prince's will, and scrupulously adhered to by his son, Richard, were in one instance disregarded. The Black Prince had asked that he be buried in the cathedral's crypt. Instead, Richard II built his tomb and memorial at the edge of the choir, as close as possible to the shrine of Thomas à Becket. The new king inherited little of his father's martial ability, but nevertheless wanted the Prince's tomb to become a place of pilgrimage in its own right. And as I stand by it, I am conscious of the power of this intention. The Black Prince was a shooting star in the medieval firmament. His martial endeavour, his courage, and the full living of a chivalric life entranced his age – and, if we properly restore his military reputation, it can also fascinate our own.

chapter one

A REALM DIVIDED

On 15 June 1330 a son was born to King Edward III and his queen, Philippa of Hainault, at the royal palace of Woodstock. The king was a little distance away at the time of the birth, and he granted a servant, Thomas Prior, a life annuity of 40 marks (£26 13s 4d) – a considerable sum in fourteenth-century England – for bringing him the happy news as he hastened to his wife's bedside. The boy was their first child, and was named Edward, after his father.

The new parents were a young and attractive couple. The seventeen-year-old king was physically striking, already almost 1.85 metres (6 ft) tall, well built, with strong regular features and long, flowing hair. A handsome young man, Edward was well suited to the clothes of the period, with their bright colours, sumptuous materials and liberal use of fur and jewels. He was a natural extrovert, a lover of display, tournaments and pageantry. But he was also intelligent and charming, possessing the ability to talk easily to people from all walks of life; a man who made an immediate impression. Beneath what seemed an easy-going nature, he was brave, ambitious and proud, with a driving, restless energy – although these qualities had not yet fully shown themselves.

His sixteen-year-old wife was even-tempered and kind. She genuinely loved her husband, and over time would accompany him on military campaigns and prove to be an exemplary mother to her children, the first-born Edward of Woodstock, the Black Prince, and then eight others who would survive infancy. She took considerably more interest in them than was usual for a queen in this

9

period. The chronicler Jean Froissart praised her as 'wise, glad-some, humble and devout'. She was hardworking and intelligent, and would become a notable patron of scholars and artists.

The days after the birth of their son were a happy time for Edward and Philippa. The king went hunting in the neighbouring forests, and, during the following month, held a tournament in honour of his wife and baby son. The queen was provided with magnificent velvet robes embroidered with golden squirrels, a reference to her favourite pet. A nurse was found from nearby Oxford, and a nurse-maid appointed to rock the baby's cradle; both were later rewarded with generous pensions.

Yet in that summer of 1330 a cloud hung over this couple. To grasp the reasons for this, we have to go back in time about five years and witness the extraordinary circumstances that led to their betrothal and marriage. For the tale of the Black Prince is very much that of a close but troubled father–son relationship, one that would exist throughout the Prince's entire adult career. To under-stand it better, we need first to look at the formative experiences in the life of his father, King Edward III, and in particular at what happened to him when he was coming of age.

†

In 1325 the future Edward III was only a young prince himself. He was about to see his world turned upside down in a traumatic and bewildering sequence of events that, in emotional terms, would leave him permanently scarred. For better and for worse, they would shape the man and monarch he would come to be.

In September of that year, the twelve-year-old Prince Edward crossed to France according to the wishes of his father, Edward II, to do homage to the French king, Charles IV, for the English-held duchy of Aquitaine. It was an occasion that allowed the young prince to make an *entrée* to the international stage and the king had prepared him thoroughly for it. The prince was expected to do his duty by his father in keeping with the principles of loyalty and obedience that had guided and informed his whole upbringing.

The act of homage – the formal, public acknowledgement by which a feudal tenant declared himself to be the vassal of his lord, owing him fealty and service – was a powerful ritual. The prince would offer his allegiance to King Charles in return for his father being granted the right to administer the duchy. The ceremony would take place in the French capital. It was intended to bring a short and inconclusive war between the two countries to an end, and the ground had been laid for it by several months of tough diplomacy. Six months earlier, King Edward's French queen, Isabella, the youngest surviving child of Philip IV 'the Fair', had gone to Paris to negotiate with Charles, her older brother, in order to bring hostilities to an end

On 31 March 1325 Isabella had sent a first report back to her husband, admitting that she was finding her brother difficult to deal with, and anticipating that the talks would take time. But now they had been brought to fruition and young Prince Edward's act of homage would formalize what had been agreed between his mother and uncle. The dispatch of the prince to Paris seemed to show the king and queen acting in common cause, with united purpose – and that is no doubt how their son saw it, as he embarked upon his journey. There was no sign in the letter, which was long and affectionate, of any disharmony between husband and wife. On five different occasions Isabella addressed her husband affectionately as 'my truest sweetheart'.

Such terms of endearment would not have surprised Prince Edward. In September 1325 he had every reason to believe that his family was a happy one. He probably knew one story about his parents' relationship particularly well. In June 1313, some eight months after his birth, his parents had visited France and were staying near Pontoise, sleeping (because of the summer heat) in a large silken pavilion. One night it caught fire and Isabella was only saved by the quick thinking of her husband, who scooped her up in his

arms and rushed outside with her. The chronicler Geoffrey of Paris
recounted the episode approvingly: it not only showed Edward's
bravery — Geoffrey adding that even though the king of England
was 'completely naked' he then ran back into the fire and rescued
others — but also his romantic nature. The chronicler said simply:
'Edward had rescued Isabella, above all else because he loved her
with a special kind of love, which can be called "courtly love". Love
made him do it.'

Geoffrey was clearly much taken with the couple's devotion to
one another: he also related how, on another occasion, they had
missed a meeting with Isabella's father, King Philip IV of France,
because they had overslept after their 'night-time dalliances'. Later
that day, Geoffrey continued, they had watched a parade together
in Paris from a specially constructed tower, 'surrounded by a large
group of ladies and damsels'. It was a blissfully happy picture.

And Edward II appeared to be a doting father as well as husband. When Isabella was pregnant with Edward's younger brother
John, in the spring of 1316, the king was quick to pay for a bay horse
'to carry the litter of the lady the queen' and gave an additional £4
for pieces of silk to make cushions for the carriage. When his first
daughter Eleanor was born, two years later, a delighted Edward paid
500 marks (£333 13s 4d) for a feast to celebrate the birth; when the
second, Joan, appeared, the happy monarch arrived at the Tower of
London, where the queen was staying, generously rewarding her
servants but dismissing the constable of the Tower from his post on
finding that a little rainwater had come through the roof on to the
queen's bed while she was in labour.

But all was not as it seemed. Prince Edward had joined his
mother at the Château of Vincennes on 22 September 1325 and
homage for Aquitaine was duly performed before the French king
two days later. After a short stay in Paris, he was expecting that — in
keeping with the instructions King Edward II had given him — he
and his mother would both return to England and report back
to his father on what had been achieved. Instead, Isabella made

an extraordinary declaration in front of the entire French court, in which all her pent-up frustrations about her marriage were unleashed. She made clear, in quite astonishing fashion, that she was no longer willing to endure what had become for her a sham:

> I feel that marriage is a joining together of man and woman, maintaining the undivided habit of life, and that someone has come between my husband and myself trying to break this bond. I protest that I will not return until this intruder is removed – and discarding my marriage garment, shall assume the robes of widowhood and mourning until I am avenged of this Pharisee.

This announcement shocked all who heard it and must have been a bombshell to the young Edward. The picture of a contented family was breaking into pieces all around him. He now learned that his father was embroiled in a highly charged relationship with the chamberlain of the royal household, Hugh Despenser the Younger, the 'Pharisee' of Isabella's stinging denunciation and, in political terms, a man who exerted a baleful influence on Edward II.

Prince Edward had little inkling of all this before his mother's announcement. Royal children were brought up under the care and tutelage of carefully chosen advisers, which to some extent insulated them from gossip and rumour. On the wishes of the over-protective king, Prince Edward had been kept away from political life and in a state of near seclusion following an incident in which he had narrowly escaped capture by a Scottish raiding party at York, in September 1322.

A long period of dissension between Edward II and his leading magnates had finally flared into open rebellion in March 1322. The revolt was put down and its ringleaders either killed in battle or executed after it (or, in the case of Roger Mortimer, sentenced to life imprisonment). In its aftermath, outright opposition was – for a few years at least – muted. Hugh Despenser's position of chamberlain meant that he controlled access to the king and watched over those who attended Edward II's court. An atmosphere of fear and suspicion was all-pervasive.

Chroniclers of the day were critical of Despenser's power and influence, which they believed was won through manipulation of the besotted monarch. Geoffrey le Baker remarked that some considered Despenser to be 'another king, or more accurately, ruler of the king… and he was so presumptuous that he frequently prevented certain nobles from speaking with Edward II'. Others went further, judging Despenser to be 'haughty, arrogant, greedy and evil', and 'more inclined to wrongdoing than any other man'.

But it was the emotional and almost certainly sexual relationship between the two that disturbed people the most. The Anonimalle chronicler criticized the royal favourite and lover for leading the king into 'a cruel and debauched life'; while another, the Westminster chronicler Robert of Reading, caught the sheer degree of infatuation involved: 'he led the monarch around as if he were teasing a cat with a piece of straw'.

Queen Isabella, from the safety of the French court, made it clear she regarded Despenser as a hated rival and dangerous foe. The previous autumn he had demonstrated to her his power over the king when he persuaded Edward II to deprive the queen of all her lands and most of her household servants. This episode, which was designed to humiliate Isabella, created a scandal: some even believed that Despenser, by imposing such drastic penalties, was planning to obtain a papal annulment of the royal marriage itself. Her outburst against Despenser showed her fury, but also her fear of the man who had 'come between her husband and herself'.

As proof of the estrangement between king and queen, Isabella dressed in the garb of a widow, and this was how she now appeared on formal occasions. Documentary records show Prince Edward dining regularly with his mother throughout October 1325; indeed, he was scarcely out of her sight. Isabella sent away the members of Edward's own small entourage, leaving him firmly under the queen's influence.

It was at this time that Edward probably learned from his mother about an earlier infatuation of his father's with another royal favourite, Piers Gaveston, that had taken place in the 1300s, before his own birth. The king's open flirtation with Gaveston had grievously hurt his teenaged queen and alienated members of the nobility. King Edward II was at considerable fault for involving himself with Gaveston in such heedless fashion – but the royal favourite was made the scapegoat for his scandalous actions. Gaveston was banished in 1311 – his third such punishment – and then, after his return from exile, executed by aristocratic opponents of the king.

Edward II subsequently claimed that the birth of his first son, in November 1312, had a powerful and positive effect on him, allowing him to put the memory of Gaveston behind him and enjoy an improved relationship with his queen. Isabella herself must have fervently wished that her husband's infatuations were a thing of the past: but the rise of Despenser had put paid to these hopes. This time, however, she was not a reticent teenager in a strange country, but a strong and determined woman with a forceful personality. And that personality was coming increasingly to the fore.

We can only speculate on Prince Edward's reaction. He must have felt considerable sympathy for his mother. How he now regarded his father we do not know. Isabella claimed that she still loved him, but that she could not return to England because of the jealousy of Despenser, which put her own life at risk. She may have genuinely believed this to be the case, but the period of mourning for her shattered marriage did not last long. At the end of November 1325, Queen Isabella began an affair with Roger Mortimer, lord of Wigmore, a rebel and enemy of the king who had escaped to France some two years earlier. This was a liaison governed by political expediency and fuelled by one driving emotion: a shared hatred of Hugh Despenser.

Isabella knew that Roger Mortimer would be a most useful ally. A major landowner on the Welsh Marches, he had also served — very successfully — as Edward II's lieutenant in Ireland. Mortimer had fallen out with the king over the power of Hugh Despenser in Wales, and in 1322 had led a rebellion whose chief aim was to remove him from the king's presence. Mortimer's uprising had failed, and he was sentenced to life imprisonment and locked up in the Tower of London. A year later he had managed to escape in spectacular fashion, somehow contriving to drug his gaolers, flee the fortress and make his way to France.

Mortimer was an ambitious magnate, brave and forceful and, like the queen, politically astute. Prince Edward, perhaps already turning away from his father in his heart, may well have been impressed by him. Both shared a love of the values of knighthood, the tournament and stories of the legendary King Arthur. And Mortimer, unlike Edward II, was a natural warrior. In the French capital, away from the poisonous intrigues of Edward's court, Mortimer would have had the chance to acquaint the prince with his father's failings as a commander. He may have told him the story of the disaster at Bannockburn, near Stirling, in the summer of 1314, where a large English force was outmanoeuvred and out-fought by the well-drilled Scottish troops of Robert the Bruce. King Edward had displayed tactical ineptitude, quarrelling with his nobles instead of uniting them in common purpose, and never got a grip on his army. And Mortimer may have gone further, making it clear that the king's bungled response to a Scottish invasion eight years later had not only brought shame on the nation, but had put both his wife and eldest son in personal danger.

Mortimer's view was a persuasive one. Although a rebel, he spoke for many within the kingdom who felt that the values of martial renown had been lost during the reign of Edward II. The Northumbrian chronicler Sir Thomas Gray certainly would have endorsed it. Gray's father had fought at Bannockburn, and in the tough, intermittent warfare on the Scottish borders. He believed that the king's worst failing was his lack of chivalry; indeed his view was that the only people who were behaving like King Arthur, the mythical British ruler whose deeds fascinated the medieval aristocracy, were Edward II's noble opponents. After the treaty of Byland, which brought the disastrous Scottish campaign of 1322 to its close, Gray, in his *Scalacronica,* had this to say of Edward II: 'And thus the king returned home, and kept himself in peace and quiet, *undertaking nothing of honour and prowess*' [author's italics].

Mortimer represented something that was lacking in Prince Edward's own father. But Isabella and her new lover moved carefully. It is likely that the couple had already decided on a plan to remove the king, and soon turned their thoughts to raising an army and invading England. The prince would be a most useful figurehead in such a scheme. By the beginning of December 1325, they had started to plot a marriage alliance between Prince Edward and one of the daughters of Count William of Hainault (one that had been briefly considered by Edward II, three years earlier, but not acted upon), an alliance that would secure from the Hainaulters, in return, money, ships and men. Count William's brother John openly offered Isabella refuge and aid against her husband.

It is unlikely that Isabella and Mortimer confided all of this to Prince Edward. Even if Edward had become disillusioned with the rule of his father and the way he had treated his mother, he may well still have retained some affection for him. Some fifty years earlier another Prince Edward, the future Edward I, who went on to become a powerful warrior and forceful king, grew disaffected with the weak and ineffective rule of own his father, Henry III, but – at a time of crisis and rebellion – stayed loyal to him. Isabella and Mortimer knew their history. Most likely, they told the prince that the purpose of the invasion would not be to act against the king, but to remove his hateful and corrupt lover, Despenser – a manifesto they were already starting to circulate among their supporters in England. The rest could wait.

Prince Edward, largely powerless as these events unfolded, was trapped in a dangerous and volatile situation not of his own making. And through their spies, Edward II and Hugh Despenser were starting to get a sense of what was afoot. Edward, growing fearful and suspicious of Isabella's intentions, tried to prise his son from the queen's side. At the beginning of December the king wrote to him in direct fashion:

> Very dear son, although you are of young and tender age, may we remind you of what we charged and commanded you at your departure from Dover. You answered then, with duly acknowledged goodwill, that you would not trespass or disobey any of our commandments in any point, for anyone. And now that your homage has been received by our dearest brother [-in-law], the king of France, your uncle, please take your leave of him, and return to us with all speed, in company with your mother, if she will come quickly; and if she will not come, then you must come without further delay, for we have a great desire to see you and speak with you. Therefore, do not remain for your mother's sake, or for anyone else's.

Young Edward was contrite. He said that he wanted to obey his father, but could not return because his mother would not let him. There may have been some truth in this, but the king's behaviour grew more intimidating. His son's lands were put under royal administration and sheriffs were instructed that both the queen and Prince Edward were to be arrested if ever they returned to England.

On 18 March 1326 Edward II wrote to his son again. He had now heard rumours that the prince might be betrothed to a daughter of the count of Hainault, and wondered if the truth of this was being deliberately concealed from him. He warned the Prince:

> You cannot avoid the wrath of God, the reproach of men, and our great indignation... You should by no means marry, nor suffer yourself to be married, without our previous consent and advice; for nothing that you could do would cause us greater injury and pain of heart. And since you say that you cannot

return to us because of your mother, it causes us great uneasiness of heart that you cannot be allowed by her to do your natural duty.

The king then spoke of his own emotional pain, talking more frankly of Queen Isabella:

You and all the world have seen that she openly, notoriously – knowing it to be contrary to her duty, and against the welfare of our Crown – has attached to herself, and retains in her company, Mortimer, our traitor and mortal foe, proved attainted and judged, and she accompanies him intimately in her own house and on her travels, in disregard of us, of our Crown, and the right ordering of the realm – him, the malefactor... And worse than this she has done, if there can be any worse, in allowing you to consort with this said enemy, making him your counsellor, and allowing you to associate with him in the sight of the world, doing so great a villainy and dishonour both to yourself and us, to the prejudice of our Crown, and the laws and customs of our realm, which you are supremely bound to hold, preserve and maintain.

This letter could not have caused the young Edward anything other than distress. But the king continued in even more menacing vein:

We are not pleased with you; and you should not so displease us, neither for the sake of your mother nor for anyone else's sake. We charge you, by the faith, love and allegiance that you owe us, and on our blessing, that you come to us without delay, without opposition or any further excuse, for your mother has written to us to say that if you wish to return to us she will not prevent it... Fair son, do not disregard our orders, for we hear much that you have done which you ought not have done.

Young Edward was now a pawn in a battle between his parents. On 19 June 1326 Edward II wrote his son a last, bitter letter, in which he angrily denounced him:

> You have not humbly obeyed our commands, as a good son ought, since you have not returned to us... but you have notoriously held companionship with Mortimer, our traitor and mortal enemy... and proceeded to make various injunctions and ordinances without our advice and contrary to our orders... You have no other governor than us, nor should you have.

The letter ended with a clear threat:

> Understand certainly, that if you now act contrary to our counsel, and continue in wilful disobedience, you will feel it all the days of your life, and you will be made an example to all other sons who are disobedient to their lords and fathers.

And with that, all communication between the king and his son ceased.

In the later Middle Ages, monarchs and nobles saw themselves as players in a larger family drama, mapped out in the lavish pedigrees and genealogies commissioned by rulers and aristocrats alike. A sense of lineage gave meaning to their actions, and within it, pride in the continuity of the dynasty was paramount. The rift between Edward II and his son meant that a link in the chain had been broken, a breach that would, in emotional terms, long outlast its immediate political repercussions. For it would impact strongly upon the young Edward's relationship with his own son, the Black Prince — the grandson of the aggrieved King Edward II — as he in turn grew to manhood.

Events now moved rapidly. Isabella and Mortimer left the French court, with the prince accompanying them, and prepared to invade England. John of Hainault furnished them with ships and a small army of about 1,500 men. The price for his help was a marriage alliance. On 27 August 1326 Prince Edward and Philippa of Hainault were formally betrothed at the cathedral church of Mons. Edward swore on the Gospels to marry her within two years, an arrangement conducted without any reference whatsoever to his father, King Edward II, and in clear opposition to his wishes. Roger Mortimer, the sworn enemy of the king, stood as guarantor of the contract.

The bishop of Exeter, Walter Stapeldon, was a trusted servant of Edward II who had conducted numerous diplomatic missions on the king's behalf. He had already met all the daughters of the count of Hainault (on an embassy on Edward's behalf in 1322), and had said of Philippa, who was then eight:

> She has not uncomely hair, which is betwixt blue-black and brown. Her head is clean-shaped; her forehead high and broad... Her eyes are blackish-brown and deep. Her nose is fairly smooth and even, save that it is somewhat broad at the tip, and also flattened, yet it is no snub nose. Her lips are somewhat full, especially the lower lip... The lower teeth project a little beyond the upper, yet this is but little seen... her neck, shoulders and all her body and lower limbs are reasonably well-shapen... Moreover, she is brown of skin all over, much like her father, and in all things she is pleasant enough, as it seems to us.

Philippa later told the chronicler Jean Froissart a romantic tale about their meeting. The fourteen-year-old Edward, she said, preferred her to her sisters and he chose her over them. That August, the young prince 'had devoted himself most, and inclined with eyes of love to Philippa rather than the rest; in return, the maiden knew him better than any of her sisters'. When his mother, Isabella, went through the form of asking him whether he would marry one of the Count of Hainault's daughters, he is said to have replied: 'Yes, I am better pleased to marry here than elsewhere, and rather to Philippa, for she and I accord excellently well together, and she wept, as I know well, when I took leave of her at my departure.'

It is an appealing picture, a young prince spending time with a group of girls, falling in love with one of them and choosing her over her sisters as his wife. It calls to mind Geoffrey of Paris's superficially pleasing vignette of Edward II and his queen happily watching a procession surrounded by a bevy of damsels. In both cases, a less romantic reality is being masked.

Philippa was the third of four daughters of the Count of Hainault. In August 1326 her two older sisters, Margareta and Joanna, had already been married for two and a half years; their double wedding — to Ludwig of Bavaria and Wilhelm of Jülich — had taken place in Cologne in February 1324. There remained two unmarried daughters of the count who could be proposed as brides for Prince Edward: Philippa, who was roughly the same age as the prince, and her much younger sister Isabella, who was little more than an infant. That Edward preferred Philippa's company in these circumstances is hardly surprising.

The betrothal was in reality the result of ruthless political calculation and had nothing to do with the whims or wishes of the two adolescents. Philippa may not have fully realized it at the time, but she was assisting in an attempted overthrow of her father-in-law by her mother-in-law, with her fiancé being used as a weapon against his own father. The betrothal was also unlawful on two counts: Edward was at the time officially engaged to someone else, Eleanor, the sister of King Alfonso XI of Castile; and his legal guardian, his father Edward II, now stood in firm opposition to the Hainault match and did not consent to it. Philippa's wish to draw a veil over all this, and sometime later make up a pleasing tale, turning the circumstances of her betrothal into a sweet fantasy, is perhaps understandable.

Yet it would be unwise to dismiss completely Philippa's version of the story. Given the enormous affection that later grew between the couple, in a highly successful marriage that would span four decades, it is probable that they did like each other very much, and that they enjoyed each other's company in 1326, whatever the cold political reasons that brought them together. And already the germ of a shared enthusiasm can be seen: a fascination with tales of chivalry and courtly love. Over time, it would grow into a skill in recreating – through pageantry, celebration and ritual – an embodiment of that world that would enchant and uplift those who witnessed it.

But in 1326 Edward and Philippa's time together was brief. Within weeks they were parted, the prince sailing with the invasion fleet of Isabella and Mortimer that landed on the estuary of the River Orwell in Suffolk on 24 September. On hearing of its arrival, the narrow governing clique surrounding Edward II and Hugh Despenser was paralyzed by indecision.

Despenser was now hated in much of the country. On 15 October there was a popular uprising in London on behalf of the rebels – a clear indication of the revulsion felt towards the king and his lover. Some of Edward II's supporters were murdered in the streets, while others fled the capital. On 26 October Isabella and Mortimer announced their right to govern on behalf of the king's son. The following day Despenser's father, Hugh Despenser the Elder, was captured and executed in Bristol. Despenser and the hapless king attempted to flee to Ireland but stormy weather prevented them from making the crossing, and they were apprehended in Wales soon afterwards. Edward II was imprisoned in Kenilworth Castle in Warwickshire, while Despenser was brought before the queen at Hereford.

On 24 November 1326 Isabella and Mortimer enjoyed their moment of revenge. Even by the standards of this brutal and bloodthirsty age, the sentence meted out to Despenser was grotesque – and the fourteen-year-old Prince Edward, being schooled in such political ruthlessness, was required to watch it. Hugh Despenser was hauled into Hereford's market square, with the queen, her lover, Mortimer, Edward and a crowd of their supporters looking on. A crown of nettles was placed on his head and a verse from the Psalms – 'Why do you boast in mischief, o mighty man?' – hung around his neck. Charges were read out against him and he was tried and sentenced to be hanged, drawn and quartered. Despenser was then half-strangled on the gallows, cut down and tied to a ladder.

In the fourteenth century an aristocrat sentenced to death for treason would normally be executed cleanly, as a final mark of respect for his rank, rather than being mutilated while still alive. No such scruples were shown in Despenser's case. His was an exceptionally cruel and humiliating punishment, for the queen was vindictive in her sexual jealousy. Prince Edward was witness to a ritual castration: on the instructions of Isabella and Mortimer the executioner first hacked off Despenser's penis and then his testicles, and flung them into the fire in front of him. Then Despenser's entrails were cut out. Finally he was lowered to the ground to be beheaded. Despenser's head was subsequently placed on London Bridge and the remains of his body cut into four and displayed on the city walls of York, Carlisle, Bristol and Dover. The warning to others was clear: Isabella had now resolved to depose Edward II and would not brook any opposition.

On 24 January 1327 a parliament was held, in the king's absence, and Edward II was forced to abdicate. The beginning of the reign of his son, Edward III, was announced by proclamation. On 1 February Edward III, aged fourteen, was crowned at Westminster Abbey; his captive father was henceforth to be styled Edward of Caernarfon. A month later the deposed monarch was transferred to a more secure prison at Berkeley Castle, in Gloucestershire.

All effective power now lay in the hands of Isabella and Mortimer; the concerns of this new regime, with Edward III as its figurehead, were purely self-interested. On 31 March 1327 Isabella and Mortimer agreed to the Treaty of Paris, the conditions of which were humiliating for the English crown: its possessions in Gascony were much reduced and it was obliged to pay a subsidy to France. The reluctant young King Edward was forced to agree to the terms. And then the Scots invaded.

Great commanders sometimes experience disasters in their youth and learn a great deal from them. Their genius is forged from failure as well as success. The military campaign that Edward III now endured was so dire that it became, in part, a catalyst for the martial successes of his later reign, and those of his eldest son, the Black Prince, who was frequently told about it. Neither would ever forget the events of the Scottish invasion.

The Flemish chronicler Jean le Bel, a member of the entourage of Jean of Hainault, was a witness to this campaign – Edward III's first – in Weardale, undertaken against a Scottish army in the summer of 1327. A truce between the two countries had broken down. Although Robert the Bruce, Scotland's great war leader, was now ill, he judged the time was right, with Edward II deposed and held as a prisoner, to test the mettle of the new regime. He summoned his leading nobles, called out his troops and ordered them onto the offensive, to harry and plunder the north of England. Le Bel was fascinated by these tough raiders:

> When they want to pass into England they are all mounted, the knights and esquires on good strong warhorses, the ordinary soldiers on little hackneys. They do not encumber themselves with carts or baggage trains and can subsist on iron rations, a sack of oatmeal tied on to their horses... So it is no surprise that they can make longer marches than most other armies. They enter into England, burn and devastate the country and round up the cattle [to take with them] for their return. They are crafty and resourceful soldiers.

The Scots' raid penetrated deep into northern England. Queen Isabella and Roger Mortimer, who had made much of Edward II's failures in Scotland in their deposition of the unfortunate king, realized that a strong response was necessary and gathered a large army at York. It would be under the nominal command of Edward III, who was given a coterie of advisers (his uncles, Edmund of Woodstock and Thomas of Brotherton, and his cousin,

Henry of Lancaster). When news of the Scottish incursion – and the havoc it was causing – was relayed to it, the royal army pushed north to Durham. Its strategy appeared deceptively simple: to trap the retreating Scots against the River Tyne and bring them to battle. But in war a great deal can go wrong with even the simplest and best-laid plans, as the young Edward III was about to find out.

The English army set out, attempting to track their opponents through the smoke of the burning villages left in their wake. But it was clear that the Scots were moving faster than they were. So, realizing this, they decided on a different plan: to outmanoeuvre their opponents instead, rising after midnight and conducting a pell-mell charge to the Tyne, so that they could hold the river ahead of the enemy. Jean le Bel and his Hainaulters were paid professional soldiers brought in to stiffen the English army. And as a professional soldier, he described what followed, on 20 July, in some bafflement:

> All began to ride in terrible haste, through moorland, rough ground, hillside and valley. Many of the army's supplies and pack horses simply got left behind in the rush. There were constant false alarms, calls that those in front were already engaged with the enemy, and all must hasten to help… But when we arrived we would find out it had only been a startled deer or some other wild animal… And thus the young king rode that day with his army, through this barren wasteland, without proper roads, paths or trails.

The baggage train was simply abandoned, battle being expected within a day. Between sunrise and sunset, when the cavalry eventually reached the Tyne, they covered some 28 miles (45 km) cross-country, without stopping, 'except to piss or tighten the saddle strappings on our horses', as le Bel remarked in matter-of-fact fashion. The advance guard crossed the river at a ford near Haydon. The majority of the tired soldiers, orientating themselves only by the position of the sun, eventually joined them, gathering along the northern bank of the Tyne and setting up camp. Le Bel continued:

> Our troops, all in a state of exhaustion, lay that night by the banks of the river, each holding his horse's rein in his hands, because in the darkness it was not possible to see any place to tether them. Our baggage was somewhere far behind us, so there was no hay, oats or forage to feed the hungry creatures. For ourselves, we only had a little bread, which we had tied behind the saddle, and that was soaked through in horse's sweat. We were not able to make fires to warm ourselves... or even remove our armour.

Things did not get any better:

> The next morning men roused themselves, with the hope of either giving battle to the Scots, or at least moving on and making a proper camp. But instead it began to rain, and soon the downpour was so strong, and the river so swollen, that it was impossible to cross it. We were unable to discover where exactly we were, or where food might be. So we had to fast that day, and our horses eat dirt or the leaves from the trees.

The king and his advisers now tried to acquire some much-needed provisions. Eventually supplies were brought in – but it only provided an opportunity for blatant profiteering, as le Bel remembered only too vividly:

> ... the next day some people did arrive, on little horses and mules, bringing badly cooked loaves in baskets, poor wine in large barrels, and other such goods to sell, which was supposed to provide relief for a large part of the army. And so, after staying in this forsaken place without any food at all, we now had to pay six or seven English pennies for an ill-cooked loaf of bread that was only worth a farthing, and to buy four gallons of wine,

which should have cost four pennies, but for which we had to pay 24 or 26.

The Scots, whom the English were supposed to have beaten to the Tyne, did not appear. And the weather refused to let up:

> In addition to these miseries, it did nothing but rain that whole week, so that saddles, clothes and leathers were all rotted and ruined and our horses left with running sores on their backs... We had no way of shoeing those that had lost their horseshoes, nor any material to cover them at night. Most of us had no protection against the damp and cold either, and for the entire week it was not possible to even make a fire, the wood being so damp and green.

And so, for seven days, the English army remained in this wretched state. Some felt sure that all was well, and they had succeeded in preventing the Scots from returning to their own country. The majority were less pleased, and a rumour began to circulate among the soldiers that those who had advised the march to the Tyne had meant to betray their king. On 26 July the containing strategy was suddenly abandoned. Tired of the 'discomfort and poverty' of its camp, the army now marched upriver, sending out reconnaissance parties to try, once again, to locate its foe.

Finally, information was obtained on the whereabouts of the Scottish army, after the king offered the reward of a knighthood to the man who brought him the news. A squire, Thomas Rokesby, won the honour cheaply: he had conducted little effective scouting but had blundered into the Scottish position and been promptly captured. The Scots released him in an act of bravado, on condition that he told Edward III and his counsellors their whereabouts, and passed on the message 'we have as much desire to fight with you as you with us'. The English soldiers moved off once more, to the south-east in the direction of the River Wear, where they at last found their opponents, encamped at Stanhope Park.

The rival forces now drew up in formation, but the Scots had the advantage of the higher ground and the protection of the river. Outnumbered by the English and in a good defensive position, they understandably showed little inclination to move. Le Bel recalled that:

> The young king rode out before the assembled host in order to give heart to our troops. He spoke graciously, exhorting us all to do well and to maintain our honour – and commanding that discipline be kept, with no man advancing beyond the army's banners until he gave the order. Soon afterwards, we all moved forward by the short step, keeping our ranks – seeing if we could entice the Scots down from the high ground. But our opponents made no move at all and it was deemed too risky to cross the river and attack them.

All was not well among the English commanders. Henry of Lancaster, the most experienced soldier, who had fought in Flanders, Wales and Scotland, wanted to take the offensive; Roger Mortimer, who held no official position within the army, nonetheless forbade it. Another uncomfortable night followed. Attempts to snatch a little sleep, curled up on hard ground in full armour, were thwarted by their foe, as le Bel related: 'The Scots, seeing that we were attempting to rest, made the most colossal racket from dusk until dawn, blowing a mass of hunting horns, at full blast, so that it seemed that they were the very devils of hell come to strangle us.'

The next day the weary English sent a picked body of archers across the Wear to try and provoke the Scots, but their attack was easily beaten off. Running out of ideas, they even sent out their heralds with a proclamation to the enemy, urging them either to give up or to offer battle. Le Bel, struck by the desperation of this tactic, found the Scottish reply darkly humorous:

> When they heard this, they took counsel, and then responded that they would do neither one nor the other. The English king

and his advisers could well see that they were in his realm and
had burned and devastated it; if this troubled him, he might
come and amend it, for they would tarry there as long as they
liked.

So, in a campaign of innumerable plans, yet another was tried.
The English moved north and attempted to blockade the opposing
army into submission. The Scots had other ideas. On 5 August the
experienced soldier Sir William Douglas led a daring night raid into
the very heart of the English camp. Le Bel — well aware that the
resolve and confidence of the Scots far exceeded that of his own
army — recorded what followed:

> Douglas, who was bold, enterprising and resilient in all military
> matters, took a picked force of about two hundred men and
> crossed the river around midnight, a good distance from our
> army, so that he could catch us unawares. He charged straight
> into the middle of us, he and his men crying out — 'Douglas!
> Douglas! You will all die, English lords!' His force did indeed
> kill more than three hundred of our men, Sir William spur-
> ring his horse forward to the king's own tent. As Edward was
> rushed to safety, Douglas triumphantly cut its ropes [leaving it
> to collapse] before riding off again.

Despite this mishap, Edward III's advisers still seemed to feel sure
that they had the Scottish army trapped and could now starve
them into submission or force them to fight. They were living in
a realm of make-believe. The swampy ground north of the river
valley was supposed to prevent any Scottish escape, but it was far
less impassable than they believed. The Scots undertook a night
march, making their way on foot and leading their horses through
the difficult marshland. Thereafter they marched back to Scotland. On the morning of 7 August the English awoke to find their
foe had gone. A hugely expensive campaign to bring the Scots to
battle had yielded no result whatsoever, and chroniclers said that

the young Edward III wept in frustration when he realized that the enemy had escaped him.

And so it all spluttered to a halt. Edward made his way back to York, 'in great desolation', as the chronicler Henry Knighton related, 'because things had not gone better for him at the beginning of his reign – and severely stricken with shame, he grieved much'. The popular verdict was blunt: the conduct of the campaign had led to 'dishonour and scorn for the whole of England'. The London-based chronicle *The Brut* even accused Mortimer of double-dealing with the enemy. The Scots had caused so much damage in their plundering raid that in the lay subsidy, a tax levied later that summer, the three northernmost counties, Cumberland, Northumberland and Durham, were deemed unable to pay a single shilling.

Jean le Bel and his Hainaulters went back home. Their wage bill alone amounted to over £41,000, emptying the English treasury. Le Bel believed the Weardale campaign showed a degree of military ineptitude difficult to imagine unless one had actually experienced it; his account would make the English the laughing-stock of Europe. He was polite about the hapless Edward III: 'Never had such a young king undertaken such a difficult and dangerous expedition,' he opined diplomatically. But King Edward would never forget this fiasco. He resolved never again to lead such a mismanaged campaign; and, later in his reign, he took the decision to harden his own son, the Black Prince, on the battlefield.

On 23 September 1327 Edward III was told that his father had died at Berkeley Castle two days earlier. The official explanation was illness, brought about by grief, as *The Brut* reported. But the timing of Edward II's death was suspiciously convenient for Roger Mortimer. While there was – in spite of the growing unpopularity of Isabella and Mortimer – little support for the former king's restoration, opponents of the new order had certainly been plotting to rescue Edward, and the regime was accordingly nervous. It is highly likely, therefore, that Roger Mortimer ordered the former king to be murdered. Some believed that he had been strangled or suffocated. However, in a ghastly echo of the scandals which had surrounded his dalliance with Piers Gaveston and then his involvement with the much more substantial sexual predator and powerbroker Despenser, rumours even circulated that he had been sodomized to death. The Benedictine chronicler Ranulf Higden, writing in the 1340s, described his fate as follows: 'Edward sometime king was brought from Kenilworth to the castle of Berkeley, where he was slain with a hot spit put through the privy place posterial.' Edward was buried at Gloucester Cathedral on 20 December.

After the traumas of the first year of his rule, the clouds above Edward III briefly lifted towards the end of December 1327. Philippa of Hainault was brought across to England, escorted by two of the king's closest friends, Bartholomew Burghersh and William Clinton, and arrived in London just before Christmas. On 26 January 1328 the couple married at York Minster. *The Brut* caught the genuine happiness of the occasion, describing how Philippa was met

> With great rejoicing, and a noble show of lords, barons and knights, high-born ladies and beautiful damsels, with rich display of dress and jewels, with jousts too, and tourneys for a lady's love, with dancing and carolling, with great and rich feasts day by day; and these celebrations lasted for the space of three weeks.

Silver, jewels and plate worth over £2,400 were purchased for the event, and lavish cloth of gold. Philippa presented her husband with a beautiful illuminated manuscript of a fourteenth-century French allegorical poem, the *Roman de Fauvel*, which contained copies of two pieces of music – secular *chansons*, light and humorous in tone – to be performed at the wedding.

Such festivities offered welcome relief from political reality elsewhere. On 4 May 1328, Parliament formally ratified the Treaty of Edinburgh, in which England was forced to renounce all rights of Scottish overlordship. Robert the Bruce was accepted as King of

Scots and a marriage alliance was made between his son David and
Edward III's sister Joan. This agreement had been decided upon by
Isabella and Mortimer and Edward was forced to put his name to it;
he subsequently showed his distaste for the arrangement by refusing to attend the wedding.

And so it went on. For the next two years Roger Mortimer
consolidated his power, ensuring his elevation to the earldom of
March and promoting the interests of his family and a narrow
group of friends. The nobility were growing increasingly restive,
but lacked an effective focus for opposition. And Edward III was
a passive figure – still young and inexperienced and perhaps not
surprisingly lacking in confidence after all that had happened to
him – controlled by Isabella and Mortimer and presiding over a
realm still fractured and divided.

†

England had been going through a long and difficult process
of transition. From 1066 it was part of an Anglo-Norman kingdom; following the marriage of Henry of Anjou (later Henry II)
to Eleanor of Aquitaine in 1152, it belonged to a larger Plantagenet
empire, stretching from the Scottish border to the south of France.
Most of these continental possessions had been lost in the thirteenth century, in the troubled reigns of King John and Henry III,
leaving Gascony (part of the duchy of Aquitaine) as a remnant. In
the last three decades of the thirteenth century the warrior-king
Edward I had attempted to forge a fresh identity for the nation, subduing Wales, attempting to conquer Scotland, and – with a strong
promotion of the Arthurian legends, drawn from Geoffrey of
Monmouth's twelfth-century *History of the Kings of Britain* – encouraging a sense of destiny among his people.

For a while Edward I had been successful. Contemporaries were
struck by the vigour of his martial enterprises. Wales was pacified by
a string of newly built castles; the king's son (the future Edward II)

was born at the royal fortress of Caernarfon and invested as Prince of Wales. In 1296 Scotland was vanquished in a whirlwind campaign. And Edward's invocation of the deeds of King Arthur (portrayed by Geoffrey of Monmouth as a resolute leader, fighting a series of battles for the cause of Celtic Britain) in celebratory tournaments, caught the popular imagination. A great military leader was once more on the throne and pride and self-belief were rekindled.

But Edward's conquest of Scotland did not last. The rebellions of William Wallace and Robert the Bruce wore away the king's strength and drained his treasury. And his son, Edward II, who succeeded his father in 1307, proved totally incompetent in military affairs, as in much else. The hopes for a new Arthur were dashed in 1314 at Bannockburn – one of the most calamitous defeats endured by the English in the entire Middle Ages.

Military affairs were only part of the story. An effective king needed to unite the political community behind him. In the thirteenth century England had gone through a period of profound constitutional change. The Magna Carta of 1215, and the Provisions of Oxford and Westminster of 1258–59, had placed restraints on royal power, and a Parliament had come into being (from 1265). A fourteenth-century monarch needed to govern with the assent of the political community, and, to provide good government, his relations with the aristocracy were crucial.

In 1330 the English nobility consisted of some fifty earls and barons (entitled to take their seats, along with the bishops, in the House of Lords) and around 400 knights (representing the shires, some of whom were allowed to take places – after a process of election – in the House of Commons, alongside designated burgesses from the towns). To command respect within the English aristocracy an English king was expected to administer justice impartially and to be even-handed in his dispensation of patronage, the grants of lands and offices within the royal gift. He also needed to be an able war leader. And above all he had to create a court that rose above faction, where all could come together, united by pride in the magnificence of their ruler and uplifted by a vision of their nation's destiny and its place within European Christendom. Edward II had signally failed in all these respects and now the regime of Isabella and Mortimer was doing little better.

In March 1330 unsubstantiated but disturbing rumours began to circulate that Edward II was not in fact dead, but had somehow escaped to the continent. On the vaguest of insinuations, Edward III's uncle Edmund, earl of Kent (the younger son of Edward I by his second marriage, to Margaret of France, and thus by implication a potential claimant to the throne), was arrested and accused of treason. Although the king wished to pardon him, he was overruled by Mortimer, who ordered Kent's execution. This decision caused such outrage that nobody could be found to carry out the sentence; eventually an obscure member of the royal household came forward to conduct the beheading. Edward's movements were being closely watched by Roger Mortimer's agents, and his correspondence was frequently opened by them. There were even rumours that Queen Isabella was pregnant with Mortimer's child, and that he was now planning to usurp the throne.

It was the birth of his own son, in the summer of 1330, which galvanized the king. What followed was described in colourful detail in Sir Thomas Gray's *Scalacronica* and *The Brut*. Plans were made in secrecy and only confided to the king's most trusted friends. In October 1330 Queen Isabella and Roger Mortimer had moved to Nottingham, intending to summon a council there to discuss affairs of state. Arriving in advance of the king, they had installed themselves in the castle, surrounded by Mortimer's men. Edward III and a group of young followers, headed by William Montagu and William Clinton, now decided that Mortimer must be seized by force; it was a risky and dangerous course of action, but they could see no alternative. As Montagu said bluntly: 'It is better to eat the dog than let the dog eat you.'

Edward and his allies moved up close to Nottingham and, as night fell on 19 October, rode hard towards the castle. Its keeper,

William Eland, informed the king that most of the garrison were keeping sentry duty on the walls or manning the gate. But Eland knew of a secret tunnel in the cliff that opened directly into the keep; he promised to lead the attackers through it. The group stole into the castle, stormed the queen's apartments, killing the few servants or guards who resisted, and burst into her bedchamber. Mortimer was found hiding behind a curtain, and, according to the chronicler Geoffrey le Baker, the queen even pleaded for the life of her lover, crying out: 'Fair son, fair son, have pity on the noble Mortimer.'

Whether Isabella actually caught sight of her son is far from clear, but Mortimer was hauled out of the castle and taken post-haste to London. The sheriffs of every county were ordered to proclaim that he had been arrested and the king was now committed to rule 'according to right and reason, as befits his royal dignity'. On 26 November, Mortimer was tried before Parliament at Westminster and accused – among other charges – of the murder of the late king. He was found guilty of treason and executed by hanging at Tyburn, 'the common gallows of thieves', as Geoffrey le Baker remarked; an ignominious end for an aristocrat. The queen was confined to Castle Rising in Norfolk, barred from all political activity and placed in a state of near banishment.

The young Edward III had decisively asserted his royal authority and a sense of relief was felt by his entire kingdom. 'It was now a time of celebration', Sir Thomas Gray recalled, 'and the king and his companions indulged to the full in tournaments, hunting, feasting and ceremony'. The Christmas court at Guildford in 1330 was a particularly splendid occasion, replete with jousting. At the tournament in Dartford, in April 1331, according to the St Paul's chronicler, the monarch 'performed very well, although he was of tender age, and battered by heavy blows – enduring all most strongly'. At Cheapside later that year, on 22 September, the same chronicler related:

> The whole market area... was enclosed with stout timber and
> planks, and the pavement was strewn with sand... And at the
> time for which the tournament was arranged, the king and all
> his knights gathered in London... There came with them many
> of the most noble and beautiful women of the kingdom, all
> wearing red velvet tunics and caps of white camel's hair cloth.

In December 1331 Edward and Philippa toured sites in the West
Country, at Cadbury and Glastonbury, associated in Geoffrey of
Monmouth's *History* with King Arthur and his queen, Guinevere.
Their love of chivalric romances formed a wellspring of their personal affection – as well as giving her husband the illuminated
manuscript of the *Roman de Fauvel* as a wedding gift, three years
later Philippa had a silver cup made for him, richly decorated with
castles, banners, mythical beasts, all surrounding the figure of
a king – and it now began to enrich their court. And they were
united by their pride in their first child. When Philippa's mother,
the countess of Hainault, visited the court in the summer of 1331
the king ensured that the baby prince was provided with a fitting
array of clothing, so that he could be properly presented to her.

And it was in one of those early tournaments that the king
adopted the badge of the sunburst, a breath of wind bursting from
the clouds to reveal a hidden sun. The medieval world was fascinated by puns and the device was a play on Edward's birthplace,
with intertwining symbols of 'winds' and 'gold' – which in French,
the language of the court, was *or* – spelling out, in symbolic form,
the word 'Windsor'. In an age acutely aware of visual imagery, it
perfectly caught the mood after the Nottingham coup.

But the king's mind was turning to thoughts of war. The Scots
had humiliated him and wreaked havoc on the northern part of
his country. King Edward was determined to exact revenge, but he
would not rush into battle. The succession of tournaments was no
mere courtly distraction; they served an important military func-
tion as training exercises, in which skill in weaponry was honed

and group fighting co-ordinated. At Bannockburn, in 1314, the English had fought a series of disparate, piecemeal engagements, unable to engage with the enemy as a whole. Edward resolved not to make that mistake again.

He was also determined to use a particularly devastating weapon, the longbow – with its rapid rate of fire and ability to penetrate armour – to best effect. English archers, left unprotected, had been routed by a Scottish cavalry charge at Bannockburn; in the Weardale campaign of 1327 they had been pushed too far in front of the army and suffered a similar fate. Edward learned from these errors. And he was struck by how, in an engagement at Dupplin Moor on 12 August 1332, a small force of English bowmen had been used effectively when protected by the army's tactical formation and by the terrain. The king realized that, in the right circumstances, they could be a trump card against the Scots.

In May 1333 Edward III was ready to put his plan into action. He marched a well-equipped and well-trained army up to the Scottish border and besieged Berwick, which had been in Scots hands since 1318, and which the king wanted to recover for the English. But he also wanted to draw the Scots into battle, on ground of his own choosing. His opponents were over-confident – underestimating both the English king and his soldiers – and fell into the trap. On 19 July the two armies faced each other at Halidon Hill, 2 miles (3.2 km) north-west of Berwick.

Edward placed his archers on the flanks of his army, where they could unleash their arrows to best effect while being protected by his dismounted men-at-arms. Anticipating a Scottish attack, and with a keen eye for the terrain, he noticed an obstacle to their advance: a large marshy creek-bed between the two forces, with steep ground rising on either side of it. It would slow the advance of the Scots and make them a target for his bowmen. Most crucially, the creek was out of sight of the enemy troops as they assembled, so they remained unaware of its existence. As a Scottish chronicler, Andrew of Wyntoun, ruefully observed:

They made their way to Halidon ready to fight, for they were
more numerous [than the English] and believed themselves to
be superior troops. They drew up for battle in good order and
advanced upon the enemy. But they had not properly considered the terrain.

The Scots resolved they would give no quarter to their foe and
pushed forward in the expectation of easy victory. It was just what
Edward had been waiting for. He had taken enormous care to give
his bowmen plenty of ammunition – the sheriffs of London sent
195 sheaves (each of twenty-four arrows) to his army, and these
were only a small proportion of the total used – and as the Scottish troops stumbled up the sides of the creek, the English archers
unleashed volley after volley upon their opponents. *The Brut* gave a
jingoistic rendition of the battle's onset:

> The English minstrels sounded their drums, trumpets and
> pipes, and the Scots let out their hideous war-cry. Each divi-
> sion of the English army had two wings of good archers, who
> when the armies came into contact shot arrows so thickly as
> the rays in sunlight, hitting the Scots in such a way that they
> struck them down by the thousands, and they began to flee in
> order to save their lives. But when the servants in the rear saw
> the scale of the defeat, they fled with all the horses, leaving their
> masters stranded.

One contingent of Scottish soldiers, 'grievously wounded in the
face and blinded by the archery', had been forced to turn back
even before reaching the English line; another, weakened by the
arrow-storm, attacked Edward's dismounted men-at-arms, but
was quickly repulsed. Their line was breaking up in disarray and
the English king sensed that the moment had come to press for
a complete victory – a victory that would ease the pain of years
of military shame and hurt. *The Brut* continued, with ill-concealed
delight:

With this, the English mounted up, and charged the enemy, overtaking them and striking them down. There one could see the valiant and noble King Edward of England and his men, and how vigorously they chased their foe. Scottish banners were hacked to pieces, heraldic surcoats bathed in blood and bodies were strewn everywhere. Small groups of men rallied, attempted to make a stand, but were always defeated. And so it came about that day, as God had willed it, that Scottish numerical superiority against the English was of little help to them – they gained no more advantage than twenty sheep would have done, when faced with five wolves.

This was a pulverizing English triumph. Of nine Scottish earls who fought in the battle, six perished. Of the 200 knights dubbed on the field, only five survived. 'So many nobles were killed,' a Scottish source lamented, 'it would be tedious to give all their names, and more saddening than useful.' English casualties were very light.

Jean le Bel, who had chronicled the disastrous Weardale campaign six years earlier, was not present at the battle, but it was clear to the chronicler that a complete transformation had taken place. He described how Edward III, 'loved and honoured by great and small alike for the great nobility of his deeds, returned to England with much joy and worship'. Thanksgiving Masses and processions were held across the country. A parade of all the clergy and citizens of London carried the city's relics from St Paul's to Trinity Church and back, praising God and their king and rejoicing at the victory. Jubilant songs were composed in the king's honour, proclaiming that he had avenged the English defeat at Bannockburn. As le Bel put it: 'Everyone said he was a second Arthur.'

At the start of the campaign, Philippa and the infant prince had accompanied Edward as far north as Durham, where they stayed in the priory awaiting the king's return. It was a joyous reunion. The couple had survived the pain and trauma of Edward II's deposition and the early years of Edward's rule; now a future of hope and aspiration was emerging. However, Edward III's memories of his late father were still contaminated by enmity and bitterness, so as he and his family travelled south they paid their respects at the deceased king's tomb at Gloucester Cathedral, in an attempt to lay these ghosts to rest.

A new opportunity was beckoning to the king and to his son – the path of the warrior. Instead of being manipulated by the machinations of others, they would seize the initiative and shape their own future. Both would fight together in a common cause, healing the pain of the past through glory in battle. And that fight would be taken to the greatest enemy of all: the kingdom of France. The shame of Edward II's reign would be expunged by the winning of chivalric renown and by fame so stirring that every European court would take notice of it. Thus was forged the destiny of the Black Prince.

chapter two

THE VISION

Details of the Black Prince's early life are scanty. He was baptized by Henry Burghersh, bishop of Lincoln and Edward III's chancellor, who was from a family that would play a prominent part in the Prince's education as he was growing up. From birth he was regarded as a future earl of Chester, the traditional estate of the king's eldest son, and provision was made for the child and his attendants through a yearly grant of 500 marks (£333 13s 4d) from the county. In practice, his small household – the group of servants who cared for him – was joined with that of the queen's, and he travelled with his mother around England or stayed with her at royal residences, Woodstock being a particular favourite.

In June 1332 the Prince's sister Isabella was born; another sister, Joan, arrived later the following year. On 18 March 1333 he was formally created earl of Chester, his first title, although its revenues were brought into his mother's household as he continued to live with her. Cutting a fine appearance was all-important in Edward III's family, and from 1334 the young Prince had his own tailor, William Stratton, who made fine silk robes for the three-year-old as he celebrated Whitsun with the queen at Woodstock.

The Black Prince's youth was spent in the surroundings of a magnificent court that delighted in tournaments, gift-giving, feasting and celebration. At the age of three the Prince also had his own almoner, an official responsible for the granting of alms and offerings. This showed that the young child was already taking part in royal visits and was expected, through his servant, to participate actively and make appropriate gifts. This was the milieu that shaped his outlook.

At the age of seven the Prince was given his own suit of armour, scaled down for size but accurately representing every item of equipment used in the joust or on the battlefield. He had his own war tent to pack and unpack, and his own sword. These were not merely expensive toys: Edward had high expectations of the Black Prince, even from such an early age, and required his son and heir to master the world of chivalry and to become steeped in its conventions. In 1336 the Prince attended his first tournament; his tailor provided a cloak for the occasion, trimmed with fur. In the following years he was first a regular spectator at such events and then (from the age of thirteen) an active participant, alongside his friends, chosen household officers and fellow warriors.

Through such martial and ceremonial events, which the Black Prince would learn to recreate in his own adulthood, Edward III hoped to instill a renewed sense of pride in his dynasty. However, in the first decade of his rule, as his heir grew to manhood, not everyone was won over. The professional soldier Sir Thomas Gray wrote rather dismissively that early in his reign the king 'led a merry life of jousts, tourneys and entertaining ladies — until more serious matters arose'. Gray was a hard man to please, a tough fighter whose outlook was forged in the bleak warfare of the Scottish borders, and even after Edward III's great victory at Halidon Hill he damned his monarch with faint praise, being unable to resist a jibe: 'When the battle was finished the king of England took himself back to the south, where he attended assiduously to *peaceful* deeds of arms' [author's italics]. Gray was echoing a comment he had earlier made about Edward II after the 1322 Scottish expedition; he was impressed by perseverance on military campaign, not courtly celebration.

Edward's tournaments were deliberately ostentatious, and their elaborate finery was not to everyone's taste. Some saw them as unnecessary and a waste of money; others felt that its participants were indulging themselves in a world of empty pride and vanity.

Such criticisms of Edward III in the 1330s and early 1340s would be repeated in relation to the court of the Black Prince in Aquitaine some twenty years later, so it is important that we look deeper into this world, and uncover its real purpose. Without this, it will be hard to comprehend either the Prince, or his policy, as an adult ruler in France acting on behalf of his father.

†

Tournaments originated in western Europe in the twelfth century and – for all the old soldier Gray's sneering – were often rough and violent affairs. In their earliest form participants were divided into two teams who fought on horseback with sword and lance in a large, marked-out arena. In the thirteenth century jousts were introduced: these were individual encounters between two knights in a clearly enclosed space, the 'lists', where they fought each other under the gaze of a crowd of spectators. There was an increasing degree of ceremony and ritual on these occasions, and at a tournament at Chauvency in Lorraine in 1285 jousting and general festivities took place over an entire week. A local poet, Jacques Bretex, left a detailed account of it, opening a window on an extraordinary world.

The event was announced weeks in advance and knights came from across a wide area to take part. Heralds spread the word and also acted as masters of ceremonies once the event began, in a fashion somewhat similar to modern-day sports commentators: identifying each competitor by his coat of arms, calling out his name before the fight and, when appropriate, praising his performance. The tournament began with an evening dance, held in the great hall of the castle and attended by all of the most important knights and their ladies. Bretex recalled that it went on until well after midnight.

The following morning all the contestants attended Mass and then everyone processed to the jousting arena outside the castle walls, where the ladies seated themselves above the lists on specially erected wooden scaffolds. Although tournaments were primarily aristocratic affairs, ordinary people from the locality also attended, helping in the work of setting up the event and waiting on the participants in the festivities that followed it. On the entry of each knight into the lists, the heralds gave a running commentary as they drew up in their fine armour and charged their opponents. In the morning events all of the knights 'broke their lances' as they hit their targets. The number of injuries was frightening: the first jouster broke his arm when his mount fell; and during the fifth encounter two horses collided with such force that their riders – who were clearly badly concussed – were feared dead.

The assembly was not daunted by such mishaps; indeed, it seemed to thrive on them. Between jousts the heralds addressed the ladies, making it clear that knights were risking life and limb to win their favour. A new group of knights arrived at noon and another later in the afternoon and the jousting continued until sunset. Then the ladies came down from the stands and the whole company went back to the castle for a banquet and a singing competition, in which everyone competed. Then there was more dancing and once again it was very late before everyone retired.

The next day champions noted for their skill and prowess were matched. The compliments from the heralds grew ever more lavish, as in this example:

> See how Sir Gerard is inflamed by courage and boldness in the fight. Nor is his ardour doused once he removes his helmet, but is transformed into courtesy, loyalty and generosity. He displays all these attributes – both in the lists and in the festivities in the castle.

The festivities became increasingly sumptuous. That evening there were plays and 'diversions' alongside the singing and dancing. The following day was an opportunity for rest, story-telling, light-hearted boasting of feats of arms performed and good-natured mocking of the claims of fellow knights.

The tournament culminated with a team competition. There was a din of trumpets, drums, horns and bugles as the contestants gathered in the appointed place, the sun glinting on the armour and trappings of the contestants. A mock battle began, in which lances were prohibited but swords and clubs were used. A chaotic, swirling fight ensued, with helmets knocked off, weapons broken and faces gashed. One group – engrossed in combat – even collided with the scaffold where the spectators were gathered. Increasing numbers of wounded were carried from the field. Before nightfall, the tournament winners were chosen from the handful of knights still standing following the mayhem. After dinner, there was more dancing (by those who were still capable of it) and songs were sung of lovers and their ladies. It was almost dawn before everyone was in bed, although who was in which bed Bretex discreetly passed over. After a few hours' sleep, Mass was once again celebrated and, after a last communal song, everyone departed.

Tournaments on the lavish scale evoked by Bretex were also devised by the English king Edward I, Edward III's grandfather. At Nefyn Castle in 1284 (a year before Chauvency), a tourney was held to celebrate King Edward's conquest of Wales. A large number of knights attended and the press was so great that the floor in the upper room set aside for the dancing collapsed. Remarkably, none of the participants seems to have been seriously injured.

Some of the ferocity of the earlier twelfth-century tournaments was now abating. Specialist armour was padded for better protection and the combat arena was more clearly marked out. Edward I set out ordinances regulating these events, limiting the number of followers a knight could bring and prohibiting them from carrying real weapons of war. He insisted that the majority of jousts were fought with blunted lances or swords. And yet, even with such provisions, the risk of serious injury or death was ever present.

Edward I's son, Edward II, showed no interest in knightly combat and discouraged tournaments. This was an unpopular move with the nobility, and his son, Edward III, reinstated them as speedily as possible – introducing ever more splendid costumes and disguises. Edward and his close personal friend William Montagu often gave each other gifts of tournament outfits and presided over rival teams dressed in costumes of their own devising, or that reflected characters and scenes from the popular Arthurian romances of the late-twelfth-century French poet Chrétien de Troyes.

The church thoroughly disapproved of these elaborately staged events and the hedonism that sometimes accompanied them. The chronicler of Meaux Abbey in Yorkshire wrote sternly that early in the reign of Edward III:

> The king and nobility of England held tournaments in various cities and towns throughout the realm, to which ladies and other gentlewomen were invited. But scarcely any married women attended with her husband but instead was chosen by some other man, who used her to satisfy his sexual urges.

Henry Knighton noted that whenever a tournament was held:

> A troop of ladies would turn up dressed in a variety of extraordinary clothing, as if taking part in a play. There were sometimes as many as forty or fifty of them, representing the showiest and most beautiful – but not the most virtuous – women of the whole realm. They were dressed in multi-coloured tunics with short hoods and wore belts – thickly studded with gold and silver – slung across their hips, below the navel.. . .

The king's friend Henry of Grosmont was a notable jouster and skilful fighter. He took part in the famous Cheapside tournament in September 1331 and was one of Edward's principal captains in the Scottish campaigns that followed it, rising rapidly to the post of king's lieutenant there in 1336. Later in his life he wrote a devotional treatise, *Le Livre de Seyntz Medicines* (*The Book of Holy Medicine*), which contained alongside its religious narrative many candid reminiscences of the sexual opportunities that tournaments afforded.

In his book, Henry of Grosmont spoke of the thrill of the tournament, of his pride in wearing finely wrought armour, and of how,
when jousting, he would stretch out his legs in the stirrups so that
watching women would get a better view of his calves. Nowhere
did he mention his wife – the marriage had been arranged when
both were young and there seems to have been little affection in
it – and she clearly did not accompany him on such occasions.
Henry was a sensual, tactile man who enjoyed a magnificent lifestyle. He loved fine clothes and jewelled rings on his fingers: when
he pawned some of his possessions to help raise a loan for one of
King Edward's military campaigns they included no fewer than
seven coronets and eleven gold circlets.

Henry of Grosmont enjoyed the hunt, as did many aristocrats.
He also loved to dance – he had his own dancing chamber at his
castle in Leicester – and thought himself pretty good at it. He was
fond of the rich food and well-spiced dishes served at banquets,
salmon being a particular favourite, and he liked getting drunk.
He drank wine, he confided disarmingly, 'to put myself and my
friends out of our senses, for it is a good feeling to be merry'. He
over-indulged in the feasts that followed a day of hard jousting, so
that his legs 'were neither so good or so ready to bring me away
as they were to get me there'. And he admitted that he had made
love to many different women, sometimes 'taking a great delight in
lust', and the excitement of being 'praised, then loved and then lost
by women'. He revelled in the erotic scent of high-born ladies and
the sexual responsiveness of commoners. At the tournament there
was no shortage of partners in either category.

Yet these reminiscences only told part of the story. Henry of
Grosmont had shared them for a reason, to portray an inner battle
against the seven deadly sins, which he compared to a castle's walls
being breached by the temptations of the Devil. His book extolled
the redemptive power of faith in Christ and advocated a morally
disciplined life. To attain this, he had put the pleasures of the flesh
behind him, becoming instead an ardent crusader, first in Spain

and then Prussia, ready 'to fight, at his own expense, all enemies of the Christian faith'.

To his contemporaries, Henry was above all a consummate soldier, tough, skilled in war and well versed in chivalry. Jean Froissart described him as 'a great and famous warrior', and even Sir Thomas Gray was won over, praising him as 'a man of honour, valiant and enterprising in all feats of arms'. As the Black Prince grew into manhood, Grosmont was no longer a dissolute courtier but one of Edward III's leading commanders; his victories in Gascony in 1345, at Auberoche and Bergerac, would establish his military reputation on an international stage.

Tournaments offered knights opportunities to gain prizes and martial renown, but above all they provided training in horsemanship, in the handling of weapons, and in individual combat and group operations, both mounted and on foot. And through them a real and lasting *esprit de corps* was formed. This truth was well understood by some medieval rulers, though not by all of them. In the twelfth century, when the English king Henry II banned tournaments, the chronicler Roger of Howden related that the king's son Richard (the future Richard the Lionheart) sought them out on the continent instead:

> For he knew that skill in battle can only be acquired through practice, and that a knight who has never seen blood flow, has not heard teeth crunch under the blow of an opponent or felt the full weight of an adversary upon him is simply unfit for war.

When Richard came to the throne, he reversed his father's decision and licensed tournaments because he saw that the French 'were fiercer and better trained in war, and he did not want the warriors of his own kingdom reproached for any lack of courage or skill'.

†

Edward III would also repudiate his own father's policy and seek to create knights of prowess and renown on the battlefield, drawing upon the legacy of the great English warrior kings and also the courtly culture of his wife's home in Hainault, where its ruler, Count William, regularly held jousts and festivities based on a recreation of the Arthurian Round Table (extolled, in Geoffrey of Monmouth, as the pre-eminent symbol of King Arthur's warrior court). In the tournament lifestyle encouraged by Edward III, there lay a mailed fist beneath the velvet glove. For amid the feasting and celebration, the Prince's father was constantly preoccupied by war. One incident was particularly telling.

In November 1334 news of a fresh threat from Scotland reached Edward III and his court. The king, undeterred by the winter weather, resolved to venture north immediately. His response showed courage and determination: Edward was seeking to banish the spectre of the terrible Weardale of campaign of 1327. The weather in 1334 was, again, atrocious, as the Yorkshire chronicler of Meaux Abbey related: 'At about the feast of St Martin [11 November] a heavy frost appeared and the snow began to fall. Ice was everywhere. No one could remember ever having seen such bad weather.' Pushing on, through wind, frost and thunderclaps, King Edward marched north with several hundred soldiers and by late November had reached Newcastle, where he picked up supplies and reinforcements. His intended destination was the fortress of Roxburgh, on the Scottish marches, at the junction of the rivers Tweed and Teviot. Although the castle's strategic position made it a natural base for operations, it had been demolished by the Scots after they had captured it in 1314, the year of Bannockburn, and it now lay in ruins.

In such a harsh winter, setting up quarters in a broken shell of a castle was hardly an attractive prospect, but Edward III was undaunted. He ordered Newcastle's carpenters to construct wooden buildings, split into sections, so they could easily be carried north and assembled on site; these included a tower, hall and out-houses.

Then the king and his followers moved up to Roxburgh, intending to camp out in their makeshift prefabricated accommodation.

Not all of them got there. Winter campaigning was challenging at the best of times, and the conditions were terrible. As the army crossed the Scottish border and reached Annandale, its constable, Sir Edward de Bohun, tried to save a man-at-arms who had fallen into the flooded river. Sir Edward rode into the Annan and attempted to lift the man up on to his horse; but the panic-stricken soldier, flailing about wildly, only succeeded in pulling his rescuer into the water as well, drowning both men. De Bohun had been a prominent leader of the Nottingham coup and was a divisional commander at Halidon Hill. His loss was hard for Edward to bear.

The king called for reinforcements from the northern counties to swell his army, but as temperatures plummeted many knights ignored the royal summons to fight. Still mindful of de Bohun's heroic sacrifice, Edward was having none of it. On 15 December he wrote to Nicholas de Mesnil, who, with twenty-eight others, had made a series of excuses to avoid turning up. The king began:

> We have been with our army, in our lands in the marches of Scotland, for the safety and defence of our realm and the people that dwell within it. The Scots have risen against us in war, with the intention of entering our kingdom and burning and destroying its lands, and they grow stronger every day, gathering all the forces they can to harm us.

Having set the scene, Edward quickly got to the point:

> Yet, although we have often sent you letters, asking that you come to us – well-provided with horses and weaponry – to help us repulse the malice of our enemies, you have continued to disobey our orders, putting our army in danger and showing an utter disregard of our commands. By doing this, you are delaying the success of our enterprise – to your considerable dishonour

and shame. We marvel at this, and are greatly angered [by your behaviour], as well we should be.

And then, in no uncertain terms, the king made clear what he now expected:

So we order you once again, on pain of forfeiture of all that you possess, and making no excuses, that you come to us with all the forces that you can muster. We shall expect you at Roxburgh, properly equipped and with food and supplies for fifteen days, by New Year's Day at the latest. And we warn you now, that if you fail to do this, disobeying our summons and once more putting us in danger – and through such inaction encouraging others in your locality to do the same – we shall inflict on you such punishment that everyone will be taught a lesson by your example.

William Dene, a clerk in the service of the bishop of Rochester, wrote approvingly:

The king of England had decided to drive back the Scots from the English border. In order to repel them he spent the winter at Roxburgh; the costs were great and the weather was particularly harsh. He took some of his magnates with him, and a group of young English knights – but all in all had relatively few soldiers. And yet, no one bore the hardship and harshness [of that winter] better than he, or laboured more willingly – and all the time he greatly comforted his army by words, gifts and deeds... And thus he inspired their resolve.

Queen Philippa travelled to Roxburgh in December and joined her husband for a week, sharing in the hardships of life on campaign and leaving her children behind for safe-keeping. It was a brave decision. What her four-year-old son, the Black Prince, later heard about this desolate place – the dramatic weather, the mix of danger and sheer excitement and the camaraderie between his father and his fellow fighters – may well have left a strong impression.

William Dene recalled how Edward III joined his men on sentry duty or by the campfire and gambled with them, joking and telling stories, to lift their morale. A comment made by the king did the rounds: 'We all drink from the same cup.' Edward was prepared to tough things out with his men. And his son seems not to have forgotten the stories he heard of Roxburgh; when he reached adulthood and planned his own campaigns, he set aside a daily sum for gambling so that he could relax with his soldiers. And at Poitiers, his most famous victory – where he shared the same hardships as his troops and stood shoulder to shoulder with them in the line of battle – the same refrain passed from man to man, according to Geoffrey le Baker: 'We all drink from the same cup.'

The scope of King Edward's Roxburgh campaign was limited: he wished to discourage the Scots from mobilizing a raiding force. But in the summer of 1335 he returned with a much larger army and penetrated deeper into the country. It was, according to William Dene, the best-ordered and supplied army seen in recent memory and it struck hard against the enemy, 'burning and destroying – and taking much booty'. The king was returning to the policy of his grandfather, Edward I: supporting a rival claimant to the Scottish throne, Edward Balliol, to undermine the regime of Robert the Bruce's young son David. Edward III's effective campaigning had already driven the eleven-year-old monarch into temporary exile in France, although his supporters continued the struggle on his behalf. But at the end of this summer campaign, on 18 August, a host of Scottish noblemen transferred their allegiance to Balliol, leaving the cause of David Bruce considerably weakened.

There now was an opportunity to negotiate a very different treaty from the humiliating settlement imposed in 1328. New proposals were set out, according to which Balliol would rule for his lifetime and then make David Bruce his heir. If Edward III had secured general agreement on this, it would have been a diplomatic triumph. But David Bruce, who had set up his court-in-exile at Château-Gaillard, near Les Andelys in Normandy, was a pawn of the French king, Philip VI. It suited Philip's purposes to encourage Scottish resistance to Edward, so David – on the advice of the French – withdrew from the negotiations and ordered his remaining followers in Scotland to continue fighting.

In the summer of 1336 Henry of Grosmont, the king's lieutenant in Scotland, struck once more against King David's partisans. At the end of June he was joined by Edward III himself. Edward had learned of French plans to send reinforcements to prop up King David's position. If these troops appeared on Scottish soil, it was a point of honour for him to be there in person to meet them.

To achieve this, King Edward had first hurried north, and then ridden non-stop from Berwick to Perth to join his lieutenant. This was an astonishing feat – covering a distance of 104 miles (167 km) in little more than two days, riding flat out, without rest, with a force of only a hundred mounted men-at-arms. Part of the dash was through enemy territory, putting the king and his companions 'in the greatest danger', as William Dene related; but, as he continued, English soldiers 'welcomed their king with tears of joy and applauded his bravery'.

Edward III was conducting military affairs with remarkable energy and the raid that he led from Perth some two weeks later displayed, if anything, even greater boldness. He had heard that one of Edward Balliol's supporters, the countess of Atholl, was besieged in the castle of Lochindorb by Bruce's soldiers, and that the countess, along with the other women of her household ('all of them beautiful ladies', Sir Thomas Gray noted, in an uncharacteristically gallant aside) and her small garrison were running short of supplies. The king decided to ride to the countess's rescue, and the course of his exploit was subsequently relayed to Queen Philippa by letter. The story began on Friday 12 July 1336:

> Our lord the king of England moved out of Perth that day so suddenly that few had even received orders to arm themselves.

He put up his tents in the fields that night, having with him only 400 mounted men-at-arms and as many archers. And the following morning he rode to the castle of Blair-Atholl, a distance of twenty miles. The day afterwards, he crossed the fastness of Atholl, passing some of the highest and most difficult parts of Scotland, and covering a further thirty miles.

Edward III was now closing in on Bruce's besieging troops, and neither they nor the beleaguered garrison had the remotest idea that he was approaching. The news-letter resumed its narrative:

> The following Monday [15 July], hearing the whereabouts of the Scottish siege force around Castle Lochindorb, where the Countess of Atholl was, the king rode hell-for-leather for a distance of sixteen miles, and then, dismissing his baggage train [with battle imminent] he advanced two miles short of the castle, within sight of the tents of the besiegers. And when the enemy suddenly saw his force, they fled in all directions.

With banners raised in triumph, Edward and his followers proudly rode into Lochindorb, to be greeted by its overjoyed defenders:

> The Countess repeatedly thanked our lord the king, telling him of the deprivation and suffering endured by herself and her ladies, adding that for everyone in the castle there no longer remained any victuals, except for one cask of wine, of little or no worth, and two bushels of grain; and that they did not even have any straw upon which they could lie down and take their rest.

The king had arrived just in time, as the news report was at pains to emphasize. On the last day alone Edward and his men had ridden some 40 miles (64 km) in total, 'over terrible paths, losing many of their horses, and they were themselves so short of supplies that hardly a side of beef was to be had for the entire army'. Now cattle were herded in from the surrounding countryside and wine, beer, bread and salt fish quickly acquired. That night 'all were refreshed, amid much rejoicing'.

The king had shown extraordinary bravery and vigour and had created a new sense of enterprise and self-belief among his warriors. He had brought the Scottish lowlands largely under his sway and conducted raids as far north as Aberdeen. It was a remarkable achievement. However, the war in Scotland did not always go his way. The following year Edward's friend William Montagu besieged Dunbar, which was holding out for David Bruce. Montagu began the siege confidently, bringing up an array of siege equipment and putting the fortress under sustained bombardment. The Scottish chronicler Andrew of Wyntoun recorded that 'Sir William Montagu was well prepared. He had a series of powerful catapults built – and they threw great stones, hard and heavy, against the walls.' The castle was held by Agnes, countess of Dunbar, and she was determined to put up a stout resistance. Well aware that King Edward had gained much kudos by coming to the assistance of the ladies of Lochinbar, and that Montagu was one of his principal captains, she decided to employ a little humour to mock his efforts. In the words of the chronicler: 'After the English had shot at the castle, a young lady, dressed prettily and well, wiped the wall with a towel in full view of the attackers – so that they could see her and be all the more annoyed.'

After a subsequent assault was beaten back, the countess leaned over the battlements, called out to her opponent in French, the language of chivalry: 'Adieu, Monsieur Montagu', and gave him a wave. The English were making little progress, and Edward, seeing the way the Scots were taunting his commander, and turning the enterprise into a propaganda opportunity of their own, grew uneasy and called the siege off.

The king now had greater issues on his mind – his thoughts were turning more and more towards the French. For Edward had resolved upon a most extraordinary step: he would claim the throne of France in his own right, and take the war to the enemy.

†

In order to understand this dramatic move, which would have far-reaching consequences for both King Edward and his son, we have to go back some ten years, to 1328. King Charles IV of France, the last monarch of the Capetian dynasty, had died in early February of that year, leaving no male heir. There were two chief claimants to the throne: King Edward III himself, through the right of his mother Queen Isabella, Charles IV's sister; and Edward's cousin Philip, count of Valois, King Charles's nearest relative in the male line. Early the following year the French aristocracy elected the count of Valois, who became Philip VI of France.

The English did not immediately contest the election. The fifteen-year-old Edward III was at this time very much under the control of Isabella and Mortimer, and Isabella was intent on maintaining her power in England, not provoking a war with France. And even after Edward had asserted his authority some two and a half years later, executing Mortimer and banishing his mother from court, his relations with Philip remained cordial. In 1332 the two monarchs had even discussed going on crusade together. What changed everything was King Philip's support for David Bruce of Scotland.

Philip VI was both surprised and dismayed by King Edward's emphatic victory against the Scots at Halidon Hill. When he offered David's exiled court protection the following year, in 1334, he was seeking to reassert both political and diplomatic authority over the new English king. At the same time, he began to demand stricter terms of homage from Edward for his holding the duchy of Aquitaine. When King Edward protested, Philip insisted that any settlement in Aquitaine be linked to that of Scotland, a prospect entirely unpalatable to the English. The French king also began to hint that he was prepared to use military force to back up his demands. From 1335 onwards there were rumours that Philip's fleet might land troops in Scotland in support of David Bruce's partisans, or even attempt an invasion of England. King Edward appeared to be caught in the grip of an ever-tightening vice.

In the short term the English king maintained military operations against Scotland and diplomatic negotiations with the French. But these were becoming increasingly fraught. As Philip was sheltering David Bruce, Edward in turn offered protection to Robert, count of Artois, who had rebelled against the French king. And when, in 1337, Philip VI threatened to confiscate English-held Gascony, King Edward put to Parliament his own rights to the crown of France.

It suited Edward's temperament to take the initiative in foreign affairs. He may genuinely have felt aggrieved that his claim had not been more strongly asserted in 1328. But the course he was embarking upon carried considerable risk. France had a larger population than England and a much richer economy. It also had a strong navy that could mount sudden counterattacks. Crucially, England's war with Scotland had not been concluded: Edward would have to seek out alliances on the continent, and these would take time and money to put into effect; and he would need to keep the support of the aristocracy and broader political community as he did so.

Sir Thomas Gray was struck by the king's new approach. He wrote of the Parliament of February 1337, where these measures were discussed:

> It was now agreed that the king should press his own rightful claim to the crown of France, renouncing all homage to Philip of Valois, his opponent, and declaring war upon him. In pursuit of this aim, envoys were sent to Germany to begin forming a series of alliances [against the French].

The Holy Roman Emperor, Ludwig of Bavaria, was Edward III's brother-in-law, but it remained to be seen whether he was seriously prepared to challenge the French. Gray also noted that Edward was rewarding his principal aristocratic supporters, mindful that much of the burden of fighting would fall upon them: 'The king bestowed his possessions liberally upon the good men among the nobility. Henry of Grosmont was made earl of Derby, William de Bohun, earl of Northampton and William Montagu earl of Salisbury.'

However, it was always dangerous to fight a war on two fronts. Gray was worried that royal resources would become overstretched once war with France began. He warned that with Edward and his aristocrats preoccupied by this new conflict 'many of the castles and fortresses won in Scotland might be lost again through lack of good governance'. He reported the concerns of William Montagu, 'at that time one of the most trusted of the king's council':

> Montagu was of the opinion that the alliance being formed with the Germans would not lead to any profitable result – and that the realm would not be able to bear the expenses of the conditions they were demanding [to give their support]. He believed they were greedily looking to enhance their own profit.

Montagu concluded by saying that in his view the war with Scotland needed to be finished first. Gray concurred, observing of the new continental alliances: 'They will cost enormous treasure, without gaining any real advantage... and cause new taxes to be levied on the kingdom, which will be a heavy burden on its people.'

Fresh horizons were opening up, whatever the risks. At the Parliament of February 1337 Edward III outlined a new role for his son, the Black Prince. The king knew that to build his diplomatic offensive properly he would need, for a while at least, to move his court abroad and base it in the counties of Hainault and Flanders, which were sympathetic to his claim to the crown of France. Edward's strategy was being undertaken with the blessing of his brother-in-law, Count William of Hainault, who had grown increasingly mistrustful of Philip VI of France and was organizing a coalition of allies on the English king's behalf. This transfer of authority would take time to put into effect and when it finally occurred some of Edward's powers would need to be delegated. He envisaged that during his absence, England would be governed by a specially appointed council. Looking ahead, the king decided that he wanted his son to lead it, as 'guardian of the realm'.

This was a surprising choice, given the Prince's age: he was six years old. His role would therefore be very much that of a figure-head, appearing at some formal occasions and being told a little about broader matters of policy; the routine of government would be left to others. Mindful of this, the king would staff the council with experienced advisers, trusted nobles and churchmen, to carry the burden of day-to-day administration. Nevertheless, he also expected his son to start learning 'on the job', gaining an education in matters of state. This was a heavy responsibility, even nominally, to place upon a young child.

Edward's decision in relation to the Prince came about after the sudden death of his younger brother, John of Eltham. John was a natural warrior, whose early career would uncannily echo that of the Black Prince. He had fought with distinction at Halidon Hill when he was only sixteen and his military skill was recognized by the grant of the office of Warden of the Northern Marches, holding the frontier with Scotland, three years later. He had already served as 'guardian of the realm', and the king, who was extremely fond of him, would almost certainly have appointed him to the post again. But on 13 September 1336, after leading a successful plundering raid into Scotland, John died suddenly at Perth. The circumstances were unclear – he succumbed to a virulent fever – and the West-minster Chronicler hinted that he might have been poisoned by one of Bruce's partisans.

The king's brother was only twenty years old. Edward III had the body embalmed, and he and his knights solemnly escorted it from Scotland to London, where John lay in state in St Paul's Cathedral. He was then buried in Westminster Abbey on 15 January 1337, the king commissioning an exceptionally fine alabaster effigy for the tomb.

Edward struggled to come to terms with his loss. The West-minster Chronicler related that he had terrible nightmares about losing his brother. Less than a month after his burial, on 9 February 1337, John's earldom of Cornwall was enlarged and granted to the Black Prince, who was invested with a new title, duke, creating the duchy of Cornwall that survives to the present day. Edward, still in the throes of grief, had determined that the Prince would carry his uncle's mantle. He wanted to create an independent household for him and was granting this additional income from the duchy to support it.

Documentary records of the time show, as one might expect in a young child, the Prince's liking for games, whether playing ball or dice; an interest in horsemanship and falconry; and an enjoyment of music, with frequent payments to minstrels. But his situation was changing rapidly. He was no longer to stay with his mother and instead was given his own retinue of servants and officials. The duchy of Cornwall estates ran beyond the county – they provided the Prince with residences at Berkhamsted Castle in Hertford-shire and Kennington in Surrey, conveniently close to the capital. Bartholomew Burghersh, a trusted servant of the king and skilful soldier and diplomat (the elder brother of Bishop Henry Burgh-ersh, who had baptized the Prince), became master of the Black Prince's household. And young Edward was expected to play a role at official events.

The Black Prince was now tutored by the scholar Walter Burley. His lessons – reading, writing, Latin and arithmetic – were designed to equip him with a basic understanding of government. He was also being schooled in philosophy and in court etiquette, and was undertaking martial training.

The king watched his son's progress carefully. Later in 1337 the young Prince met with two cardinals, sent by Pope Benedict XII in an attempt to stave off all-out war between England and France. He greeted them outside London, dressed in a new robe of purple velvet and wearing a hat specially made for the occasion, with a scarlet border sewn with pearls, and escorted them into the city followed by a great company of nobles. The king ensured that his son's wardrobe was appropriately sumptuous, with a view to the public appearances he was now starting to make. He had a variety of elegant hats embroidered with silver roses and a wide ribbon belt with 37 pieces of enamel and 234 pearls sewn on to it. He was given finely woven tapestries, suggesting that he had his own rooms or even a town house for his use. On one of these was a design of branches, with roses and mermaids bearing his coat of arms. His household staff now included a number of pages and valets and a butler. When he was ill, he was attended by one of the best London physicians, and a minstrel was rewarded for playing to him to cheer his recovery.

Open hostilities between England and France were not far off. Edward III went abroad in July 1338, moving most of his household to Antwerp, which became his base of operations, and leaving his eight-year-old son as 'guardian of England'. All acts of government were witnessed in the Black Prince's name, he appeared at certain state occasions and the remnants of the royal court gathered around him. His mother and sisters had crossed with the king to Flanders.

For much of the period of Edward III's absence the Prince stayed in the Tower of London. On 20 July 1338 orders were issued to provision it with a garrison of twenty men-at-arms and fifty archers and to strengthen its defences with palisades. With the king away, it was feared the French might launch a surprise naval assault on the capital and the Prince – as guardian – was pitched into the heart of these dramatic events. Sure enough, in October Philip VI's fleet sacked Southampton, Plymouth and the Isle of Wight; in London, the city authorities were ordered to drive wooden piles into the bed of the Thames to deter the approach of the enemy.

It seemed as if the Black Prince was co-ordinating the defence of England's capital, following his father's instructions 'that our city is to be closed and fortified against hostile attacks'. That, of course, was illusory: the real work was being carried out by others, the governing council headed by the earls of Arundel and Huntingdon, and John Stratford, the Archbishop of Canterbury. But he was being given a first taste of leadership and command. Messengers were now hastening back and forth across the Channel, carrying official documents from the king to his governing council in England. Edward's main concern was money. Shortly before his departure, he had put the economy on a war footing and on 4 August 1338 he was already complaining to the English council that they were not sending him enough cash:

> We made it known to you that on our arrival at Antwerp we expected to find here treasure and supplies, for our own people and for the endeavours that we are about to undertake, and instead we discovered that no goods had arrived whatsoever, and if we had not been able to raise a loan from some of our friends in these parts we would have been perpetually dishonoured to the peril of ourselves and the realm of England.

The aggrieved king demanded everything now be sent to him 'in all haste', adding that he wanted his councillors 'to take these matters as much to heart as you possibly can'. The Prince was to some extent cushioned from the king's anger. There is a measure of confidence in his first surviving letter, written to his mother on 21 October 1338. He was clearly proud to have been entrusted with the position of 'guardian of England'. His composition was guided by one of his clerks, but the stress caused by his father's relentless demands is also evident. The Prince opened with a conventional greeting:

> My dearest and most respected lady, I humbly commend myself to your highness with all the reverence I know and ask for your blessing. My most respected lady, I am much comforted by the news that you are well and I pray to God that he will long protect you by his grace.

Then the royal cash crisis reared its head:

> And, my dearest lady, as to what you lately ordered me in my letter, that I should apply all possible care and speed to hasten

the sending of the money and wool due to be sent to my lord
the king outside his kingdom of England – may it please you to
know, most honoured lady, that I and the council of my lord
[the king] have put such efforts into carrying out your orders
that the last wool [tax] is completely collected and will be sent
to him as quickly as anyone can with all the money.

The wool monopoly scheme had been concocted by Edward III's
ministers in 1337. The crown was to purchase the country's annual
wool crop at a standard price and then resell it on the continent at
a considerable profit. A consortium of merchants was to run the
operation and split the proceeds with the English government.
This sum was in theory supposed to fund King Edward's war effort.
In practice, there was a considerable financial shortfall. The Prince,
aware of his father's wrath, concluded in a fashion that was both
harassed and determined: 'But no other aid can be raised by any
means, and I have written to tell him this in my other letters. My
most respected lady, may the Holy Spirit have you in his keeping.'

The king was struggling to bring his continental allies
together, and was losing more and more time in the process. There
was no doubting his energy as he travelled around Germany and
Flanders in a frantic round of diplomacy. But, as time went on,
Jean le Bel observed that the lavish hospitality of Edward's newly
established court at Antwerp was failing to yield concrete results:
'The noble King Edward put on a magnificent display and greatly
feasted his allies and honoured them and afterwards he drew them
into counsel very courteously and laid his business before them
in order to learn their intentions, and asked that they meet their
commitments quickly.' But the English king was met with a web of
obfuscation. Le Bel continued:

These lords responded to King Edward that they were not properly ready, or well counselled enough, to respond to what he
had asked for. They would go back to their own people, and

then return at a future date, and give a much fuller answer. The king saw that he would not get anything from them at that time — so he agreed a date with them for their return. .

When the agreed date drew near there was a fresh round of excuses:

Edward's allies now told him that they would be ready and equipped [to join an army to fight the French] as they had promised, but first the King must do something about the Duke of Brabant, because he was the most important amongst them [in this confederation] and yet he seemed to be making his preparations with little enthusiasm.

So Edward turned to the duke of Brabant:

The noble king arranged to speak with the duke, seeing that he showed no zeal in getting himself ready, and showed him the response which the allies had sent him, telling him in all friendship that he [Brabant] must not fail him... When the duke heard this he was entirely confounded — and said that he must seek counsel on the matter.

And so it went on.

The king was doing all that he could. Another son, named Lionel, was born to him at Antwerp on 29 November 1338. The birth was celebrated with proper magnificence, but it seemed as if Edward might father a whole brood of sons before his allies stirred themselves to any great degree. Sir Thomas Gray, one of Edward III's entourage in Flanders, was once again unimpressed by the festivities, saying of the king's sojourn in Antwerp: 'He stayed fifteen months there, without making any war, but only jousting and living the fine life.'

Edward's life was not in fact as fine as Gray imagined it to be. The king was now borrowing heavily from the Italian banks of the Bardi and Peruzzi, and running up massive debts. It was well over a year before the alliance took firm military shape, and an

Anglo-German army, with additional Flemish contingents, came into being. The Holy Roman Emperor and king of the Germans, Ludwig of Bavaria, had recruited soldiers from Savoy to Silesia to add to Edward's host. But the cost of putting the royal strategy into effect had been astronomical, and the governing council in England remained under enormous pressure throughout Edward's stay abroad.

In October 1339 the Black Prince opened Parliament on behalf of his father. Its proceedings were dominated by an ugly row over the surrender of Perth to the Scots. The harassed King Edward believed that the garrison commander, Sir Thomas Ughtred, should have held out longer and had the money and supplies to do so, and brought criminal proceedings against him. Ughtred, a competent and reliable soldier, was furious: the supplies had never arrived and he insisted that Parliament clear his name. Ughtred's honour was eventually satisfied, but it was all too clear that resources were desperately overstretched.

Parliament broke up a few weeks later without agreeing to provide the king with any further revenue. On 1 November Edward wrote to his son and his advisers. The king began on a note of exasperation:

> The cause of our long stay in Brabant we have often made known to you before and it is well understood by each of you now. Lately hardly any [financial] aid has come to us out of our realm of England, damaging us and leaving the people with us in dire straits and our allies exceedingly unhappy with the whole business.

Edward then turned from fiscal frustrations to military matters, and his mood became more bullish. His army had at last gathered, he had resolved to meet his foe in combat, and he had invaded northern France in order to offer battle to the French king. After all the delays, Edward was determined to provoke a reaction from his opponent, and his raiding tactics were savage. He announced

bluntly to the Prince and his councillors: 'On the eve of the feast
of St Matthew [20 September 1339] we began to burn the Cambrésis [an area around the town of Cambrai] and continued to torch
the area for the following week until the region was completely
laid to waste – and all its wheat, cattle and other goods taken or
destroyed.' Edward then moved deeper into France, expanding the
destructive range of his army: 'Each day we pushed forward, our
men burning and destroying for twelve leagues [20 miles] on either
side of our line of advance... we wanted to wreak as much havoc
as we could.'

King Philip VI assembled his own army and responded to the
English king's challenge; meanwhile, King Edward's unwieldy
coalition was showing signs of strain. On 23 October the rival forces
lined up near the small town of Buironfosse. Edward was ready for
the encounter: 'That day we were in the fields well before day-break
and took up a position for him and us to fight', he told the Prince.
'Some enemy scouts were captured, who told us that the French
vanguard was not far away and ready to go into battle.' But King
Philip declined to meet him in combat, and instead went over to
the defensive:

> He ordered deep ditches to be dug around his camp and great
> trees to be chopped down, to prevent our coming to him. We
> stayed in battle array all day, until the evening, until it was clear
> that nothing would be happening... And the following day we
> offered him battle again, but we heard no news of him. Finally
> [a day later, on 25 October] we found out that the enemy had
> scattered and retreated in great haste and fled from us.

Edward and his Anglo-German army then pulled back to Flanders. It had hardly been an impressive campaign, although he had
challenged his opponent to battle and seen him retreat, thereby
presenting Edward with a propaganda opportunity. On 26 January
1340, in the marketplace of the city of Ghent, Edward formally
declared himself king of England and France by holding aloft his

shield upon which the coats of arms of England and France were now joined; a bold statement of intent from an image-conscious king. Onlookers now saw that the leopards of England were quartered (the heraldic term for dividing a shield and its coats of arms into four equal parts) with the French lilies. It was a watershed moment. 'From now on Edward styled himself king of both realms in all he did,' remarked Jean le Bel.

†

Edward III returned from Flanders on 21 February 1340, his financial resources exhausted. His visit to England was destined to be brief: he simply wanted to extract more money from Parliament. He had at last negotiated alliances against the French, in Flanders and Brabant, and plans were afoot to cement these through marriage, with his son the Black Prince to be contracted to Margaret, daughter of John, duke of Brabant. The king also began to assemble a war fleet and planned to return to Flanders with a new army. But his incessant financial demands were leading to mounting criticism of his foreign policy, and he desperately needed a tangible military success.

The Black Prince, meanwhile, continued to alternate personal pleasures with ceremonial duties. The end of April 1340 found him at Byfleet, relaxing with his companions: he lost 12d at 'single-stick', a form of gambling, to John Chandos — the first appearance in the historical record of the man who would become his mentor and chief military adviser. At Kennington on 25 May he presented one of his father's chief allies in Flanders, the marquis of Juliers, with a gilt and enamelled cup. By early June he was in Bury St Edmunds, where he made an offering at the shrine of St Edmund — with his father's forthcoming voyage in mind — and before the relics of the abbey church. He then travelled east to Holbrook, overlooking the estuary of the River Stour, where Edward III's fleet was gathering.

It was a dramatic occasion. The English king was planning to ferry his troops to the city of Bruges, to join with his Flemish allies and begin a new offensive. He had assembled more than 100 ships. But the French had anticipated this course of action and were blockading his passage at the estuary of the River Zwin with a flotilla twice as large. Many felt that Edward's fleet was too small and his opponents would be too strong for him. John Stratford, archbishop of Canterbury and chancellor of England, urged the king to wait. The chronicler Robert of Avesbury caught the moment:

> The Archbishop warned Edward that his adversary, Philip of France, realizing his plan, had assembled a great navy to resist him at the Flemish port of Zwin. He advised him to wait and provide himself with a larger force – by crossing immediately he could easily perish along with all his men. The king said that he would cross anyway.

Stratford knew that the French held the advantage at sea. Their vessels, adapted from the Mediterranean galley, were fast and easy to manoeuvre. England did not have a purpose-built navy; merchant ships – known as cogs – with deep draughts and round hulls were requisitioned and converted for service as warships by the addition of wooden 'castles' at bow and stern and crow's-nest platforms at the masthead, from which archers could shoot at enemy craft. They could carry plenty of troops, but were cumbersome and unwieldy on the open sea. Fearing a calamity, Stratford threatened to resign his chancellorship if Edward did not delay his embarkation. Avesbury continued the story:

> The king then called his admiral to him, and asked him how dangerous it would be to cross. He replied in much the same way as the Archbishop had earlier. At which King Edward said angrily: 'You and the Archbishop have composed a sermon against me. I will cross regardless – and if you are afraid, when there is nothing to fear, you can stay at home.'

The admiral, Sir Robert Morley, reluctantly agreed to join him, and 'by speaking soothing words' the king brought Stratford round as well. But the danger was very real: the French had been further reinforced by Genoese galleys, and were now waiting for him across the Channel. On 22 June the English fleet was ready to sail. The young Prince was rowed out to King Edward's ship, the cog *Thomas*, to say goodbye. He spoke briefly to his father and some of his captains before they sailed. He understood that they were all in grave danger.

The Prince then travelled back towards London, through Colchester and Chelmsford, tipping the park-keepers of various landowners as he went. He was trying to take his mind off events by enjoying some hunting, but he found it hard to relax. He had heard reports that the French would now intercept his father's fleet and destroy it in a major sea battle. One of his messengers was left behind at Harwich, 'to find out about the rumours of the king's crossing and about his enemies'; this individual even hired boats in order to widen the search for any news that might be had. Another spent six days at Orford on a similar mission. The Prince clearly feared for his father's life.

However, Edward III's defiant decision to cross the Channel and confront his enemies was far from mere bravado. The king trusted the quality of his men-at-arms and the archers crammed aboard his ships, many of them hardened by the war in Scotland. He also knew that many of the enemy vessels were crewed by sailors with little fighting experience. It was vital that he engaged the French on his terms and dictated the shape of the battle — and by taking the initiative the king showed his readiness to do this.

While the Prince was anxiously waiting, the rival fleets were at last coming into view off the coast of Flanders, near the town of Sluys. *The Brut* related:

> The king and his fleet sailed forward at the break of day [on 24 June], and when they saw enemy the sight was almost too

horrible to look at. The French ships were strongly bound together with large chains, [and were equipped with] castles, wooden breastworks and barriers. But nevertheless King Edward said to all those who were around him: 'Good lords, my brothers, do not be dismayed – but be of good comfort. Those who give battle for me today will be fighting for a just cause and will have the blessing of God Almighty – and each shall keep whatever he may gain.' And when the king finished his speech those around him eagerly sought out and engaged the enemy.

King Edward knew how to encourage his men, and he was assisted by the lack of unity among his opponents, for command of the French fleet was divided. The Genoese admiral Barbavera rightly argued that they should break the chains and put to sea; the constable, Béhuchet, countermanded his orders, insisting instead on maintaining a defensive formation. Sensing his opponents' indecision, Edward seized the initiative. He sent his ships towards the French flank in groups of three, two packed with archers, the other with men-at-arms. The tactic proved highly effective; King Edward's men, taking advantage of the enemy's immobility, used grappling hooks to engage ship after ship, with the archers raining arrows down upon the deck and the men-at-arms then boarding each vessel.

After a hard struggle, the whole of the French first line was captured. Those in the second began to panic, some abandoning their ships and jumping into the sea. 'The battle was fierce and dire', a London chronicler related, 'and it lasted from noon through much of the night'. But it ended in total English victory. Banners bearing the arms of Philip of Valois were cut down and replaced by King Edward's leopards and lilies. There were few English losses; most of the French fleet was captured and thousands of its sailors drowned.

Four days later, on 28 June 1340, the Black Prince received a letter from his father:

Very dear son, we know well that you are anxious to receive good news from us, and to hear what has happened since we left England. God, by his miraculous power, gave us victory over our enemies, and we thank Him as devoutly as we can for it. And we tell you that the number of ships, galleys and barges of our enemy amounted to 190, all of which were captured, except twenty-four in all which fled, and some were later captured at sea. And the number of men-at-arms and other armed men [of the French] amounted to 35,000, out of whom 5,000 escaped; and the rest, as we are told by some whom we captured alive, are dead and their bodies are all along the Flemish coast.

No one had expected the English to win this fight. *The Brut* related a joke doing the rounds among Edward's captains: 'So large a number of Philip's men were drowned there, that if God had given the gift of speech to the fish of the sea, from thence forward they would have spoken French because they had eaten so many.'

†

Sluys was a stunning naval victory, but it did not yield the decisive political opportunity Edward III had hoped for. He besieged the town of Tournai, intending once more to draw Philip VI into battle. Philip, however, refused the bait and the English king simply ran out of money. While French chroniclers criticized King Philip's lack of fight, their English counterparts complained about King Edward's profligate spending. 'The king's triumph at Sluys did not fully salvage his reputation,' William Dene remarked, 'for he had styled himself king of France but not yet obtained the kingdom.' That endeavour would have to wait.

The king's vision of winning the crown of France was born, but its birth-pangs came at enormous cost. Edward had spent nearly half a million pounds – a sum that most rulers would not see in an entire lifetime – and his default on debts would bring down the two Italian banking houses, the Bardi and Peruzzi, which had loaned him much of the money: the Peruzzi was bankrupted in 1343, shortly after the king's repudiation of his loans, and the Bardi went into liquidation two years later. Edward returned to England in a fury and vented his anger on his hapless ministers; the king's expenditure, and a further clash between him and his chief minister, the chancellor and archbishop John Stratford, came close to provoking a constitutional crisis. Edward made a more modest return to France the following year, intervening in the War of the Breton Succession. To some extent this was a sideshow; a more realistic and prudent policy now had to be pursued.

With King Edward in Brittany, the Black Prince was once more briefly appointed 'guardian of England'. On 5 December 1342 Edward wrote to his son with the usual instruction 'to stir up our chancellor and treasurer to send us money'. The king was cautiously optimistic:

> Dear son, know that we have laid siege to the city of Vannes, which is the best town of Brittany after that of Nantes and [through its capture] we can best compel and restrain the country to our obedience... We hope, by the power of God, to have success, for since our coming into these parts he has given us a good beginning.

But the city did not surrender. Edward was forced to conclude another truce – and was back in England by March 1343. On his return, the Prince's intermittent guardianship of the realm was finally brought to an end. In recognition of his services, some two months later, on 12 May, the king formally created him Prince of Wales.

The following year, 1344, the king announced his intention of reviving Arthurian glories by instituting a Round Table of 300 knights. A magnificent tournament was held at Windsor and on 20 January Edward solemnly swore that he would found a Round Table 'of the same kind and status as that laid down by lord Arthur, once king of England'. He ordered his carpenters and masons to rebuild the Round Tower at Windsor Castle to provide a fitting setting for it. But Edward knew that to achieve real success against France he would have to remodel his army, reform its organization and refine its tactics; and this he set about doing.

A few details of the Black Prince's life can be glimpsed from a fragment of his household accounts in the period 1344–5. There are notes of substantial payments for the buying of horses abroad, one servant travelling to Brabant to buy thirty-two horses in all. Later in his career, the Prince would show a keen interest in horse-breeding, owning no fewer than seven stud farms, and would enjoy making gifts of warhorses to his closest companions. Sir John Chandos was given money to arm himself for a tournament at Winchester, an event which the Prince seems to have attended. His establishment, headed by a group of experienced soldiers, diplomats and administrators, numbered in all about 120 men.

Peace talks with France conducted at Avignon in 1344 had ended in failure. In 1345 Edward launched a series of military enterprises against Philip VI. The earl of Northampton was sent with a small army to Brittany; Henry of Grosmont was dispatched with a force to Aquitaine. The king set out for Flanders on 3 July 1345, intending to negotiate a fresh alliance against the French king, and on this occasion the Black Prince joined him. They left the port of Sandwich together and sailed for Sluys, where they met Jacob van Artevelde, the Flemish leader, and discussed the organization of a new military campaign. But Artevelde was assassinated in a riot in the town of Ghent on 24 July, and on hearing this news Edward and his son returned at once to England.

Plans were now put into effect for a major military campaign in Normandy the following year, one in which the Black Prince would take part. Now aged fifteen, the Prince had been offered a vision of chivalric leadership, built up through his father's tournament lifestyle and military successes against the French and Scots. The king himself had found a noble quest – to win the crown of

France that he saw as rightfully his – and his son hoped to play a full part in bringing that about. The Prince had been schooled in the government of the realm; he would now join his father on the battlefield.

chapter three

INITIATION

In the summer of 1346 Edward III surveyed a number of tempting military possibilities. He might join the small English army already operating in Gascony under Henry of Grosmont and bring it substantial reinforcements; or he might make a more substantial intervention in the Low Countries, joining a contingent under Sir Hugh Hastings that had been dispatched to Flanders. But Edward, wishing to provoke his adversary, Philip VI, as much as possible, decided to strike elsewhere. He would land his main force in Normandy and lay waste the duchy's rich agricultural lands, deliberately ravaging the estates of the French aristocracy, in order to goad Philip and bring him to battle. The king believed that his 14,000-strong army was up to the task.

The king had been planning his attack for many months. Commissioners of array – officials responsible for selecting soldiers for the army – had been busy in every English county. Hundreds of ships had gathered at Portsmouth. And Edward had decided to recruit the core of his force on a new and more professional basis, through the retinues of his most experienced captains. They would contract with him, through a legal document known as the indenture, to serve for an agreed wage, over a set period of time and with a specified number of knights, men-at-arms and archers, both mounted and on foot. The king expected all to be properly equipped and trained.

On 12 July 1346 Edward III landed at Saint-Vaast-la-Hogue on the Cotentin peninsula. Upon disembarking, the king tripped and fell face forward on the sand. His companions were alarmed but Edward was quick-witted enough to claim that this was a good omen: the land of France was welcoming him as one of its own.

The story may have been apocryphal, but upon his arrival in Normandy, King Edward knighted his son, the Black Prince, and gave the sixteen-year-old command of the vanguard – a responsible and honourable position within the army. The Prince's division would lead the way, responsible for reconnaissance and scouting, and would be the first to clash with enemy soldiers in the army's path. The king selected a host of experienced captains to support his son, including the earls of Northampton and Warwick. But his intention was clear: he would train the Black Prince in the art of war. The Prince would not be insulated by rank or class from the risks of combat, but would take on all the dangers borne by his fellow fighters. Edward wanted his son to win honour and renown; if he survived the campaign, it would mark his initiation into a warrior elite.

King Edward maintained a tight control of his army, and disciplinary ordinances were now read out to the troops. Mindful of his claim to the French crown, the king adopted a carrot-and-stick approach: if civilians surrendered promptly, their lives and property would be spared, but if they did not, they would suffer the consequences. The army was going to pillage the lands of France, but only on the king's terms.

After five days of preparation, Edward's soldiers began their march. The Prince's master of household, Sir Bartholomew Burghersh, was with him in the vanguard and caught the mood of excitement at the head of the army, writing home on 17 July:

> We have arrived well and in good heart, in that part of Normandy called the Cotentin, and on our arrival my lord the Prince was knighted. The town of Barfleur has been taken and the earl of Warwick skirmished with the enemy, and won the day honourably. Many other knights have engaged the French

in combat – such enterprises are going on the whole time. Now the enemy soldiers, who were supposed to be defending the region, have withdrawn into their castles and fortified towns... The king and his army are setting out into the country to establish his rights by conquest, as God shall give him grace.

The ritual of knighting was the formative moment in a warrior's life. By the fourteenth century, it had grown in its full form – when time and circumstance allowed – from a simple blessing into a special ceremony accompanied by a lavish feast. Knighting on a battlefield, or at an important moment on a military campaign, was rather different, but even here the occasion held considerable power: it was a designation of valour, bestowed by lords well tested in battle and witnessed by the entire army. At the moment of his becoming a knight, it is appropriate to dwell on the Black Prince's inner thinking as well as his outer experience. In medieval chivalry, campaigns and battles evoked a world of ritual and symbolism, alongside the harsh realities of combat.

†

As the English army began its march, the Prince would certainly have reflected on becoming a knight. And the writings of one particular knight, the Frenchman Geoffrey de Charny, may well have echoed his thinking, for Charny was a contemporary of the Prince, and the two men's paths would later cross in dramatic circumstances. Geoffrey de Charny was a skilled soldier and man of high moral values. His *Le Livre de Chevalerie*, dating from around 1350, illuminates the underlying principles of how a knight should behave.

Charny believed that prowess on the battlefield was the greatest quality a knight could display and would win him honour. And he believed that prowess was a gift from God which required ceaseless thankfulness. Prowess embodied a whole cluster of warrior virtues: great strength, toughness, skill in weaponry – on horseback and on foot – and courage and determination. And it was on these virtues that a knight's reputation was based. As the chronicler Jean Froissart said: 'As firewood cannot burn without flame, neither can a gentleman achieve honour or worldly renown without prowess.' Charny put it more simply: 'He who does more is worth more.'

Geoffrey de Charny's understanding of chivalry was suffused with a sense of piety and of the importance of righteous suffering. He stressed how hard it was to be a knight, to work the body to the limits of its endurance and constantly risk it in battle. A warrior saw 'arrows and lances rain down upon him; his friends' bodies sprawled on the ground all around. He is on horseback and could escape, but to flee would be a loss of honour.' Charny concluded rhetorically: 'Is he not a great martyr who puts himself to such work?'

Charny was honest about the drudgery of constant campaigning and the fear of fighting men who regularly faced each other in battle. Yet he also drew a veil over the cruelty and viciousness of war and instead cast a mantle of virtue over the knightly profession. He insisted that war, for all its violence, was pleasing in the eyes of God. His description of knighthood caught the mentality of the fourteenth-century warrior class. Charny began:

> When someone is knighted he should first of all confess his sins and put himself into a fit state to receive communion. And on the eve of the day when he is to be knighted, he should wash and cleanse his body of all the filth of sin and evil living, and leave this filth behind in the water. So he should get out of the bath cleansed in conscience, and should go and lie in a brand new bed with clean white sheets and should rest there like one who has come through great travails by sin and many torments by devils. And the bed symbolizes the sound sleep of conscience when it has appeased our Lord for all that it has done in the past to anger him.

De Charny then moved on to the next stage of the ceremony:

Then the knights should come to the bed to dress him; and he should be dressed in new linen clothing and everything else should be new; just as his body has been washed of filth and sin, so the new clothes signify that he should keep himself clean and spotless of sin in the future.

He went on to expand on the ritual's meaning:

Then he should be dressed by the knights in scarlet robes, signifying that he is sworn to shed his blood for the faith of Our Lord and to defend and maintain the laws of the Holy Church. And then the knights should bring him black hose as symbol that he came from the earth and to earth he must return and that he must expect to die; nor can he know the hour of his death, so that he must trample on all pride. Then the knights should also bring a white girdle, and fasten it on him, as a sign that he should always be surrounded by chastity and cleanliness. And put a scarlet cloak upon his shoulders as a sign of humility.

After a church vigil, the prospective knight was left alone, so that he could pray to God for forgiveness from sin:

The next day the knights take him to hear Mass devoutly… And the one who is to confer the Order [of knighthood] upon him shall put a gilded spur upon his foot, signifying that just as gold is the most coveted metal, so it is put on the foot to take away all covetousness from the heart. And he shall gird a sword upon him; just as the sword has two cutting edges, so he must keep and sustain right, reason and justice on all sides and never betray the Christian faith or the rights of the Holy Church.

This was the interior world of a knight – one that sought meaning and moral value in a profession founded on violence and suffering. The Chandos Herald, who wrote a book on the Prince's life, said of him:

From his childhood, he never thought of anything but noble deeds, courage and loyalty. It was how he was brought up… And above all was endowed with prowess. And when the king his father crossed the sea to Normandy, he surrounded his son with knights of great courage and renown. He was noble and valiant… and above all, he loved the Holy Church well, and the Holy Trinity.

Over time, the Prince would grow into a man of deep and genuine piety. But now, at the age of sixteen, all around him was bustle and excitement. As son and heir of the king, the eyes of the army were on him — and in this campaign there was honour to be won through acts of valour.

On 17 July 1346 the English army swung inland, burning and pillaging as it went, accepting the surrender of Carentan and capturing Saint-Lô. When King Philip was brought news of the invasion, his first actions appeared decisive and resolute. He sent out summonses to his nobles, ordering them to join him with their levies, and then went to the Abbey of Saint-Denis where he unfurled the *Oriflamme,* the royal banner of war. The Scottish king David Bruce had returned to Scotland five years earlier, in 1341, after several years of exile in France following the disaster of Halidon Hill. With Edward absent from his kingdom, Philip urged David to go onto the offensive and invade England.

But Edward III had taken a leaf from Philip's book. Accompanying his expedition was a turncoat French nobleman, Geoffrey of Harcourt. Harcourt had been incriminated in a plot to wrest control of the duchy of Normandy from Philip's eldest son, and his punishment was to be expelled from the country. Edward seized upon this opportunity, warmly welcoming Harcourt to his court and inviting him to join his army. Harcourt, out for revenge, strongly advised the English to land in Normandy, well knowing that the duchy was unprepared for war.

Geoffrey of Harcourt also urged King Edward to lay the countryside to waste. Edward did not need much persuading. He immediately gave Harcourt permission to strike out some 20 miles (32 km) from his army, with a picked force of men-at-arms and archers, burning and destroying. A French chronicler recorded: 'They found the country rich and fertile in all things, the granaries full of corn, the houses containing all manner of riches – they put the buildings to the torch and carried the livestock – sheep, pigs, oxen and cows – back to the king.'

With Harcourt ravaging the land on one side of Edward's army, to balance matters the king sent his constable, the earl of Warwick, to do exactly the same on the other. And so the army continued its advance:

> And the noble king of England and his son the Prince led their host forward by short stages, always finding provisions and lodgings with ease, for the people of the country had been taken unawares and had hidden nothing away. They were truly astounded, for they had not known war for a long time, nor seen men under arms – but now they saw soldiers kill without pity, rob houses and burn and lay waste all around them.

There was a mounting sense of panic as Edward and his men bore down on Caen. With Philip VI still in Paris, the constable of France, Raoul de Brienne, count of Eu, attempted to organize a defence, summoning local nobles and calling out the town militia. King Edward struck hard and fast, before the count's preparations were complete, launching an attack as soon as he reached the town, on 26 July. The Prince gained his father's permission to lead the assault. Jean le Bel described its onset:

> At first there was determined resistance, but when the townspeople saw the banner of the king of England and so many fine soldiers – the like of which they had never seen before – they

were so afraid that nobody in the world could have prevented their retreating into the town, whether the constable liked it or not.

The Prince and his men advanced on Caen shortly after dawn and were soon fighting inside the town. The constable did the best he could, reinforcing the castle and deploying the remainder of his troops on the vital bridge over the River Orne that linked the two halves of the town. Le Bel recorded that it 'was much strengthened with a stockade and a portcullis'. The French made a determined stand there but were outflanked by the Prince's soldiers. Caen's defences had not been properly maintained; the town 'was badly walled, and with the river low, the English were able to cross it in many places and surround the defenders'.

The Prince's troops closed in on the gatehouse. The count of Eu retreated to its upper floor. The attack was led by low-born archers and their blood was up: they raced after him, cutting a swathe through his fellow fighters. For a few moments there was no one of rank among the press of English, and the archers hacking their way towards the count did not seem to be taking prisoners. All appeared lost. But then, glancing out of the window, the count recognized one of the combatants standing outside. It was Sir Thomas Holland, one of the Prince's lieutenants, with whom he had fought on crusade in Prussia. The count of Eu called out to him, and Holland and his companions immediately pushed their way through the throng and accepted his surrender. It was a fortunate reprieve for the relieved Frenchman.

The order allowing the capture of prisoners was normally given towards the end of an engagement – it was hard to fight wholeheartedly while shepherding a group of surrendered opponents. But Holland was not waiting for a battle signal: his coming to the rescue of a worthy opponent was a chivalric gesture from a bold warrior who was fast gaining a reputation for martial prowess. We will hear more of Sir Thomas later.

Others were not so lucky as the count of Eu. According to the conventions of war in the Middle Ages, the inhabitants of a town that failed to surrender forfeited all rights to humane treatment. Angered by Caen's resistance, King Edward allowed his troops to sack the town. Jean le Bel recorded grimly: 'Each man saw before his eyes his mother and sister murdered, his wife and daughter violated, houses robbed and burned.' A churchman in Edward's retinue wrote to Queen Philippa in somewhat self-satisfied fashion, showing little compassion for the population's suffering:

> A great number of the French were slain, knights and squires, and many ordinary citizens, in the streets, houses and gardens. It cannot be said how many were killed, because the bodies were stripped of clothes and belongings and could not easily be recognized. No person of rank was lost on our side, except one squire who was wounded and died two days later.

On 29 July Bartholomew Burghersh wrote home again, relaying more news from the Prince's vanguard. The English army was now occupying Caen, and Burghersh believed their opponents had been thoroughly intimidated from the outset of the campaign: 'After we left La Hogue, where our landing took place, and we began our raid, no one of substance dared to challenge us, either in the towns or the countryside, until we came to Caen.' Burghersh went on to describe the tactic that had won them the fight:

> And when we came as close to the town as we could, the archers went straight to the bridge and assaulted it with volleys of arrows... And then they fought hand to hand with the enemy at the barriers and they conducted themselves well and nobly, defeating all who opposed them, to the very last man... and thus we entered the town.

And then there was the yardstick of those killed or captured – to the medieval mind, the measurement of success for any military engagement:

The constable of France surrendered to Sir Thomas Holland, with all the men that were with him, and the chamberlain, the count of Tancarville, was captured by one of the Prince's own knights – so he is now the Prince's prisoner. And between 120 and 140 valiant French knights were killed or captured... and five thousand squires and citizens of the town were slain in the fight... So far, our affairs have gone as well as possible, praised be the Lord!

Burghersh was proud that the Prince and his followers had played a prominent part in defeating the enemy garrison. In the words of the Chandos Herald: 'He took the bridge at Caen, carrying the town by force, and he fought well there – because at his young age he was eager to gain fame and a good reputation.' The mood within the army's vanguard was upbeat, and Burghersh concluded on an optimistic note:

The king has stayed two or three days in the town, which is full of supplies, provisioned his men and now intends to march directly against his adversary, to bring matters to whatever end God will decree. Our ships have come into the estuary [of the Orne] which leads to Caen and have destroyed about a hundred enemy vessels, as well as doing much damage in the country [through sending out raiding parties] by burning and other means. That is all the news I have at the moment.

Edward's army continued its easterly march through Normandy. The towns of Bayeux and Lisieux surrendered without resistance. Philip VI hurried up from Paris to Rouen to block the crossing points of the Seine and bar the English king's entry into the Norman capital. The chronicler known as the Bourgeois of Valenciennes related that, in an act of bravado, Sir Thomas Holland left the English army on 7 August with only two fellow fighters and rode hard to the southern end of Rouen's bridge, in the city's outer suburbs. In an adrenalin-fuelled escapade, Holland charged through a group of surprised French soldiers, killing several of them. He then waved his banner at the astonished citizens and cried out 'St George for England!' before galloping off again.

However, Rouen was not the English king's target. Instead, Edward turned south, following the left bank of the Seine, and advanced towards Paris. The French were caught off guard. They shadowed Edward's movements from the other side of the river, destroying bridges at Pont-de-l'Arche, Vernon and Meulan, but made no real attempt to halt his progress. At La Roche-Guyon there was further evidence of English boldness:

> Sir Robert de Ferrers took a handful of men, crossed the Seine secretly in a small boat and attacked the very strong castle there. The garrison resisted – but when the small group of soldiers managed first to enter the outer bailey and then take the inner one by storm they lost heart and gave up the fight.

The garrison commander was astonished by these desperados. It made no sense to him that a small group of men should attack a well-defended castle. So he sought a rational explanation: the entire English army must be following up behind them. It was not. But instead of retreating into the safety of the keep the bewildered French simply surrendered. There was a gallant finale: 'The castle was full of noble ladies, whom Ferrers released unharmed and without shame or injury... and then he returned to the English army to tell the king of his exploit.'

Philip VI was still gathering his army. At first the beleaguered monarch had resolved to fight the English as quickly as possible. Then he lost confidence, and decided to recruit more troops instead. The French king's hesitancy was now attracting criticism. 'Although we were pillaging and burning throughout the whole region... yet he [Philip] did not dare to cross the waters of the Seine and meet us [in battle] as he should have done, for the proper defence of his kingdom', wrote Richard de Wynkeley, King Edward's chaplain. Jean le Bel was more scathing: 'The king of

France looked more to his own safety and comfort than protecting his realm... Such conduct will only lessen his standing amongst his people.' And this was Edward's objective, to humiliate his rival and demonstrate to his subjects that Philip had failed in his regal duty to protect them.

King Edward and his soldiers drew ever closer to Paris. Its frightened citizens could now see the pall of smoke marking the progress of the English army. The Carmelite friar Jean de Venette, author of a chronicle of this period of the Hundred Years War, was in the French capital at this time:

> The English king marched to Saint-German-en-Laye, looted the town and set alight its royal palace. He also burned the nearby villages. He even destroyed the Tower of Montjoye, which the king of France had rebuilt magnificently not long before. This could all be seen from Paris by anyone able to climb up a turret. The fires, the closeness of the English to the capital, amazed and astonished everybody in the city. No one thought they would ever see such a thing.

Michel Pintouin, a monk of the Abbey of Saint-Denis, said bitterly: 'These were the principal residences and special abodes of the king of France — their destruction brought great dishonour to our kingdom.'

On 14 August Philip VI was at last ready to act. He sent a letter to Edward, now at the town of Poissy — only 18 miles (29 km) from the French capital — challenging him to battle. King Edward was delighted by this turn of events. He responded: 'At whatever hour you approach, you shall find us ready to meet you in the field — with God's help, it is the thing we desire above all else.' But he did not intend to fight with his supply lines over-extended but rather on ground of his own choosing. Now that his opponent had committed himself to an engagement, he decided to draw the French army further north. To do this, he needed to outmanoeuvre Philip.

Edward sent the Black Prince and the army's vanguard to raid the suburbs of Paris. It was a dangerous assignment — the Prince's force would be a considerable distance ahead of the main army and likely to bear the brunt of any enemy attack — but his son carried it off successfully. The king wanted the French to believe that all his troops were intending to push south, deeper into French territory. But this was a feint. As Philip moved to block this imagined threat, the English king ordered his carpenters to start repairing the broken bridge at Poissy, over the Seine. He was going to strike northwards instead.

Philip did not expect the English to change their line of march so suddenly, and was taken by surprise when they did so. Believing the river impassable to Edward III's soldiers, he had only left a weak militia force to defend its far bank. Edward and his army now showed consummate skill and professionalism. They repaired the bridge during the night, carrying out the work so quietly that the sentries opposite had no inkling of what was afoot. At first light on 17 August the work was complete. The English cavalry thundered across, scattering the astonished defenders in all directions.

King Edward now moved rapidly north. In the army's vanguard, the Black Prince was spoiling for a fight. On 18 August he asked his father's permission to attack a nearby town, but the king refused him, warning that the main French army was too close and he did not want to lose time or lives. On 19 August the Prince's vanguard clashed with troops of Philip VI's ally, Jean of Luxembourg, the blind king of Bohemia, hurrying to join the French king. Philip himself was chasing after Edward with the main body of the French army. Three days later, on 22 August, the English reached the small town of Airaines, in Picardy — 100 miles (160 km) north of the bridge at Poissy. They were now just 7 miles (11 km) from the River Somme. Philip and Jean of Luxembourg had joined forces and were 15 miles (24 km) to the east of them, at Amiens.

The French once again destroyed all the bridges, and once again they were outwitted by the English king. For Edward had learned of a ford across the river, at the hamlet of Saigneville, on the approaches to the Somme's tidal estuary. Here a strip of hardened white clay ran along the length of the riverbed, and a line of men twelve abreast could move across the river with the water coming up only to their knees. The ford's local nickname was *Blanchetaque* ('white-tongue'). On the following day the army rested. Scouts were being sent out in all directions, and the king was conferring closely with his chief war captains. The English soldiers had been confident on this campaign. But now unsettling rumours were spreading among the men. Some spoke of the sheer size of the French force pursuing them; others that all the crossing points of the river were held by the enemy and that their supplies were running low.

Shortly after dawn on 24 August, St Bartholomew's Day, the army was ordered to break camp and move towards the river. At around 7am the English soldiers drew up in battle array on the left bank of the Somme. They were less than 8 miles (13 km) from the sea, the river had widened substantially and there was a heavy swell on the water. On the opposite bank enemy soldiers seemed to be gathering. And as the army waited, the numbers of this opposing force grew larger.

A medieval commander would relay written orders to a hand-picked group of captains or speak words of encouragement to those noblemen around him that he liked and trusted. He might, in special circumstances, ride along a troop formation and stop and chat to small groups of ordinary soldiers. But to reach out to an entire army, touch men's hearts, communicate a cause and uplift spirits, a sense of theatre was required. And what was about to happen on that summer morning would be one of the most dramatic episodes in the history of medieval warfare.

†

To understand the significance of the situation, we first have to remember what the king knew. He knew of the existence of the ford, and its exact location, although the strip of white clay, lined with stones, could only be seen with the naked eye when the tide was at its lowest point and the observer was close to the water's edge. He knew that the ford was only passable at low tide and that a crossing could only be made for a short period of time before the water rose again. He knew that local drovers used it to move across their cattle, but a crossing by an army of thousands, many of its men in heavy armour, and a waggon train of supplies following up behind, had never been undertaken. He knew also that local troops had been seen on the other side of the river, and that his men would almost certainly have to fight their way onto the far bank.

Above all, Edward would have known that if he got this wrong — on a narrow causeway with little room to manoeuvre — with a large French army coming up behind him, time running out and the water level rapidly rising and the far bank securely held by the enemy, he would face utter catastrophe. All would now depend on the plan of action worked out between the king and his most trusted captains. The Black Prince was now one of this select group and he was sharing in its counsel, alongside the king's most experienced fighters. However, the majority of the army had no knowledge of it.

The army kept its discipline. A column of heavily armoured knights, all on horseback and led by the earl of Northampton, formed up. They plunged into the river, but to everyone's amazement the water reached only the knees of the horses. Mounted English archers rode along the causeway, following up behind the charging knights. They loosed volley after volley towards the enemy. And then Northampton and his men crashed into the French defenders on the far side of the river. The enemy broke and ran.

The water level was starting to rise. The Black Prince and the vanguard moved across the causeway. A mass of soldiers got into position behind them. The carts and waggons of the baggage train were pushed, pulled and hauled down to the river's edge. The tide had turned and the river was rising substantially. Blanchetaque had disappeared beneath the water. And then the soldiers of Philip's vanguard came into view on the left bank of the Somme. But the crossing was now impassable for another twelve hours.

On the afternoon of 24 August there was clearly much discussion within the ranks as Edward's soldiers marched through the rolling countryside of Ponthieu. Chronicle accounts reveal men asking each other how the king had learned about Blanchetaque. Some wondered whether a reconnaissance patrol had found it; others said that a local man had revealed its location for a cash reward. The majority believed that it could be explained only by divine intervention: it was a sign that Edward had been chosen by God to lead them against the French.

In fact, the county of Ponthieu was Edward's ancestral land, inherited from his mother long before he claimed the kingdom of France. The king had already visited it twice, in 1329 and 1331, and he had even spent time hunting there. According to the well-informed chronicler of Meaux Abbey in Yorkshire, Edward had been alerted to the existence of the ford long before he reached the Somme. It is entirely possible that King Edward, with his keen eye for terrain, had also noted an ideal site to fight a battle – a long ridge, with a forest behind it, overlooking the village of Crécy – on one of his earlier visits to Ponthieu. A clue that this was in the king's thoughts, even at an early stage of the campaign, is found in an order dispatched by Edward to the English council on 29 July 1346. The king was about to leave Caen, march eastwards to the River Seine, and then turn south towards Paris. He requested that the council provide him with fresh troops and supplies, particularly bows, arrows and bowstrings. But crucially, he asked that these be sent to the small port of Le Crotoy, on the mouth of the Somme estuary, a short distance from Blanchetaque and only 15 miles (24 km) from Crécy, strongly suggesting that Edward already had Crécy in mind as a battle location. Here he believed his army could hold its ground against the French.

If this battle site was already part of the king's plans, it is also highly likely that he knew of the crossing place at Blanchetaque which would allow him to reach it. It was a sign of Edward's showmanship that he chose not to disclose the existence of the ford to most of his army until the first riders actually started crossing it, thus allowing the drama of the occasion to work to his advantage. The chroniclers Adam of Murimuth and Robert of Avesbury said that many ordinary soldiers felt they had witnessed a miracle and began to liken Edward III to Moses, the Old Testament leader and prophet. One story was in everyone's mind, whether read in the scriptures, heard in sermons or seen on church wall-paintings: that of Moses leading the Israelites out of their Egyptian captivity. The Red Sea seemed to block their path. But, miraculously, it had parted long enough for the Israelites to cross it, but not for the Egyptians to pursue them. The similarity with Blanchetaque was striking.

Edward III may well have seen the benefits in being likened to such an illustrious leader; if so, by staging this piece of elaborate theatre at Blanchetaque, he was inviting such a comparison. He still bore the quartered arms of England and France on his banners, but his claim to the kingdom of France seemed remote to many: it was the king's business, not theirs; and some resented the increase in taxes that accompanied Edward's continental ambitions.

Now, however, at the end of this momentous day, the king had made his claim real to ordinary soldiers. They saw Edward as a leader of almost superhuman power, capable of leading his people out of a state of slavery to the ambitions of the French. Gascony was held by the English – and the French had asserted their overlordship of it in a manner that was humiliating to Edward and his people. They had threatened England with their fleet and encouraged the Scots to invade. After Blanchetaque, the logic was clear enough: King Edward – by claiming the crown of France – wanted to set his people free. And for everyone in the army, that was a cause worth fighting for.

The clash of arms was not far off. The next day, Edward slowed the army's marching pace and English soldiers camped in the forest of Crécy. The king's chosen battle site was near by. On 26 August Edward drew up his forces between the villages of Crécy and Wadi-court on a ridge of high ground overlooking the valley. Behind the ridge was woodland, preventing the enemy from attacking the rear; agricultural terraces gave the site additional protection from the front.

Edward III now made his battle dispositions. He ordered all his troops to dismount: the army would fight on foot. His son, the Black Prince, was given command of the right wing; the earl of Northampton the left. The king took the central division, and also found a vantage point, a windmill near the top of the ridge, where he could oversee events. Edward decided each division would contain an equal proportion of men-at-arms and bowmen. Chron-iclers were fascinated by these preparations, which revealed a way of fighting not seen before in medieval warfare. Missile-bearing troops were normally deployed in front of the main body of the army, not within it.

Understandably, given its novelty, there was some confusion around the exact system of deployment. Jean le Bel recalled that the king did not place his archers on the flanks of the army, but chose to spread them along his battle line. Geoffrey le Baker said that within each division, the majority of archers were placed slightly to the side of the men-at-arms, 'rather like wings': 'in such formation they would not hinder their fellows, and be able to catch the enemy with their cross volleys'. Most likely, the majority of bowmen were placed on the flanks of the division, with a few clumped together along the line, able to loose their arrows and then retreat behind the men-at-arms.

To further strengthen his position from attack, Edward created a protective circle – a *laager* – where he drew up his waggons behind the army and where all the horses could be kept safely. He also gave out orders to 'quickly dig a large number of pits near the frontline, each a foot deep and a foot wide, so that when the French cavalry approached their horse would stumble upon these obstacles'; these were hidden from his opponents in the grass and foliage.

Edward also brought up a number of primitive field guns. These early artillery pieces were recent inventions – guns and gunpowder had been employed for only a few years, and then only at sieges – and the king's use of them on the field of battle showed his interest in the latest military technology. It was something of an experiment: only a few had been brought, and they fired bolts and grapeshot rather than large projectiles, but the king hoped that the noise at least might unsettle the French horses. They were carried into position on small carts and deployed on the army's flanks.

The king, his son and principal captains heard Mass and then did the rounds, encouraging their men, Edward lifting his soldiers' spirits 'by words, gifts and deeds'. The enemy was not far off. The French troops had fully assembled at Abbeville and their scouts quickly found the English army and reported its position to the king. On the afternoon of 26 August Philip VI's army was on the move. A long column of French troops snaked along the road from Abbeville to Crécy. There were so many of them that the French king began to lag further and further behind his vanguard.

The correct course of action was to carry out a thorough reconnaissance of the English position, bring the entire French army up, rest it overnight, and then fight the battle the following morning. But the aristocrats thronging the roads ahead of Philip were impatient to start the engagement as soon as possible. Jean le Bel reported that it had become a matter of honour to fight the English without further delay. All royal orders to the contrary were simply disregarded:

> None of the lords wanted to turn back, and refused to do so
> unless those ahead of them did so first. But those in the front
> of the line were not willing to either, for it seemed shameful to
> them. So the entire column kept moving forward, as a matter of

pride, and continued in this fashion until the English came into view, well-arrayed in three divisions, calmly awaiting them. And then it became a point of honour to attack them at once.

Realizing what was happening, and hoping to retain at least a semblance of authority within his army, Philip now threw caution to the winds. He sanctioned an immediate assault on the English position, even though he had not yet reached the battlefield. To support his vanguard, Genoese crossbowmen and some light infantry were pushed forward along the congested roads. The main attack was to be a series of massed cavalry assaults on Edward's forces, although Philip was not yet able to see where his troops would be fighting or impose order on his army. Experienced military professionals in his entourage looked on aghast. The chronicler of St Omer commented ruefully that 'the king did this against the wishes of all those who knew the ways of war', while Froissart was blunt in his summing up of the battle's chaotic opening:

> There is no one [I have spoken to] who has been able to understand or explain the terrible confusion that reigned on the French side. All one can say is that the battle began in the late afternoon without any attempt to observe the position of the enemy or deploy accordingly – in fact, without any proper preparation whatsoever.

The first victims of this self-inflicted chaos were the Genoese crossbowmen. They arrived on the battlefield without their pavises – the large shields that protected them while they loaded their crossbow bolts – and short of ammunition. These were still gridlocked in a traffic jam of men and equipment, several miles behind them. Nevertheless, they advanced in good order. But, as Froissart related, they were met by massed volleys from Edward's waiting bowmen:

> The English archers poured out their arrows on the Genoese so thickly and evenly that they fell like snow. When they felt

these arrows piercing their arms, their heads, their faces, the Genoese – who had never experienced such accurate shooting before – were thrown into confusion and began to fall back.

More and more French cavalry had been building up behind them and suddenly their patience snapped. In desperate haste to get to the English line they simply charged through the retreating crossbow-men. Le Bel was appalled: 'The cavalry did not wait, but attacked in disorderly fashion, all mixed together, so that they trapped the Genoese between themselves and the English, and trampled them down, or tumbled over them like pigs in a heap.'

The first French attacks quickly foundered. The English bowmen shot into the thickest press of the enemy, wasting none of their arrows: 'They impaled or wounded horses and riders, who fell to the ground in great distress, unable to get up again without the help of several men.' The barbed arrowheads tore at the horses' flesh. 'Some would not go forward,' le Bel continued; 'others leapt into the air as if maddened; many balked and bucked horribly'. The ground was soon littered with bodies.

But now, in the early evening, the main French division arrived.

So far, Edward's battle plan had worked perfectly, and his arch-ers had done him sterling service. The longbow – the yew bow used by his archers – had a draw weight of well over 45 kg (100 lbs) and called for real strength and skill to be used properly. The weapon was very accurate in the hands of a person properly trained – and also very powerful. A bow with a draw weight of 68 kg (150 lbs) could drive a heavy 60 gram (2 oz) arrow some 210 metres (230 yards), a lighter arrow 275 metres (300 yards). A broadhead arrow – of the sort commonly used against horses – would penetrate mail with ease, while a narrow pointed 'bodkin' shaft could be lethal even through plate armour.

These were the great strengths of the English bowmen. Their weakness was their vulnerability once hand-to-hand combat began. While some archers might wear a 'brigandine' (a jacket with metal plates riveted to the fabric), or a 'jack' (a similar garment but with the plates sewn into the fabric), or a mail shirt – the vast majority wore only doublets and perhaps leather jackets, and even lacked protective headgear. So within an English army, the archers needed to be properly protected to be fully effective. At Crécy Edward III had chosen a superb site for his bowmen – a ridge shielded by the woodland behind it and the man-made ditches in front of the archers' position.

Edward had also taken enormous trouble to integrate his archers into the battle formation. He began military reforms, setting up a system known as 'indentured retaining', whereby captains contracted to recruit soldiers for the crown on a legal, professional basis, creating continuity of service and *esprit de corps*. Bowmen would form up in companies fifty or a hundred strong, each with a leader of proven quality. The earl of Northampton's victory at Morlaix in 1342, during the War of the Breton Succession, was a testing ground for combined operations between English bowmen and men-at-arms.

The main French army now appeared. It contained as many as 25,000 knights, squires and mounted soldiers, nearly double the size of Edward's host. Its cavalry had resolved to smash the English once and for all – and, if anything, the failure of the vanguard made them even more determined, willing to fight on into the dusk and the hours of darkness. Soon Edward's troops would be hit by wave after wave of mounted attacks. And his bowmen could only maintain concentrated fire for a limited period of time.

Each bowman had forty-eight arrows in two sheaves. Edward had supplies in reserve, kept in the waggons behind the archers' positions, and these would be brought up as fighting commenced. A skilled archer could loose at least seven or eight aimed arrows per minute. It was likely that these volleys would be carefully controlled – the psychological impact of massed, co-ordinated shooting would be far more terrifying than 'firing at will'. But the arrow-storm could only maintain its full intensity for around twenty minutes or so. As Edward became locked in a battle of attrition with a desperate opponent, the effectiveness of his bowmen would be reduced.

The protective ditches in front of the English army would begin to fill with dead horses and their riders, and as they did so, Edward's men-at-arms would receive an increasingly savage battering from the French cavalry squadrons. Horsemen would hit the battle line with the impact of a tidal wave. Men would lower or drop their weapons, link arms with their fellows and feel the breath knocked out of them as the enemy crashed into their position. They had to hold firm at all costs. Once the French found a break in the line, more and more of their cavalry would pour through it, surrounding the English fighters. And after holding firm, as the enemy turned to retreat, they had to strike at the horses with whatever weapon came to hand. The cavalry would pull back, then wheel round and attack once more. There was a limit to the amount of punishment the English army could take.

Edward was alert to this danger, and had chosen the battle site with special care. Agricultural terracing ran along a lower section of the ridge, impeding the French cavalry and forcing them into a narrow passage to the right of the English position. This restricted their advance and broke their momentum before their horsemen could finally fan out again. At the neck of the passage — forming a stopper to the bottle — was the Black Prince's division. Here the enemy pressure would be greatest.

Where there was danger, there was also opportunity, for the terrace channelled the enemy into an increasingly constricted space. As more and more troops crowded into the gap, it could become a killing ground, with the press so great that the French would be unable to swing their weapons, move or even breathe.

At Dupplin Moor in 1332 — Edward III's first victory against the Scots — the small English army had drawn up in a defile with their men-at-arms holding a front only 180 metres (200 yards) wide, and the archers on slightly higher ground on either side of them. The key to their position was its funnelling effect. One chronicler noted that they could only be approached through a 'straite [constricting] passage', beyond which the men-at-arms were formed up, 'with the archers disposed so that they could attack the enemy on the flank'. When the English line held firm, the Scottish forces collided with each other, losing momentum and coherence, and presenting an easy target for the bowmen. The mass of the Scots, pushing into a narrow field of combat, hemmed in by their opponents, bunched together by the force of the arrow-storm, succumbed to mass suffocation. A chronicler observed:

> The forward troops of the Scots, badly wounded by the arrows and driven up close to their second division, jammed together in a small space, one being crushed by another. Suffocated by each other – and beaten by that, rather than blows of the sword – they fell in a remarkable way, in a great heap. Pressed against each other in this way, and squeezed against each other as if pressed by ropes, they perished miserably.

At Crécy, Edward understood that if the Black Prince became a target for the French, attracting more and more of their troops in an effort to overcome him, the press would build in the constricted space in front of his division. In the fading daylight, with little or no effective command or control from Philip VI, more and more of their soldiers would push up behind their fellows. As the French cavalry moved further into the funnel, and closer and closer to the Prince's banner, the sheer mass would push people towards the centre. Men and horses would start jostling at the back, unable to move easily. A deadly calibration would occur: too many people, not enough room, a quick reduction in space, a massive increase in density, a sudden restriction in forward movement. At that point, the sheer number of men trying to advance on the English would become life-threatening. In this scenario, French strength would therefore become a weakness, their numerical advantage working against their own side rather than eroding the English position.

It is unclear how much of this the Black Prince understood, or was told by his father. He was brave and wanted to stand firm and win honour. But the pressure that would be brought to bear on his division, and the threat to his own life, was considerable. However, if he could hold his ground, Edward III could bring about a situation that would crush the life out of the French.

As dusk began to fall, the French launched wave after wave of attacks on Edward's army. The Black Prince and his men formed a breakwater in a sea of French cavalry. Geoffrey le Baker described the scene:

> The young Prince displayed marvellous courage, standing in the front line against the enemy, running through horses, felling knights, crushing helmets under his blows – and all the while he encouraged his men, pulling fallen friends to their feet and setting everyone an example.

The ground in front of the Prince's division was littered with the bodies of fallen men and horses, but still the French pushed forward. His troops were now really hard pressed – and one of his knights went to Edward III, who held a small reserve of soldiers behind the army's main position, and appealed for help. The king asked whether his son was badly hurt or slain, and was told that he was not, but was under such fierce attack that he needed assistance. According to Froissart, Edward replied:

> Go back to him and those who sent you and tell them, from me, that they are not to send for help again, whatever happens, as long as my son is still alive. Tell them that my orders are that they should let the boy win his spurs, for I wish the day to be his, if God wills it, and that he and his companions shall have the honour of it.

The sheer weight of numbers began to tell: 'French knights and squires broke through the line of archers and began to fight the remaining men-at-arms with swords and lances.' The Black Prince himself was beaten to the ground. The standard went down – but one of the Prince's servants, Sir Thomas Danyers, plunged into the French line and recovered it. The soldiers of the count of Alençon closed in on King Edward's badly concussed son and tried to haul him away, but his men fought them off. The king was now so concerned that he disregarded his previous command, and sent in a selected group of knights to try and save the Prince. As these small reinforcements arrived, his son recovered consciousness, picked himself up and carried on fighting.

Night had fallen and the battle continued under the moonlight, but the French attacks were now faltering. Philip VI had fought bravely, having two horses slain under him and being wounded in the face by an English arrow. As his army began to disintegrate around him, he reluctantly left the field with his personal bodyguard. The English had won an incredible victory.

The following morning the heralds counted the tally of the dead. They included Philip VI's brother, the count of Alençon; a number of other great French lords; and, according to Edward III's own estimate, 80 noblemen, at least 1,542 knights and squires, and a large number of their ordinary soldiers. English casualties amounted to fewer than 300. The extent of the slaughter on the French side was unprecedented. Jean le Bel commented that no one could remember so many princes dying in a single encounter. And Geoffrey le Baker described the grim manner in which most of the French had perished: 'When they attacked the English, the front line was cut down by swords and spears, but the majority were crushed to death, without a mark upon them, in the middle of the French army, because the press was so great.'

Edward III's brutally effective tactics had been vindicated. The battle was a defining moment of his kingship, an act of personal revenge on Philip VI (after the forceful terms of homage imposed upon him early in his reign) and a stunning military accomplishment. For Thomas Bradwardine, one of the chaplains present in the king's army, Crécy's outcome was a sign of divine intervention, and in his victory address to Edward III and his captains he stated: 'For it is God who worketh in you, both to will and to accomplish according to His divine grace.' Many would have agreed with him.

The following morning Edward III and his son went together to look at the carnage of the battlefield. Edward asked the Prince what he now thought of going into battle and fighting. His son did not reply. But when they found the body of Jean of Luxembourg, the king of Bohemia, and his followers, both were deeply moved. Jean of Luxembourg was one of the foremost warriors of his age, generous and charismatic – a noted chivalric figure, 'worthy and valiant in arms' and a close friend of Philip VI. He had contracted an eye disease, ophthalmia, while on crusade in Lithuania, and – despite two operations by Philip's personal surgeon, Guy de Chauliac – his sight could not be saved; at the time of the Crécy campaign he was nearly blind. But Jean had resolved to go into battle one last time. In the gathering dusk, he and his followers tethered their horses together, and rode with him to the English line 'so that he might make a few [sword] strokes against the enemy'. They were all found dead, in a heap, in front of the Prince's division, their horses still tied together.

Jean of Luxembourg died courageously. And his fellow knights had shown their master absolute loyalty: they had not abandoned him, but rode with him to certain death. The Prince stopped and looked at his fallen opponent. He took Luxembourg's badge of the ostrich feather and resolved to use it as his own, as a tribute to Jean's bravery. (Although not 'Ich dien', which together with 'Houmont' – 'I serve' and 'High courage' – was a motto of the Prince's own devising, first used by him in 1363.) He was also struck by the leather cords around the horses, which bound them together – a telling symbol of comradeship. These fighters were at one in life; they were at one in death.

John of Arderne, a fourteenth-century military surgeon who accompanied the Black Prince on campaign, was intrigued enough to draw the device of the ostrich feather in the margins of his medical treatise on the treatment of anal fistula (composed in 1376, the year of the Black Prince's death). Arderne was a well-informed source, and he commented: 'Edward the eldest son of King Edward III bore an ostrich feather above his [heraldic] crest. He took the feather from the insignia of the king of Bohemia, who was killed at Crécy.'

Many of the knights who fought with the Prince at Crécy, including Sir John Chandos and Sir James Audley, would become lifelong friends and companions. 'We would like you to know', the Prince wrote to Sir Thomas Ferrers, his justice of Chester, on 12 September 1346, 'that God watches over us and has shown us such grace that we have made a good and honourable feat-of-arms in this present expedition.' The Black Prince had embodied the quality of prowess that Geoffrey Charny so admired. He had won his spurs.

chapter four

BEAUTY AND
THE BEAST

An Irish chronicler, John Clynn, recounted a disturbing vision that took place in the year 1347. It occurred in the Cistercian monastery of Tripoli in North Africa and its content was soon circulating around Europe. A monk was celebrating Mass before his abbot, when, before communion, a spectral hand appeared and began writing on the cloth on which the bread and wine had been placed. Its message appears opaque to a modern audience, and would have been disturbing to a medieval one. Fragments of prophecy and bizarre symbolism were woven together into a strangely compelling warning:

> The lofty cedar of Lebanon shall be set ablaze and Tripoli destroyed... Woe to Christianity! There will be many battles and great slaughter, fierce hunger, mortality and political upheaval...the eastern beast will subjugate the whole world by its power... there will be a coming of the Antichrist. Be watchful.

In the fourteenth century, people were fascinated by prophecy and fearful of God's punishment, in which the appearance of the Antichrist, in the Book of Revelation, would herald the end of the earthly world. The threat of the 'eastern beast' and what it represented soon took on a particular and quite terrifying meaning. For in the year that followed Clynn's vision, merchants returning from the Black Sea carried a virulent new form of plague into Italy. Giovanni Boccaccio wrote:

In the year 1348 the noble city of Florence, which for its great
beauty exceeds all others, was visited by the deadly pestilence.
Some say that it afflicted the human race because of a malign
conjunction of the planets, others that it was a punishment, signifying God's righteous anger at our iniquitous way of life. But
whatever its cause, it had originated some years earlier in the
East, where it claimed countless lives before it unhappily spread
westward, growing in strength as it swept relentlessly on, from
one place to the next.

The disease was bubonic plague – spread by fleas living off rats –
which infected the lymphatic system, causing buboes and internal
bleeding; there was also a pneumonic strain, caught through direct
contact with the afflicted, that struck at the lungs. So lethal was
the disease that a person could go to bed well and die before they
woke. So rapidly did it spread that to a French physician, Simon
de Covino, it seemed as if one sick person 'could infect the whole
world'. By January 1348 it had appeared in Marseilles, in southern
France. Moving along coasts and navigable rivers, it was carried
through the ports of Languedoc to Spain, and northwards, up the
River Rhône, to Avignon, where it had arrived by March. At the
same time, in Italy, it had spread from Sicily to the ports of Genoa
and Venice, and thence to Florence and Rome. Between June and
August it reached Bordeaux and Paris, and then spread to Burgundy and Normandy.

The plague reached England shortly after the Black Prince's
eighteenth birthday in June 1348. He was profoundly marked by the
experience. He lost one of his sisters to the disease (and two more
when it returned thirteen years later), alongside trusted servants
and fellow soldiers. The devastation and death wreaked by the pestilence shaped his outlook as much as the Battle of Crécy did. To
understand this fully, we need to examine the course of events in
Europe following the English victory in 1346, and, in particular, to

consider developments in the lives of the Prince and his father in the months before the Black Death reached English shores.

†

In the early summer of 1348 England was basking in the glory of a string of military successes and had negotiated a favourable truce with France. The mood in the country was celebratory. It seemed, to one chronicler, 'that a new sun was rising, illuminating a realm of abounding peace, plentiful goods and glorious victory'. Two years earlier, in September 1346, Edward III — fresh from his triumph at Crécy — had laid siege to the port of Calais. The town was well defended, with strong walls and wide moats, and held by an experienced commander, Jean de Vienne, but Edward was determined to take it, building makeshift huts for his soldiers, bringing in reinforcements from England and Flanders and making use of cannon, catapults and scaling ladders. Philip VI of France, fearful of Edward's army and reluctant to risk another battle, had called upon Scotland for support, impressing upon David II 'that the land of England is without defence, for most of its soldiers are with its king... If you act with speed and energy you can inflict great damage.'

King David had duly responded, invading England with more than 12,000 soldiers. But on 17 October 1346, at Neville's Cross, near Durham, his army was decisively defeated by a force of local levies half its size under the command of the archbishop of York. Once again, the English longbow was used to devastating effect and in the hand-to-hand combat that followed the Scottish king was captured. He would remain a prisoner in the Tower of London for the next eleven years. The threat from Scotland had been neutralized at a stroke.

In Gascony, Henry of Grosmont took advantage of Philip VI's caution and led a spectacular raid into Poitou, storming the towns of Saint-Jean d'Angély, Lusignan and Poitiers. There was little resistance from the French. At Poitiers, Grosmont's forces 'carried off gold, silver and countless precious objects' and, according to Jean Froissart, the loot was so plentiful that the soldiers 'only helped themselves to garments if the fabric contained gold or silver thread, or was trimmed with fur'. The army returned to Bordeaux at the end of October 'much laden with good things'.

In the north, Edward III tightened his grip on Calais. This was a difficult siege operation, and as the king struggled to supply and pay his troops through the winter months he was faced with desertions and an outbreak of disease in his war camp. At the beginning of March 1347 the Black Prince suddenly fell ill, and one of his physicians, William Blackwater, was paid a £5 advance on his wages, 'that he may quickly come to the Prince, as ordered'. As his condition worsened, he was taken to the hospital of St Elizabeth in Bergues, some thirty miles east of Calais, a religious community enjoying the protection and patronage of the counts of Flanders. With the towns of Bruges, Ghent and Ypres in revolt against Philip VI and supporters of the English cause and a small Anglo-Flemish force protecting the eastern flank of Edward's army, this was a safe haven for the ailing Prince – and the English king was concerned enough about his son's condition to leave the siege and visit him there.

However, the Black Prince was to make a full recovery. On 13 March a much relieved King Edward promised to found a nunnery and hospital 'for the care of poor people' on the island of Cadzand, near Sluys, as a mark of gratitude for the care his son had received; the Prince also set his seal to the agreement. At the end of the month both rejoined the siege – and by the beginning of June it was clear that the defenders were running short of food. Philip VI finally brought up another army, but Edward simply blocked off the approaches to Calais and denied him the means of relieving the garrison. In early August Philip's forces withdrew and Edward then accepted the surrender of the town. Calais would remain in English hands for more than 200 years hereafter. Its capture was another formidable success for the Plantagenet king.

By October 1347 Edward III had negotiated a truce with France and was back in London. His priorities for the following year were to celebrate his military successes and re-establish his authority over Parliament. The king won an increase in taxation, to be levied over the next three years, reform of the judicial system was agreed upon and the truce with France confirmed. And as the plague spread across France, Edward — perhaps not fully comprehending the horror of it all — held a series of splendid tournaments. In February 1348 he jousted at Reading garbed in the costume of an eagle; in May he ordered fine robes of blue and white for himself, the Black Prince and a chosen body of knights. Further events were held at Eltham and Windsor.

At the Windsor tournament, on 24 June 1348, the Prince arrived with a substantial retinue, for whom he provided robes and heraldic trappings — for the king and his son were now spending a considerable amount on special badges and costumes. In a suitably chivalric gesture, the various French noblemen held prisoner in England after Crécy were allowed to take part, as was King David, and the 'favour of the field' — the award for best jouster — was granted to Raoul de Brienne, count of Eu. The Prince's delight in music was evident in the feasting that accompanied the event: he gave a warhorse to a minstrel who had pleased him. Noble prisoners were allowed to take some of the comforts of home with them into foreign captivity, and he also bought musical instruments — four silver gilt and enamelled pipes — from the count of Eu.

And through this love of ceremony, a symbolic motif was emerging. A number of costumes worn by King Edward, the Black Prince and their companions were decorated with embroidered garters. Edward III knew that Alfonso XI of Castile had founded a military order whose members wore white surcoats with a vermillion sash. In 1343, Henry of Grosmont had met the knights of this select band during a visit to Castile, and on his return to England he shared his impressions with the king. The Order of the Sash embodied principles of chivalry and loyalty to the monarch on the field of battle and it inspired Edward to seek his own symbol to bind a fighting elite in common cause.

For most of the fourteenth century the garter was a male item of clothing; it was not worn by women until the late fifteenth century. It was, in its simplest and most practical form, a piece of material a man tied in a knot round the upper part of his thigh to hold up his leggings. However, from early in Edward III's reign garters also began to appear as fashion statements, expensive decorative items, often made of fine silk and sometimes attached to leg armour. Such garters were meant to be visible and were worn for show. In 1332 Edward's armourer and master of costumes, John of Cologne, made a pair of pearl garters for the king to wear at Woodstock. In 1337, when the seven-year-old Black Prince was first equipped with his own suit of armour, he was also provided with a pair of garters made of red velvet. Henry of Grosmont was particularly fond of them: in his *Le Livre de Seyntz Medicines* he confessed his pride in looking good in the jousting lists: 'garters suit me well, in my opinion'.

By the summer of 1348 the garter was being used not merely for decoration but as a chivalric badge; at the Eltham tournament King Edward appeared in a blue robe displaying twelve garters and the motto *Honi soit qui mal y pense* – 'Shame on him who thinks badly of it'. Garters appeared frequently in the Black Prince's own household accounts, where one item read 'twenty-four garters made for the Prince to be given to the knights of the Company of the Garter'.

The royal household records are fragmentary, but they strongly suggest that, in the months before the arrival of the plague, King Edward and the Black Prince were planning to create an order of knighthood to rival that of the Castilian Order of the Sash. Such an order needed a home – a place where its members could meet – and on 6 August 1348 the king demanded the urgent completion of his new chapel at Windsor Castle, to be dedicated to St George, and to be attended by a chosen body of twenty-four warriors.

In the meantime, the Black Prince had set up his own full household, with knights and squires, keepers of the armoury, grooms for his warhorses, priests for his chapel, a barber and barge-master, clerks of the kitchen, heralds and messengers. He prepared to take an active role in managing his estates. He had won his spurs – and his independence.

The Prince had adopted a lifestyle that was characterized by generous gift-giving to his intimates. His New Year presents for 1348 had included an enamelled gold cup for his father and a brooch set with three rubies for his mother. His sisters Isabella and Joan received elaborate jewelled clasps. Joan's was particularly appealing: it was designed in the form of a woman, with a single ruby above her head, and three diamonds around her body, the whole thing surrounded by a garland of pearls and emeralds. Members of the Prince's household also received jewels: Bartholomew Burghersh and his son (of the same name) were given ruby and sapphire brooches, John Chandos an ornate clasp and the Prince's physician, John Gaddesden, a rose of gold – this being an allusion to his famous treatise, *Rosa Medicinae,* written more than thirty years earlier.

Gaddesden, originally a physician at the court of Edward II, had gained fame by curing the Prince's father (then a two-year-old child) of smallpox, without leaving a trace of scarring on his face – a procedure he described in his *Rosa Medicinae.* This was the first work by a doctor wholly trained in England, and a valuable compendium of contemporary medical understanding, offering as it did a mixture of fourteenth-century science, herbal remedies and folklore. Such knowledge was about to be put to its sternest test.

✝

In August 1348 the plague finally crossed the Channel into southern England. A chronicler wrote grimly that:

> The grievous pestilence penetrated the seacoast by Plymouth and Southampton, and came to Bristol, where the whole strength of the city was smitten. Few survived more than two

or three days – and afterwards, this cruel disease broke forth across the kingdom. It struck at young and old, rich and poor, righteous and unrighteous. Reaching London about the Feast of All Saints [1 November] it slew many people daily – and filled the cemeteries with its victims.

In 1349, the plague moved to the north of England and then into Scotland and Ireland, and on to Scandinavia. It had passed through most of Europe by 1350, although it would return intermittently through the remaining years of of the fourteenth century. The chronicler Jean Froissart estimated that in this first terrible outbreak 'a third of the world died'. A third of Europe's population amounted to about 20 million deaths.

Across Europe, the effects of the plague were apocalyptic. In Avignon, in southern France, at the height of the plague it was said that 400 died daily, 7,000 infected homes were shut up and a single graveyard received 11,000 corpses in six weeks. When graveyards filled up, bodies were flung into the River Rhône until mass burial pits were dug. In London, corpses were piled up in such pits in layers until they overflowed. Everywhere the sick were dying too fast for the living to bury.

Amid a growing fear of contagion, people died without the last rites being administered and were buried without prayers. Pope Clement VI found it necessary to grant remissions of sin to all those who died of the plague, because many did so unattended by priests. An English bishop gave permission for laymen to make confessions to each other, as was done by the Apostles, adding that if no priest could be found to administer extreme unction, 'then faith alone must suffice'. These were desperate measures.

Documentary evidence revealed the scale of the catastrophe: at Givry, a prosperous Burgundian village of 1,200 people, the parish register recorded 615 deaths in the space of fourteen weeks, compared to an average of thirty deaths a year over the previous decade. Before the coming of the Black Death the largest cities in Europe,

with populations of about 100,000, were Paris, Florence, Venice and
Genoa. Ghent and Bruges in Flanders, Cologne on the River Rhine,
and the Italian cities of Milan, Naples and Rome had some 60,000
inhabitants each, while London hovered around the 40,000 mark.
The plague swept through them all, killing between a third and a
half of their inhabitants.

A chronicler of Tournai in Flanders described an ever-expanding
rate of mortality:

> First the plague began in one parish, then the others – and
> every day the dead were carried into churches, first five, then
> ten, then fifteen, then twenty or thirty. The bells began to toll
> in the morning and evening, then day and night. And everyone
> in the city, men and women alike, began to be swept up in a
> growing wave of terror – no one knew what to do.

In Siena, where half the population died of the plague, work was
abandoned on a project to expand the cathedral into a massive
basilica, and never resumed, owing to the loss of masons and
master workers and 'the melancholy and grief' of the survivors.
A city chronicler described how fear of catching the disease froze
all other instincts: 'Fathers abandoned their children, wives their
husbands... and no one could be found to bury the dead for money
or friendship... I buried my five children with my own hands, and
so did many others likewise.'

The horror was unimaginable, as the Siennese chronicler made
clear:

> I do not know how to begin to tell of the cruelty and the pitiless
> ways of the plague. It seemed that almost everyone became stu-
> pefied by seeing such overwhelming pain. And it is hard for the
> human tongue to recount the awful truth. Indeed, one who did
> not see such ghastliness can be called blessed. The victims died
> almost immediately. They would swell beneath the armpits
> and around their groins and collapse while talking... Great pits

were dug and piled with the multitude of the dead. And they died by the hundreds, both day and night, and all were thrown into those ditches and covered with earth. And as soon as they were filled, more were dug.

Bodies were heaped upon bodies, with only a thin layer of dirt separating them. Even the possessions of the afflicted became a serious danger. Gabriel de Mussis, a lawyer from Piacenza in Italy, noted:

Some Genoese, who were already infected with the plague, sold their merchandise, whereupon the purchaser, his family, household and all his neighbours contracted the disease. One man, wanting to make his will, died along with the notary, the priest who heard his confession and the people summoned as witnesses. All were buried together the following day. The pestilence has claimed countless victims in this fashion: men of the church, noblemen, young people, women – particularly those who were pregnant. It is too distressing to keep reciting this. I am overwhelmed – I cannot go on.

Flight was the chief recourse for those who could afford it. The urban poor died in their small houses, and 'only the stench of their bodies informed neighbours of their death'. In the countryside, peasants dropped dead on the roads, in the fields and in their homes. A chronicler from Meaux Abbey in Yorkshire wrote that 'the pestilence was so strong that men and women dropped dead while walking in the streets, and in many villages and households not one person was left alive.'

Survivors fell into apathy, leaving ripe wheat uncut and livestock untended. Across England, sheep – mainstay of the precious wool trade – died in their hundreds of thousands. The chronicler Henry Knighton reported 5,000 dead in one field alone, 'their bodies so corrupted by the plague that neither bird nor beast would touch them'. Knighton continued:

Sheep and oxen strayed through the fields and amongst the crops, and there was no one to drive them off or to collect them, but they perished in uncounted numbers throughout all districts for lack of shepherds, because there was such a shortage of shepherds and labourers... And there was a great cheapness of all things for fear of death; for few now took account of riches or possessions of any kind. A man could have a horse that was formerly worth forty shillings for half a mark [6s 8d], a big fat ox for four shillings, a cow for twelve pence, a large pig for five pence.

And so few servants and labourers were left, Knighton added, 'that no one knew where to turn to for help'.

Although the death rate was highest among the anonymous poor, the plague claimed plenty of victims from the ranks of the high-born. King Alfonso XI of Castile was the only reigning monarch killed by the plague, but King Peter IV of Aragon lost his wife, Eleonor, his daughter Marie and a niece within the space of six months. In France, Queen Jeanne and her daughter-in-law, Bonne of Luxembourg, were both killed by the disease. And Edward III would lose his second daughter, Joan, as she travelled to Spain to marry Pedro, the heir of Castile.

Joan, who had been brought up in a safe and happy family environment with the Black Prince, three other brothers and three sisters, set sail for Bordeaux in July 1348. Rumours of the plague were already circulating before the disease reached English shores, but the deadly danger it represented was not yet fully understood by the royal court. The fifteen-year-old princess left Portsmouth in a little flotilla of four ships, carrying her attendants and belongings. These included her wedding dress, made from luxurious thick silk woven with gold thread; a suit of red velvet — with twenty-four buttons of silver gilt and enamel — and five corsets, woven with gold patterns of stars, crescents and diamonds. There were other dresses, embroidered with roses and lions — the symbol of the English monarchy — and ceremonial garments and clothes for everyday

wear and riding. She was accompanied by a Spanish minstrel, sent
as a present by her husband-to-be, two senior royal officials, servants and a retinue of 100 archers. Joan even had her own portable
chapel on board ship, with a beautifully decorated altar cloth and a
couch carved with dragons and a border of vines. No expense was
spared to make her passage to Castile as comfortable as possible.

Joan's visit to the capital of English-held Gascony was meant to
be a pleasant break in her journey to Spain. It turned into something rather different. On reaching Bordeaux, the English royal
contingent were met on the quayside by the mayor, who informed
them that the city was in the grip of a terrible disease and that it
was too risky to land. Joan's advisers brushed the warning aside.
Within days, the leader of her party, Robert Bourchier, a former
chancellor of England, had succumbed to the pestilence. He developed tumour-like buboes that started the size of almonds and
grew to the size of eggs; his skin was covered in dark blotches; he
developed a hacking cough and began to vomit incessantly: every
part of his body gave off a disgusting stench. With her entourage
falling sick all around her, the princess fled in panic to the nearby
village of Loremo. But her retreat into the Gascon countryside did
not save her, and she died on 2 September 1348.

By the time Edward III learned of his daughter's death, the
plague had reached England. The king ordered prayers and processions throughout the realm in the vain hope of deliverance from
the disease. And he wrote a highly personal letter to the king of
Castile, comparing his daughter to a martyred angel:

> With a deeply grieving heart, we have to tell you that destruc-
> tive Death, who seizes young and old alike, sparing no one,
> and reducing rich and poor to the same level, has lamentably
> snatched our dearest daughter, whom we loved best of all, as
> her virtues demanded. No fellow human being would be sur-
> prised to learn that we are inwardly desolated by the pain of
> such a bitter loss. But we, who have placed our trust in God and

our life in his hands, where he has held it closely through many great dangers, give thanks to him that one of our own family, free of all stain, whom we have loved with a pure love, has been sent ahead to heaven, where she can gladly intercede for our offences before God himself.

The calamity was felt intensely by Edward and his family. But it was an agony that struck at every part of society. The chronicler of Meaux Abbey in Yorkshire recorded that only ten of the community's forty-two monks survived the plague; in the village of Halesowen in Shropshire half of the adult male population perished, along with a third of the women and large numbers of children; among London's merchant community, all eight wardens of the Company of Cutters and four from the Goldsmiths died before July 1350. Sir John Pulteney, master draper and four times mayor, was a victim; likewise Sir John Montgomery, governor of Calais.

Within the space of three months William Wakebridge, a prosperous yeoman farmer from Derbyshire, lost his father, wife, two brothers, two sisters and a sister-in-law. The catalogue of death was listed by a grief-stricken Wakebridge, who endowed a chantry chapel in memory of those who had perished, asking that the priest 'say masses for the souls of the deceased every day – for ever'. Graffiti carved on the church tower of St Mary's Church in Ashwell (Hertfordshire) spoke of 'the most wretched, fierce, violent pestilence... only the dregs of the people remain to tell the tale'.

The epidemic would later be called 'the Black Death', a term first coined in a medical text of 1631 and only widely used from the nineteenth century. In 1348 it was known simply as 'the Pestilence' or the 'Great Mortality'. How the contagion spread mystified contemporary observers. In October 1348 Philip VI asked the medical faculty of the University of Paris for a report on 'the affliction that threatens the very survival of humanity'. The doctors, unable to break free from the shackles of astrology, ascribed it to a malign conjunction of the planets Saturn, Jupiter and Mars. The deadly role of the two bubonic plague carriers, the rat and the flea, was not fully understood; and nor was the pneumonic form of the plague, which was communicated through the air. Guy de Chauliac, physician to three successive popes, speculated that the pestilence might even be spread by sight — that looking at a plague victim was sufficient to cause a person to fall ill, as if the power of infection could transmute into beams of light.

In medieval medicine the health and temperament of each individual were believed to be dictated by the balance of the bodily fluids known as the four humours — black bile (melancholic), yellow bile (choleric), phlegm (phlegmatic) and blood (sanguine) — in various permutations with the signs of the zodiac. All human temperaments were considered to belong to one or another of the four humours, each of which governed a particular part of the body. Plague sufferers were treated by various measures designed to draw poison from the body: bleeding, purging with laxatives, lancing, cauterizing or applying hot plasters. Medicines ranged from potions of myrrh and saffron to pills of powdered stag's horn. None of them was of much use.

Doctors advised that floors should be sprinkled with sweet-smelling herbs and that hands, mouths and nostrils should be washed with vinegar and rosewater. Pomanders made of exotic compounds were to be carried when going out. Sewage disposal was far from adequate in the fourteenth century: although privies, cesspools, drainage pipes and public latrines existed, they did not replace open sewers, and the contents of the latter frequently seeped into wells and water sources. And as street cleaners and carriers died of the plague, cities became ever more polluted, increasing the risk of infection. Edward III wrote to the mayor of London, complaining bluntly that the roads were 'putrid with human faeces and the air poisoned, to the great danger of those passing through, especially in this time of infectious disease'. The king ordered that the streets be cleaned 'as of old'.

Strict quarantine was imposed in some cities. As soon as the

plague spread to the Tuscan cities of Pisa and Lucca, their neighbour Pistoia forbade any of its citizens visiting or doing business in
the stricken cities from returning home. Draconian measures were
adopted by the despot of Milan, Giovanni Visconti, who ordered
that all houses where plague was discovered be walled up, with
their occupants inside, enclosing the healthy, the sick and the dead
in a common tomb.

For most people the only explanation was to regard the disease
as a form of divine judgement on human sinfulness. The leader of
western Christendom, Pope Clement VI, announced in a proclamation of September 1348 that 'God is afflicting the Christian people
with a pestilence, which is a chastisement from Heaven'. Clement
himself had managed to escape such punishment, preserving his
health by burning aromatic substances to purify the air around
him. His doctor, Guy de Chauliac, ordered two huge fires to be lit
in the papal apartments and required Clement to sit between them
through the heat of the Avignon summer. The treatment worked,
perhaps because it discouraged the attentions of fleas and required
the pope to remain isolated in his chambers.

Clement VI was an intellectually inquiring pope and a patron of
the arts and sciences, and he encouraged dissections of the dead 'in
order that the origins of the disease might be known'. He was also a
pope of prodigal spending habits with a taste for sensual pleasures,
who indulged in the purchase of over 1,000 ermine gowns for his
personal wardrobe. As a result of a conflict between the papacy and
the French crown, the papacy had moved from Rome to Avignon
at the beginning of the fourteenth century and seven French popes
in succession resided there in affluence and splendour. Clement VI
completed a great papal residence, the Palais des Papes, on a rocky
outcrop overlooking the Rhône, a huge mass of roofs and towers
constructed in castle style around interior courtyards. It had banqueting halls and gardens, money chambers and offices – and even
a steam room for the pope, heated by a boiler. The tiled floors were
intricately decorated with flowers, fantastic beasts and elaborate

heraldry. 'I am living in the Babylon of the West,' the Italian human-ist Francesco Petrarch wrote in the 1340s, 'where the Popes are clad in purple and loaded with precious stones, the cardinals are rich, insolent and rapacious and prelates feast at licentious banquets and ride on snow-white horses decked in gold.'

Many ordinary people, in the face of the catastrophe of the plague, turned away from the church entirely, indulging in hedon-istic behaviour and seeking out scapegoats. In Germany, southern France and Switzerland, the Jews were a particular target. The first attacks occurred in the spring of 1348 in Narbonne and Carcassonne, where Jews were accused of poisoning wells, dragged from their houses and lynched. In Savoy, formal judicial procedures began in September, and thereafter the accusations against − and attacks on − Jews spread rapidly across western Europe. To his credit, Pope Clement attempted to check the hysteria, stating clearly that the plague was afflicting all peoples, including Jews, that it raged in places where no Jews lived and that elsewhere they were victims like everyone else. But his voice was scarcely heard.

The populace became fascinated with a lay order known as the Flagellants, who rose up spontaneously at this time of crisis. By re-enacting the scourging of Christ upon their own bodies, by making their blood flow, the Flagellants hoped to atone for human wickedness and earn another chance for mankind. Organized in groups of several hundred, they marched from city to city, crying aloud to Christ and the Virgin Mary for pity, while the watch-ing townspeople wept and groaned in sympathy. The chronicler Robert of Avesbury described their arrival in London:

> They appeared at St Paul's and at other points of the city, clothed from their thighs to their ankles, but with their chests stripped bare. Each had a knotted scourge in his right hand, in which sharp nails had been fixed. They marched barefoot, whipping themselves until the blood ran − and all the while chanting and singing.

For a short period, bands of Flagellants roamed Europe. Their leaders grew in confidence, assuming the right to hear confessions, grant absolutions and impose penances. But their movement did not halt the plague and soon church and state took action against them. Philip VI prohibited public whipping on pain of death, and the Flagellants vanished just as quickly as they had come, 'like night phantoms or vanishing ghosts'.

As the plague cut a swathe through English towns and villages, many aristocrats and bishops chose to retreat to their country estates. In November 1348, as the pestilence continued to ravage northern France, the king and the Black Prince travelled to Calais to reassure the garrison there. In December, with hundreds dying in the capital each day, Edward set up court in the Tower of London. His friend and fighting companion Sir Walter Mauny purchased a large cemetery at Smithfield and set up a chapel there, so that the dead could at least be buried on consecrated ground. This was exceptionally brave leadership in the face of adversity.

By the spring of 1349 the king had been forced to close the law courts for the remainder of the year and cancel the next meeting of Parliament, but on 23 April 1349, St George's Day, at Windsor Castle, he inaugurated his chivalric order, the Order of the Garter. There were twenty-six members in all, the king and the Black Prince and twenty-four specially chosen knights. In the words of Geoffrey le Baker:

> The king held a great feast at his castle at Windsor... All those together with the king were clad in russet gowns, spangled with gold and with armbands of Indian blue. They had similar garments on their right legs, again in blue, embroidered with the badge of the Garter. Dressed like this, they solemnly heard a ceremonial Mass... and then in due order seated themselves around an ordinary table... calling themselves the Company of the Knights of St George of the Garter.

The king and the Black Prince drew up the list of founder members together. The Order's statutes record the presence of great earls – Henry of Grosmont, earl of Lancaster, the earls of Salisbury, Stafford and Warwick – with the barons John Lord Beauchamp, John Lord Grey of Rotherfield, the lords Lisle and Mohun and a plethora of knights, including the Prince's friends Sir James Audley and Sir John Chandos and his standard bearer, Richard FitzSimon. There was Bartholomew Burghersh the younger, son of the Black Prince's master of household and Nigel Loring (who would become the Prince's chamberlain), knighted for his bravery at Sluys. Others included Thomas Holland (of whom we will be hearing more shortly) and his brother Otto, Sir Roger Mortimer (the grandson of the original Mortimer, family honours having been gradually re-acquired following his death and disgrace), Hugh Courtenay, Walter Paveley, Miles Stapleton, Thomas Wale and Hugh Wrottesley. There was a Gascon, Jean de Grailly, leader of the pro-English nobles in the region, a Picard, Eustace d'Aubrecicourt (who had helped the king during his time in Flanders) and a Dutch squire, Henry Eam, a personal friend of the Prince (who was formally retained in his service in 1348).

Selection was based on acts of valour, not rank and all those chosen had seen active service. The Order's numbers were fixed (the sovereign, the prince of Wales and twenty-four Garter knights) and on the death of a member another would replace him (Hugh Courtenay and Richard FitzSimon succumbed to the plague later in 1349 and the earls of Northampton and Suffolk were elected in their stead).

Members of the Order were required to celebrate the Feast of St George together each year, to wear their garter in public on formal occasions and never to pass through Windsor without hearing Mass at the Garter Chapel. The Order's statutes were primarily religious and struck a serious and solemn tone:

> Each year on St George's Eve shall be held a meeting of all the companions of the Order of Saint George, at the castle of Windsor, whether they be within the kingdom of England or outside it, but that they may conveniently be able to come thither and there they must attend church service.

To found an order of knighthood in a time of plague was a strikingly defiant gesture and, over time, many legends grew up around it. One of these legends centred upon a twenty-year-old woman, Joan of Kent, described by Jean Froissart as 'the most beautiful lady in England, and the most amorous'.

†

Joan's career was certainly remarkable. She was a grand-daughter of Edward I and young cousin of Edward III. In 1330, when she was two years old, her father, the first earl of Kent, had been executed for treason at the insistence of Roger Mortimer (see page 35). After Mortimer was removed from power the king and queen showed Kent's young daughter considerable sympathy. She was brought up first in the royal household and then with the children of Edward's close friend, William Montagu, earl of Salisbury. At the end of January 1341 she married Montagu's son and heir, a teenage boy about the same age as herself.

Nothing seemed untoward. The wedding was publicly celebrated and had the full approval of the king. The young couple were granted the castle and lordship of Mold in north Wales, not perhaps the most romantic-sounding of abodes, but after Salisbury died in a jousting accident two years later, Joan's husband became an earl and she a countess. As the new earl of Salisbury joined the king on the Crécy expedition, a promising career seemed to be beckoning. In later accounts, an exciting future seemed to be opening out for his wife as well. According to the early Tudor historian Polydore Vergil, a ball was held to celebrate the capture of Calais a year later, and it was here that the young countess made a pulse-racing *entrée*:

> Her arrival was greeted with great enthusiasm, particularly by the king. Every man was left awe-struck by her beauty; King Edward could not stop looking at her, for he thought that he had never before seen so noble or so fair a lady. He was pierced to the heart by a pulsating love, one that endured for long afterwards.

Edward chose the countess as his dancing partner and, whether as a result of some strenuous royal cavorting or an incident that happened before they took to the floor, Joan of Kent was seen to lose her garter. (Vergil was seemingly unaware that this was solely a male item of clothing in the mid-fourteenth century.) The king picked up the piece of blue velvet, smiled and tied it around his leg, remarking to the company: '*Honi soit qui mal y pense!*', 'Shame on him who thinks ill of it!' This was how, nearly two hundred years after the event, Polydore Vergil explained the origin of the Order of the Garter: it had all come about through a fourteenth-century 'wardrobe malfunction'. Sadly there was no contemporary evidence whatsoever for Vergil's story. But truth would prove stranger and more sensational than fiction.

In October 1347, one of the heroes of the Crécy campaign, Sir Thomas Holland, made a startling revelation. He announced that Joan's match with the earl of Salisbury was invalid because he had in fact married her first, in May 1340 (some eight months before her marriage to the earl). The two of them had consummated the relationship and had kept their marriage secret. Holland went on to claim that later, when he was on crusade in Prussia, Joan – 'not wishing to contradict the wishes of her relatives and friends' – had been married to the earl 'by their arrangement'. Salisbury, aided and abetted by Joan's mother, refused to acknowledge Holland's claim and the following year, in 1348, appealed to the pope.

If we assume Sir Thomas Holland's account to be true, the clandestine marriage took place when Holland was twenty-five and Joan only twelve. It was conducted in the utmost secrecy, with no priest present, although Sir Thomas later claimed he could produce witnesses. And it was then immediately consummated, Holland not even waiting until his new 'wife' was fourteen – the usual medieval practice within an aristocratic marriage – before having sex with her. Then, in this version of events, with her husband out of the country, Joan was forced into a second marriage, which she did not want.

The nineteen-year-old earl of Salisbury confined his wife to Mold Castle. In Holland's eyes, this was further proof of coercion – although it could equally be read as a desperate attempt by the earl to save his marriage. Whichever version was correct, in 1348 Joan was in no position to attend any celebratory balls or drop any garters.

Historians have generally told the story of Joan's supposed first marriage from Sir Thomas Holland's viewpoint, thereby lending legitimacy and respectability to his version of events. His marriage to Joan has been portrayed as a love match, thwarted by a conspiracy of Joan's relatives and friends, led by her mother Margaret. But the insalubrious reality is that Joan was still a child and Holland an adult more than twice her age when he claimed to have married and bedded her. Joan became known to posterity as 'the Fair Maid of Kent', but the contemporary sobriquet 'the Virgin of Kent' was perhaps more telling in its mockery.

There were in fact substantial problems with Holland's story. It is unclear how he gained access to Joan in the first place. In May 1340, when she was only twelve, she was being closely chaperoned by the Montagu family. If a binding marriage had taken place between Holland and Joan and had been consummated before his departure on campaign in 1340, it is surprising that, on learning of Joan's marriage to the earl of Salisbury on his return to England in late 1341, Holland did not appeal at once to the English ecclesiastical

courts. His subsequent behaviour is even more puzzling. If Sir
Thomas considered that he had been supplanted by the earl of
Salisbury and had suffered a considerable injustice, it is remarkable
that he chose, in 1345, to become steward of the earl's lands, a post
that would require him to work closely with Joan's new husband.

Sir Thomas's direct appeal to the papal court was a highly
unusual, not to mention expensive, course of action. If his case
stood up to scrutiny, it would have been considerably cheaper,
and quicker, to have taken it before an English ecclesiastical tri-
bunal. Sir Thomas knew that the earl of Salisbury was short of
money – the revenues from the young earl's inheritance, apart
from lands specifically granted to him in north Wales, were still
in the king's hands because Salisbury was underage – and Holland
now had plenty of cash of his own, having sold his ransom rights
to the count of Eu to Edward III for 12,000 florins (around £1,800).
And every Englishman knew that the Papal Curia was notoriously
corrupt and susceptible to bribery.

An alternative scenario was not hard to construct, and it went
something like this. Joan had begun an affair with Sir Thomas *after*
Holland became steward of the earl of Salisbury's estates, the earl's
frequent absences providing them with ample opportunity to consummate their relationship. They then concocted the story of a
clandestine marriage as a way of getting rid of Salisbury. In this
version of events, Joan was not a girl of twelve but a young woman
of seventeen, and was falling for a proven warrior and crusader, a
man daring enough to ride into the centre of French-held Rouen
with only two companions and flaunt the banner of St George at
his astonished opponents. The earl of Salisbury would have understood how they felt.

According to this scenario, Joan's family – headed by her
mother Margaret – were not the coercive mafia suggested by Sir
Thomas Holland. Instead, they were genuinely shocked by their
daughter's behaviour. Margaret stuck by her daughter's spurned
husband because she sympathized with him, and simply did not

believe Holland's story. The Welsh chronicler Adam of Usk wrote of Joan's 'slippery ways' in her marital affairs.

Edward III attempted to stay impartial in these proceedings, with little success. In November 1347 he sent his old friend Elizabeth Montagu, the earl's grandmother, to Avignon, possibly to sound out Holland's chances of success with the pope. After her return, he granted Salisbury a portion of his inheritance so that he could fight the case. But both the king and the Black Prince liked and admired Sir Thomas Holland, their former comrade-in-arms, and were genuinely fond of Joan; neither had warmed to the new earl of Salisbury.

For the earl, keeping Joan in seclusion could only be a temporary strategy, as Holland submitted a second petition to the papacy. In May 1348 Pope Clement VI ordered the archbishop of Canterbury to secure Joan's release so that she could give evidence. Joan's testimony would be crucial to the proceedings; without her confirmation of Holland's petition, the court could not make a judgement. Yet it seems that, for a few months at least, she lost her nerve and made no comment on the case. Her attorney, David Martyn, failed to submit anything on her behalf when he attended the court on two successive occasions and matters stalled. In the autumn a new official, Cardinal Bernard d'Albi, was appointed to oversee the case. Joan chose a new attorney, perhaps at Sir Thomas's prompting, and submitted at last that she had voluntarily married Holland and consummated their union; her marriage to Salisbury had been forced upon her by her family and she had only agreed to it out of fear.

Joan's mother was furious when she learned of this and broke off contact with her daughter. Edward III invited the young countess to spend Christmas with the royal family. Only too mindful of the daughter he had lost, and the pestilence that was afflicting his realm, the king was happy to have his beautiful cousin in his company again. So too was the Black Prince, who gave her a finely worked silver beaker, addressing her by her childhood nickname 'Jeanette'.

In April 1349, the case was still before the papal court. That same month, the earl of Salisbury and Sir Thomas Holland were both elected founder members of the Order of the Garter. At the tournament following the Feast of St George, on 23 April 1349, the knights were organized into two jousting teams of twelve, one under the king, the other under the Prince. Salisbury and Holland were on opposing sides and quite literally fighting over the same woman. The countess may not have actually dropped her garter for Edward III, but she was the centre of romantic attention at the Order's inauguration.

But the driving force behind this new order of knighthood was not sexual frisson but high-minded kingship, the comradeship of veterans of Crécy and Calais and a belief in Edward's claim to the crown of France. And that, fundamentally, was what the Garter motto was referring to. Edward III knew how to have a good time but he also cared passionately about the dignity of the monarchy and at a time of unparalleled crisis would do nothing to besmirch it. Mindful that some commentators had criticized tournaments as magnets for sinful behaviour, he did not mention them in the Order of the Garter's statutes, the focus of which was instead placed firmly on religious observance. Edward well understood that too much talk about sensual pleasure would undermine the moral purpose of his chivalric body.

The case between Salisbury and Holland dragged on, and was finally decided on 13 November 1349, when a papal decree pronounced Joan's marriage to Salisbury void, and ordered that her marriage to Sir Thomas Holland be properly celebrated in a church ceremony, which took place shortly afterwards. Joan bore Holland five children over the next few years; the eldest, named Thomas after his father, and the second son, John, would later be companions of the Order themselves.

†

As the Black Death passed through Europe, its effect was traced in an explosion of artistic imagery and a revival of interest in a thirteenth-century legend, 'The Three Living and the Three Dead'. This told of a meeting between three young nobles and three decomposing corpses, who say to the aristocrats: 'What you are, we were. What we are, you will become.' The Black Prince would incorporate these words, on the theme of the inevitability of death and decay, in his own tomb and memorial at Canterbury Cathederal.

The Order of the Garter was not the first order of knighthood, nor would it be the last. But it was the only one formed in the midst of a plague outbreak. At the core of its identity was a spiritual purpose, strongly emphasized in its statutes, to properly commemorate the dead:

> It is recorded that on each morrow of St George's Day, before the companions take leave of each other and depart, a requiem mass is to be celebrated for the souls of all the faithful departed, and that the whole society [of St George] shall be there in its entirety.

As the Black Death made its lethal progress across Europe, physicians endeavoured to tend the sick and priests ministered to the dying. But it was the soldier who was perhaps best placed to understand one fundamental aspect of the disease – namely the suddenness of the death it brought about, which left no time for a person to seek absolution from sin and guarantee their soul's safe passage to the next life. An unprepared death was one of the pestilence's particular terrors and a point of connection between the plague victim and the warrior, for the soldier's worst fear was that he would die unconfessed in battle, and thereafter not be buried in consecrated ground but flung into a mass grave. His dread was rooted in the medieval belief in Purgatory, a place of limbo, where unconfessed souls were trapped in an intermediate state between Heaven and Hell – one increasingly associated, in the thirteenth and fourteenth centuries, with pain, fire and suffering.

In time of war or plague proper religious observance could not always be followed. But soldiers understood the spiritual horror engulfing Europe. Those military men who could afford it petitioned the papacy for the right to use private confessors and portable altars, at which Mass could be celebrated. In the Black Prince's household, Sir Nigel Loring and Sir John Chandos were both granted this privilege. And the spiritual needs of ordinary soldiers in the Prince's army were also catered to: John Lyons, Chandos's chaplain, was granted permission (as the papal registers clearly stated) to receive confession from all English soldiers, 'because in the past, being ignorant of the language [used by a native priest, speaking French or Gascon] they have died imperfectly confessed'.

The statutes of the Order of the Garter stipulated certain spiritual obligations of its members. As has been described, all had to attend the annual service at Windsor on St George's Day, and on the following day participate in a Requiem Mass. The Requiem Mass, also known as the Mass for the Dead, was offered for the repose of souls – taken from a place of suffering to one of rest; it began with the words *Requiem aeternam dona eis, Domine* – 'Grant them eternal peace, O Lord'. This symbolic act of remembrance was reinforced by the sponsoring of hundreds of additional Masses, paid for by the founder knights and performed by priests in chapels and churches all over the country.

Such was the power of numbers and repetition over the medieval mind – a repetition, it was believed, which assisted the soul in climbing a Purgatorial ladder out of the realm of fire. On the death of one of the Order's warriors, the king would have 1,000 Masses said for the Garter knight's soul. Other members of the order were required to provide them according to rank, ranging from 700 from the Black Prince to 100 from an ordinary knight. In the arithmetic of the king's Masses alongside those of all the other Garter knights, around 5,000 would be said within three months of a knight's death – a very large number, even by fourteenth-century standards.

This intercession meant that if a knight died on campaign without leaving a will, which would have specified that Masses were to be said for the soul of the deceased, his soul would not languish in Purgatory. When Sir John Chandos died intestate in 1370, his companions in the Order paid for at least 5,300 Masses to be said. In 1372, the Black Prince's brother, John of Gaunt, provided 500 Masses for the soul of Sir Walter Mauny, 'our most dear companion and knight of the Order of the Garter', who was elected to the Order on the death of John Lord Grey, and twenty years earlier had endowed a large consecrated burial ground for plague victims at Smithfield.

The reciting of so many Masses – baffling to modern sensibilities – chimed with the deeply felt piety of the medieval era. The Order of the Garter's desire to remember the dead properly extended beyond its own fellowship: its annual Requiem Mass 'for the souls of all members who have died and for all Christians', went further, offering assistance to all souls languishing in Purgatory. And this gave the Order a unique spiritual identity and moral authority.

The plague was still wreaking havoc across the country in the summer of 1349. In August of that year Edward wrote to the English bishops, castigating the survivors of the plague for their lack of charity and calling on them to pray to God for his mercy:

> We are amazed and appalled that the few people who still survive have not been humbled by this terrible judgement... and charity has grown more than usually cold in them. This seems to presage a much mightier calamity unless God, who has been offended by their guilt, is pacified by the performance of penance for sin and by the prayers of the faithful.

But that autumn – to what must have been a general sense of joy and relief – the pestilence at last began to dissipate. And Edward soon found himself presented with a new opportunity to return to the offensive in France. Officially, the two countries had ceased hostilities following the advent of the plague and were bound by a temporary truce. On Christmas Eve 1349, however, Edward III learned of a plot to betray Calais to the French. He responded with confidence and panache. Within a few days he had assembled a scratch force of Garter knights, household servants and English archers and crossed over in person, as the chronicler Geoffrey le Baker related:

> The king, anxious to keep the town, which he had won by great effort and over a year's siege, hurriedly crossed the Channel, accompanied by his eldest son, the Prince of Wales, Sir Roger Mortimer and a handful of others, and arrived only a few days before the date set for the plot. When he reached Calais, he prepared a crafty welcome for the French.

Edward had learned that the town gates were to be opened to the enemy, in return for a large bribe. However, the officer concerned had betrayed the conspiracy to the English king. Edward could have simply reinforced the garrison, putting an end to proceedings. Instead, he devised something rather more elaborate, appearing to let the plot go ahead and preparing a hand-picked reception committee for his opponents, led by himself and the Black Prince. Geoffrey le Baker was fascinated by the cleverness of Edward's stratagem:

> Under the vaults inside the gateway of the portcullis and around it he stationed knights, building a thin wall in front of them, not cemented but made of dry stone and plastered level with the adjoining walls, and carefully faked to look like old work so that no one would suspect that there were men hiding in there.

One senses the king's delight in these preparations, as if he was engaging in an elaborately staged tournament rather than simply wishing to repulse the French. But Edward was also testing the mettle of some of his new Garter companions, and engaging in some military action after the horrors of the plague was doubtless a relief to him. And he knew that the surprise assault on the town was to be led by the famous knight and author Geoffrey de Charny. And on this occasion Charny appears to have been less than chivalrous, for he had conceived an audacious if not entirely honourable plan of bribing the captain of Calais's citadel, a Lombard named Aimery of Pavia. De Charny had reasoned that the Italian would prefer financial enrichment to honourably serving Edward III, but he had miscalculated: it had been Aimery of Pavia who had given away details of the plot to the English.

There was more to come, as Geoffrey le Baker made clear:

> Then he [Edward] had the great beam of the drawbridge partly sawn through, yet left so that armed horsemen could still ride over it. He also had an opening made in the tower above the bridge, and a large stone placed there; a trusted knight was put in hiding there, who was to break the sawn-through drawbridge at just the right moment by throwing down the stone.

Edward III had arrived in person at Calais with his son and a few trusted companions to spring a most ingenious trap. He entered the town secretly and kept a low profile. The French had no idea he was there. The king told Aimery to accept the bribe and tell Charny's agents that the castle would be handed over to them at midnight on 31 December. Timing was everything. Edward and the Black Prince intended to meet their opponents in person, in a clash of arms that would mark the beginning of the New Year. And remarkably, the knight hidden above the drawbridge had instructions to let a reasonable number of the French through before breaking it: the king wanted a fair and satisfying fight.

Things started well for the English. Geoffrey de Charny and his advance guard entered Calais as planned, only to find themselves suddenly cut off from their followers still outside and surrounded by a mass of English soldiers. De Charny, who had borne his banner proudly into the town, shouted to his fellows that they must stand and fight bravely but most of the French attempted to flee, chased by Edward and his knights who, not content with overpowering the advance guard, then launched themselves on the enemy soldiers outside the gate. Employing judicious understatement, Geoffrey le Baker remarked of Edward's assault:

> I dare not say it was wisdom or military prudence that led the king to pursue the enemy, but it was royal courage nonetheless to carry out such a dangerous feat, and by the grace of God he came out of it with honour.

The king of England – fighting incognito, in unmarked armour – and about thirty companions (half men-at-arms, half archers) had rushed outside the gates of Calais in pursuit of their foe but the hunters now found themselves hunted. 'The French suddenly realized that only a handful of men were following them', Baker continued in sober fashion, 'and reformed their ranks: more than eighty men-at-arms were now facing the king's sixteen'.

King Edward was cut off on a causeway – and in real danger of being taken prisoner or killed. His archers were about to flee when Edward turned to them, revealing his identity, and said: 'I am Edward of Windsor – shoot for me!' Galvanized by this exhortation, they held off the enemy for a while. The Black Prince, seeing the danger, then hacked his way through to his father's side, with many of the English garrison following him. The French withdrew, leaving many dead and others taken prisoner.

Edward had indeed emerged 'with honour' from the escapade, but only just. Before leaving Calais, Edward held a banquet for Geoffrey de Charny and the other captured French knights, at which the first course was served by the Prince. De Charny received a mock dressing-down for unchivalrous behaviour. Another captive, Eustace de Ribemont – who at one stage of the fight had traded blows with the king – was praised for his courage and spared having to pay a ransom. But on the royal party's return to London, the biggest plaudit was reserved for the king's son. 'My good lady,' Edward said to Queen Philippa, 'be sure to entertain the Prince well, for I would have been taken by the enemy if it had not been for his great valour.'

This was the defiance of plague survivors – willing to meet death head-on, without fear. And that summer, a new threat was seen off. After the untimely death of Princess Joan, King Alfonso of Castile had struck up an alliance with the French, and early in 1350 a large Castilian–Genoese merchant fleet, on its way to Flanders, attacked and sank English shipping, throwing the crews overboard. Edward resolved to meet it in battle on its return and gathered his forces. On 29 August 1350, while his men were waiting for their opponents off Winchelsea, the king decided to perform a stunt to lift his troops' morale, as Jean Froissart describes:

> The king posted himself on the forepart of his own ship: he was dressed in a black velvet jacket and wore a small black beaver hat which suited him well. He was (as I was told by those who were there) as joyful as his fighting comrades had ever seen him. He made his minstrels play a German dance which Sir John Chandos, who was present, had recently brought back [Chandos had been on crusade in Prussia]. For everyone's entertainment, he asked the knight to sing with his minstrels – and all took great pleasure in hearing him. And, from time to time, Edward looked up at the forecastle where he had placed a lookout to tell him when the Spanish came into view. And as the king enjoyed himself in such fashion, all those who could see him relaxed too. Then the lookout came running up with the news that the Spanish fleet was coming – and the music ceased.

A signal was given and the English ships drew together. King Edward's force, ranging from small barges to great merchant vessels, was crammed with men-at-arms and archers. Most of the Garter knights were present, and alongside the king and the Black Prince were Henry of Grosmont, the earls of Warwick, Northampton and Salisbury – all of whom were given squadrons to command – Reginald Lord Cobham, Sir John Chandos, John Lord Lisle, Sir

Walter Mauny and Sir Thomas Holland. As a sensible precaution, Salisbury and Holland were posted to different parts of the fleet.

King Edward had ordered a thousand large shields to be made for the protection of the bowmen on board his ships. They were painted white and displayed the royal coat of arms encircled by a blue garter. They must have presented a striking spectacle, placing the Order of the Garter at the heart of the English war effort.

Edward III trusted the quality of his fighters, but the Spanish ships were longer, broader and taller – in Geoffrey le Baker's vivid phrase 'like castles towering over cottages' – and the English would need to ram and board them. The king set an example, ordering the captain of his flagship to steer directly at the first Castilian vessel. The two collided, the Spaniards' forecastle collapsed and its occupants were thrown into the sea. Within minutes, the king's ship had smashed into another galley. But soon the Prince's ship was in deadly danger, as Froissart related:

> His vessel was grappled and held by a much larger Spanish ship. And the Prince and his men had much to suffer, for their ship was split and holed in many places, so that the water entered at great speed – and it was only by much bailing that it was prevented from sinking immediately. The Prince's men fought right bitterly to overcome the Spanish ship, but they did not succeed – for it was stoutly defended.

It was Henry of Grosmont who saw the danger the Black Prince was in. He brought his ship round to the other side of the Spanish vessel, and grappled it. The Prince attacked once more, this time from the other side, and the Castilian ship was at last boarded and overcome, its crew flung overboard. Moments later, the Prince's own ship sank.

The battle concluded at dusk. The Spanish fleet had been routed: seventeen Castilian ships were captured, twenty-seven had fled and the remainder were sunk. To celebrate the victory Edward knighted eighty squires. In the battle's aftermath, with so many

Castilians and Genoese consigned to a watery grave, the clash was nicknamed 'Les Espagnols-sur-Mer.'

†

By the summer of 1350 the plague had departed. Between a third and a half of England's population had died; the pestilence had carried away so many that survivors could demand higher wages and better working conditions. Landlords therefore found their revenues substantially reduced. An attempt to hold wages to the amount paid before the plague – the Statute of Labourers of 1351 – proved impossible to enforce and did not succeed in keeping wages down.

The Black Prince, as a great landowner, had his share of these troubles. His Welsh revenues, which had brought in nearly £5,000 a year before the arrival of the pestilence, declined sharply: income from the coal and lead mines dropped by 95 per cent; tolls on boats and fishing dried up completely. Sir John Wingfield was appointed steward of all the Prince's lands in 1350, and Wingfield was relentless in his pursuit of local officials and in the maintenance of hard-driving, cash-generating policies, sending out a stream of instructions, some even written 'from our bed' or 'from the chimney-corner of our house'. Yet the Prince showed himself to be a tough but fair landlord. In September 1351 he instructed his receiver in Cornwall 'to deal equitably and rightly' with tenants over disputed payments, adding that he wished them protected from 'oppressions and extortions'.

When he saw genuine suffering, the Prince remitted rents of those working on his lands to alleviate their poverty and encourage them not to abandon their holdings. He was prepared to give a fair hearing to men who appealed to him for redress. In May 1352 the lead miners of Holywell in Flintshire complained of an infringement of their franchise, for which they had been paying him 20s a year. The Prince was sympathetic and instructed his officers to 'examine well the conditions granted to the said men, ascertain whether they do what they ought for them and do them right, so that they have no cause for reasonable complaint'. And hearing of the misdeeds of one Cornish knight, whom he had retained in his service, but who was now oppressing the peasantry, he dismissed him on the grounds that his conduct 'has been and still is outrageous and offensive to us, and our subjects, ministers and tenants'.

In the summer of 1353, the Black Prince's agents in Cheshire were struggling to carry out their duties amid conditions of local unrest; one of his bailiffs, Hugh Hamson of Northwich, was murdered while 'on the prince's service'. In response, the Prince announced his first visit to the county and his wish to hold judicial sessions there on 26 June. He said it was the result of 'grievous clamours and complaints' that had reached him, 'of wrongs, excesses and misdeeds' which needed his presence to put right. He arrived in Cheshire with his great council, which included all his principal officers: Sir John Wingfield, Sir Richard Stafford, Bartholomew Burghersh the younger, Sir Nigel Loring (the chamberlain of his household) and Sir John Chandos. In anticipation of armed attacks on his justices, the Prince arranged for the retinues of Henry of Grosmont and the earls of Stafford and Warwick to be stationed near by. As it transpired, they were not needed, for he won over his opponents without violence or coercion.

On 15 August 1353 (the feast of the Assumption) a magnificent banquet was held at Chester Castle to which many of the Cheshire gentry were invited. The Prince explained why he had come to the county; as he later expressed in a charter grant, 'the particular unrest disorder and feuding within Cheshire has compelled us to see what was behind such lawlessness and put an end to it'. He understood the sensibilities of local custom and that Cheshire was fiercely independent, for as a county palatine it held special autonomy from the rest of the kingdom. He would make money out of these proceedings (by levying judicial fines) but he would offer something concrete in return. He would listen to people's grievances and attempt to redress them. He would begin public works schemes, improving river navigation on the Mersey and the Dee. And, above all, he would grant Cheshire new privileges and enshrine them in a charter of liberties. He turned to those around him and asked, simply and directly, for their support.

On 19 August the community of Cheshire offered a fine of 5,000 marks (£3,333 13s 4d) payable over four years, to which the Black Prince agreed. Payment was to be made by all, 'in accordance with their wealth in lands, goods and chattels', with the exception of members of the church and poor people with an income of less than 20s a year, who did not have to contribute. The Prince concluded his visit on 10 September 1353 by granting a charter of liberties to the county.

†

A contemporary poem, *Wynnere and Wastoure* (*Winner and Waster*), written in alliterative verse in the mid-fourteenth century, is thought to have been composed by a member of Sir John Wingfield's retinue and was possibly performed at the great banquet at Chester Castle on 15 August 1353. *Wynnere and Wastoure* was a dream poem, and in his dream the author saw two armies drawn up on a plain, with Edward III camped above them. The king sent his herald to intervene and the leaders of the armies – Winner (representing financial prudence) and Waster (prodigality and excess) – then presented their respective cases for King Edward to judge.

Intriguingly, the poet makes a reference to the chief justice, Sir William Shareshull, who headed the Prince's commission, and to a fear of armed resistance ('... and Shareshull with them, that said I rode out with power to disturb his peace'). The broader themes of the debate in *Wynnere and Wastoure* were certainly topical: the search for money, the exploitation of revenues, the surveys and statements of account jostling with the desire to share the fruits of this wealth.

They may have been, in part, a response to criticisms already circulating about the Black Prince's extravagant lifestyle. On 23 December 1348 the Prince spent no less than £105 on an evening's gambling with his father, and his debts were mounting. In August 1350, about to embark for the sea battle off Winchelsea, he drew up his will, with a request to the king that if he perished in the fight his executors be allowed to gather revenues from his properties for a further year, in order to pay off all the sums he owed.

Winner upbraided Waster's tendency to indulge in tourneys and feasting on a whim, a whim that then required borrowing a lot of money:

> 'You use up all my goods with wassailing on winter nights,
> With your extravagant spending and arrogant pride:
> There is no source of wealth flowing through your hands
> That is not given and granted before you have got it.'
> But Waster retorted:
> 'With our feasts and fine fare we feed the poor.
> It gives pleasure to our Lord, who created Paradise,
> When all Christ's people have a share, and it pleases him more
> Than if it is heaped up and hidden, and hoarded in chests,
> So the sun cannot see it in seven years.'

The debate about spending and saving ended inconclusively (the surviving text of the poem breaks off with the king only part way through his judgement). However, the poem offers an intriguing commentary on the social and economic problems afflicting mid-fourteenth-century England. There was, of course, value in both Winner's and Waster's point of view, something that the Black Prince and his fellow landowners would have well understood. To recruit men into his service, a great lord needed to be generous, whether in feasting or gift-giving or making payments to secure men's allegiance, by annuity (an annual payment of a fixed sum) or an indenture of retainer (a more formal, legally binding agreement). But alongside such displays of largesse, for a lord to continue to reward his servants, and give them a share of his patronage, he needed to avoid the burden of heavy debt.

We can only speculate whether the poem was describing, or intended for, a real event. It created a resplendent setting, and one that the Black Prince would certainly have been familiar with. In the banqueting hall described in the poem, the Order of the Garter's insignia is everywhere prominently displayed:

> The roof and its rafters all arrayed in red,
> Adorned with medallions dazzling and bright,
> And about each one a blue garter, glittering with gold.

Similarly magnificent red hangings, decorated with eagles and stars, would later be gifted by the Prince to St George's Chapel, Windsor, the spiritual home of the knights of the Garter.

Wynnere and Wastoure, if read aloud to an assembled audience, represented the kind of entertainment that the Black Prince enjoyed. It was a well-crafted and sophisticated work which addressed the financial and ethical dilemmas of its time. The author of the poem and the Chandos Herald both lamented that a real appreciation of poetry had declined, along with its capacity to transport an audience. Once lords had given a place at their feasts to skilled 'makers of mirth', they complained, but now they had been supplanted by young entertainers performing knockabout comedy.

Whether the Prince heard the poem recited, or was simply familiar with its broader content, he may well have reflected upon the moral issues it raised. As his career unfolded, the poetical debate offered him an invitation: to amend his chivalric lifestyle and temper his natural generosity with a measure of fiscal prudence. And within that invitation was an implicit warning. If he failed to do so, he might one day be confronted by an opponent who had mastered this skill — and was prepared to use it against him.

†

On 31 December 1353 the Prince went to the royal palace of Eltham for a tournament, accompanied by Sir James Audley and Sir John Chandos. Soon afterwards, evidently dissatisfied with his armour, he ordered four new pieces, 'which the prince has devised', to be ready for the next jousts 'in accordance with the instructions of Roger, the prince's smith'. In the summer of 1354 he toured his Cornish estates, saying that 'he wished to be better acquainted with his tenants from these parts before he next went abroad', receiving their homage and settling outstanding disputes. The Prince returned to one of his favourite residences, the castle of Berkhamsted (in Hertfordshire), which he had ordered substantially repaired and improved, restoring its great tower and curtain walls, and erecting a new timber palisade around the park.

The Prince was genuinely concerned for the well-being of his tenants in the aftermath of the Black Death. But the beauty of the decorations and insignia of the Order of the Garter, forged at this time of suffering and loss, and conjured so effectively by the author of *Wynnere and Wastoure*, was never far from his thoughts. His prowess would soon be demonstrated once more against the enemy, the Valois kingdom of France.

chapter five

THE GREAT RAID

In January 1355, Queen Philippa gave birth to a fifth son, Thomas of Woodstock, and two months later, after the 'churching', the ritual period of purification, a lavish celebratory tournament was held in London. The Black Prince jousted alongside his close friends Sir John Chandos and Sir James Audley, giving them armoured breastplates for the occasion, covered in black and red velvet – a typically generous gesture. A knight from Gascony also attended: Jean de Grailly, known as the Captal de Buch.

De Grailly, one of the founder members of the Order of the Garter, requested an audience with Edward and Queen Philippa. He told Edward that he spoke for knights within the duchy of Gascony who were supporters of English rule, and that they all wanted to see something done about one of their enemies, the count of Armagnac. The Chandos Herald caught the moment:

> The Captal de Buch came from Gascony, a valiant and noble man, bold and very brave, and popular with everyone. He was given a warm welcome, and the prince was very glad of his arrival. One day he said to the king and queen: 'Sire, you know how many noble knights in Gascony are your friends and how they fight hard on your behalf, but they have no captain of your blood. If your advisers thought fit to send one of your sons, they would be all the bolder.'

It was quite clear which son de Grailly was referring to. Apart from the most recent arrival in the royal family, baby Thomas, the other three boys – Lionel, John and Edmund – were only aged sixteen, fifteen and fourteen respectively, and as yet had no military experience between them. Later in the year, the king would take Lionel and John with him on his short Calais campaign of November 1355 and knight them, but they were scarcely ready for an independent command. The Black Prince, on the other hand, was immediately enthusiastic.

The Gascons faced a threatening opponent in the experienced warrior and diplomat Jean, count of Armagnac. Armagnac had been appointed by the French king, John II, as governor of Languedoc. Methodical and well organized, Armagnac had taken the initiative, invading Gascony and capturing a number of towns and small fortresses. He was a rich, powerful and intimidating aristocrat, and by the end of 1354 he was winning Gascon nobles over to the French cause.

De Grailly well knew the Black Prince's bravery at Crécy and felt that his appointment would inspire his fellow Gascons and revitalize the war effort there. Ten years earlier Henry of Grosmont had led a highly effective campaign on his arrival in the duchy as king's lieutenant, and de Grailly hoped that the Prince would now emulate it. The two men had already struck up a firm friendship: they were the same age and both were chivalric adventurers.

The Black Prince was captivated by the idea of a Gascon expedition and impatient for action. On 24 April 1355 he wrote a letter to his steward in the duchy of Cornwall, saying that he had 'urged the king to grant him leave to be the first across the sea', in other words, to lead a campaign abroad in his own right. However, Edward III did not rush into the appointment. He knew of the courage his son had displayed at Crécy and Calais and was aware of the importance of giving him his own command. However, it was a question of timing.

At first, the king was thinking of sending a more experienced commander, the earl of Warwick, to Gascony. He was swayed by his son's enthusiasm and de Grailly's advocacy but wanted to consider his options carefully, in the light of the diplomatic situation. Earlier that year negotiations with the French at Avignon had broken down and the king now wanted to make a strong military intervention, with the English supporting an uprising organized by the dissident nobleman Charles of Navarre (ruler of the kingdom of Navarre and also an aristocratic landowner in France) in Normandy and launching a plundering raid of their own from Calais. He took the matter to his council, where by 24 May a final decision was made, as part of a broader plan to renew action across the whole of France. On this day, according to Robert of Avesbury, 'it was ordained that the Lord Edward, Prince of Wales, the oldest son of the king, would cross the sea to Aquitaine'.

England and France were quickly moving towards a full-scale resumption of war. The truce that had nominally existed since 1347, although constantly broken by both sides, was renewed in 1353 and again in 1354. Edward offered to renounce his claim to the French throne in return for substantial territorial compensation. The French king John II was less and less willing to compromise with the English. In the winter of 1354, in tortuous negotiations at Avignon, Henry of Grosmont, Edward's representative, managed to run up an expense account of £5,600 as a result of the extravagant enter-taining expected at the papal court. But King John refused to ratify the treaty of Guînes, which would have given Edward sovereignty over an enlarged Aquitaine in return for surrendering his claim to the crown of France. A further clash now seemed inevitable. Henry of Grosmont would be sent to Normandy with an army; Edward III would bring another to Calais later in the year. Amid this rush of military activity, orders were also given in England for the prepara-tion of the Black Prince's expedition.

The indenture between Edward III and the Prince, formally appointing him king's lieutenant, was sealed on 10 July. It set out his powers and the remit of his expedition, giving him full authority to act 'as if the king were there in person', in all matters concern-ing the government and administration of Gascony, the making of truces and local agreements. It also stated that 'the Prince shall be granted a sum of money sufficient for the conciliation of the people of the country and such other purposes as he shall think proper for the king's profit'. The 'conciliation of the people' meant reassuring the king's loyal subjects and winning back the doubters; this would be achieved by bold military action.

The expedition was delayed while necessary shipping was found for the army. It consisted of about 2,600 soldiers – half of them men-at-arms, half of them archers. More would join when it reached Gascony. The Prince was looking to create a fast raiding force. He was accompanied by members of his household and administrative staff, by a substantial aristocratic contingent – including the earls of Warwick, Oxford, Suffolk and Salisbury, Reginald Lord Cobham (elected to the Order in 1352) and John Lord Lisle – and by the knights Sir John Chandos and Sir James Audley, who were his special advisers.

The Order of the Garter was the pulsating heart of this new enterprise. Fourteen Knights of the Garter – more than half the Order – would join him for the campaign and all his divisional commanders would be Garter knights. This was a potent mix of military experience and youthful enthusiasm and all felt a strong sense of loyalty to the Black Prince. The leading lights of the Order included the earls of Warwick and Suffolk and Reginald Lord Cobham. These men had many martial endeavours under their belt and on Edward III's Crécy campaign had been members of the king's council of war. The great strength of the English military command was its closeness and sense of trust, and the Order of the Garter embodied these qualities: these were men who enjoyed working together and could take important decisions with speed and confidence.

Sir John Chandos, a Garter knight and personal friend of the Prince, was praised by the chronicler Jean Froissart for his innate sense of chivalry. Froissart recorded Chandos's first exploit, single combat with a French squire at the siege of Cambrai, where onlookers were impressed by his courage. He fought at the naval battle of

Sluys in 1340, and six years later at Crécy he served in the vanguard under the Prince's command.

Thirty-five-year-old Chandos was a leading light of the Derbyshire branch of his family. Always urbane and diplomatic, he was a man passionately committed to the cause while not taking himself too seriously (he had already displayed his sang-froid at Winchelsea in 1350) a characteristic that perhaps captures the spirit of the Garter knights as a whole. Sir John Chandos received regular gifts of jewellery, robes and horses from the Prince, who clearly enjoyed his company and valued his judgement, and was a member of his inner council. The two would be inseparable on campaign and Chandos's herald would later write an account of the Prince's life, one of our principal sources for the period. Two other Garter knights and members of the Prince's household, Nigel Loring and James Audley, both had an appetite for this new martial enterprise, having fought with Henry of Grosmont in Gascony ten years earlier.

The Black Prince spent most of July and August at Plympton Abbey in Devon, making his preparations for the expedition. Sir John Wingfield, the Prince's chief councillor and 'governor of all his affairs', joined him, bringing a businesslike efficiency to the arrangements. 500 archers were brought down from Cheshire, another 100 from Flintshire. Two Cheshire knights, Sir John Danyers and Sir Ralph Mobberley, advised the Prince on their recruitment. The two men had joined the Prince's council of war for very different reasons. Danyers wanted to get back into favour: he had been seriously rebuked by the Prince's administrators three years earlier. Now he secured a pardon for all fines and transgressions in return for good service. Mobberley, on the other hand, wanted to make money: he was a landowner in east Cheshire struggling with the declining income from his estates and was looking to gain profit from the war. Both knew their localities well.

The Prince wanted a good return for the wages he was paying out for his troops. On the recommendation of Danyers and Mobberley the captains of the bowmen were hand-picked, and if they did not show up at the army's mustering point they were pursued with the full weight of the law. Thomas Brescy of Chester had received pay but had failed to appear; the Prince's officials in Cheshire were instructed to find him and order him to Plymouth 'with all speed'. If he made excuses or tried to disobey the summons they were to arrest him and confine him to Chester Castle.

A small number of desertions once the troops had reached the Devon coast were also dealt with firmly. When it was discovered that Richard Wynstanton had left the Black Prince's force with £6 of wages in his pocket orders were immediately sent out for his arrest 'until he has given satisfaction for the money'. Thirty-nine archers who went missing were imprisoned and had their possessions confiscated. The Prince realized an army's discipline was created the moment it gathered; thus he rewarded those who performed their duties well and punished those who did not, setting an example to others.

The Prince had his advisers draw up a schedule of his likely expenditure. He was naturally generous and a firm believer in the principle of largesse, that a great lord should share his wealth with his closest followers. For this, he needed to have ready cash at his disposal. At the end of June, London merchants were instructed 'to buy gold for the Prince's use during the expedition, so that he could easily make payments overseas'. But for such largesse to be effective, a clear financial plan was put in place. In August, the Prince's servant John Henxteworth was brought in to keep the accounts; his surviving financial records provide a valuable source of information. Money was collected, costs allocated and a two-month campaign budgeted for, down to wages for the grooms caring for the horses.

There was a clarity to these arrangements, but one also senses the demands imposed by a chivalric lifestyle: the gift-giving, the conspicuous display, whether on the tournament field or military campaign, and the financial pressures created. As the commander became more successful, these demands would only grow.

Military endeavours always gave an opportunity for display, for a leader to dress to impress – and the Black Prince would be meeting many of the Gascon lords for the first time. The Prince, always concerned to look his best, brought his own personal tailor, minstrels to provide entertainment and a daily allowance set aside for gambling with friends and fellow fighters. He also purchased a fine new saddle for his favourite warhorse: hard riding was to be expected once they reached France.

Sir Robert Neville of Hornby (Lancashire) was master of the Prince's horses, providing mounts, harnesses, saddles and fodder for the arduous campaign abroad. It was a responsible position and also a costly one. Sir Robert ran up heavy expenses on the job, despite being granted an annuity of 100 marks (£66 13s 4d) by the Prince, and was falling increasingly into debt. In the summer of 1351 he had mortgaged his Lancashire estates to Henry of Grosmont in return for a loan of £140; two years later he was also borrowing from London merchants at a high rate of interest. Neville expected to be very busy on campaign; he also hoped to be able to amass a substantial haul of booty to recoup his losses.

By mid-August everything was ready on land, but a steady south-westerly prevented most ships from putting to sea until early September. The delay created problems: the troops still had to be supplied and paid for and to do this the Prince, already hard pressed financially, had to raise yet more money. The fleet finally set sail from Plymouth on 8 September 1355, enjoying a fast crossing without opposing winds, and reaching Bordeaux a week later. The Collegiate Church of Saint-Seurin noted with evident relief that 'the Prince with a great army entered the city that day'.

The Prince lodged in the archbishop's palace next to the cathedral, and took immediate counsel with his military advisers and Gascon noblemen. They knew that plans to dispatch Henry of Grosmont to Normandy with another army had been postponed, and that if the king sailed to Calais later in the year it would only be for a short campaign. Gascony had become the main theatre of operations and the Prince was free to choose an enterprise of his own liking. But he sought advice, and his English and Gascon captains wanted to strike hard into French territory, seeking battle with the enemy if at all possible.

On 21 September the Prince took his oath as lieutenant of Aquitaine in the cathedral of Saint-André, before the mayor and citizens of Bordeaux. He swore to be a good and loyal lord, maintaining all the city's customs and privileges, while the citizens in their turn took the oath of fidelity to him. The ceremony was witnessed by prominent Gascon supporters of English rule: Bernard-Ezi, lord of Albret, and his son Amanieu; Pierre de Grailly and his brother Jean; Bertrand de Montferrand; the lords of Pommiers, Lesparre and Mussidan; and canons from the cathedral chapter. All those present knew military operations would commence shortly.

This was a formal occasion in which the Prince swore his oath on the Gospels and was required to read out the full text of his appointment in Latin, which, however necessary, was hardly going to set the crowd alight. But what followed did: the Prince left the cathedral and stood in the square outside it. This typically spontaneous gesture had an immediate effect. Geoffrey le Baker, who drew on a soldier's diary of the time, recorded that 'the whole population came running to meet him'.

The Prince now made clear the direction and purpose of his campaign. He did so in highly personal terms: he spoke to the throng of inhabitants, telling them of his hatred of the count of Armagnac — 'that he had conceived great anger against him in his heart' — and of his determination to put him in his place. The Prince normally spoke in French or English, but he may well have rehearsed his short oration and delivered it in Gascon, a dialect of Occitan. If so, it was an astute and crowd-pleasing gesture.

The Prince said that the Anglo-Gascon army would take the war to the enemy and punish and chastise Armagnac and his supporters. They would march east, ravage Armagnac's lands and give the count a taste of his own medicine. It was all refreshingly direct and

the Gascon lords were delighted by it. In the words of the chronicler Henry Knighton: 'They rejoiced greatly at his words, replying
that as he had offered to be their lord and protect them, they would
join him in his undertaking and fight with him to the death.' The
Prince later described these events (in a letter to William Edington,
the bishop of Winchester) in more matter-of-fact fashion:

> It was agreed that we ought to march into Armagnac, because
> the count was the leader of our adversary's troops and his lieu-
> tenant in Languedoc, and he had done more damage to the
> liegemen of our most honoured lord and father the king than
> anyone else in the region.

It was late in the campaigning season but the Gascon nobles were
now bringing in their retinues, hungry for action, and a full army
was quickly assembled. It was 5,000 strong and all, including the
archers, were on horseback. There was a bustle of activity. Additional arrows were loaded on to the waggons. Extra foodstuffs were
purchased for the first stage of the campaign, including wheat, fish,
salted meat and wine, and hay for the horses. Canvas was bought
for the repair of the army's tents and 200 kilograms (450 lbs) of wax
candles were gathered to illuminate the war camp at night. Spare
buckles were ordered for the Black Prince's helmet and additional
lances were stocked in his armoury. Pewter medicine bottles were
bought for the Prince's physician; his confectionery was stored in
wooden coffers; gambling dice would provide a little relaxation.

The ordinary soldier was not forgotten. Twenty-four Cheshire
archers were granted 40s towards their expenses in Bordeaux and
those who had lost horses, taken sick on the sea voyage, had their
mounts replaced. The Prince made a gift of shoes and leggings to
William Lawton, a bowman in Sir Ralph Mobberley's company.

On the morning of 5 October all was ready. The Prince attended
a solemn Mass at the Collegiate Church of Saint-Seurin; he wanted
to inspire his troops on the road ahead, and carefully placed his
sword and banner on the altar for blessing. Then he raised them

aloft before his assembled captains. It was said that Count Roland, the great warrior of the Emperor Charlemagne, had performed such a ceremony on the very same altar. It was a powerful piece of ritual with a deft theatrical touch, linking the Prince with a martial hero of the past and binding his men together in a common cause. That afternoon, the whole Anglo-Gascon army rode out of Bordeaux, following the road along the Garonne valley.

The start of a campaign was often an exhilarating moment. The Prince and his followers were undertaking a *chevauchée,* which literally meant a ride on horseback, but in the fourteenth century was the term used for a brutal plundering raid, pillaging and burning over a certain breadth of land on either side of the route taken by the column. It evoked images of fire, slaughter and devastation — the laying waste of territory whose inhabitants' only crime was to have the wrong man as their overlord. It was the means of denying that lord the stores and wealth with which to make war, a way of humiliating him, of showing his vassals that he was incapable of protecting them.

A *chevauchée* was an operation that combined elements of economic, psychological and propaganda warfare with the threatened violence of the protection racket, and it was the poor and defenceless who suffered the most. The overlord lost face; his subjects lost food, shelter, savings, life and limb. And yet, however shocking for us, in undertaking a *chevauchée* the Prince was following established and accepted military practice of the time. It was what the Scots had done on their raid into northern England in 1327, what his father Edward III had done in the Cambrésis in 1339 and Normandy in 1346. His army was bound by a common purpose: to ravage the enemy's lands and if at all possible bring him to battle.

War was an expression of chivalric ideals and military policy, but it was also an outlet for greed and violence. One of the Prince's captains, Sir Robert Marney of Layer Marney in Essex, was a competent solder who had fought in the retinue of the earl of Northampton in Scotland and Gascony, at the siege of Tournai in 1340 and at the Battle of Crécy six years later. He was rarely out of trouble with the law. In 1342 he was accused of breaking into an Essex park belonging to the earl of Hereford with a gang of ruffians and poaching game. Marney was locked up in the Tower for a while, and, on his release, committed a fresh misdemeanour: a local knight, John Fabel, alleged that Sir Robert had abducted him by force, kept him prisoner and forced him to sign away his inheritance and bonds worth £1,000. The threat of litigation and of being outlawed prompted Sir Robert Marney to put his own goods into safe-keeping with friends and sign up for the Prince's expedition. The gentry of Essex must have breathed a collective sigh of relief — now the French would be on the receiving end of Marney's unruly behaviour.

Adam Mottram was a small landowner in Macclesfield and gaoler of the castle there. He had been charged with assault, housebreaking and abduction on the Prince's visit to Chester in 1353, and got out of his difficulties by promising to take a group of archers on the campaign. Richard Mascy of Tatton, convicted of rape and armed affray, also made a deal with the Prince's officials, in which all fines were remitted in return for his war service. These were tough and resilient men, habituated to violence. In the context of the *chevauchée*, however, this violence would be channelled, for the army kept its discipline on the march.

The great punitive column set out with a train of horses and carts behind it. For the first few days, the Black Prince and his soldiers were passing through friendly territory and lived off what they had brought or could buy. They made their way through forests of tall trees and out into an arid land of heather and gorse, putting their horses through their paces. On 9 October they reached Arue, 70 miles (112 km) south-east of Bordeaux, overlooking a steep valley — the edge of the lands of their great enemy, the count of Armagnac.

At Arue the Prince called his men together. He gave out extra wine to the troops. He dubbed new knights, signifying that military operations were about to begin. He split the army into three divisions: the earl of Warwick and Reginald Lord Cobham would take command of the vanguard, the Prince the main body, and the earls of Suffolk and Salisbury the rearguard. And he ordered all banners to be unfurled.

The Prince valued the fighting experience of the men around him and was confident in his delegation of command. His army was happy to see the forty-one-year-old Thomas Beauchamp, earl of Warwick, leading the way. Warwick was an experienced soldier, who had fought in most of Edward III's campaigns in France and Scotland, and a ferocious fighter. On the Crécy campaign, he was first off the boats at La Hogue, where he and a small band of soldiers routed a much larger force seeking to oppose the English landing. At the battle itself, Edward III placed him in the vanguard alongside the Black Prince, where the two traded blows side by side. Chroniclers vied with each other to give him plaudits. For the abbot of Abingdon he was 'a most energetic warrior'; for Thomas Walsingham 'a spirited fighter'; and on one occasion the mere news of the arrival of 'the devil Warwick' was enough for the French to take to their heels.

The army now rode in columns, spreading out over a wide distance. On 12 October it entered the lands of the count of Armagnac and began burning. A huge pall of smoke rose above the advancing soldiers and fires raged for many miles around them. Three small towns, Gabarret, Géou and Panjas, were set alight on the first day, but at Monclar, where the army camped for two days, the fire was started accidentally. It burned so fiercely that the Prince had to withdraw into the fields to escape from the heat.

The Black Prince was leading an army of English, Welsh, Gascons and mercenaries from Germany and Spain. He maintained discipline but he also reached out to his men through humour. After abandoning a burning house at Monclar he joked that he would spend the remainder of his nights sleeping in his tent, as it was known to be the safest place on campaign: a reference perhaps to the occasion in 1327 when his father fled his war camp with moments to spare, as Sir William Douglas charged through it and hacked down the royal tent ropes. The Prince granted his tailor Henry Aldington the sum of £29 7s 'for his services on 15 October, and seeing some soldiers raising their eyebrows at his fine clothing, he played to the gallery and knighted Aldington before the whole army. However, the Prince's rituals were also solemn and dignified. The army spent a whole day in mourning for a fallen comrade, the captain and Knight of the Garter John, Lord Lisle (who died from wounds received in an assault on the small fortress of Estang). Such moments transcended divisions of nationality or class and created a real sense of solidarity among the troops.

For the next eleven days the army wrought havoc on the count of Armagnac's estates. An attractive region of low hills and shallow valleys, dotted with villages and small castles – a 'noble, rich and beautiful place', as Geoffrey le Baker described it – was put to the torch. The walls of its fortresses had been put up quickly and cheaply, and long before: they were no match for the Anglo-Gascon army, which burned a broad track across the entire province. Skirmishers fanned out from the main line of march for a distance of some 10–15 miles (16–24 km) and stripped the surrounding villages and fields, bringing back food and fodder, jewels and money, and destroyed all that they did not choose to carry off.

The road began to rise steeply as the army left the small town of Beaumarchés, winding along a high ridge. The army was now some 115 miles (185 km) south-east of Bordeaux. From here, they could see for miles on either side, and groups of Anglo-Gascon horsemen scouring the cultivated lands and settlements were clearly visible. The Prince had ordered, out of piety, that all church property was to be spared. Geoffrey le Baker reported that the town of Bassoues was left undamaged because it belonged to the bishop of Auch. Everything else, however, was fair game for his soldiers. 'We have ridden hard across this land of Armagnac, harrying and wasting the region,' the Prince reported home, 'which has given great satisfaction to the subjects of our Lord the King.'

There was no sign of Jean, count of Armagnac. The count had made his initial preparations diligently, warning towns to strengthen their defences, calling out the local levies and hiring Italian mercenaries to strengthen his forces. His followers had been instructed to wear a white cross badge for easy identification. At the end of September he had ordered that villagers bring the harvest in as quickly as possible, so that it would not be plundered by the Prince's army. Stocks of provisions were gathered in safe places and those living in the countryside were told to be ready to take refuge in the nearest fortified castle.

On 8 October the Genoese mercenaries arrived and the first reinforcements were sent out to those garrisons likely to be in the path of the Anglo-Gascon army. However, the quality of the French troops was not high, and arguments broke out between them and the Italians. The count of Armagnac, anxious not to give the Black Prince an opportunity for the victory he clearly craved, became more defensive. He gathered his soldiers and shut himself up in Toulouse. It was a strong walled city and his spies had reported that the Black Prince's army was not carrying much siege equipment. So Armagnac destroyed the bridges over the River Garonne and hoped that the momentum of the Prince's campaign would fizzle out.

The French king, John II, was unhappy with this cautious strategy. It seemed to be allowing the English too much initiative, so he sent in reinforcements. As the Prince's soldiers laid waste the lands of Armagnac, the marshal de Clermont and constable Jacques de Bourbon joined the count with their own retinues. Together they substantially outnumbered the Prince's army. Seeing this, Bourbon argued for an aggressive strategy; Armagnac, pointing to the poor quality of many of their soldiers, favoured a defensive one. For the terrified local population the trio seemed paralyzed by inaction.

The Black Prince's army was moving steadily eastwards, at the rate of 7 or 8 miles (11–13 km) a day, from one valley to the next, over dome-shaped hills, with the snow-tipped Pyrenees visible to the south after the army left Mirande, some 20 miles (32 km) east of Beaumarchés. They sacked and burned Samatan, 'as great a town as Norwich', Sir John Wingfield wrote with grim satisfaction. On 26 October the Prince reached the small town of Saint-Lys, about 15 miles (24 km) south-west of Toulouse. The French commanders assumed that he would either turn back or attack the city. He did neither.

The Prince halted for a whole day while his scouts rode out, gathering information. They returned with the news that the count of Armagnac, still sheltering behind the walls of Toulouse, 'had broken all the bridges on both sides of the city'. There was nowhere to cross the Garonne and Ariège, and these rivers barred his path eastwards. The Prince made the surprising decision to march eastwards nonetheless, towards the unpassable rivers and leaving an enemy force on his flank that greatly outnumbered his own.

On 28 October the Anglo-Gascon army set out. It was a good day's march to the banks of the Garonne, close to the village of Portet, and the Prince and his troops reached it by early evening. His men gazed at the mass of water ahead of them. It was 'swift, rocky and terrifying', Geoffrey le Baker recalled. Some of the troops thought of Blanchetaque, on the Crécy campaign, and the Black Prince had a similar piece of theatre in mind. 'There was no man in our host who thought a ford was there,' Sir John Wingfield remarked innocently. But the Prince and his closest advisers knew differently.

Arnaud Bernaud was the Prince's chief guide on the campaign and was handsomely paid for his work. He recruited men with local knowledge of the places they passed through. The Prince's account book recorded the payment of a substantial reward of 22s to two local guides before the army left the Garonne earlier in the month – almost certainly because they had told him about the crossing point further upriver.

It was put about that no man on horseback had ever managed to cross the Garonne at this place. But the order was given to cross nonetheless, and men, horses and waggons splashed into the water, most of them making it safely. Sir John Wingfield, who was in on the secret, remarked laconically: 'By the grace of God we found it [the ford] anyway.' The Prince and his men then achieved a further success by crossing the River Ariège, which was seen as 'even more dangerous'. His decision to ford the rivers individually, south of Toulouse, rather than face their added breadth and depth after the Ariège joined the Garonne a small distance further north, was proved to be absolutely the right one.

It was the crucial moment of the campaign, and the Black Prince's boldness paid handsome dividends. 'They were very stiff and strong to pass,' the Prince wrote home. He had lost some men and matériel in making the crossings, but the gain was immense. With the rivers behind him, not only did he gain total independence of movement, but his army's morale was substantially boosted. And the sheer audacity of the Prince's action threw the caution and lack of initiative of the count of Armagnac into stark relief. A chronicler of Toulouse reported that the inhabitants of the city were so angry at Armagnac's failure to confront the Anglo-Gascon army they demanded the count foot the bill for all the war damage. The Prince struck east, leaving the French troops far behind him.

The army was now marching across a great plain, extending as far as the eye could see, following the old Roman road across the county of Languedoc. This was rich agricultural land and a region entirely unprepared for war: most of the towns only had the most rudimentary defences and there was therefore no effective opposition to the Prince's army. His men became bolder, attacking the larger and stronger towns in their path. Avignonet was captured on 31 October; Castelnaudary a day later. Jean Froissart described the assault on Castelnaudary:

> When the English arrived, they spread out around the town
> and their assault parties began to throw themselves against the
> walls. Their archers would form attack groups and fired volleys

of arrows so dense that the defenders could no longer hold their positions. Then the assault parties pressed their advantage, and poured in and took the place. There was tremendous slaughter and violence – with the whole town infested with invaders. It was sacked and pillaged, and everything in it was carried off. The English did not bother with mere bales of cloth when there was so much plate and gold coin to be taken. When they had captured a townsman or peasant they demanded ransom from him – and if he would not pay they left him mutilated. Then they abandoned the town – burning and ruinous – with its citadel demolished and its walls thrown down.

There was now real concern among the French. The town notary of Montpellier, drawing on the reports of spies sent out to watch the invading army, described the ravaging progress of the Prince's forces: 'From the moment the English crossed the Garonne, just below Portet, they have been burning and pillaging every town, village and castle in the vicinity.' Montpellier was 150 miles (240 km) east of Toulouse and seemingly well out of range of the Black Prince's *chevauchée*. But his Anglo-Gascon army, meeting little or no effective resistance, was gathering momentum at an alarming rate. Amaury, vicomte of Narbonne, who personally undertook several reconnaissance missions, witnessed the same levels of brutality and violence:

Large numbers of the enemy are now raiding both day and night – advancing on our towns and villages in columns, lighting the path ahead of them with burning torches. It is a terrifying sight. We have never seen such destruction.

The Prince's soldiers were, at this stage, considerably to the west of Narbonne but a wave of panic was sweeping Languedoc. The chronicler Robert of Avesbury described people 'fleeing in terror as far as Avignon, with such property as they could carry, in order to put themselves under the protection of the Pope'. The English were astonished by the ease of their advance. 'Every day', the Prince wrote, 'our troops captured towns, castles and fortresses.' On 3 November 1355 the army arrived before Carcassonne, one of the principal towns of Languedoc. The distant view of the city impressed the English. 'It was a fair city to look upon and a great one', wrote the Black Prince. 'It was larger, stronger and more beautiful than York', was the appreciative judgement of Sir John Wingfield.

It would not stay beautiful for much longer, however. Carcassonne was divided into two parts – the *cité*, a fortress town with a double circuit of walls, overlooking the River Aude, and the *bourg*, a more recent addition, on the other side of the river, that had largely grown up in the mid-thirteenth century. The citadel, perched 45 metres (150 ft) above the right bank of the river, was too strong to be stormed and could have withstood a siege for months. The *bourg* had no walls and was virtually indefensible. When the English arrived, the population fled, leaving the Prince's troops to take possession of it without opposition, and they helped themselves to everything left behind.

When a short truce was agreed, the citizens sent a delegation to parley with the Prince. The city was rich and prosperous, and they offered him a large sum of cash to be left alone. The Black Prince was out to make a profit from the campaign and had already taken money from some of the smaller towns on his route in exchange for sparing them the horrors of pillage and burning. And the citizens of Carcassonne were promising him a lot of money – he would receive 250,000 gold crowns (around £37,500) if he spared the *bourg*.

But here at Carcassonne the Prince wanted to make a bigger point. He knew that his father had hesitated before appointing him to the command. The king was not sentimental, even with his own family, and would judge his son's *chevauchée* firmly on its results. Time was not on the Prince's side: the expedition had been delayed and was operating late in the campaigning season, and the weather could turn at any moment. The Prince's commission was for a six-month period, and would only be renewed if King Edward believed that it had advanced his war effort. And that war effort centred on his claim to the crown of France.

Carcassonne was a major French city, and the Prince realized that a propaganda gesture here would have maximum impact. He therefore did not take the city's gold crowns; instead, he told the townspeople that he had come for 'justice not money', and as they were in rebellion against their lawful ruler they should surrender. The inhabitants, whose 'rebellion' was their refusal to recognize the Prince's father's claim to the French throne, were having none of it. They would now pay the price of their loyalty to King John, for the Black Prince was determined to draw attention to the French king's failure to defend Carcassonne and damage his prestige among his subjects; and he also wanted to show up the military failings of the count of Armagnac, King John's lieutenant of Languedoc.

On 6 November the Black Prince's forces systematically razed the *bourg* to the ground. 'We spent the whole day in burning, so that it was completely destroyed', the Prince wrote bluntly, and then his army moved on. This was a ruthlessly calculated act, and one undertaken by the Prince primarily to please his father.

The Mediterranean now lay only some 35 miles (56 km) away. To march from sea to sea, with flame and sword, would reveal English strength and French weakness in the most emphatic fashion. The Prince's army now passed through the flat, sandy basin of the River Aude. As the weather changed, the conditions grew foul, but it rode on through driving rain and cloying mud, without slackening its pace, reaching Narbonne on 8 November. Once again, the Prince's troops occupied the city's *bourg* with virtually no resistance. The Anglo-Gascon army had now covered nearly 250 miles (400 km) since leaving Bordeaux and was within sight of the Mediterranean Sea.

However, their stay in Narbonne was not a comfortable one. The garrison of the nearby *cité* bombarded the Prince's soldiers day and night with catapults, causing serious casualties. When, on 10 November, they began to shoot flaming arrows into the wooden houses, the Prince and his men decided to withdraw. They retreated through burning streets, pursued by angry mobs of townspeople who attacked stragglers and smashed some of the army's waggons. It was the first significant resistance that the Prince had encountered.

From Avignon, 120 miles (193 km) north-east of Narbonne, Pope Innocent VI had been watching the Black Prince's progress with alarm. He now sent messengers appealing for the truce between England and France to be reinstated. But the Prince, acutely conscious of the negative impression such discussions might have on his father, whatever their final result, did not want to halt at this point in his campaign. He kept the papal messengers waiting for two days, and then, on 12 November, he firmly rebuffed them:

> The Pope sent two bishops to us, but we did not begin any negotiations with them, for we did not want to be party to any treaty without knowing the wishes of our most honoured lord and father the king, particularly since we had news that he had crossed into France with an army. So we sent letters back, saying that if they wanted to negotiate they should go to him, and we would do whatever he commanded.

These delaying tactics were successful. Edward III had indeed landed at Calais with another English army at the end of October. He ventured out to offer John II battle on 6 November, but John chose not to respond to his challenge. Then he heard news that the Scots had invaded northern England. On the day that the Prince told the papal envoys to meet with his father in northern France, King Edward had sailed back to England.

King John II was deeply angered by the failure to defend Carcassonne and demanded that his commanders take more resolute action. Stung by his rebuke, the vicomte of Narbonne gathered troops to oppose the Black Prince's army. The Prince held a council of war and decided it was time to return to Gascony, but he remained prepared to fight the enemy. In the expectation of an imminent engagement, his army first swung north, spending the night at the castle of Capestang, and the Black Prince knighted a number of his followers. But there was to be no clash the following day: it seemed that Jean, count of Armagnac, lacked the confidence to face his opponent in battle and rather than join with Narbonne, had withdrawn his forces to the city of Toulouse.

The Anglo-Gascon army now began its return. On Sunday 15 November the Black Prince chose to participate in a religious ceremony; eloquent proof, in the middle of a military campaign, of his contempt for Armagnac's generalship. On Sunday 15 November, confident that the French would do nothing to hinder him, the Prince visited the Abbey of Notre Dame at Prouilhe, 15 miles (24 km) west of Carcassonne, where he and his principal captains were 'devoutly admitted' as lay brothers of the Dominican foundation. Geoffrey le Baker was impressed by the sheer size of the religious establishment and the wealth of its lands, noting that 'in separate cloisters, a hundred friars and preachers and 140 women recluses are able to live off the profit of its estates'. According to tradition, the Virgin Mary had appeared before St Dominic in a vision at Prouilhe and handed him the rosary, a memory aid for counting prayers. But while the Prince was visiting this religious community, the remainder of his army burned four French towns in twelve hours. Its opponents did nothing to stop them.

Two days later the Prince made another visit to a religious house. He met with the count of Foix at the Cistercian Abbey of Boulbonne, 5 miles (8 km) north-west of Belpech, the chief monastic house of the region and mausoleum for the count's family. The count, Gaston Fébus, was twenty-four years old, a year younger than the Prince. He was a charismatic young man, charming, humorous and learned, the future author of a manual on hunting and another on the art of prayer. He ruled the principalities of Béarn and Foix on the northern slopes of the Pyrenees, and his support was worth having. In typically flamboyant fashion he had bestowed upon himself the name 'Fébus', an allusion to the sun god Apollo, who, like the count, had a mane of unruly blond hair and loved the hunt. His principal residence was the Pyrenean castle of Orthez – a place of enchantment, its pentagonal keep rising high above a steep wooded hillside. Some thirty years after the Black Prince's expedition, the chronicler Jean Froissart visited Fébus there:

> I knew that if I was granted the good fortune of coming safely to his castle, and being at leisure there for a while, I could find no better place in the world to be fully informed of all the news, for a great many foreign knights and squires abide there, and gladly return for the sake of his noble welcome.

Orthez was an impressive and well-appointed place. It boasted a deer park within its walls and an imposing great hall, where banquets were held and gifts given to every visitor, for Fébus was a most attentive host ('I wanted for nothing during my stay there,' Froissart remarked). While life at Orthez was governed by elaborate court protocol, Fébus himself had an easy formality of manner and liked to do business sitting in the shade of the castle vineyard. This was a place where the visitor could forget his cares and troubles for a while and revel in an atmosphere of music-making and story-telling.

Fébus was fascinated by the world of chivalry and Froissart's gift to him was prudently chosen: he gave the count three hounds – Hector, Tristan and Roland – named respectively for heroes of Greek, Arthurian and Carolingian legend. Froissart had also brought him his new work, *Méliador*, a verse romance describing the quests of a knight at Arthur's court:

> The rapport between the two of us was thus: I had brought with me a book called *Méliador*, that the count was most eager to see, and every night after supper I read him some of it… While I read no one dared speak one word, for he wanted me to be clearly heard and he took great pleasure from hearing me well.

Fébus was a skilful and enthusiastic huntsman, and what would shine through his *Livre de chasse* (which he wrote between 1387 and 1391) was the *experience* of hunting: its intimacy with nature (including the pleasure of seeing dawn rise over the mountains), the camaraderie of working with huntsmen and their hounds and the physical challenge of tracking and killing one's prey. His work was at times lyrical, almost mystical in its reverence for the hunt – and as such it reflected the attitudes of most of the fourteenth-century aristocracy. Fébus told Froissart that the three great passions of his life were hunting, love and making war. He had his own war-cry, 'Fébus go forth!', and go forth he did, on crusade (once, in Prussia, with his cousin and friend Jean de Grailly) and – more often – to wage war against the count of Armagnac.

In November 1355, Fébus was already intensely jealous of Armagnac and this was the main reason the Prince's fighting companion Jean de Grailly had arranged their meeting. The vendetta between the families of Armagnac and Foix had started during the previous century, when both were vying for power in the foothills of the western Pyrenees. When John II appointed the count of Armagnac to be his lieutenant in Languedoc, Fébus was deeply offended and promptly withdrew from the French court. Armagnac then attacked Gascony, but Fébus in turn ravaged the count's lands. The feud between the two men would continue unabated, and would culminate in a battle at Launac in 1362 (seven years after the meeting between Fébus and the Prince) in which Fébus routed Armagnac's army, captured the count and imposed a crippling ransom on him.

Gaston Fébus was fiercely independent. His personal motto said it all: 'Touch me if you dare!' He had announced to one of Philip VI's representatives that he considered his lands of Béarn to be held 'by no man on earth, but of God alone'. The French king was so astonished that he called for a clerk to take down the count's words verbatim. Fébus was also a man of considerable charm. Froissart said of him: 'He was in the whole world the lord most eager to see strangers and hear their news... He welcomed me with very good cheer, and said to me laughingly that he knew me well, although he had never seen me, for he had often heard about me.'

When the Black Prince met Fébus at Boulbonne (and Geoffrey le Baker gave an exact time for it, at 1pm.) there was a deal to be struck: on the Prince's side that he would refrain from ravaging the count of Foix's lands and on Fébus's that he would continue to undermine the authority of the count of Armagnac. That was the business end of the matter, and it was concluded quickly . The Black Prince, Fébus and a few chosen companions then spent the rest of the afternoon on an impromptu hunting expedition, leaving the army to await their return. While the Prince and his host enjoyed the pleasures of the chase, Jean, count of Armagnac and hundreds of his soldiers cowered behind their walls and ramparts. The Prince's account book recorded gifts made to Fébus's squire and huntsman as mementos of the occasion.

The Anglo-Gascon army then proceeded to Carbonne, 20 miles (32 km) south of Toulouse. The Black Prince crossed the Garonne once more, in the pouring rain, by repairing a broken bridge across which his cavalry advanced in single file, much to the astonishment of the local people. On 20 November his troops wheeled north-west, and a scouting company under Sir John Chandos and Sir James Audley fell upon a larger group of Frenchmen, capturing thirty of their knights and dispersing the remainder. Despite the disparity in numbers, it still seemed as if the English were on the attack. Jean, count of Armagnac, had received further reinforcements, and at last ventured out of Toulouse: he now had so many men that his force marched in five columns instead of the usual three. But he still appeared reluctant to launch a large-scale assault or risk a pitched battle.

Late on the evening of 21 November, again in driving rain, the Black Prince encountered a French force blocking his path at Gimont. He withdrew his men to the shelter of the nearby village of Aurimont and gathered them again at first light, only to find that his enemies had once more melted away. The Prince, who was still up for the fight, stood his ground: 'We were in proper order before sunrise, and we waited there for much of the day, hoping that battle would take place. It was clear that the enemy did not want to fight us, so we decided to return to our own lands.' Rivers were rising and becoming more difficult to cross, but there were no further signs of opposition. On 28 November the Prince's army reached Mézin, arriving back on Gascon soil. Banners were furled and some of his force disbanded. On 2 December, at La Réole, the Black Prince ordered the remainder into winter quarters. His soldiers had amassed so much plunder that, according to the Florentine chronicler Matteo Villani, nearly 1,000 waggons were needed to carry it all.

The seneschal of Carcassonne, Thibault de Barbazan, attempted to reassure the terrified inhabitants of Languedoc, who feared the Prince might reappear and inflict yet more devastation upon them. On 15 December he set out with a group of commissioners on a tour of inspection. His assessment was blunt: 'The Prince of Wales and his soldiers had been allowed to pass too easily into the region,' he wrote, 'where they found many places poorly fortified and weakly defended, which they easily captured and set alight.' Yet Barbazan did not vent his anger on the Prince's army but on those of his compatriots who had neglected their responsibilities. 'They have not maintained the defences, and installed strong garrisons, as they were required to do,' he concluded, 'and have grievously failed their countrymen and the king himself.'

On 16 December William Jodrell, described by the Prince as 'one of our archers', was given leave to return home and see his family. Leaders of companies of bowmen were granted a cash bonus. The Cheshire squire John Stretton decided that he would settle in the duchy. Within a few years he had acquired properties and married a Gascon heiress, Isabeau de Saint-Symphonien. Richard Mascy of Tatton, formerly guilty of rape and armed affray, also gained enough wealth to become a man of means.

The Black Prince spent Christmas at Bordeaux amid great fes-
tivity and rejoicing. In strategic and military terms, the expedition
had been a success. The Prince outlined his achievements in a letter
sent to the bishop of Winchester on Christmas Day, knowing that
its contents would be circulated throughout the realm and would
make a considerable impression. A letter written by the Prince's
counsellor Sir John Wingfield was similarly triumphant in tone:

> My lord rode over the whole country for eight whole weeks...
> You may know for certain that since this war has begun against
> the French king, he has never received such loss and destruc-
> tion as in this raid. For the districts and fine towns that have
> been laid to waste in this expedition provided the king of
> France more every year, to maintain his war against us, than
> did half his realm... According to the records we have found,
> the towns around Toulouse, Carcassonne and Narbonne that
> we destroyed provided each year about 400,000 gold crowns in
> war subsidies. Our enemies are wonderfully confounded.

Some of these figures may have been exaggerated, but Wingfield,
an experienced administrator, was making a good point. The vital
economic base of the French war effort in the south had been seriously weakened and the revenue that had been lost was essential
for John II's long-term military prospects. And Wingfield believed
there was an opportunity to win back those Gascon lands still in
French hands, because enemy morale was now so low.

The Prince and his advisers knew that his expedition would be
compared to that of Henry Grosmont, king's lieutenant in Gascony ten years earlier. Grosmont had set the bar high – winning
towns through skilfully conducted siege operations and defeating
the French in two pitched battles. But the Prince's great *chevauchée*
had caught the imagination of its participants, and the newsletters
conveyed their excitement to the audience back home. Crucially,
he kept up the military pressure, sending out raiding parties in the
New Year, and soon Gascon lords who had transferred their loyalty

to the French were returning to English allegiance. The Prince had restored morale within the duchy, and that was the main objective of his campaign.

The *chevauchée* had provided proof in abundance of the Black Prince's military ability. He had the intuitive gift that great generals possess, of sensing the mood of his soldiers and transforming it. On his arrival in Gascony the Prince had realized that some of his troops were frightened. Fear is corrosive and can paralyze the will of an army: the Roman writer Vegetius, whose book on warfare was read avidly by the medieval aristocracy, warned the commander to look out for fear in his men – in their facial expressions, language and gestures: 'Say anything', Vegetius advised, 'by which the soldiers' minds may be provoked to hatred of their adversaries, by rousing their anger and indignation.' The Black Prince instinctively understood Vegetius's advice. He turned his men's fear of their opponent, the count of Armagnac, into anger and ultimately – as the campaign progressed – into open contempt.

The Black Prince would later be accused of inhuman cruelty on this expedition from the Atlantic to the Mediterranean, some modern French historians even suggesting that it was this behaviour that had won him the nickname of the 'Black Prince'. Without doubt, he had conducted a brutal raid that had terrorized the civilian population. Geoffrey le Baker, who listed the many places sacked and 'burnt to ashes' over the two months of the campaign, referred repeatedly to people 'fleeing in sheer terror'. Yet, as we noted earlier, the Prince was following the established and accepted military practice of the time, and the fact that he did so more thoroughly and effectively than many others is beside the point. He maintained discipline within his army and forbade plundering of church property. The rest was fair game. In his own eyes and those of his fellow knights, on both sides of the Channel – all of whom observed a common code of chivalry – there was nothing disgraceful in his conduct and no contemporary ever criticized him for it.

The qualities of friendship and brotherhood-in-arms were particularly important in the chivalric world. Before embarking upon his great raid the Black Prince told the Gascons he had assigned a day for the army to muster, 'where everyone who was willing would come and stand with him, and those who failed to do so would no longer be considered his loyal friends'. The Prince's view of life was governed by his friendships, and for his warrior friends he would do anything – and that was both his great strength and also a weakness.

It is easy to see how the Black Prince became friends with Gaston Fébus, count of Foix. The two men shared many of the same interests. But beneath the charm and the love of chivalry that he shared with the Prince, Fébus was performing a difficult political balancing act with the kings of France, England, Navarre and Aragon. His overriding concern was to safeguard the independence of his own principality of Foix-Béarn and all was subordinated to that aim. As a result, he was a slippery and unreliable ally.

As well as cultivating a friendly alliance with Fébus, it also made sense for the Prince to stir his men's anger against the count of Armagnac. But although he had never met the man, the Prince's disdain for his adversary – perhaps influenced by his fighting companion Jean de Grailly, who was caught up in the feud between Armagnac and the count of Foix – appeared deeply felt and personal. He went out of his way to humiliate him.

If the Prince had taken time to form a more dispassionate opinion of the counts of Foix and Armagnac, he might have admired Fébus less and Armagnac more. Armagnac was different from the Prince in many ways, but he possessed many admirable qualities. Armagnac was a rather older man, fifty at the time of the great raid of 1355. He did not come from an emotionally close family: his parents had died when he was young, and he was brought up first by grandparents and then guardians. He had suffered from serious illness throughout his life, and on two occasions, in 1333 and 1347, had drawn up his will believing that he was on the point of death. Like many great aristocrats, Armagnac could be touchy on matters of personal pride, aloof and distant. He was, however, highly intelligent and a capable administrator. In his youth he had been an enthusiastic warrior. He had fought with the Black Prince's chivalric hero Jean of Luxembourg, king of Bohemia, in Italy – and Armagnac and Luxembourg subsequently became friends. But he had been taken captive in a clash outside Ferrara, forced to endure years of imprisonment and a crippling ransom, and that experience had made him cautious. And that caution bred a military weakness.

One of the Prince's military advisers on the raid of 1355 was the seneschal (steward) of Gascony, Sir John Cheverston. Cheverston had faced Armagnac a year earlier, when the count had invaded Gascony and besieged Aiguillon, south-east of Bordeaux. Armagnac had occupied a strong position around the town and set up his dispositions with considerable care. But Cheverston had undertaken a daring flanking manoeuvre, bringing a force around the count's position and attacking him from behind. The seneschal noticed that Armagnac was thoroughly disconcerted by this, and had immediately withdrawn his forces. He most likely informed the Black Prince that Armagnac seemed to lose confidence when faced by a sudden and bold response from his opponent. If so, the Prince took note: his daring crossing of the River Garonne, south of Toulouse, may well have been prompted by Cheverston's advice.

And yet, one can exploit a military advantage without hating one's enemy. Although Jean, count of Armagnac, was on the opposing side, he was someone the Black Prince might need to work with in the future. The Prince had fought his campaign on behalf of his father's right to the crown of France. But in the negotiations at Guînes a year earlier Edward III had been prepared to cede that claim, in return for a territorially enlarged Gascony held in full sovereignty – the duchy of Aquitaine possessed by his Plantagenet forebears. If such a duchy was created, and ruled over by the king or his son, Armagnac's lands would fall within it.

Sensing such a possibility, shortly after Edward III claimed the French throne at Ghent in January 1340, Armagnac had opened direct negotiations with the English king, with a view to transferring his allegiance to Edward's cause. The negotiations had foundered on the issue of the compensation Armagnac would receive for his French lands, which would be confiscated after he rendered homage to King Edward. But the very fact that they had taken place at all should have made the Prince more careful. If a newly enlarged duchy of Gascony was created, modelled on Plantagenet Aquitaine, Jean, count of Armagnac, would be its most important nobleman. His co-operation and support would be favourable to its survival; his alienation would undermine its chances of success.

Such considerations did not seem to figure much in the intoxicating chivalric arena the Prince had now entered. The raid of 1355 had showed his remarkable skill as a warrior. He had honed his Anglo-Gascon army into a formidable fighting force, one that was tough, resilient, and displayed instinctive co-operation in a crisis. And that durable sense of chivalric brotherhood, the self-belief felt by men united in common cause under an inspiring leader, would lay the foundation for the Prince's greatest ever military triumph the following year.

These strengths concealed an abiding weakness. When the Black Prince stood in the square outside Bordeaux's cathedral of Saint-André, and spoke from the heart about his hatred of the count of Armagnac, the Gascons felt his courage and passion. It cut through the niceties of political calculation: men vowed to stand and fight with him to the death.

However, a lack of nuanced political judgement fed an enmity that the Black Prince would have done well to avoid. His dislike of the count of Armagnac would come back to haunt him and would contribute to the defining failure of his career.

chapter six

POITIERS

The Black Prince left Bordeaux on 25 June 1356 and rode to the mustering point of his army. Only too aware of the importance of his endeavour, he wrote to John de Trillek, bishop of Hereford:

> Reverend father in God, we truly believe it will be through the prayers of good and devout people within the Holy Church that the quarrel we are about to pursue in these parts [of France] on behalf of our honoured lord and father the king will come to a most favourable conclusion. We earnestly entreat you, putting our trust in you, that you will do as we request, in your own personal devotions, and by commanding all those within your diocese – priests, vicars and others – to go twice each week on procession, praying for us, and also to pray daily for us in masses, or by some special prayer chosen by you. Through you doing this, we will be more likely to uphold the rights of our sovereign lord [in the days ahead].

The chronicler Geoffrey le Baker was struck by the intensity of the Prince's spiritual preparation for the campaign:

> He urged those who were about to set out with him against the enemy to protect their bodies with armour and their souls with penitence and the sacrament of the Eucharist, so that they would be ready to fight those who had rebelled against his father, by living in worldly fame and dying in eternal honour, with God and his Saints taking all credit for the victory.

This was the inner world of the knight that Geoffrey de Charny had so eloquently evoked, in which – for some individuals at least – deeds of gallantry were balanced by personal piety and religious devotion. While the mood among his troops was upbeat, the Prince chose to strike a sober and reflective tone. He was aware of the importance of what lay ahead, but he also knew that it was a path fraught with danger. His task, 'to uphold the rights of our sovereign lord', had been made clear a week earlier when his servant Sir Richard Stafford arrived in Bordeaux with reinforcements and instructions from the king.

An ambitious new strategy was being devised. Edward III, delighted that his son had laid waste to a swathe of territories in southern France the previous year, was now envisaging a campaign on a far larger scale. In it, he hoped to land at Calais or in Normandy with a substantial army and join with another English force, led by Henry of Grosmont.

Normandy was in revolt, the unrest being stoked by the plotting of Charles of Navarre and the French king faced a crisis in his relations with his aristocracy. Edward sensed an opportunity to exploit France's difficulty, and turn the war to England's advantage. His plan was to engineer a means of drawing King John into battle, either near Paris or in Normandy, and defeat him. He therefore ordered the Black Prince to advance from Gascony and in the first instance, attack John's forces south of the River Loire.

This would be a most expensive scheme. To keep three armies in the field, maintain the scattered garrisons across France and provide for the defence of Calais and Aquitaine would cost nearly £100,000, exhausting Edward III's entire annual revenue from taxation and customs duties. However, given the financial efficiency of his administration, this was a risk the king was willing to take. And from an English point of view, it was becoming essential to try to engage the French royal army and defeat it. The Prince's 1355 campaign had won plunder and prestige, but Edward was no nearer his aim of forcing King John to recognize Plantagenet overlordship of Gascony. A decisive battle was needed – one that would conclude the war in England's favour.

To bring this about, the English would co-ordinate attacks into central France from three directions: Normandy, Calais and Gascony. Their military administration was certainly up to the task. Warfare under Edward III was never conducted in a haphazard fashion: drafts, orders and instructions from the king's reign showed his thoroughness in all military matters.

†

During the Middle Ages, large-scale military operations were often hampered by a lack of accurate maps; it was not until the sixteenth century that cartography became an important military science. In the fourteenth, itineraries were kept – alongside records of distances – and guides recruited. By following roads and rivers, and by taking local advice, it was often possible to work out appropriate routes, but without maps it was much harder for commanders to construct a mental image of their forthcoming campaign. In particular, it was difficult to co-ordinate the movements of different armies, and a 'fog of war' was sometimes created in which participants struggled to see the bigger picture, and instead concentrated on tactics and prowess on the battlefield. As the pace at which armies moved varied enormously, it was far harder to anticipate events.

A small mounted force could operate surprisingly quickly. When Edward III took a small expedition to rescue the countess of Atholl in 1336, he was able to cover 40 miles (64 km) in a single day, although – not surprisingly – a good many horses were lost in his gallop to Lochindorb Castle. A large army was an entirely different matter: its pace was determined by the slowest and most heavily laden waggons of the baggage train. In 1346 it was difficult for Edward III's forces to march more than 12 miles (19 km) a day, and on the Black Prince's expedition in 1355 his army averaged little more than 10 miles (16 km).

In these circumstances, it was important to have reliable information on rivers and river crossings, and it is clear in campaign after campaign that these were a major determinant of events. On the Crécy campaign of 1346 Edward's dramatic crossing of the Somme at Blanchetaque allowed him to gain the initiative and choose the place to fight the enemy. In 1355, the Black Prince's sudden fording of the Garonne gave him the advantage over the count of Armagnac. A year later, plans for the Black Prince's forces to join with those landing in Normandy depended on him being able to cross the River Loire, without being hampered by a high water level or well-defended bridges.

In June 1356 there was real optimism about the English war effort, nonetheless. The Black Prince was acquitting himself well as king's lieutenant. After concluding his successful two-month *chevauchée* deep into French territory in the autumn of 1355, he spent the twelve days of Christmas feasting his senior commanders and then sent them back to prepare for more action. The count of Armagnac had been humiliated and the lands of Languedoc ravaged. The Prince now moved swiftly to the second phase of his campaign — to win back the lands around the shrunken borders of Gascony (reduced by the campaigning of Armagnac in the previous year). He advanced his personal headquarters to Libourne, 25 miles (40 km) north-east of Bordeaux. In January 1356 his troops took the initiative once more, splitting up into separate raiding parties and again taking the war to the enemy. To the north, they probed beyond the Charente, the river that marked the limit of Gascon jurisdiction. To the north-east, Jean de Grailly captured the important town of Périgueux. The earl of Warwick and Sir John Chandos advanced south-east up the Garonne as far as Agen. 'They did many excellent deeds,' Geoffrey le Baker said happily, 'sallying out from the places assigned to them and performing feats of arms.' Sir John Wingfield, the Prince's chief councillor, had chronicled the damage inflicted by the autumn *chevauchée* with considerable zeal. He now listed the results of this new burst of military activity:

Five fortified towns have surrendered... and seventeen castles. Sir John Chandos and Sir James Audley took the town of Castelsagrat by assault, and they have stayed there with their men, and have enough of all kinds of supplies to last until the summer... The Prince and I are at Libourne, and there are more than three hundred armed men in the town... And they have raided towards Agen, burning and destroying all the mills and have broken bridges across the Garonne. Jean, count of Armagnac, who was in the town of Agen with his men, did not poke his head out once.

...

The earls of Suffolk and Salisbury, the lord of Mussidan and other Gascons... are at the moment in the area of Rocamadour; they have been away for twelve days and have not yet returned... The earl of Warwick has taken the towns of Tonneins and Clairac; at the moment he is somewhere near Marmande, trying to destroy the enemy's provisions.

...

The Prince is awaiting more reports, which he expects to receive shortly – and then is going to decide what the best course of action is.

These were tangible successes. John II was losing support in the region and by April six Gascon lords had returned their allegiance to Edward III. When Pope Innocent VI appealed to the Black Prince to spare Périgueux in return for a ransom, he received the blunt reply: 'We will continue in what we have set out to do – to punish, discipline and tame all the inhabitants of the duchy of Aquitaine who have rebelled against our father.'

King Edward was keen to reinforce his son's army further. He instructed the chamberlain of Cheshire that:

three hundred archers be sent speedily to the Prince in Gascony, in the company of Sir Richard Stafford, and that two hundred of them be from the county and the remainder elsewhere, as ordered. And of these, choose the best mounted archers that can be found, selected and arrayed with all possible haste.

There would be no difficulties persuading soldiers to enlist. Pay was reasonable, and the rules for the division of plunder and ransom clearly spelled out. Wages were calculated by the day and there was usually a substantial advance on enlistment. Captains and leaders of companies also received a bonus for every thirty men they recruited – and those able to produce 100 men or more were even more generously rewarded.

New supplies of weapons were needed and the Black Prince sent one of his servants back to England to purchase 1,000 bows, 2,000 sheaves of arrows (each sheaf containing twenty-four arrows) and 400 gross (57,600) of bowstrings. He also bought fresh horses. The Prince's receiver in the duchy of Cornwall was ordered to provide thirty of the strongest baggage animals available, and to recruit grooms to care for them. The earls of Warwick, Suffolk and Salisbury, who were accompanying the Prince on the campaign, also had new mounts dispatched to them from England.

Yet, for all the energy and drive showed by Anglo-Gascon forces, the grand plan they were about to take part in was large on ambition and short on specific detail. The political situation in France was changing on a day-to-day basis, and it took time for Edward III, in London, to gain accurate intelligence of what was afoot, and even longer to pass this news on to the Prince at Bordeaux. The turbulent events that had rocked the French kingdom that spring, and which the English king hoped to exploit, had their roots in a dinner party that had taken an unexpectedly violent turn.

On 5 April 1356 the king's son, the eighteen-year-old dauphin Charles, was entertaining members of the Norman nobility at a banquet at Rouen castle. Suddenly the doors flew open and the king and his armed retinue charged into the room, crying: 'Let no one move or he is a dead man.' The king personally seized hold of one aristocrat, Charles of Navarre, accusing him of treason, and then grabbed Jean of Harcourt so roughly that he tore his doublet from his belt. When the dauphin Charles begged his father to refrain from violence against his guests, he was curtly told: 'You do not know what I know – these are wicked traitors whose crimes have been discovered.' The extent of these crimes was never revealed. But next morning Jean of Harcourt and three other Norman lords were executed, and Charles of Navarre was thrown into prison.

It was the fifth year of John II's rule and he was struggling to assert his authority over his kingdom. He had come to the throne in August 1350 with a strong belief in the need to reverse the defeats of his father's reign. John was tall and well built, with striking reddish-gold hair. He loved tournaments, introduced new military ordinances and created his own order of chivalry, the Order of the Star, to rival England's Order of the Garter. A cultivated man, he commissioned French translations of the Bible and the Roman historian Livy; he even carried books in his baggage when on campaign.

King John had a vision of a revitalized French army heroically standing its ground and defeating the English. A royal ordinance of April 1351 imitated some of Edward III's military reforms a decade earlier. New rates of pay were brought in for his soldiers and a clearer system of command was introduced, setting out each man's position in the host, the captain he would be responsible to and prohibiting him from leaving the battlefield without a specific order. And in January 1352, the 500 companions of the Order of the Star were required to swear an oath that they would never retreat in battle more than about 600 yards, 'but rather die or be taken prisoner'.

However, it took more than rules and regulations to make a good army. Both kings were devoted to chivalric honour, but Edward III had a rapport with his aristocracy that John II lacked. He was impetuous, did not think through the consequences of his actions and was sometimes needlessly cruel. Within three months of becoming king in August 1350 he had executed the constable of

France, Raoul de Brienne, count of Eu, a man of powerful connections within the nobility and 'so courteous and amiable in every way that he was beloved and admired by great lords, knights, ladies and damsels'.

The count of Eu had bravely defended Caen against the English in 1346. Captured by Edward III, he was put to ransom four years later. On his return to France, King John – believing rumours that Eu had struck a deal with the English – had him executed (on 19 November 1350) without trial or judicial procedure of any kind. If Eu had indeed been guilty of treason – and the facts of the case are obscure – the king needed to make plain the reasons for his decision, but John II, described by contemporaries as 'an all-too hasty man', was either too wilful or too wooden-headed to see the need for good public relations. The killing of the count had the disastrous effect of alienating many members of the French aristocracy; the situation was about to degenerate even further.

King John now gave the office of constable to his favourite and boyhood friend, Charles de la Cerda. The French king and his wife Bonne of Luxembourg (the daughter of Jean of Luxembourg, king of Bohemia) had produced a family of four sons and five daughters, but Bonne had died of the plague in September 1349. In an echo of King Edward II's relationships with Piers Gaveston and Hugh Despenser, it was now rumoured that de la Cerda was the object of the king's 'dishonest affection'. John's friendship with de la Cerda created the same poisonous mistrust between king and aristocracy, and in January 1354 Charles of Navarre recruited a group of henchmen, led by his brother Philip and Jean of Harcourt, and stabbed the royal favourite to death while he was staying at an inn in the village of L'Aigle in Normandy.

King John neither forgave nor forgot de la Cerda's murder, taking his revenge at that fateful dinner party in April 1356. But de la Cerda's death had been widely welcomed within the realm and there was little sympathy for the king's belated and brutal response. Jean's executions provoked a backlash among the aristocracy, leading to open rebellion. At the end of May 1356 Philip of Navarre and Geoffrey of Harcourt renounced their homage to the French king and appealed to Edward III for help.

John II was strongly criticized within France, with one chronicler saying that 'King John was widely believed to be at fault in the manner in which he killed those lords, and because of this much ill-will was directed against him, by the nobles and the people, especially in Normandy'. A whole series of grievances were coming to a head. John's financial officers were regarded as incompetent and corrupt; the currency was altered or devalued no fewer than eighteen times in the first year of his reign alone. And the French king's policy of avoiding a major battle against the English until his military reforms were complete was further damaging his reputation; it would now have to be jettisoned in favour of a more proactive approach. For Edward III, who had recently returned from a successful campaign against the Scots, an incredible opportunity seemed to be opening up, if he could move quickly enough to exploit it.

†

At the beginning of June 1356 Edward sent a small army under Henry of Grosmont to land in the Cotentin peninsula and offer support to the rebels. Grosmont was now one of Edward's most experienced commanders and as a sign of special favour had been created duke of Lancaster, the first promotion to that rank outside the royal family. But the number of troops available was limited: Grosmont sailed for Normandy with only 500 men-at-arms and 800 archers.

Edward began preparing his own army. When he learned that King John had delegated the defence of France south of the Loire to his son, the count of Poitiers, he urged the Black Prince to seek him out and bring him to battle. This was a bold course of action: the sixteen-year-old count had a formidable entourage of military advisers – including Jean de Clermont, the marshal of France, the experienced captain Jean le Meingre (otherwise known as Bouci-caut) and the seneschals of Poitou, Saintonge and Toulouse – and several thousand troops had already gathered around him. For the Prince to be successful, the broader military situation needed to remain advantageous to the English, allowing them to keep the initiative and dictate the shape of events.

By 6 July the Black Prince had set up his military headquarters at the town of La Réole, south-east of Bordeaux, assembled his force of English and Gascon soldiers and was ready to begin his cam-paign. Enthusiasm was high, the archbishop of Bordeaux recording in wonderment that 'all the knights and their retinues had left the city for the Prince's mustering point' – and the date (the eve of the feast of the Translation of St Thomas à Becket) would come to a hold a special significance.

Events were proceeding apace in Normandy. On landing, Henry of Grosmont gathered more troops at the Abbey of Montebourg in the Cotentin, received reinforcements from Geoffrey of Har-court, Philip of Navarre and the professional captain Sir Robert Knolles, who brought a contingent from the Breton garrisons. These increased his army's strength to around 2,500 men. At the end of June he marched on eastern Normandy, in support of the towns loyal to Charles of Navarre that were now in open revolt against the French king. Grosmont's distinguished martial reputa-tion evidently preceded him; as he approached Breteuil, on 4 July, the besieging forces of John II simply melted away. Two days later he installed his army at Verneuil.

King John now brought the full royal army up from Dreux and challenged Henry of Grosmont to battle. The French king had many more men and Grosmont, after some deliberation, retreated, returning to Montebourg on 16 July with a fine haul of booty and prisoners. In turn, John II offered pardons and amnesties to the garrison of Dreux to bring about a speedy surrender. The English campaign in the north was petering out.

By 22 July the Prince had moved up to Bergerac, on the
Dordogne, with his newly gathered troops. But instead of striking
immediately into enemy territory, he was delayed for two weeks
by an unforeseen and troubling development, and it was only on 4
August that he finally left the town. Jean, count of Armagnac, had
flung aside his earlier caution and was now acting with remarkable energy and purpose; conscious that he was lucky to have kept
the post of king's lieutenant of Languedoc after his dismal showing against the Prince's *chevauchée,* he had set about redeeming his
reputation.

Armagnac appeared a man transformed: he sent out teams of
spies to monitor the Prince's movements and began recruiting a
much larger army. Most strikingly, he decided to go on the offensive, telling John II that the best way to deal with the continuing
threat posed by the Black Prince was to invade Gascony. By late
July Armagnac had done just that, placing a substantial number of
towns and fortresses across the south-west under siege and sending
raiding parties out over a wide area.

At Bergerac the Gascons' earlier enthusiasm waned. They had
welcomed the Black Prince as a protector, not as someone who
would strip the duchy of troops when it was under threat. The
Prince was determined to follow his father's orders, but in doing so
he found himself forced into difficult negotiations with his Gascon
subjects. Eventually an uneasy compromise was hammered out.
The Prince would divide his army, leaving over 2,000 men under
the seneschal, Sir John Cheverston, to defend Gascony from Armagnac's incursions. He also promised to compensate any town
damaged by French attack.

This was not an auspicious beginning, and by 4 August, when
the Prince marched out of Bergerac with his reduced army, the
broader picture had also changed substantially. Some of Henry of
Grosmont's force had been disbanded, and Grosmont himself was
now in Brittany, conducting small-scale military operations west
of Vannes on behalf of the Montfort party, allies of the English, in

the War of the Breton Succession (against supporters of Charles of Blois, *de facto* duke of Brittany). And King Edward, for a variety of reasons, no longer felt it was essential to cross the Channel. He had received the homage of the French rebels Geoffrey of Harcourt and Philip of Navarre in London, and placed them under the protection of the English court. An Aragonese fleet, in alliance with John II, had arrived off the mouth of the Seine, and was ready to blockade any attempted sea crossing. Edward III's great enterprise had simmered, but had never come to the boil.

The Prince, however, was entirely unaware of these developments. His army's strength was now around 6,000 men, many of them on horseback. Moving at a steady rate of 10 miles (16 km) a day, up through the Périgord and the Limousin, it passed through the towns of Brantôme and Rochechouart, inflicting as much damage as it could. Froissart described the Prince's progress:

> The Prince and his army... rode forward at their ease and gathered provisions of all kind in great profusion, being astonished to find the Limousin so rich and plentiful in all things. They burned and pillaged the whole land, and when they entered a town that was well-stocked with food, they rested there a few days to refresh themselves, and at their departure destroyed what remained, smashing barrels of wine, and burning fields of wheat and oats, so that their enemies could not have anything.

The Prince intended to move fast, never stopping long enough for his opponents to catch him at a disadvantage, avoiding well-fortified castles or towns, swiftly taking those that were only lightly garrisoned or whose walls had fallen into disrepair, and using their stocks of food or wine to replenish the army. The baggage train was light. Waggons carried booty and fresh stocks of weapons, but it was expected that the army would live off the land. Apart from a few minor skirmishes, the Anglo-Gascon army had encountered little resistance. However, the Prince began to feel uneasy. He placed his trusted companions Sir John Chandos and Sir James Audley at the head of his scouts. And, as Geoffrey le Baker recorded, he kept a personal watch over his men:

> The Prince himself took charge of the camp, seeing that it was moved each day after the road ahead was inspected, and provided with defences against night attacks. He also saw that the usual night watch was kept, and went around the sentries himself, with a few of his most valiant comrades, and visited each part of the army in case something out of the ordinary exposed it to danger.

Still believing that his first objective was to attack the count of Poitiers, the Black Prince tried to ascertain the whereabouts of his father's army. As he made clear:

> We wrote to our lord and father the king that we were intending to ride towards our enemy in France [John II], and we made our way through Périgord and the Limousin directly to Bourges, where we expected to find the [French] king's son, the count of Poitiers. The chief reason for our going there was that we expected to hear that the king [Edward III] had crossed [the Channel], but since we did not find either the count or a great army there, we moved towards the Loire, and sent our men to see if we could cross it.

The Anglo-Gascon forces arrived at Issoudun in Berry on 24 August; the garrison looked on helplessly from the great keep as the Prince's soldiers wrecked the town so thoroughly it would remain uninhabitable for years. A scouting party set out for Bourges, but found that the count of Poitiers had withdrawn his troops back to the Loire. The French were regrouping.

John II had received the submission of Dreux on 20 August, and then moved south, to Chartres, to recruit more troops. The French king's attention was now fully focused on the Black Prince. He wanted to block his adversary's progress and gather enough men to bring his army to battle and destroy it. In pursuit of this, the count of Poitiers received fresh orders from his father to hold the line of the River Loire until he and the dauphin reached it with the main French army — an army that was growing all the time.

The Prince began to sense that something was seriously wrong. On 28 August, he crossed the River Cher and occupied Vierzon. He sent Chandos and Audley on a scouting expedition ahead of him, to Aubigny, on the Loire, and they returned with disconcerting news. The campaign in Normandy was over. King John was now raising a much larger army to meet him in battle. There was no sign that Edward III had landed in France. The River Loire was well guarded. And there was no news of Henry of Grosmont.

John II had struggled to recruit a full contingent of troops for his Normandy campaign. Many of his subjects sympathized with the rebels, and enthusiasm for the royal cause was muted. But the opportunity of bringing the Black Prince to battle had a galvanizing effect — the ruthless raiding tactics he had employed in the previous year's *chevauchée* had succeeded in uniting the French against him. Stung by the Prince's presence near the Loire, in the heart of France, nobles responded to the royal summons, whatever their sentiments towards John II. 'No knight and no squire remained at home', a chronicler wrote, 'and here was gathered all the flower of France.'

With John II at the mustering point for the new army, at Chartres, were his four sons, aged fourteen to nineteen; the new constable, Gautier de Brienne; the two marshals, Arnoul d'Audrehem and Jean de Clermont; 26 dukes and counts; and 334 lesser noblemen. It was one of the largest French armies of the fourteenth century — 'a great marvel', an English chronicler wrote uneasily, 'the equal of which had never been seen amongst their nobility'. Its size was already three times greater than the Prince's force and more troops were on their way.

On 28 August the Aragonese fleet, co-ordinating its actions with the French, appeared off the coast of Kent. English shipping, gathered to ferry Edward's army across the Channel, was now ordered to take refuge in the nearest safe harbour. Its mariners were mustered for coastguard duty along the south coast. It was clear that Edward III would not be joining his son on the Loire. Concerned for the Prince's safety, he ordered Henry of Grosmont to attempt to do so instead.

The Black Prince's indenture with his father for the lieutenancy of Gascony had contained an emergency clause. It stated:

> The king has promised that if it shall happen that the Prince is besieged or beset by so great a force of men that he cannot help himself unless he be rescued by the king's power, then the king will help him one way or another, provided that he can be assisted easily. And the duke of Lancaster [Henry of Grosmont] has also pledged his faith to give all the help and counsel that he can in making such a rescue.

Edward III expected his captains to stand on their own two feet. But he had conceded in his indenture that if his son were facing overwhelming odds he would send him assistance, just as he had at the crisis point of Crécy. This clause now came into effect. Edward, able to communicate directly with Henry of Grosmont by sea, passed on the order to his most trusted captain. His spies were warning him that the French were massing in large numbers and intended to engulf his son's forces. It was clear that the Black Prince needed all the help he could get.

The Prince had paused for several days at Vierzon. He was better informed about the enemy's intentions than his father's dispositions. The main French force was gathering some 95 miles (153 km) ahead of him and the count of Poitiers's army was 65 miles (105 km) to his east. In contrast, Henry of Grosmont's soldiers, still in Brittany, were more than 270 miles (435 km) to his west and Edward III was still in England. The Prince's understanding of the rapidly changing situation depended on the military intelligence available, and this — as has been explained — grew increasingly uncertain over longer distances.

Fourteenth-century communications were far from straightforward. Roads were poor and, in a time of war, messengers and spies were often captured by the enemy. The Black Prince was north of the River Cher, 280 miles (450 km) from English-held Gascony. His main sources of information were his scouts and what could be gleaned from the interrogation of enemy prisoners. From these, he learned that King John had ordered his army to assemble at Chartres by 3 September. After a few days of preparation it would advance towards him. To meet this threat, it was becoming clear that the best course of action – with no news of Edward III's landing in France – was to move in the direction of Henry of Grosmont's forces. Accordingly, the Prince swung his own troops westwards.

John II was facing serious financial problems and would have struggled to maintain a large army in the field for any considerable length of time. But the vulnerability of the Anglo-Gascon forces allowed him to plan for a quick, decisive campaign, and he now ordered his mounted detachments to ride out and harass the enemy. On 31 August the Black Prince's vanguard collided with a large reconnaissance force under the French captain Boucicaut. It was the first serious encounter between the Prince's forces and King John's. Froissart described the clash in vivid terms:

> Some of the French troops set up an ambush near Romorantin and lay quietly in wait for their foe. They let the English pass through, and then saddled up and charged straight at them. Hearing the horses' hooves, their opponents swung round and instinctively made gaps in their line so that the French would pass through it without causing too much damage. A sharp engagement followed, in which numerous knights and squires were unhorsed on both sides and many were killed. When the rest of the English came up the French retreated inside nearby Romorantin Castle.

The Black Prince now ordered his troops to capture Romorantin. Given that its castle was a strong fortification, whose four towers and impressive ramparts and gatehouse were protected by a large moat fed by the river Sauldre, this was a risky decision to take. The Prince would lose time in conducting what was a relatively small-scale siege operation; and all the while the main French army was not far away and would soon be on the move. But the Prince, always an instinctive commander, felt that his men's morale was faltering and that the best remedy was to involve them in some action. And importantly, he also needed to dispatch messengers to try to make contact with Henry of Grosmont. On 1 September the Prince's army went onto the attack. Froissart recalled the ferocity of the first assault:

> All the men-at-arms and archers prepared for battle – and made a sudden charge on the walls of Romorantin. The offensive was fierce and powerful, the English archers sending over such a hail of arrows that scarcely any defender dared show themselves on the battlements. Then the men-at-arms flung themselves forward, some plunging into the moat up to their necks, others floating across it on makeshift rafts. All began to hew at the wooden gate with pikes and pickaxes. Above them, the French threw rocks and stones and emptied pots of quick-lime over their heads.

The outer walls were scaled and the gate broken open, and the French retreated into the keep. The next day, three successive assaults were beaten off. The Prince now announced that his army would not move until Romorantin fell; he brought up his catapults and unleashed incendiary weapons. Geoffrey le Baker described the bombardment:

> The Prince gave orders that stone-throwing machines should be made. These machines, manned by specially trained troops, destroyed the roof of the tower and the battlements with large rocks. They also set fire to the tunnel which the miners had dug – which reached to the foundations of the castle.

The garrison had seen enough and Romorantin surrendered shortly afterwards, the prisoners including Amaury, lord of Craon, the French king's lieutenant in Poitou. An English chronicler noted that 'the Prince, through his personal involvement in the siege operations, gave great encouragement to his men'. The brisk action at Romorantin had had the desired effect of lifting the army's spirit. And soon there was more good news: contact at last had been made with Henry of Grosmont, 'of whom', the Prince happily related, 'we were given certain tidings that he would in all haste draw himself towards us'. Help was on its way. And if Grosmont managed to cross the lower Loire in time for his and the Prince's army to form a united front they might, despite King John's great numerical advantage, defeat him through the superior quality of their soldiers.

On 7 September the Prince's Anglo-Gascon army reached the Loire, camping in the suburbs of Tours with the great river spread out before them. The Black Prince and his soldiers were once more full of confidence. Henry of Grosmont and his mounted troops had covered an astonishing 125 miles (200 km) in four days – and were at a crossing point of the Loire further downriver, at Les-Ponts-de-Cé, south of Angers. The weather was mild and sunny. And the two English armies were now only 70 miles (112 km) apart.

News that Henry of Grosmont was approaching was a shot in the arm for the Prince's soldiers. He was famed for his speed of movement and the fear that he provoked in the enemy, whether in battle or man-to-man combat. Some would have recalled his dramatic rescue of the Prince six years earlier, during the sea battle against the Castilian fleet, or perhaps another escapade that had taken place in 1352. Returning from a crusade in Prussia in the summer of that year, Grosmont quarrelled with the German magnate Duke Otto of Brunswick and accepted a challenge to a duel; it was a time of truce between England and France and it was decided to hold the event in Paris under the auspices of King John. Grosmont was granted a safe-conduct and crossed to Calais with a retinue

1. The embodiment of valour.

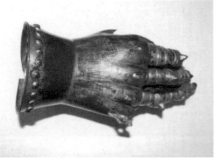

2. Accoutrements of a warrior:
the Black Prince's gauntlet.

3. The helm (from his achievements
at Canterbury Cathedral).

4. Berkhamsted castle — one of the Prince's main residences in England.

5. The ridge at Crécy, viewed from the French approach. The Black Prince's division was centre left.

6. 'A fair city to look upon': Carcassonne, one of the targets of the Prince's great raid in 1355.

7. King John II of France (from a fourteenth-century
painting on wooden panel).

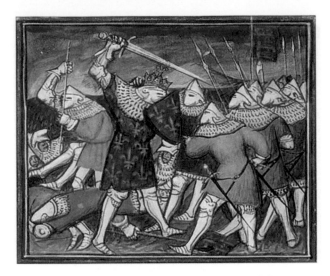

8. The closing stages of Poitiers: the French king is surrounded by assailants (from an illuminated manuscript of Froissart).

9. The abbey of Sauve-Majeure: its records contain an early news report of the battle.

10. Divine strength: Samson subduing the lion (from a roof boss in the Black Prince's chantry, Canterbury Cathedral).

11. 'The most beautiful woman in the realm of England': Joan of Kent (from a roof boss in the Black Prince's chantry).

12. Wax seal showing the Prince's achievements: shield, helm, cap and crest (Canterbury Cathedral Archives).

13. The Black Prince's psalter: the marginal decoration
at Psalm 101 depicts John II's surrender at Poitiers.

14. Remains of château of Angoulême,
centre of the Prince's administration of Aquitaine.

15. Gold *pavillon* minted by the Prince as ruler of Aquitaine.

16. An ill-fated alliance: alabaster statue of Pedro of Castile.

17. The unfolding battlefield (from the English approach). Nájera is in the centre; Huércanos, where the flanking march was undertaken, to the right.

18. A formidable adversary: Charles V of France.

19. 'Flower of all chivalry'.

of fifty knights, in full pomp and ceremony. He was met by the marshal of France, Jean de Clermont, who escorted him with great honour to Paris, where crowds of people thronged to see him. King John received him in state at the royal palace of the Louvre and entertained him magnificently. The event was a sell-out. A special fighting arena was built, with an elaborate dais for the French king and his nobles and wooden seating for the ordinary spectators. On the day of combat, it all proved too much for Otto of Brunswick. Geoffrey le Baker reported:

> Henry of Grosmont rode into the lists, saluting the king of France and the assembled peers and nobles, in a most seemly manner. He waited for his opponent, properly mounted and equipped, in full martial array... But when Otto of Brunswick appeared he was shaking so much he could hardly stay on his horse. He struggled to fasten his helmet properly and could not even keep his lance steady. Seeing the state he was in, the French king abruptly brought proceedings to a close and sent Otto away.

No doubt this amusing story did the rounds in the Anglo-Gascon army. Sensing the upsurge of morale, the Black Prince sent his troops on a raid up to the city walls of Tours, hoping to provoke the garrison to sally out and engage in battle. But the defenders wisely stayed put, and then the rain came. 'The weather had been fine and calm since the beginning of the campaign,' said Geoffrey le Baker, 'but it now thundered and rained for three days – and the sheer heaviness of the downpour made the Loire a raging torrent.'

With the sudden change in the weather, the burgeoning hopes of the Anglo-Gascon army were dashed. The burning tactics of the Prince's troops were rendered ineffective by torrential rain that immediately put out the flames. The French had destroyed most of the bridges over the Loire and in these terrible conditions it was impossible to ford the swollen river. The Black Prince was unable to advance further north; nor could Henry of Grosmont cross the

Loire and move south to join the Prince's army. The defences at
Les Ponts-de-Cé, in the suburbs of Angers, had been reinforced and
were simply too strong for Grosmont's troops. Both leaders sent
out reconnaissance patrols, and one night these leading elements
were close enough to see each other's campfires across the river.
But the Loire remained impassable.

On 11 September the Black Prince heard the news he had been
dreading: John II's army was on the move. Using a bridge at Amboise
that had been kept intact, it had succeeded in crossing the Loire.
'So many men were now following the French king,' wrote the
author of the *Grandes Chroniques* (an account of the reigns of John II
and Charles V, probably compiled by Charles's chancellor, Pierre
d'Orgemont), 'it seemed he had sufficient strength to defeat the
rest of the world'. King John was now only 20 miles (32 km) east of
the Prince, and more enemy troops were advancing from Saumur
to the west. Behind his line of retreat the garrisons of Poitou were
being mobilized. The French king now ordered Jean, count of
Armagnac, to bring his army up from the south, cutting off the
road to Gascony. The Prince was in the utmost peril.

On the afternoon of 11 September the Black Prince gave the
order to retreat. He turned south, crossed the rivers Cher and
Indre, and camped for the night at Montbazon. At this difficult
moment, with disappointment, uncertainty and fear besetting his
army, an emissary from Pope Innocent VI – Hélie de Talleyrand,
cardinal of Périgord – suddenly appeared.

In the autumn of 1355, the Prince had rebuffed papal messengers
in the midst of his raid into the Languedoc. Now Pope Innocent –
sensing that a major battle was in the offing – was redoubling his
efforts to restore a truce between England and France. The timing
could not have been worse. The French were in a position of overwhelming strength and both sides knew it. King John did not want
a mediated settlement; he wanted to destroy the Anglo-Gascon
army. As for the Black Prince, he was undertaking a difficult retreat,
and could not afford to fritter away time in pointless discussions.

Although the English remained deeply suspicious of the Avignon papacy, Edward III and his government nevertheless recognized Innocent VI as a worthier candidate than his predecessors. He was a genuine reformer. Instead of commissioning countless expensive works of art to adorn his palaces he sold off most of his paintings. He cared passionately about reuniting the Christian jurisdiction within Europe, and reversing the schism between the western and eastern churches. But he was still a Frenchman, born Étienne Aubert in a village in the Bas-Limousin, a former bishop of Noyon and Clermont, and as pope resided in a French city. For most Englishmen, Pope Innocent was not an impartial intermediary but a puppet manipulated by the French monarchy.

These suspicions had formed a year and a half earlier, when Henry of Grosmont arrived in Avignon on Christmas Eve 1354, accompanied by an impressive retinue of 200 riders, for a fresh bout of peace negotiations. On Christmas Day there was a sumptuous banquet for the English and French delegates, but in the weeks of diplomacy that followed no truce was ratified. The English chroniclers blamed the French for insisting that they retain overlordship of Aquitaine; they accused Innocent VI and his cardinals of failing to act as honest brokers and of conniving with them.

The man Pope Innocent chose to lead his latest diplomatic initiative, the cardinal of Périgord, was from a well-established French aristocratic family. Périgord was well travelled, cultured, a literary patron and had wide political experience. He was also, in the opinion of the Florentine chronicler Matteo Villani, 'proud and haughty', and heartily disliked in England. A bishop at twenty-three, a cardinal at thirty, he had at one time or another held as many as nine English benefices – in London, York, Lincoln and Canterbury – and his exploitation of these incomes, while still residing in Avignon, was strongly resented and drew vociferous complaints from Parliament. 'At a time of war', the House of Commons declared, 'this money should be kept within England, not sent to France.'

The Black Prince's encounter with the cardinal of Périgord was disconcerting. When the Prince announced that a mandate for discussion could only come from his father, the cardinal responded by saying that Edward III had already given it. He produced letters of authorization from English emissaries at Avignon, dated 4 August, in which King Edward empowered his son to negotiate an extension to the truce. Edward III, satisfied with English endeavours in Normandy, was now willing to buy time and consolidate his influence in the western part of the duchy. This was the first the Prince had heard of such a plan and the news must have been bewildering to him. The fact that Edward had delegated authority to him to treat for peace, on the same day that he had marched out of Bergerac with his army, burning and plundering the French lands in his path, revealed an alarming breakdown in communications between father and son.

The discussions at Montbazon were brief. However, it was clear that the cardinal of Périgord would be back, with more prelates in his entourage, and that more time would be lost in fruitless negotiations before battle commenced. French forces were growing all the time.

On 13 September the Anglo-Gascon army moved south to La Haye and a day later reached Châtellerault. The Prince was moving at speed – he had covered 45 miles (72 km) in three days. Châtellerault marked the upper limit of navigation on the River Vienne, a tributary of the Loire. King John II was barely 15 miles (24 km) away, at Loches, gathering even more troops. Despite the proximity of the French, the Black Prince waited three days at Châtellerault, hoping against hope that there still might be news of Henry of Grosmont's army. Grosmont had made a valiant effort to join him but had been thwarted by the weather and by unexpectedly strong French defences along the Loire. Reluctantly, he was now pulling his forces back into Brittany. The Prince would have to fend for himself.

The situation was desperate. The small Anglo-Gascon army was entirely on its own and its troops were growing despondent: they were fearful of the sheer size of the French army and bemoaned the fact that they had split their forces and left behind thousands of good troops at Bergerac. But it was now, as he stared calamity in the face, that the Black Prince cast off the shackles of an over-ambitious campaign and a strategy that had never been entirely clear to him, and showed his true mettle as a commander. He trusted his gut instinct and reached out to his soldiers. First of all, he let them know he was up for the fight, and that, in such difficult straits, there was no place for caution or prevarication. On 16 September, he announced to his troops that he was ready to face the French king in battle.

Boldness is often the best remedy in adversity. The Black Prince once more launched his men into action. 'We determined to hasten towards him [John II]', the Prince wrote (in a letter to the mayor and aldermen of London), 'along the road which he would have to pass, and fight with him there.' He reorganized his troops into battle formations and bore down upon the bridge over the Vienne at Chauvigny, east of Poitiers, hoping to launch a surprise attack on John's forces. He found the majority of John's soldiers had already safely crossed the river, but was able to engage with part of the French rearguard – 'some 700 mounted men-at-arms' by the Prince's own estimation – and defeat it. According to Bartholomew Burghersh the younger, 240 of the enemy were captured or killed in this small action. All knew that a major battle was now imminent.

The French king had cut across the Prince's line of march and was now west of the Anglo-Gascon army. Before the engagement, he entered Poitiers and joined with yet more reinforcements. According to one English chronicler the Prince had around 3,000 men-at-arms and the same number of archers; the French 'such a huge, growing number' that it was scarcely possible to count them all. He was certainly outnumbered by at least three to one, if not more – and while he had faced similar odds at Crécy, here the French would be advancing together, rather than being flung into the fight in piecemeal fashion. The Black Prince and his men camped on the edge of the forest of Nouaillé, 6 miles (10 km) south-east of their opponents. When a reconnaissance patrol saw the vast horde of enemy soldiers – reporting that 'all the fields outside Poitiers are covered with their men-at-arms' – the Prince simply replied: 'Well, in the name of God, let us now study how we shall fight with them to our advantage.'

He did just that. He had decided that his whole army would dismount and fight on foot and he knew that the ground he chose for battle would be all-important. Ideally, he wanted to protect his position on the flanks, shielding the archers from the enemy cavalry. He had with him as one of his advisers the renegade Poitevin nobleman Amanieu, lord of Pommiers (who had abandoned his lordship of Pommiers-Moulons in Poitou-Charente for a life of brigandage). As the Chandos Herald recounted, he was famed for his eye for terrain; his military skill was such that the Prince hastened to recruit him for his army. Awaiting the French, the Prince looked for the advantage of high ground, and a relatively narrow approach to it, so the enemy could not easily deploy the full weight of their forces. If possible, this approach would be broken by ditches, hedgerows or clumps of trees, to prevent the French horsemen from gaining full momentum. There also, ideally, needed to be an obstacle behind the army – a river or stretch of woodland – to prevent any of King John's forces from circling round and attacking his men from the rear.

In the aftermath of Crécy the French had refined their battle tactics, relying on combined infantry and cavalry attacks rather than an all-out mounted assault. At a small battle at Mauron, in Brittany, in August 1352 the English commander, Sir Walter Bentley, had placed his men on a gently sloping hill, with the archers protected by a small hedge. Most of the French dismounted, leaving their cavalry to attack the archers with the men-at-arms following up behind. Had these attacks been co-ordinated properly Bentley could well have been in trouble. On the English right, the French mounted knights managed to break through, scattering the archers in panic, but their infantry was too slow in closing with Bentley's troops and the opportunity was lost. The English counterattacked and won the day. But the warning was there.

There was much to take account of, and all of it in unfamiliar territory. However, at Poitiers, the Prince made excellent use of reconnaissance and deployed his army in a strong, natural position. He occupied an 800-yard (730-metre) ridge of high ground running across a bend in the River Moisson. His flanks were protected by thick woods on one side and a steep escarpment on the other, and the frontal approach was impeded by sunken lanes and thick hedges. His forces were spread four to five men deep, with the archers on the wings of each division. He placed the vanguard, under the earls of Warwick and Oxford, to his left, his own division in the centre, and the rearguard, under the earls of Suffolk and Salisbury, to the right. Waggons from the baggage train were used to shield his army's flanks further.

Geoffrey le Baker described the Prince's choice of battle site:

The Prince surveyed the scene and saw some high ground, encircled by hedges and ditches, bramble-thickets and vines. He placed his army upon this hill, below which lay a broad, deep valley, and a marsh, watered by a stream. The space occupied by the vanguard and centre was also protected by a particularly thick hedge, which ran down to the marsh.

Froissart was similarly impressed: 'The English cunningly drew up their forces behind thick hedges of thorn, and dug ditches in front of these, to prevent any sudden cavalry attacks.' The chronicler gave credit for the choice of location to the Prince's friend and fighting companion Sir James Audley, 'a prudent and valiant man, who had suggested how the army might be drawn up'. The *Chronique Normande* noted instead the presence of the Prince's adviser, Amanieu of Pommiers.

The Anglo-Gascon forces readied themselves for battle. On the morning of 18 September the French had learned of their

whereabouts. King John heard Mass in his tent and held a brief
council of war with his nobles:

> Then it was ordained that all men should draw up in formation,
> and every lord should display his banner. The command was
> given – to set forth in the name of God and Saint-Denis. Trum-
> pets sounded throughout the host and every man mounted his
> horse and followed the king's standard, which could be seen at
> the head of the army, swirling in the wind. There were many
> noblemen riding out to battle and their fine armour and trap-
> pings made a fair picture – for here was all the glory of France.

King John brought his troops into the valley below the Prince's
army and sent out a reconnaissance force under one of his best captains, Eustace de Ribemont. Six years earlier, at Calais, Ribemont
had been praised by Edward III for the courage he had shown in a
man-to-man fight against the English king. John II now instructed
him 'to ride out to inspect the array of Englishmen, advise us on
their numbers and by what means we should fight them, whether
on foot or on horseback'. He returned with the news that the
Anglo-Gascon force was small, but was occupying a strong defensive site and that its hedges gave excellent protection to the archers.
Taking account of this, Ribemont recommended that the cavalry
be placed on the French army's flanks, 'to break open the archers'
position', and that the main formations then advance on foot, 'to
engage with and defeat the English men-at-arms'.

John II took Ribemont's advice, ordering the majority of his
men to dismount and form up in three divisions. The first would
be under the command of his eldest son, the dauphin; the second
under his brother, the duke of Orléans; the third and largest under
Jean himself. He selected the groups of horsemen, and appointed
two of his noblemen, Arnoul d'Audrehem and Jean de Clermont,
to lead them. But before proceedings could begin, the cardinal
of Périgord and a large body of churchmen rode out onto the
battlefield.

The cardinal was making a last-ditch attempt to stop this clash of arms, but neither side wanted him as an intermediary. The French were confident of victory; the English mistrustful that any meaningful terms would be offered to them. But it was a Sunday, and a high-profile papal delegation asking for a halt before battle commenced could not simply be ignored. So both sides reluctantly called a short truce. The discussions appear to have been somewhat lacking in hard-headed realism. King John opened proceedings by demanding that the English give up all the towns and castles they held, free any prisoners without ransom and not take up arms against him for another seven years. Not to be outdone, the Black Prince demanded, in reply, one of the French king's daughters in marriage and a substantial dowry.

At the heart of John II's retinue was the celebrated knight Geoffrey de Charny, proud bearer of the sacred *Oriflamme*, the battle standard of the kings of France. It was intended to strike fear into the hearts of an enemy, for until it was lowered no prisoners would be taken. But Charny's suggestion that the engagement be decided by a combat of 100 champions from each side was vetoed by other French commanders. Instead, they proposed that the Black Prince and his principal captains simply surrender to avoid further bloodshed.

This was more knightly banter than serious negotiation. And, as it proceeded, the French took in more reinforcements – even being joined by some of the knights from the cardinal's own retinue, much to the indignation of the Prince's followers. For their part, the English knuckled down and improved the ditches and field defences around their army. They were unimpressed by the cardinal, whom they saw as a mere mouthpiece for John II. A joke began to circulate among the ranks: 'Since the Pope is clearly a Frenchman, we pray that on the day of battle Jesus Christ will show himself an Englishman.'

The two armies were less than a mile apart. As the truce continued to hold for the rest of the day, rival soldiers watered their horses from the same stream. In one encounter, Sir John Chandos came face to face with the marshal of France, Jean de Clermont. Clermont was unhappy that Chandos's coat of arms was similar to his own. 'I have as much right to wear it as you,' Chandos responded. 'This is idle boasting,' Clermont retorted. 'You English can invent nothing new, but take for your own all the good things that rightfully belong to others.' Chandos looked the marshal of France in the eye and said: 'You will find me tomorrow in the front line of our soldiers, ready to show by my skill in arms the truth of what I have just said.'

The papal negotiators left at sunset. There was never any real hope of an agreement being reached and the Black Prince now walked through the English encampment, talking to his soldiers, listening to their concerns and offering words of encouragement. The great strength of his Anglo-Gascon army was its cohesion and unity: some had fought with the Prince at Crécy; many more had joined his raid across southern France the previous year. It was vital that it kept its discipline and resolve.

The Prince urged his captains not to let their men stray too far from the standards — the rallying points for the army — and made clear that taking prisoners would only be permitted towards the end of the battle, after an agreed signal was given. He did not want his men distracted by shepherding captives to the rear during the heat of the engagement. There was no concealing the daunting odds they had to face. He spoke to clusters of soldiers, praising their courage. 'In this endeavour, we are all fellow companions,' he said. And he repeated the words his father had spoken at Roxburgh in December 1334: 'We all drink from the same cup', expressing the simple yet powerful sentiment 'We fight together, in victory or to the death'. The Prince knew that his army was tired and hungry. Supplies were low: it was crucial that battle began the following morning, without further postponement. He decided, after consultation with his senior captains, that if the French delayed their attack he would provoke them into making it nonetheless.

The sun rose on the morning of 19 September shortly before 6am. There was a bustle of activity in both camps, with men calling out to their squires, donning their armour, archers filling their quivers and readying their bows, horses being led out by their grooms. Scouts on both sides were already observing the enemy. The Prince spoke to his fellow fighters:

> If fortune allows this day to be ours, we shall be the most honoured people in the world. And if we fail in this, our just quarrel, the king, our kinsman and friends will surely avenge us. Let us do our utmost this day, in the name of God and St George, and acquit ourselves as all good knights should.

Then the Black Prince gave a signal. The earl of Warwick started to gather carts and horses in front of the army, and move them in a southerly direction, as if he was undertaking a withdrawal. 'We were aware of our shortage of food, and the risk that the [French] army would watch us for a while, rather than immediately giving battle', the Prince wrote. 'So at half Prime [about 7.30am] we began to shift our forces, in full view of the enemy, as if we were intending to make a retreat – hoping to provoke them into starting the fight.'

This was in fact a clever feint. Arnoul d'Audrehem, one of King John's cavalry commanders, was the first to see Warwick's troops on the move, and immediately warned Jean de Clermont, who was with the horsemen on the other flank, 'that the English are fleeing, and if we do not immediately charge at them they will get away from us'. Clermont was not so sure – the other wing of the Anglo-Gascon army was still holding its position – and he suspected a trick. But Audrehem chided him for being slow to respond. Clermont, still angered by his encounter with Sir John Chandos the previous day, regarded this as a slight upon his honour and his patience snapped. 'I shall out-distance you in the attack,' he retorted, 'so that the point of your lance will not even reach my horse's rump.'

The French yelled out their battle cries. 'Then the uproar began', the author of the *Grandes Chroniques* wrote, 'with shouts and

a clamour of voices, as the cavalry readied itself for the charge.'
The Prince immediately ordered Warwick to return to his original
position. The tactics of provocation had worked and now his army
steadied itself. The enemy's heavy cavalry was thundering towards
the great hedge that protected its position, and behind it, men-at-
arms and archers braced themselves for the shock of combat.

Eustace de Ribemont had advised the French king that 'the
boldest, toughest and most enterprising riders should be chosen'
for the cavalry assault, and that their mounts should be 'well-
barded' – fitted with horse armour – to protect them from the
English bowmen. The attack was supported by crossbowmen and
infantry armed with javelins, who moved up behind them to provide covering missile fire. The first volleys from the Black Prince's
archers were ineffective, as Geoffrey le Baker described:

> The French cavalry had been formed up with one clear design –
> to ride down our bowmen. They were well-armoured and the
> horses only offered our archers a target on their fore-quarters,
> which were well protected by steel plates and leather shields.
> The arrows aimed at them shattered or glanced off, falling on
> friend and foe alike.

The first riders smashed through the hedge and began fighting with
the men-at-arms and archers. The Anglo-Gascon line was thin
and began to buckle and more cavalry were approaching. Behind
the horsemen, the first division of French infantry was starting to
move forward. It was a frightening spectacle – a vivid mass of sound
and colour: 'The French foot soldiers began their advance', le Baker
continued, 'to the sound of trumpets, tabors, horns and clarions,
banners and pennons unfurled in the wind, shining bright in gold
and silver, purple and ermine.'

The best armies respond instinctively to a crisis. Only those
horses in the front line of the French cavalry were armoured, and
the English bowmen now shifted their position, so that they could·
aim at the parts that were less well protected. Geoffrey le Baker

described the violent effects of their marksmanship: 'The archers moved to one side and shot at the hind-quarters. When they did this they quickly wounded the horses, who reared up, threw their riders and turned back on their own men, knocking more than a few of them to the ground.'

Now the bowmen were making their mark and the force of the mounted assault began to slacken. More and more horses, maddened by the pain of barbed arrows that tore at the flesh, careered back into the path of the advancing French infantry. The cavalry that had broken through the Black Prince's defences was surrounded and cut down. Arnoul d'Audrehem was wounded and captured; Jean de Clermont fought bravely to the death. The archers started shooting at the approaching foot soldiers.

The French infantry were now taking serious casualties. 'A hail of arrows fell on the enemy,' Geoffrey le Baker related, 'loosed by English bowmen now in a state of desperate fury. Our opponents joined shields together and lowered their heads to protect themselves from the rain of missiles.' King John's troops pushed on, reaching the Anglo-Gascon army, tearing large gaps in the hedge and fighting bravely with the Prince's soldiers. The *mêlée*, the clash of dismounted men-at-arms, was a slugging match, in which attackers and defenders collided with the force of a wave hitting a breakwater. The fight surged backwards and forwards and the Prince, fearing his line was about to break, sent in most of his reserve. It was a bloody struggle – but after two hours of combat, the French began to pull back. There was now a brief pause. According to Geoffrey le Baker, the Black Prince's men were utterly exhausted:

> They carried the wounded away from the front line, and laid them under bushes and hedgerows, out of the way; others, having broken or damaged their weapons, took the spears and swords from those they had overcome – and the archers, lacking arrows, made haste to draw them from the poor wretches

that were slain or half-dead. There was not one of them who
was not wounded or greatly wearied by the labour of battle.

The dismounted French men-at-arms pressed on. For a moment, it
seemed as if their advancing second line was dissolving. The duke
of Orléans could be seen leading three of the king's sons off the
battlefield. But the remainder were in fact reforming around King
John's division, which was now preparing to attack. This force was
substantially greater than the entire Anglo-Gascon army and all its
men were fresh.

As the French troops came into view, there was a gasp of horror
on the Anglo-Gascon side. The experienced commander Robert
Ufford, earl of Suffolk, attempted to steady his soldiers' nerves:
'passing through each rank, encouraging his men, restraining
the young knights from advancing against orders and bidding the
archers not to waste their arrows'. The fifty-eight-year-old Ufford
was the oldest nobleman in the Black Prince's army and a trusted
and experienced councillor. He had fought for Edward III in Scotland and in France, and according to Jean Froissart advised Edward
of the suitability of the battle site at Crécy. In that encounter, he
fought with the Black Prince's division and showed considerable
bravery. Geoffrey le Baker paid tribute to the veteran's unshakeable
prowess: 'He distinguished himself by strenuous deeds from youth
to old age.' According to a number of chroniclers, his calmness at
Poitiers steadied those around him.

Robert Leigh of Adlington, leading a contingent of 108 Cheshire
archers, was at his best in a crisis. On one occasion he had been
hauled before the justices at Macclesfield and charged with a litany
of offences. Seeing the judgement going against him, he had struck
down two officials and fought his way out of the courtroom. But
now, even Leigh was dismayed. The French king's division was so
large it threatened to break the Anglo-Gascon line with the force of
a battering ram. As the soldiers realized this, their resolve started
to crumble. One captain blurted out that men should flee while

they still could, or else they would be overwhelmed by the enemy. The Black Prince rounded on him: 'You lie, you fool, and speak the worst slander possible, if you say that we will be defeated whilst I am still alive.' But sheer defiance alone would not restore the strength of his army. And there seemed nothing else to give.

The Black Prince and his followers gazed at the advancing French. According to the Chandos Herald, 'King John brought up such a great power that it was a wonder to behold.' The Herald reported that the Prince looked up at the heavens and prayed aloud:

> Mighty Father, I believe that thou art King above all Kings and through thy son, Jesus Christ, thou did endure death on the cross for us all, to redeem us out of hell. My Father, who art true God of Heaven, I believe I have good right in this quarrel. Through the power of your Holy Name, guard me and my people from evil.

His fighting comrades, Jean de Grailly, John Chandos and James Audley, all founder members of the Order of the Garter, stood in silence around him. For a few moments, all was quiet. And then came a flash of inspiration.

It was a memory of a shared conversation between the Prince and de Grailly, about a small military engagement at Limalonges, in Poitou, seven years earlier. On that occasion, Jean de Grailly — one of the captains in a raiding army of English, Gascon and renegade Poitevin knights — remembered how their soldiers were instructed to dismount and take up a good defensive position. But the French then did something unusual. They launched a frontal cavalry attack and at the same time sent a small group of horsemen around the battlefield, to strike the largely Gascon army from the rear. This was a clever ploy, but the combined attack slightly miscued. The flanking force broke through the waggons of the Gascon baggage train and drove away all the horses. But the main mounted charge went in too early and was beaten off, allowing the foot soldiers to reform. The French were repulsed, with some 300 of their men killed or taken prisoner, and their remaining horsemen then pulled back. There was a stand-off until evening and after dusk the predominantly Gascon force retreated in good order.

It was a small clash of arms with an inconclusive result. The French quickly forgot about it. But de Grailly did not. Nor did the army's commander, none other than Amanieu of Pommiers. They remembered the confusion the tactic had caused – how even experienced soldiers were momentarily disorientated. And they had shared these impressions with the Prince. Suppose they try it themselves, with the French infantry on the move and the attacks properly co-ordinated? De Grailly would take a picked force of Gascon cavalry round the flanks. The Prince would order every man with a horse to mount up for the main assault. The archers would provide the covering fire. It was a gambler's throw of the dice, with everything staked on the last roll.

Froissart caught the moment in the words of Sir John Chandos: 'The French king will hold his position – he will not think of retreat. Let us ride straight for him – it is there that the battle will be decided.' Sir James Audley asked for the honour of leading the main cavalry attack. The thirty-eight-year-old Audley was the illegitimate son of an Oxfordshire knight, a man of modest origins who had risen in wealth and status because of his skill in war. He had shown great courage and ability at the Battle of Crécy and the siege of Calais, where he fought as a member of the Black Prince's retinue. He now took on, without hesitation, what was in effect a suicide mission. He would ride directly towards John II, accompanied by only a four-man retinue, all of whom fully expected to die in the assault. The Prince gave his assent.

Great commanders know when to break the rules; great armies know how to carry out their orders. In the fourteenth century English armies usually dismounted and fought on foot: they waited for their opponents to attack them. Now, however, they would be doing the exact opposite – just when the French were least expecting it. De Grailly gathered his men. He would raise the banner of St George when he got into position: it would be the signal for everyone to charge.

Trumpets sounded. Orders were passed along the ranks: for men-at-arms to get on their horses; for archers to provide covering fire. The soldiers were confused. They did not know what was happening or what they were doing. But as the line of horsemen formed up, and Audley and his four companions rode out in front of it, suddenly every man understood.

Armies are weakened by fear and galvanized by anger. But when soldiers fight out of love, love for their comrades, love for their cause, they gain a power and unity of purpose. Jean de Bueil, a French soldier who fought in the last stages of the Hundred Years War, wrote a semi-fictional account of his martial experiences, entitled *Le Jouvencel* ('The Youth'), in which he caught a timeless truth:

> You love your comrade so much in war. When you see your quarrel is just and your fellow soldiers are fighting well, tears rise to your eyes. A great sweet feeling of love and compassion fills your heart... And then you prepare to enter the fray, to live or die by their side – and for love, not to abandon them. And out of that arises such a feeling of exhilaration that he who has not tasted it is not fit to say what a delight it is. Do you think that a man who has experienced this fears death? Not at all – he feels strengthened... Truly he is afraid of nothing.

When the Anglo-Gascon troops saw Sir James Audley take up his position every man felt proud: proud of Audley's courage, proud of what they had achieved against a far larger French army and proud to be charging towards the hated *Oriflamme* banner. The earl of Warwick turned to the earl of Salisbury and said: 'Let us slay some Frenchmen this day in Poitou.' If a soldier had to face death, what better way than in one glorious assault against the enemy commander: to kill or capture the French king or die in the attempt.

A surge of energy ran through the army. Fear, doubt and fatigue dissolved. Men looked at each other. Mounted knights steadied their horses and gripped their weapons. Bowmen nocked their arrows. Disparate thoughts and feelings slipped away. Every soldier became united in common purpose. They would give their all, every ounce of strength – for death or victory.

The French infantry were still advancing. King John's forces were now within extreme bow range. They could see that their opponents had mounted their horses. Some quickened their pace; others slowed to receive the attack. Their orderly formation was starting to break up.

On the ridge of high ground, the Black Prince glimpsed Jean de Grailly's uplifted banner in the distance. 'He suddenly burst out of hiding,' Geoffrey le Baker recounted, 'having followed a track around the battlefield. Now he signalled to the rest of the army.' The small Gascon force – some sixty mounted men-at-arms and 100 archers – was ready. The Prince gave the order to his own line of cavalry. The horsemen began to move forward, first at the walk, then the trot. As they gathered speed, they shouted the war-cry that bound the army together: 'Guienne et St-Georges!' ('For Gascony and England!'). Arrows rained down upon the French foot soldiers. Audley reached the enemy line first and hacked his way towards the French king. His comrades plunged after him.

The French had been mesmerized by the main English cavalry attack. No one had noticed Jean de Grailly's mounted force moving up behind them. And now it struck with the force of a hammer blow. There was a wave of shock, then confusion and then panic. There were shouts of betrayal, accusations of cowardice – and men turned and ran.

The sheer impact of the charge knocked the French king's contingent out of the battle line. 'Our army entirely lost its formation,' the author of the *Chronique des Quatre Premiers Valois* related, 'dented out of shape by the ferocity of the attack.' The Black Prince was everywhere, 'hewing at the enemy, lifting up his fallen comrades',

Geoffrey le Baker wrote proudly. John II was a brave man, and so were his fighting companions, knights of the Order of the Star, who had sworn never to retreat in a clash of arms. They gathered around their monarch in a small meadow, close to the river Moisson. Sir Geoffrey de Charny – 'the most worthy and valiant of them all', according to Froissart – held the *Oriflamme* banner high. He would defend it with his life.

The Prince ordered his bowmen to join the fray once their last arrows were shot. The English archers flung down their bows, rushed forward and joined in the hand-to-hand fighting. 'Armed with swords and shields they attacked the heavily armoured enemy', Geoffrey le Baker reported, 'anxious to buy death dearly, since they had expected to meet their end that day.' Ahead of them, more and more English and Gascon cavalry were converging on King John's position. 'The French king did many marvels in feats of arms', related Matteo Villani. 'He wielded a great axe and fought in the thickest press of his enemies.' His was a courageous last stand, and Geoffrey le Baker spoke of it with genuine admiration:

> It was a stubborn force of the bravest men. The standards wavered and the standard-bearers fell. Some were trampled upon, their innards torn open; some spat out their own teeth. Many were stuck fast to the ground, impaled [by lances]. Some had lost arms; others wallowed in the blood of their comrades. Men slipped and were crushed by those falling on top of them.

Geoffrey de Charny was cut down and the sacred *Oriflamme* banner fell from his hand. King John and his youngest son, fourteen-year-old Philip, were surrounded by their opponents. 'There was a great eagerness to capture the king,' Froissart related:

> Those who were near him, and knew him, cried out: 'Surrender yourself, surrender yourself – or you are a dead man.' A young knight from St Omer, Denis de Morbeke [Moerbeke], had been banished from France for committing a murder, and

had switched allegiance, going into the service of Edward III.
He rode right up to the French king, and told him to give him-
self up... King Jean gave him his right-hand glove and said:
'I surrender myself to you.'

In truth, there was a scuffle over King John as English and
Gascon soldiers, not wanting him to be captured by a Frenchman, attempted to drag him away from Moerbeke. The earl of
Warwick and Reginald, Lord Cobham, intervened and escorted
John II to safety. Sir John Kentwood had an easier task taking the
French king's son Philip captive. Philip had been too young to fight,
although he had loyally stood by his father's side, warning him of
approaching opponents. Kentwood was handsomely reimbursed,
receiving 4,000 marks (£2,666 13s 4d) for the prince.

The signal had been given allowing the taking of prisoners,
but the last stages of the battle were chaotic. An English knight,
Sir Maurice Berkeley, chased rather too vigorously after a mass of
fleeing Frenchmen and was himself captured by the enemy. One
Frenchman, the Count of Danmartin, recalled trying to surrender
to a succession of opponents. He was first captured by a Gascon
squire.

> He called on me to give up and I did so at once. I gave him my
> word so that he would protect me. He said that I should be quite
> safe and need have no fear... Then he handed me over to the
> keeping of a man of his and left me. Then another Gascon came
> up and demanded my pledge. He tore of a piece of my surcoat
> and then abandoned me like the last man. I shouted after him
> that since he was deserting me I would pledge myself to anyone
> else who came up who would be willing to ensure my safety.
> 'Protect yourself, if you can', he shouted back.

Danmartin eventually became a prisoner of the earl of Salisbury,
who had acquitted himself well in the battle. Geoffrey le Baker credited him with the choice of the strong defensive position along the

hedge, which proved invaluable in the opening stages of the battle, and with courageously repulsing d'Audrehem's cavalry attack. He had lost his first wife, Joan of Kent, to Sir Thomas Holland; he was able to present King John's illuminated Bible – taken as booty from his tent – to his second, Elizabeth Mohun, whom he pointedly referred to in his dedication as *la bonne comtesse* ('the good countess'). He returned home a war hero.

The Black Prince put up his banner at the top of a tree as a rallying point for his troops. 'A red pavilion was set up underneath it,' Froissart recalled, 'and a drink was brought to the Prince and all those lords who were about him.' The field was strewn with enemy dead. 'When the trumpet call summoned our men together again,' Geoffrey le Baker said:

> They pitched their tents in the cornfields and the whole army at once turned to the care of the wounded, rest for the weary, security for their prisoners and refreshments for the hungry. Realizing that some were missing from their midst, they sent out search parties to find them, and bring them back, alive or dead.

Fourteen French counts were captured, twenty-one other great lords and a thousand others whom Froissart described as 'worthy of ransom.' The French dead totalled 2,500 men-at-arms and a larger number of other ranks. No Anglo-Gascon nobleman had been killed; although casualties among the infantry and archers were unknown. The surprise tactic of mounting up the army, and throwing in a second cavalry attack from the rear, had been a devastating success. The bowmen had provided crucial support. And so ended what the Chandos Herald called 'this great and terrible battle'.

Many English archers took four, five or even six men captive. In fact, the English and Gascons had so many prisoners that they decided to ransom most of them immediately. Froissart had this to say about the treatment of French prisoners and the spoils of war that accrued to their captors:

Knights and esquires who had been captured found their opponents most courteous. Great numbers of them were ransomed
that day, or released on their honour – to return to Bordeaux
the following Christmas and pay what was due. It can well be
imagined that all those who were with the Prince in this victorious battle became rich in honour and possessions, as much
by the ransoms of their prisoners as by the gold and silver, plate
and rich jewels and chests stuffed full of beautifully orna-
mented belts and fine gowns. Of ordinary pieces of armour, and
helmets, they took no notice whatsoever.

That evening, during the course of the celebratory feasting that followed the battle, Sir James Audley was found, seriously wounded,
lying next to a hedge; he was carried into the English camp. Geoffrey le Baker said that 'he was placed on a broad shield and carried
with enormous care to the Prince's lodgings – half-dead and
barely breathing'. The Black Prince excused himself from his royal
prisoner and tended to Audley personally. 'The Prince brought him
back to life through his care and attention. He comforted Audley
by telling him that they had captured the French king, which the
wounded man could hardly believe.'

The Prince then returned to the dinner and served King John
personally: 'He waited on the king's table with every mark of
humility and refused to sit with him, saying he was not yet worthy
of such an honour, and it would not be fitting.' According to Froissart, in a vignette that became justly famous, the Prince then
remarked to the French king:

> Do not feel aggrieved, Sire, if God has chosen not to favour you
> today. I assure you, my father the king will treat you as honour-
> ably and amicably as he can and will agree sensible terms – you
> will make a lasting friendship. It seems to me you should be of
> good cheer, even though the battle has gone against you, for
> you have earned a reputation for high prowess and surpassed

the finest in your army in the way you fought today. I am not saying this to flatter you. All your companions agree with me in awarding you the prize and laurels – if you will accept them.

In reality, it was the Black Prince who won 'the prize and laurels', both for the manner of his victory and for his gracious treatment of his prisoners after it. The Prince believed the military engagement was won through the grace of God and saw its outcome as nothing short of miraculous. In a letter to Reginald Bryan, bishop of Worcester he pointed out the campaign had begun on 6 July, 'the eve of the Translation of St Thomas à Becket', and he believed the saint's intercession played a part in the victory. If his humility in the aftermath of Poitiers reflected his piety, his bravery on the day of battle was undeniable. 'He was as courageous and as cruel as a lion', Froissart said, 'and took great satisfaction in fighting and defeating his enemies.' The cult of chivalry was formed around the precepts of bravery in combat and proper treatment of prisoners in the aftermath of battle – and on both counts, Poitiers would form the core of the legend of the Black Prince as chivalrous hero.

After recouping its strength, the Anglo-Gascon army began its march back to Gascony on 22 September, laden with booty and prisoners. The earls of Warwick and Suffolk rode ahead with a force of 500 men-at-arms to secure the road, but the French offered no resistance. Following the defeat and the capture of its king, the country seemed to be in a state of shock. Jean, count of Armagnac, captured the mood of despondency when he wrote to the town of Nîmes:

Dear friends, it is with great sorrow that I must tell you that several days ago our lord the king met the Prince of Wales in battle and – as God sometimes tests our faith by inflicting the greatest of misfortunes on us – was fated to suffer defeat, despite being surrounded by some of the finest knights known to us in these times, who were all at his side.

Armagnac's letter also recorded that the French king had suffered two wounds to the face in the fighting. There was no doubting John II's courage – indeed, he became a hero to his countrymen, who accused many of the nobility of abandoning him and fleeing to save their own skins. The estates general of Languedoc declared a year of mourning and prohibited the wearing of gold, silver, pearls and decorated robes. The mayor of Poitiers banned all feasts and festivals. 'These losses did great damage and irreparable harm to the realm of France,' wrote the author of the *Chronique des Quatre Premiers Valois*.

When the Prince and his distinguished prisoner made their formal entry into Bordeaux on 5 October the mood was rather different, as the Chandos Herald recalled:

> Nobly were they received and welcomed by all the people, with crosses and processions. All the clergy came to meet them, and the ladies and damsels, old and young, down to the humblest serving made. There was such joy that it was marvellous to behold.

There was enormous pride that an Anglo-Gascon force had won such a resounding success. The abbey of Sauve-Majeure, 20 miles (33km) south-east of Bordeaux – a religious community that the Prince was on good terms with – noted in a battle report (probably gleaned from returning soldiers) that the triumph had been 'brought about by the might of the Gascon lords'.

In England, 'great thanksgiving was made in all the churches' when Edward III announced the victory on 10 October. The king had received news of his son's triumph at Poitiers from a groom of the Prince's chamber, Geoffrey Hamelyn, who brought King John's helmet and tunic as proof of victory. Ten days later the Prince dispatched his chamberlain, Sir Nigel Loring, and other members of his staff with letters for King Edward, the bishop of Worcester and the mayor and aldermen of the city of London, describing the campaign more fully. The Prince was not yet able to return to England, for there was much administrative work to do. He opened discussions for a truce with France and, on his father's behalf, started negotiations for the purchase of the principal aristocratic prisoners. But he found time for some private pleasures, acquiring a lion for his private menagerie.

On 12 October the Black Prince received a visit from the cardinal of Périgord, who told him that the Frenchmen from his retinue who had joined King John's army on the eve of battle had done so without his knowledge. According to Geoffrey le Baker the Prince was unconvinced, but the two men parted cordially. Remembering that the cardinal had relayed humiliating terms on the eve of battle, requiring him to surrender all his lands and prisoners, he drew up, in mock seriousness, a grant putting all of Périgord's family estates in Poitou under English protection. Poitou did not yet fall under English jurisdiction, but the Prince could see which way the wind was blowing.

The Black Prince and King John signed a two-year truce at Bordeaux on 23 March 1357. On 19 April the Prince and his captive, their servants and retainers, finally set sail for England. Their voyage lasted two weeks. The anonymous chronicler of Canterbury wrote:

> In the month of May 1357 the Prince of Wales brought the King of France and other captives over by sea. The voyage had been kept secret, and they arrived in a large ship accompanied by a naval squadron. On 3 May they disembarked at Plymouth, and from there the Prince conducted his prisoners — day by day — through all the main towns of England, until he reached the outskirts of the capital.

The Prince was sharing the fruits of his victory with the English people, parading before them King John, his youngest son Philip, and thirteen other great French noblemen. And part-way through their progress, Edward III and his son devised a little joke. As they passed through a forest, 500 men suddenly appeared, bearing bows and arrows, swords and shields. The French king was amazed. The Black Prince told him with a straight face that 'they were men of England, foresters... and it was their custom each day to be thus arrayed'. This shamelessly stage-managed event was a piece of 'chivalric sport': the image being conveyed to the French was that England was a country full of hardy bowmen, living rough, but ready to follow the Prince back to France should he so command.

The Black Prince's triumph at Poitiers would have far-reaching consequences. The ransom money from the French king and his nobles would replenish the English treasury, and King John's captivity offered a remarkable opportunity to negotiate a favourable end to the war. The magnitude of what the Prince had achieved was clear to everyone.

In London, the citizens made preparations for the Prince's arrival in the capital. On 24 May houses were decked with tapestries and the streets crowded 'with a multitude of people'. The Canterbury chronicler continued:

> Outside London, the mayor, aldermen and citizens waited to escort the Prince. Each of the city guilds had turned out bodies of horsemen, all dressed in their finest robes. There was a large throng of spectators. And as they escorted the Prince's entourage into London there were scenes of great rejoicing. The water in the main city conduit was replaced by wine, and all could drink as much as they wanted. It was wonderful to see.

Warmed by the free wine, the Londoners roared their delight at the Prince's achievement and also at the chivalric modesty he displayed in mounting King John on 'a well-apparelled white courser', while contenting himself with 'a small black horse'. The Prince celebrated his victory with his customary largesse: lands and cash were given to his fighting companions; horses and armour to the rank and file. Alan Cheyne and William Trussell, members of the Black Prince's bodyguard, were given grants of £40 a year. The captain Baldwin Botecourt received the Prince's manor of Newport for his 'good services'; Nigel Loring a large cash grant; and one of the wounded, William Lenche (who lost an eye in the fight) rights to a ferry at Saltash. Sir James Audley received the most generous gift of all – an annuity of £400.

And so the procession wended its way past St Paul's, Ludgate and Fleet Street. The Canterbury chronicler captured the happiness of the moment – when the Black Prince rode in triumph through the city at the summit of his career as England's warrior-hero:

> In the middle of Cheapside, by the goldsmiths' quarters, there were two really beautiful girls, placed [above the main thoroughfare] in a cage with a canopy above them, fastened by an elaborate series of ropes – a tableau designed with wonderful artistry by the goldsmiths – and the girls scattered gold and silver leaves upon the heads of the Prince, the King of France and all those who rode with them.

chapter seven

PRINCE OF
AQUITAINE

Edward III now held the kings of both France and Scotland captive. David II would shortly be released, after ransom terms had been agreed; John II's freedom would require careful negotiation. In the interim, the French king was treated with the utmost respect and courtesy, as chivalric convention dictated, and installed in the Savoy Palace in London. To honour the Black Prince's success, Edward put on a series of celebratory jousts that ran for many months, first at Smithfield, then at Bristol – the first night-time tournament ever seen in England – and finally, on the anniversary of the founding of the Order of the Garter, at Windsor.

It was the culmination of a heady period of rejoicing. On St George's Day, 23 April 1358, King Edward put on the most splendid tourney of them all. King John watched the proceedings from the royal dais and Edward gave safe-conducts to all foreign knights who wished to compete. His open invitation, at a time of truce between England and France, attracted the dukes of Brabant and Luxembourg and a number of the Black Prince's Gascon friends and allies. For the Prince, it was a joyous occasion: he paid out more than £100 to the assembled heralds and minstrels and distributed presents of armour. A surprise guest at this Garter tournament was King Edward's mother Isabella, now a frail old lady of sixty-two. In the twilight of her life, the king chose to make peace with the past and brought her back into the orbit of the royal court, giving her permission to move to Hertford, closer to the capital. The king of France, her kinsman, was allowed to visit her there.

After her political banishment in 1330, Isabella had set up a strange court-in-exile at Castle Rising in Norfolk, an imposing residence to which she added a west range comprising a residential suite and private chapel. Edward III gave her a generous income of £3,000 a year 'to provide for her estate'. Her freedom of movement was restricted and she was allowed little political influence. In the year after her banishment she may have suffered a form of nervous breakdown, for large payments were made to a team of physicians who tended her. If so, she made a reasonable recovery, for she subsequently had long periods of lucidity, receiving guests, doing business and managing her properties. The king sent her gifts and made the occasional visit. But when Philip VI of France suggested her as a possible mediator in peace negotiations, in 1348, Edward was having none of it; he sent Henry of Grosmont instead.

Over time, Castle Rising took on a rather other-worldly appearance. Isabella put down black carpets in her rooms and decorated them in striking colours. She kept a pair of lovebirds in her bedroom, which she fed on hemp-seed, and had a well-stocked bathroom full of ointments and cosmetics. Her attentive household of eight ladies-in-waiting and thirty-three clerks and squires helped to manage her affairs; a doctor and surgeon were kept in residence. Isabella enjoyed music and had a sizeable library, where she pursued her interest in astrology and alchemy. She was also an avid reader of Arthurian romances.

And the queen mother loved to entertain. In the year that King John was brought back to England Isabella was visited by her son, by her grandson the Black Prince (on three occasions), by Roger Mortimer, 2nd earl of March (her lover's grandson, who now enjoyed the confidence and favour of Edward III), and her daughter Queen Joan, whose ill-fated marriage to King David of Scotland had been effectively brought to an end when the Scottish king was captured at the battle of Neville's Cross in 1346, and then, still in captivity, managed to find himself a mistress.

There was more than a whiff of eccentricity about the ageing

She-Wolf of France. She became a lay member of the Poor Clares, a Franciscan order founded by St Clare of Assisi, and sometimes wore the garb of that order. The Poor Clares were a spiritual body that embraced poverty as a path to joyous communion with God and forbade the ownership of property, and yet Isabella continued to maintain a lavish lifestyle. She seems to have been simultaneously aware of the need to seek salvation for her soul, but reluctant to surrender the riches that adorned her body and decorated her home.

In the year 1358 alone, Isabella spent an astonishing £1,400 (almost half her annual income) on jewellery, amassing a dragon's hoard of precious stones, glittering crucifixes, rosaries, amulets and gold rings – and 'a large brooch containing a thousand pearls'. Fascinated by alchemical medicines believed to prolong life, she took an *elixir vitae*, dosed herself up on a host of remedies and appeared at the St George's Day tournament wearing a silk dress threaded in silver, shimmering with 300 rubies and 1,800 pearls. It was a remarkable advertisement for a life of holy poverty.

Such oddities aside, there was a healing element in Isabella's return to court. It was satisfying for her son, King Edward, who had banished her in the aftermath of humiliating treaties with Scotland and France, to welcome her back, some thirty years later, with the king of one of these realms recently released on payment of a large ransom, and the other still securely held in his custody. Edward's action may well have been prompted by the realization that his mother did not have long to live (she had been seriously ill in March 1358). But this moving act of reconciliation between the Plantagenet English king and his mother born of French royal blood carried with it an undoubted political advantage in that it helped Edward's negotiations with the captive John II.

The Black Prince enjoyed his grandmother's company. In 1354 he had invited Isabella to spend Christmas with him at Berkhamsted Castle, and following his return to England after the victory at Poitiers he visited her regularly. In her will, Isabella would leave all her properties to the Prince, including Castle Rising.

On 8 May 1358, King Edward and King John came to an agreement about ransom payments and also set out a broader political settlement. According to one chronicler, the two men 'embraced each other many times, exchanged rings and dined together'. Under the terms of the treaty they signed, John II agreed to pay the sum of 4 million French crowns (around £670,000) for his release and recognized Edward as the sovereign ruler of Aquitaine, Calais and Ponthieu. These were substantial concessions: Aquitaine was defined as extending from Poitou in the north to Bigorre, on the slopes of the Pyrenees, in the south, and from Quercy in the east to the Atlantic coast in the west. In return for these territorial gains, Edward would renounce his claim to the throne of France.

From a French perspective, this was a humiliating and scarcely palatable outcome. Most of his countrymen had forgiven King John the many failings of his reign, believing that he had been deserted by his noblemen, whom they saw as the real villains of Poitiers. But while John was elevated by some to the status of a distant chivalric hero, others were left to struggle with the challenge of governing a country bankrupted by war and suffering constant political unrest.

In England, the French king was allowed to go hawking and hunting whenever he wished. He was at liberty to receive visitors and enjoy the pleasures of court life, although a guard was assigned to him to prevent any attempted escape or rescue. His accounts show expenses for horses, dogs, falcons, a chess set, an organ, a harp, a clock, venison and whale meat from Bruges, and fine garments for his son Philip and his favourite jester, who received several ermine-trimmed hats decorated with gold and pearls. In captivity, King John maintained an astrologer, a 'king of the minstrels' with accompanying musicians, commissioned books with fine bindings and even held a cockfight.

The papal mediators who had encouraged this bout of diplomacy were delighted with the agreement, which they believed opened the way for France and England to heal the divisions of war and join

forces in a crusade against the Ottoman Turks, who were menacing Constantinople and the eastern Mediterranean. For the Black
Prince, who had formed a genuine friendship with King John, and
enjoyed playing chess or gambling with him, the terms offered a
glittering future: if Aquitaine became an independent principality,
Edward III would surely be looking to his eldest son to govern it.

However, for the treaty to be binding it had to be ratified by
John II's son, the dauphin Charles, in Paris. Charles was attempting
to assert his authority in the face of a governing council imposed
upon him by Étienne Marcel, the provost of the Parisian merchants,
and was also struggling with the interminable plotting of Charles
of Navarre (who had escaped from prison on 9 November 1357). And
at the end of May 1358, a peasant uprising, known to posterity as the
Jacquerie, broke out all over France.

✝

On 28 May 1358, in the village of Saint-Leu near Senlis, north of Paris,
a group of angry peasants gathered for a meeting. They blamed the
aristocracy for their miseries and for the capture of the French
king, 'which troubled all minds'. They asked themselves: what had
the knights and squires done to liberate him? Emotions were running high and needed an outlet. 'The common people groaned',
wrote the French Carmelite chronicler Jean de Venette, 'to see the
money they had so painfully furnished for the needs of war dissi-
pated in games and ornaments for the nobility. They believed that
the nobles had shamed and despoiled the realm.'

That night a group of about 100 peasants armed with staves and
knives attacked a nearby manor house, broke into it, killed the
knight, his wife and children, and burned the place down. It was a
spontaneous outbreak of violence, and it spread quickly, attracting
new adherents every day, armed with scythes, pitchforks and axes.
Soon it had become a popular movement with its own leaders.
Thousands rose up all over the Île de France, the Oise valley and

parts of Picardy and Champagne. 'The peasants continued killing and burning without pity or mercy,' Froissart wrote. 'They were like enraged dogs.'

At the outset, many nobles panicked, abandoned their homes and goods, and fled with their families to the nearest walled town. The dauphin Charles seemed overwhelmed by it all and in the opening days of the revolt took little decisive action. Then, alarmed that Étienne Marcel and the merchants of Paris appeared sympathetic to the peasants' grievances, the dauphin sent his family to Meaux, north-east of Paris, for safe-keeping. It was a disastrous error of judgement.

Thousands of rebels were now ransacking government property in the environs of Paris. Learning that the dauphin's wife, sister and infant daughter, together with some 300 ladies of the French court and their children, had been placed in a fortress called the Market of Meaux, where they were guarded by only a small force, they converged on the city 'with great will to do evil'. On 9 June 1358 an army of around 10,000 enraged peasants appeared outside Meaux. The mayor and magistrates, who had sworn loyalty to the dauphin and promised to allow no 'dishonour' to his family, completely lost their nerve and opened the gates to the rebels. A frightening horde poured into the city streets and prepared to storm the fortress by sheer weight of numbers. The spectre of rape and death hung over the dauphin's family.

But as a torrent of peasants swept towards the fortified Market of Meaux — situated on a strip of land between the river and the canal — a small band of knights was galloping to the rescue. Gaston Fébus and Jean de Grailly, cousins riding home together from crusade in Prussia, had learned of this deadly menace. One was fiercely independent, the other — an architect of the victory at Poitiers — strongly loyal to England; neither man was a friend of the House of Valois. But the danger threatening these women and children overrode all other considerations. For a moment, the spirit of chivalry shone, a comet flaming through a darkened sky.

A bridge connected the fortress with the rest of the city. As the rebels swarmed onto it, a portcullis rose at its far end, and twenty-five mounted knights, led by De Grailly and Fébus, readied themselves for the charge. Unwisely, the peasants chose to stand and fight on the narrow confines of the bridge, where superiority of numbers counted for little. Wielding weapons from horseback, the knights cut down their opponents, trampling them, toppling bodies into the river, forcing the rest back across the bridge. They charged again and again, hacking furiously, killing the commoners until they were exhausted from the slaughter. Hundreds were slain and the rest fled into the countryside.

Meaux became a turning point. The French nobles roused themselves and pursued the rebel forces. 'They flung themselves upon hamlets and villages, chased the peasants and miserably slaughtered them,' an anonymous Norman chronicler recorded bleakly. The uprising collapsed as quickly as it had begun. But France was suffering terribly. The twenty-year-old dauphin Charles cut an increasingly forlorn figure, ineffective in government and unable even to protect his own family – a man who had been saved by one of his sworn enemies. The English believed they had little to fear from him.

†

The Black Prince spent the summer of 1358 travelling round his estates. In August he visited Cheshire, where his officials had levied substantial fines on the foresters of Wirral and Delamere the previous year. The money was now due and he wanted to supervise its collection. The Prince had appointed a panel of judges to investigate his rights. He was looking to make money, and now was prepared to do so in the teeth of local opposition. One of his foresters, Robert Foxwist, was physically threatened while gathering information for the inquiry and had to be placed under special protection. The Prince recorded that 'diverse men in our lordship

of Macclesfield and elsewhere in the county of Chester, hardened
ill-wishers of Robert Foxwist, are threatening him in life and limb,
so that he dare not continue with his work'.

The work that Foxwist was undertaking for the Prince was
critical to his purpose – full exploitation of his rights depended on
the unglamorous end of estate management, secret information-
gathering and informing on others. He continued: 'Foxwist
hath great matters to prosecute against diverse persons in our
county of Chester, and many things in hand for our profit.' The
Prince instructed his officials to take all steps necessary to protect
Foxwist's life, adding that he knew who was behind the threats:

> And if any harm or damage of body should happen to the said
> Robert, I know very well to whom to impute it, and will never
> take any fine or ransom from the guilty party, of whatever rank
> he be, but will have judgement appropriate to the deed.

The Prince's business manager, Sir John Wingfield, had warned
him in July 1357 that he was pushing people too hard, and that the
investigation might be subverted by 'a great confederacy of those
living amongst the forests, in an attempt to ensure no indictments
were made'. On his deathbed, the Prince seems to have regretted
his actions, to the extent that he surrendered his forest rights in
the Wirral altogether. But on 22 September 1357 judicial proceedings
began at Chester and Macclesfield. The inhabitants of Delamere
forest accepted a communal fine of £2,000; those of the Wirral
£1,000. In August 1358 the first instalments were due.

The Cheshire episode demonstrated that the Prince's exercise
of lordship was all too often driven by the demands of his chivalric
lifestyle, and its conspicuous spending and extravagant generosity
was drifting out of control. On this occasion, he more resembled
a war chieftain providing for his fighting band than a landlord
inspecting his properties.

Remarkably, in the aftermath of a battle that had generated the
richest haul of prisoners and booty ever seen in England, where

many of his friends and followers had made their fortune, the victor himself was, in the short term at least, substantially out of profit. The Black Prince's own income from Poitiers should have been considerable. He was entitled to a share, either a third or a half, of all ransoms collected by those knights retained by him, and there were also his own prisoners and those whom he had bought outright from their captors: the latter included King John's son Philip as well as the count of Sancerre and the lord of Craon. On the strength of this anticipated revenue, the Prince had commenced a vigorous building programme on his return to England in 1357.

At Kennington, the Black Prince's chief residence near London, he ordered most of the existing manor house to be pulled down and replaced with a fine palace, with a new vaulted hall, chamber, kitchen, chapel and servants' quarters. He used his father's best architects. The great hall was begun by the master mason Henry Yvele in 1358: it was to be 27 metres (90 ft) long and 15 metres (50 ft) wide, with two spiral staircases, a buttressed entrance porch and three fireplaces, decorated with statues. The floor was probably covered with glazed tiles and the roof was also tiled. The Prince's chamber lay at right angles to it. South of the hall lay the 'great garden' and to the west of the chamber was a private garden. The design, following the latest fashion, was modelled on the great hall built by John, count of Poitiers (soon to be duke of Berry), for his palace at Poitiers.

At Wallingford Castle in Oxfordshire, the Prince instructed that a new hall, kitchen and prison be built, as well as a room for the hearing of pleas. Improvements were also made to the great tower, the Prince's rooms and chapel. And new gardens were laid out, running alongside the River Thames. At Lostwithiel in Cornwall he began major improvements to the fortified manor house.

It was entirely natural for the Prince to undertake these ambitious building projects. He had won a great victory and was now displaying his magnificence for all to see. And he was generous in his religious patronage. The Prince made large grants to Vale

Royal Abbey in Cheshire, for the completion of its church and monastic buildings. Vale Royal had been founded by the Prince's great-grandfather, Edward I, who wanted the abbey to be a symbol of power and prestige built on the back of his military victories in Wales. Royal masons under the leadership of Walter of Hereford, one of the foremost architects of his day, started work on an elaborate Gothic church the size of a cathedral. It was to be cruciform in shape with a high central tower. The east end would be semi-circular, with thirteen radiating chapels; south of the church would stand a cloister, surrounded by domestic buildings of a scale and grandeur to match the church itself.

At first all went well. King Edward I made a generous initial endowment and large donations of cash and materials to begin the work. But soon things began to go seriously wrong. The king increasingly needed money for his great castle-building programme in Wales and resources for Vale Royal completely dried up. By the end of the thirteenth century the building work had stopped. When the Prince first visited the abbey in 1353, only the east end of the church and a section of the cloister buildings had been completed. Large parts of the structure remained a shell.

The unfinished project caught the Black Prince's imagination. A contract was drawn up with the architect William Helpston, by which the Prince, who had already given 1,000 marks (£666 13s 4d) towards the project, was to pay a further £860 towards the building of the rest of the church. The plan was very ambitious. Vale Royal was to be the largest Cistercian abbey church in the kingdom, 3 metres (10 ft) longer than Fountains Abbey in Yorkshire and the second largest in the entire order, with a complex and magnificent design, including the construction of an elaborate cluster of chapels around the church's east end. In the late 1350s work began on completing the shell of the nave and making the east end even grander. The chronicler Henry Knighton was impressed: 'The Prince was inspired by this wonderful example of ecclesiastical architecture and resolved to complete King Edward I's work as an act of pure charity.'

The chronicler Thomas Walsingham praised Henry of Grosmont's liberality in the aftermath of his campaigns in Gascony in
1345–6. But Grosmont's fine palace at the Savoy was built from a
cash supply already realized. Much of the Black Prince's hoped-for
income from Poitiers did not materialize. Important French prisoners, including the duke of Bourbon, the marshal d'Audrehem
and the count of Joigny, were transferred from the Prince's custody
to that of the king, because he had been unable to raise sufficient
money to pay for them, despite having agreed to buy them from
their original captors. His unrestrained generosity, both in the purchase price of prisoners and rewards to his followers, was one of the
most appealing features of his military leadership, but it was also
denuding him of the profits of victory. Thus he was little better
off when the business side of the expedition was wound up and, as
a consequence, was finding it increasingly difficult to live within
his means.

The Prince's second visit to Chester had been prompted by an
alarming cash-flow problem. By the late spring of 1358, his finances
were in such poor shape that Sir John Wingfield was forced to order
the chamberlain of Cheshire, John Burnham, to come to London
without delay, telling him to bring with him all the money in the
county treasury and not to pay any further assignments that year.
Those who attempted to claim sums owed to them were to be told
that no further payments could be made because the money had
all been spent. Similar instructions were given to the chamberlains
of north and south Wales and the receiver of Cornwall. This diplomatic lie, if uncovered, would have been so damaging to the Black
Prince's reputation that all involved were sworn to the strictest
secrecy.

✝

On 22 August 1358 Isabella, the queen mother, died after a short but
severe illness. Her body was brought to London for burial at the

Franciscan church of Newgate, in a service overseen by the archbishop of Canterbury, Simon Islip, and attended by the entire royal
family. In her last hours, Isabella had asked to be buried in her wedding dress and requested that Edward II's heart, placed in a casket
some thirty years earlier, be interred next to her. Her final wishes
were honoured.

In November 1358, the first instalment of King John's ransom
failed to arrive. Edward III threatened to resume the war, knowing
that the two-year truce agreed by the Black Prince and the French
king at Bordeaux in March 1357 would shortly run out. However,
King John accepted a revised treaty, signed at London on 24 March
1359, by whose terms he added to the territory already conceded
the county of Boulogne, along with Normandy, Maine, Anjou
and Touraine, the entire Angevin empire of Edward's Plantagenet
ancestors. The French king was then allowed to travel to the countryside to enjoy the spring weather, occupying the apartments that
had recently been Isabella's at Hertford Castle. King Edward, for the
time being at least, cancelled his mobilization plans. It remained
to be seen whether the dauphin would accept such extravagant
demands and humiliating terms. But the English clearly felt that,
with France dissolving into a state of anarchy, they had their
opponents at their mercy.

After Poitiers, the Black Prince had released those English, Welsh
and Gascon soldiers whom he could no longer afford to pay. With
a truce agreed between the two countries, these troops were left
to fend for themselves. And fend for themselves they did, for these
men had acquired a taste for loot. Mercenaries from Germany
and adventurers from Hainault joined these bands of demobilized
soldiers, who gathered in groups of twenty to fifty, appointed a captain and moved northwards, to operate in the area between the
Seine and Loire. More men appeared: remnants from the retinue
of Philip of Navarre, leftovers from Henry of Grosmont's forces,
Breton men-at-arms. They were masters of the art of terrorizing
a region, their speciality burning and plundering. They became

known as the Free Companies. The French called them *routiers* (members of a *route* or gang).

The *routiers* had been active long before the battle of Poitiers, but the loss of the French king and so many of his nobles gave these disenfranchised warriors their opportunity. After the truce of 1357 their forces swelled, merged, organized and spread. Their activities were well-planned: they conducted reconnaissance, made use of spies and favoured the dawn raid. They would seize a poorly defended castle, using it as a stronghold from which they exacted tribute and raided the countryside. They imposed ransoms on prosperous villages and burned the poor ones, robbed abbeys of their valuables and grew rich on such easy pickings. These bands of brigands attracted Frenchmen ruined by the war, men at odds with society, those who had fallen into debt or wished to escape local vendettas or judgements by the courts. They now shared in the ravaging of their own country.

The most notorious of the French brigand leaders was Arnaud de Cervole, nicknamed the 'Archpriest' because of a clerical benefice he had once supposedly held. Wounded and captured at Poitiers, he had been released after paying his ransom. On returning to France in the anarchic months of 1357, he made himself commander of a band of freebooters. Settling in Provence, his force grew into an army of some 2,000 desperados. In the course of one raid conducted by Cervole, Pope Innocent VI felt so insecure in Avignon that he negotiated for immunity in advance. The 'Archpriest' was invited to the papal palace, where, in the words of one amazed chronicler, 'he was received as reverently as if he had been son of the king of France'. After dining several times with the pope and his cardinals, Cervole was given a pardon for all his sins and the sum of 40,000 gold crowns (around £6,000) to leave the area.

Cervole's equal among the English was Sir Robert Knolles, 'a man of few words', whom Froissart judged 'the most able and skilful man-at-arms in all the companies'. He had risen through the ranks in the Breton wars and, after service with Henry of

Grosmont, had plundered Normandy with such ruthlessness that during 1357–8 he amassed booty worth more than 100,000 crowns (more than £15,000). During the next two years he established himself in the valley of the Loire, where he gained control of forty castles and burned and sacked from Orléans to Vézelay. In a raid through Berry and the Auvergne his company left a trail of ravaged villages, whose charred gables were known as 'Knolles' mitres'. Thomas Walsingham said simply: 'He was an unconquerable soldier, dreaded by the whole of France for his might in war.'

The Free Companies turned chivalric values on their head. In the chaos of the times, the 'bold and amorous' Sir Eustace d'Aubrecicourt, a knight of Hainault, a founder member of the Order of the Garter and companion of the Black Prince at Poitiers, turned brigand with such élan that he won the love of the widowed Isabelle of Juliers, niece of Queen Philippa of England. Jean Froissart described how he set up a fiefdom of thieves:

> Aubrecicourt maintained himself in the Champagne, of which he was virtual master. He could assemble, at a day's notice, more than a thousand fighting men. He and his gang made raids almost daily, sometimes towards Troyes, sometimes towards Provins and Châlons. The whole of the region between the Seine and Marne was at his mercy. This Sir Eustace performed many feats of arms and no one could stand up to him, for he was young and full of enterprise. He won great wealth through ransoms, the sale of towns and cities and the safe-conducts that he provided – for no one was able to travel without his authority.

Isabelle of Juliers was enthralled by it all, as Froissart related in somewhat tongue-in-cheek fashion:

> The Lady Isabelle fell deeply in love with Sir Eustace for his great exploits as a knight, of which accounts were brought to her every day. While he was in the Champagne, she sent him fine warhorses with love letters and other tokens of great affection,

by which the knight was inspired to still greater feats of bravery
and accomplished such deeds that everyone talked of him.

These feats included trafficking in stolen castles, which were sold
back to their owners for a lucrative profit. Isabelle married her
now-wealthy hero in 1360. 'May God pardon him for his misdeeds',
Froissart concluded.

In response to French complaints that the English companies
were violating the truce, Edward III ordered them to disband,
but, in reality, with peace terms yet to be ratified by the dauphin's
regime, the English king was quite willing to let the companies
keep up the pressure on France.

To defend themselves against the threat posed by the Free
Companies, villagers turned their stone churches into fortresses,
surrounding them with trenches; they manned the bell towers
with sentinels and piled up stones to throw down on the attackers. 'The sound of the church bells no longer summoned people to
praise the Lord,' a chronicler recorded, 'but to take shelter from the
enemy.' Some peasant families spent nights with their livestock on
islands in the Loire or in boats anchored mid-river. In Picardy they
took refuge in underground tunnels dug into the walls of caves.
With a well at the centre and air holes above, the tunnels could
shelter twenty or thirty people, with spaces for cattle hollowed out
of the walls.

'Misery was heaped upon the population,' Jean de Venette
wrote. 'What more can I say? Harm, misfortune and danger befell
us French for lack of good government and adequate defence.'
He blamed the nobles, 'who failed to protect the country from its
enemies', and above all the dauphin Charles, who, according to
Venette, 'applied no remedy' and 'gave no thought to the people's
plight'.

†

On 19 May 1359 Edward III's third son, John of Gaunt, married Blanche, daughter of Henry Grosmont, at the royal palace at Reading. The mayor of London ordered jousts to be held in celebration of the wedding, and the English king, who had recovered his liking for impersonations, held the field with his sons Edward, Lionel, John and Edmund and nineteen other lords, disguised as the capital's twenty-four aldermen, on whose behalf the invitations to the event were issued.

A decade later, Geoffrey Chaucer would famously evoke Blanche's virtues in his *Book of the Duchess,* written in her memory. He spoke of her golden hair and wide eyes, 'good, glad and sad', her honesty in everything, her kindness and wonderful beauty. In one striking passage he described how:

> I saw her dance so comely,
> Carol and sing so sweetly,
> Laugh and play so womanly,
> And look so debonairly,
> So good speak and so friendly,
> That certain I am that evermore,
> Ne'er has seen so blissful a treasure.

Six days after the marriage, on 25 May, the dauphin Charles took the English terms to the Estates General of France, which rejected them outright as 'neither tolerable nor practical', and granted him a subsidy to defend the realm. It would soon be needed.

In June King Edward began recruiting a force of more than 10,000 men, one of the most substantial he would lead abroad. His intention was to march to Rheims, where he would make good his claim to the kingdom of France by being crowned in the cathedral and anointed with the holy oil of Saint-Rémy, with which the French kings had been consecrated since the time of Clovis at the end of the fifth century. He made no effort to conceal his plans from the French, believing there was little they could do to stop him. If they sent a relief army to Rheims he was confident of defeating it in battle. In Edward's eyes, his planned coronation would come to pass, and he would impose the treaty agreed with King John by force.

Edward III, his four grown sons, his greatest nobles and war captains and his formidable army paraded the virility, pride and confidence of a country at the height of its power. They were opposed by the twenty-one-year-old dauphin Charles, a pale, thin man with an ill-proportioned body, who suffered from severe head-aches, toothache, heartburn and constant digestive problems. He was intelligent but no fighter. His right arm was disabled by gout; his left by an abscess, supposedly the result of an attempt by Charles of Navarre to poison him a year earlier. His realm was exhausted by the war, riven by discord and ravaged by the Free Companies. There did not seem a great deal for the English to worry about.

The expedition of 1359 was funded entirely from the king's and his magnates' own resources, without recourse to taxation. The Prince's own retinue was a substantial one of 143 knights, 443 squires and 900 mounted archers. Chandos, Botecourt and Burghersh the younger were all with him; Audley would join him later. However, the money needed to pay and equip his soldiers put his already fragile financial resources under colossal strain.

In the summer of 1359 the Prince's officials were still desperately searching for cash. In June the auditors of his lands in north Wales and Cheshire ordered that all sums due by midsummer be col-lected immediately 'in view of the Prince's great need of money for his next expedition'. In July, he pawned jewellery that had belonged to the king of France to the earl of Arundel, as security for a loan of £2,000. Further loans were received from a consortium of mer-chants, Italian financiers, the bishops of Lincoln and Winchester and prominent London aldermen. In August came an unprece-dented order to the receiver of Cornwall to sell all stocks of wood, 'as the Prince urgently needs money at present'. On 25 September the chamberlain of Cheshire was asked to raise additional revenue by selling all confiscated lands in the Black Prince's possession. By October, Sir John Wingfield had raised the sum of 20,000 marks

(£13,333 13s 4d) secured on the Prince's entire body of properties.

Sometimes, however, the imperative of securing the services of good fighting men trumped even the fiscal needs of the cash-strapped Prince. On 11 July 1359 Sir John Hyde, a landowner in east Cheshire and retainer of the Prince, went to see his master. Hyde did not appear to be in a good negotiating position. He had been fined 100 marks (£66 13s 4d) in the forest investigation of 1357 and the sum was still outstanding. In the judicial sessions of 1353 he had been found guilty of mutilating one of his servants and now he was accused of involvement in a murder. But Hyde, an experienced soldier who had fought at Crécy and Poitiers, played the few cards in his hand well. He needed part of his fine cancelled, he told the Prince, payment of the remainder delayed and a general pardon issued, 'or he would not be able to go overseas'.

A compromise was reached, albeit one weighted heavily in favour of Sir John Hyde. The Prince — although desperately in need of money — reduced the sum owed by £40, and suspended payment of the remainder. A second fine, of 200 marks (£133 13s 4d), for Hyde's involvement in the murder, was cancelled. On 16 August the Prince retained Hyde for war service for half a year, paying him 10 marks (£6 13s 4d), and subsequently issued a general pardon for all offences committed before the start of the campaign. Despite his thuggish and generally reprehensible behaviour in Cheshire, Hyde was simply too valuable a soldier to lose.

The Black Prince's officials drew up a list of debts and payments to be made on his own personal authority. These included the sums of £387 to his painter and £340 to his embroiderer, who was making tapestries for Kennington's great hall. Despite the Prince's continuing monetary travails, the renovation of his palace was proceeding apace.

The Black Prince arrived at Sandwich on 16 September 1359 and began to muster his troops. Sir Thomas Gray, another experienced fighter, remembered that new recruits flocked to the Prince's banner: 'They came in astonishing numbers... commoners, young men who until this time had been held of little account... many beginning as archers, but hoping to become knights and captains.'

It was growing late in the campaigning season. An advance force was sent across the Channel under Henry of Grosmont on 1 October, to harry the French and gather supplies; another, under Roger Mortimer (now restored to the earldom of March), was dispatched three weeks later. Finally all was ready. On 28 October 1359 Edward III and the Black Prince sailed to France with the main army. On 4 November, their soldiers marched out of Calais. There was a tangible sense of optimism: the English held the military ascendancy and were dictating the shape of events. The Anonimalle Chronicle (a well-informed, patriotic source, possibly based at St Mary's Abbey, York) noted happily: 'After Poitiers, a hundred Frenchmen did not dare meet twenty Englishmen in the field and offer battle to them.' The Italian Francesco Petrarch, who was at the French court on diplomatic service for the duke of Milan at this time, observed:

> In my youth the English were reputed to be feeble fighters, inferior even to the miserable Scots, but now they are the most warlike of peoples. They have overthrown the military glory of France in numerous and unexpected victories... and devastated the whole realm with fire and sword.

The English army on the move was certainly an imposing sight. Its knights rode out in their best armour and equipment; the mounted archers kept good order and discipline. In the baggage train were masses of carts, hand-mills for grinding corn, ovens for baking the flour into bread, forges for repairing weapons and armour and shoeing horses, collapsible leather boats, ornate canvas tents and even thirty falconers with their hawks and 120 hounds with their harriers. Jean le Bel caught the scene:

> Edward rode out from Calais with the best supply train ever seen. It was said that there were 6,000 handsomely fitted waggons, all

brought over from England. And he set out his forces so splen-
didly that they were a pleasure to behold. He commanded his
constable to ride half a league ahead of him with some heavy
cavalry, the finest-looking in the whole army, and a thousand
[mounted] archers. Then came the king's own division, consisting of 3,000 cavalry and 5,000 archers, in full battle array,
ready to fight, and behind it came the baggage train, stretching
out fully four miles, and carrying everything needed for camp
or combat... And in the rear rode the Prince of Wales and his
brother [John of Gaunt]: in their division they had 2,500 heavy
cavalry, superbly mounted and richly armoured.

The Prince kept good discipline on the march, allowing no stragglers to fall behind and instructing his men to 'ride at a good pace'.
The English army's three columns moved in parallel lines, some 10
miles (16 km) apart from each other, then struck out further afield.
'They passed through Picardy and Artois', the Anonimalle chronicler related, 'with their forces well-arrayed, destroying everything
in their path.'

However, the dauphin was one step ahead of them. He pursued a scorched-earth policy, ordering all those who were able to
take refuge in the towns and leave nothing in the countryside of
value to the English. Villages and farm buildings were burned by
Edward III's troops but there was not much to be had in the way of
plunder. His army fanned out over a wider and wider distance – at
times its columns were 20, even 30, miles (32–48 km) apart. There
was little sign of the enemy. The weather was increasingly wet with
rain falling every day and most nights. Supplies were running low
and there was little fodder for the horses.

The English troops skirted around the major towns that lay in
their path, knowing that they could not easily storm them, and
on 28 November the army regrouped at Saint-Quentin on the
River Somme, then made for Rheims. On 4 December Edward
set up his headquarters in the Benedictine abbey of Saint-Basle,

10 miles (16 km) south-east of the city. The Black Prince was based at Saint-Thierry, 5 miles (8 km) to the north-west of Rheims; Henry of Grosmont at Bétheny to the north-east. These dispositions were important. This was a loose blockade, cutting off the routes to Laon, Rethel and Châlons, but significantly, leaving the road to Paris open. King Edward was goading his rival to come to the city's rescue

This was a different operation from that of Tournai or Calais, for there were no sea or river communications to supply the English army and Edward III had not brought a siege train – a clear indication that he never intended a long investment of Rheims. Edward had received intelligence that the dauphin was gathering a relief force. With his army encamped around the city, he hoped for a quick surrender or to meet the French in battle. He promised 'to treat the inhabitants kindly, and make Rheims the most magnificent and important town in France if he could be crowned there', reported Matteo Villani. And Edward gave clear orders that his men were not to destroy or damage property in the surrounding area 'on pain of hanging'. As Henry Knighton put it, 'the troops behaved as if they were on their own soil'. The city's gates stayed firmly shut.

Edward III knew that the archbishop of Rheims, Jean de Craon, favoured the English cause. But the archbishop no longer held much influence within the city, for the dauphin, anticipating Edward's strategy, had appointed an experienced soldier, Gaucher de Châtillon, as Rheims's captain. Gaucher treated Jean de Craon as suspect, and watched him closely. He also repaired and strengthened the city walls, armed and trained its citizens in military drill and stockpiled supplies. He believed he could hold out for a long time and that the English army would run out of food well before the inhabitants of Rheims did.

The besieging force celebrated Christmas in style, as the chronicler Henry Knighton recalled, with 'every lord making merry with others as though he were on his own estates in England'. The festivities were enlivened when the freebooting captain Sir Eustace d'Aubrecicourt seized the nearby town of Attigny, and, finding 3,000 barrels of wine there, sent most of it as a present to the English army. Raiding parties were sent further afield, to storm small towns and gather supplies. It was rumoured that the dauphin was succumbing to nervous strain, losing hair, fingernails and the use of his right hand. He sent out a relief force but then recalled it.

But the English also began to suffer. There was not enough food or proper shelter for the horses, and illness began to spread among the cold, wet and hungry troops. On 3 January 1360 the Prince lost an able captain, the Cheshire knight Sir Ralph Mobberley. 'He died at the beginning of the time of sickness', Sir John Wingfield noted grimly. More fatalities followed.

On 10 January Edward III held a council of war. Foraging parties had returned, reporting that there was no longer enough food or livestock in the region to support the army. It was clear that Rheims was ready to withstand a long siege and there was little prospect of engaging with French forces. The English had ridden some 170 miles (274 km) through France without facing any effective opposition and had humiliated the dauphin, who had failed to assist one of the principal cities of his realm. Now they needed to look after their own troops. King Edward decided to march south, crossing the Marne and Seine, and advance into the lands of the duke of Burgundy. Supplies would be more plentiful and the soldiers could recover their strength.

King Edward now envisioned a broader strategy: he would exploit tensions that existed within France arising from growing frustration with the House of Valois. If possible, he would make a deal with the thirteen-year-old duke of Burgundy – Philip de Rouvres – and his advisers. He would open negotiations with other disaffected French nobles, including Charles of Navarre. When spring came, he would advance on Paris.

On 11 January Edward III's forces left Rheims and turned southeast, towards Châlons and Troyes. They rebuilt the bridge over the Marne and marched into the northern Champagne. They were still losing men to sickness, the most notable casualties being Roger Mortimer, the constable of the army, and the earl of Oxford, who had fought alongside the Black Prince on the Poitiers campaign three years earlier. But food was at last becoming more plentiful.

An advance party under the Essex captain John Harleston captured the fortified hill village of Flavigny-sur-Ozerain, north-east of Dijon. Perched on an outcrop of rock, and girded by strong walls and towers, Flavigny was considered impregnable. The French had decided to stockpile provisions there, believing that they would be completely safe. But Harleston and his followers captured the place in a daring attack. 'They found enough food', Jean Froissart commented approvingly, 'to sustain the entire English army for a month.'

John Harleston was a captain in the Free Companies who made a seemingly effortless transition from brigandage to royal service in times of truce or war. Praised by the chronicler Thomas Walsingham for his skill with weapons and leadership of men, Harleston was reputed to hold banquets where his dining tables were adorned by more than 100 stolen church chalices. But his ingenuity in seizing Flavigny gave the English army a welcome reprieve.

At the beginning of March Edward set up camp at Guillon, 60 miles (97 km) west of Dijon, and opened discussions with the Burgundians. While negotiations were under way, the king also found time to enjoy a little hunting. He also paid £16 towards the ransom of a young squire, a budding poet who had been captured by the French in a small skirmish after the army left Rheims. The man's name was Geoffrey Chaucer.

On 10 March 1360 the English and Burgundians came to an agreement. Edward III was paid a substantial indemnity, representing three months of his army's wage bill. In return, he promised to leave Burgundian territory and launch no further raids upon it for the next three years. The chronicler Matteo Villani believed that a secret diplomatic treaty was concluded. In it, the councillors of the young duke of Burgundy promised Edward that, if he was crowned at Rheims, they would give him their support. Such an assurance could not be made openly – the consequences for the Burgundians if Edward should fail would be too serious. But if such an understanding was reached, it represented a diplomatic coup nonetheless, showing deep disenchantment on the part of the Burgundians with the rule of John II and the regency of his son.

Spring was approaching. 'The weather turned as fair, pleasant and warm', a chronicler wrote, 'as anybody could remember it at this time of year.' On 15 March the dauphin attempted a diversion, landing a small force of soldiers on England's south coast, near Winchelsea. The local levies were called out and the French soon withdrew. On the same day, Edward III left Burgundian territory and swung his army north-west, towards Paris.

The tempo of the English advance quickened and morale and self-belief rose. At Auxerre, some of the Black Prince's troops were surprised by the enemy while foraging for food. They turned the tables on their foe, as Sir Thomas Gray related:

> Five English squires, without armour except for their helmets and shields, were attacked in a cornmill by fifty French men-at-arms. But they defeated their opponents, taking eleven prisoners, after which even the French in nearby garrisons called this in mockery: 'the combat of the five against the fifty'.

One Scottish chronicler said of Edward III's progress towards Paris: 'No one in the kingdom of France dared lift his head against him.' However, the dauphin had persuaded Charles of Navarre to remain loyal, and Edward's harsh renegotiation of King John's terms of release had solidified opposition to his demands within the French capital. On 31 March Edward set up his headquarters at Chanteloup-en-Brie, 20 miles (32 km) from Paris. The Black Prince's advance guard moved up to Longjumeau, a mere 12 miles (19 km) south of the city. Jean de Venette witnessed the terror felt by some of the local inhabitants:

On Good Friday [3 April] smoke and flames surrounded Paris. Much of the rural population had fled inside the city. All were in a most pitiable state. On Easter Sunday I saw priests offering them communion in churches, chapels – any consecrated spot they could find.

On 7 April the Black Prince's troops reached Vanves and Gentilly, only 3 miles (5 km) from the dauphin's palace in the centre of the city. Banners were unfurled, trumpets and clarions sounded and heralds rode up to the walls, challenging the French to battle. When there was no response, the English taunted the defenders, accusing them of cowardice. But the dauphin held his nerve – he would not be provoked into a fight. On 10 April he sent out peace negotiators but Edward sent them back. Two days later the English king set fire to the city's suburbs. 'The Prince marched close to the walls from sunrise to midday,' Sir Thomas Gray recalled, 'setting alight all that remained standing.' It was a gesture of defiance and frustration – King Edward would never again come so close to Paris.

That afternoon the English army pulled back from the French capital. Edward planned to march to Brittany and replenish his forces there. But the following day, Monday 13 April, disaster struck his army. The English had undertaken a long march in the direction of Chartres and were in the open countryside. The weather had been mild, but suddenly the temperature plummeted, the sky blackened and a strong wind rose. Then a ferocious storm broke over the shocked and frightened soldiers. 'It was a foul day', the chronicler of *The Brut* wrote. 'A tempest of frightening strength was unleashed. Dark clouds and an icy mist engulfed the army.' There was no cover on the wide plain. The troops were battered by huge hailstones and drenched by freezing rain. The cold was bitter. As the army struggled on, men fell to the ground, where they would later freeze to death. Horses died in their hundreds and part of the baggage train had to be abandoned. 'The storm was so overpowering', said Froissart, 'that it seemed as if the heavens would crack, the

earth open and swallow everything up.' The day became known as
Black Monday.

Edward's army was left deeply shaken. No one had ever
experienced anything like it. Medieval soldiers were naturally
superstitious, and to the rank and file the storm seemed to be an
event of terrible ill-omen. The king and his commanders were also
strongly affected. Froissart said that Edward was 'humbled' by what
had happened. He had lost fellow aristocratic fighters: Robert, Lord
Morley, and Guy, son of the redoubtable earl of Warwick. And the
sudden violence that had erupted from the sky was unnerving.
Could it be that it was a message from God – and that the Almighty
was displeased by King Edward's conduct of the war in France?

On 1 May, as Edward and his forces passed Châteaudun, some
80 miles (130 km) south-west of Paris, a new peace overture was made
by the dauphin. This time, the English took it seriously. Henry of
Grosmont met the French ambassadors and then reported back to
the king. His words to Edward were frank, and spoken from the
heart:

> My lord, this war that you are waging in the realm of France is
> exceedingly costly for you… All things considered, if you con-
> tinue to follow your plan, and offer battle with no takers, you
> may use up your whole life without succeeding in it. If you take
> my advice, you should get out of it while you can, take the offers
> that have been made to you and exit with honour. For we could
> lose in a day more than we have won in twenty years.

Edward listened to Grosmont's advice. According to Froissart,
the king had spent time in prayer and reflection, and afterwards
decided that if reasonable terms were offered he would be willing
to make peace. The dauphin now felt a similar sense of urgency,
'seeing how the realm could not long endure the great tribulation
and poverty the English were inflicting'. Negotiations between
England and France began at the village of Brétigny, near Chartres,
and a treaty was agreed on 8 May 1360.

Its terms were modelled on the earlier agreement between Edward III and King John II at London in May 1358, which was now fully accepted by the dauphin's government. Edward renounced his claim to the crown of France and to the former Plantagenet possessions of Anjou, Maine, Touraine and Normandy. In return, he would hold Aquitaine (an enlarged Gascony that included Poitou, the Saintonge, Limousin and the Rouergue) and, in the north, Ponthieu, Calais and Guînes, 'in all freedom and perpetual liberty, as sovereign lord and liege and neighbour to the king and realm of France, without recognizing the king or crown of France as sovereign over him, nor paying him homage, showing obedience or being in subjection to him'. The transferred territories repre-sented about a third of the territory of modern France.

King John's ransom was reduced to 3 million gold crowns (around £500,000). On payment of the first instalment, the French king would be released and hostages delivered as surety for the remainder. To ensure the continuance of peace, the two kings would renounce their present alliances — France with Scotland, England with Flanders — and do their utmost to resolve the quarrel between conflicting claimants to the duchy of Brittany, which Edward III now recognized was to be held in homage to the French crown. The campaign was over — and the treaty won from it, although far less than Edward had demanded a year earlier, was still a consider-able achievement. In its aftermath, the English army returned to Calais and then sailed back across the Channel. Edward III and the Black Prince were in London by 19 May.

Events now moved quickly. On 14 June King John II put his seal to the agreement and a celebratory banquet was held. At the end of the month the Black Prince escorted the French king to Dover, which they reached on 6 July. King John was taken to Calais and over the next few months the first instalment of his ransom was delivered and some practical problems raised by the treaty resolved. A final ratification was sealed on 24 October 1360 by Edward III, the Black Prince, John II and the dauphin. The following day

King John left English-held Calais and returned to France.

News of Brétigny was greeted with an outpouring of relief in both countries. People called it 'the great peace'. For the English, the burden of war taxation was lifted and a period of prosperity beckoned. The treaty was seen as a product of 'sound deliberation and great prudence', as Froissart put it. For the French, King John wrote:

> Our country has suffered too much through this war... Mortal battles have been fought, people slaughtered, bodies destroyed and souls lost... And it seems to us that even greater evil might ensue in time to come. There has already been too much anguish and sorrow... and for this reason we have consented to this treaty, ratified and approved it.

England had restored its martial standing among the nations of Europe. Humiliation was replaced by pride, shame by a sense of honour. To mark the triumph of Poitiers, Edward III had wished to make his eldest son prince of Aquitaine; now this would come to pass. His son's rule over this principality would be the reward of victory and mark a glorious new beginning.

The devil remained in the detail, however. The treaty of Brétigny would not come fully into effect until the provisions of an ancillary document were met. This document contained two items known as the renunciation clauses. One required the French to hand over all of the promised territories, particularly those in the newly enlarged Aquitaine. The other required the English to withdraw all their garrisons from northern France.

For all the progress made at Brétigny, there was still a residue of suspicion and mistrust. And the treaty called on both sides to make difficult compromises. The French were handing over territories that resented being forced into English overlordship; while for their part the English were disbanding garrisons that had fought loyally for their cause. The first clause took two years to be implemented, delaying the Prince's commission of authority for Aquitaine and his arrival in the duchy. The second clause never came into being at all. Edward's hesitation in properly enacting it would prove a grave mistake – and one that would have serious repercussions for his son.

In the immediate aftermath of the treaty, the renunciation clauses did not trouble either side too much. For towards the end of 1360 a fresh cataclysm erupted: the return of the Black Death. It had reached northern France by September, claiming the life of the queen of France, and, a month later, the dauphin's three-year-old daughter and her infant sister. Another of its early victims may have been Joan of Kent's husband, Sir Thomas Holland, appointed captain-general of all royal forces in northern France, although all we know is that he died suddenly at Plouigneau in Brittany on 26 December. He was a soldier of international repute, a veteran of Crécy and Calais, a great crusader and one of Edward III's foremost war commanders. He left two sons, three daughters and an exceptionally beautiful thirty-two-year-old widow in Joan of Kent.

The reappearance of the pestilence hit France's economy badly. According to a royal ordinance, plague and the devastation of war had reduced the sixty hearths of the small town of Buxeuil in Burgundy to ten, 'and these have been pillaged and ruined by our enemies, so that little or nothing remains'. By the spring of 1361 the plague had crossed the Channel and spread to southern England. 'A great mortality oppressed the people,' Henry Knighton wrote bleakly. 'It was called the second pestilence and both rich and poor died, but especially young people and children.'

In this new outbreak, the Black Prince lost two of his sisters, Mary, countess of Brittany and Margaret, countess of Pembroke, aged sixteen and fourteen respectively; also his business manager, Sir John Wingfield. He also mourned the passing of one of England's greatest warriors, Henry of Grosmont, whom he much admired and respected. The Prince attended Grosmont's funeral at Newark on 14 April and placed two pieces of golden cloth on the bier. As a gesture of defiance, Edward III held the annual Garter feast at Windsor on 23 April, installing his sons Lionel, John and

Edmund to fill the vacancies left by victims of the plague. More than 800 Garter brooches were distributed among the townsfolk. But in May, with the pestilence rampaging through London, the work of all law courts and government departments was suspended until the autumn. By then the Prince had made a remarkable decision.

In the summer of 1361 the thirty-one-year-old Black Prince, the most eligible bachelor in Europe, chose to wed Joan of Kent, his cousin 'Jeanette'. As heir to the throne, his father had wanted him to marry young and secure the succession, to marry a foreign princess and forge a continental alliance. 'Now he could have aimed as high as he wished,' a chronicler wrote, 'for there was not an Emperor, King or Prince beneath the whole of Heaven who would not have been overjoyed if he had entered their family.' But the Prince married for love.

In the words of one contemporary observer, Ranulph Higden, 'this match greatly surprised many people'. It was certainly made secretly and impulsively, in the early summer, after which the Prince sent his squire, Nicholas Bond, to Avignon to obtain the necessary licence for the union. A papal dispensation was needed because Edward and Joan had a common grandfather, King Edward I, and were therefore cousins, related in the second and third degree.

On 8 September the pope gave his assent, with the proviso that if a marriage contract between the Prince and Joan already existed it was to be dissolved and then undertaken anew. A suitable penance was imposed (the endowment of a chantry with two priests) and the couple plighted their troth once more, this time in a public ceremony. On Sunday 10 October 1361 the marriage of the Prince and Joan, countess of Kent was formally celebrated at Windsor. The king, queen, John of Gaunt and Edmund of Langley, and the earls of Warwick and Suffolk were in attendance, and a 'large number of lords, ladies, clergy and laymen in plentiful multitude'. The earl of Salisbury did not appear on the guest list.

The marriage did not meet with universal approval. The anony-mous chronicler of Canterbury, for example, struck a critical note:

A papal dispensation had been granted to the couple – and well they needed it. Joan, the daughter of the late Edmund earl of Kent, was the Prince's cousin – which otherwise would have prevented the match on grounds of consanguinity. In addi-tion, they had a spiritual relationship, one that also might have acted as an impediment to marriage, as the Prince had stood as godfather to two of the countess's sons.

The chronicler went on to claim that the archbishop of Canter-bury, who conducted the wedding service, did so against his will: 'The archbishop said he was doing this against his conscience, and only because he had been compelled to do so.' But others were more accommodating. The Anonimalle chronicler emphasized Joan's royal ancestry (she was, after all, the daughter of Edward III's uncle, the earl of Kent) and her charm and grace. The judgement of the Chandos Herald was that 'Joan was beautiful, pleasant and discreet and kindled an abiding love in the Prince's heart'. Not wishing to be outdone, a Valois chronicler praised Joan as 'one of the loveliest women in the world'.

Indeed, the French had a field day with the story. The author of the *Chronique des Quatre Premiers Valois* told how, after Holland's death, there was such competition to marry his widow that 'many noble knights who had greatly served the King of England came to ask the Prince to speak on their behalf'. The Prince agreed to the request of one named Brocas. But when he approached his cousin, she – 'who was subtle and wise' – replied that she would never marry again. As he persisted in pleading Brocas's case, the Prince 'became more and more attracted to the countess'. She began to weep. 'Then the Prince took her in his arms and comforted her.' She begged him not to press her to marry Brocas. 'For I am devoted to the most valiant man on earth... and it is impossible for me to have him.' When the Prince urged her to say who it was, she at last confessed:

'It is you — and for love of you, no other knight shall ever be at my side.' Then the Prince, greatly consumed with passion, said: 'I swear to God that as long as I live I shall have no other woman but you.'

If this full-blown story of sudden infatuation and calculated enticement is unlikely to reflect reality, because the Prince already knew Joan well and had seen her often, it may contain a germ of emotional truth nonetheless. Froissart believed that the couple's love was mutual, and he saw them together often enough. She was rich and beautiful and the man she had loved was dead. It was obvious that she ought to remarry, and the best choice for a second husband was the most sought-after man in England and heir to the throne.

Whatever the Prince's motivation in marrying Joan, it is worth noting that he declared his love for her at a time of plague, when, as the Florentine writer Giovanni Boccaccio observed, survivors often flung away their inhibitions and lived life to the fullest, as if there was no tomorrow. The Prince can fairly be said to have followed his heart, and his relationship with Joan seems to have been characterized by both emotional intensity and sexual fidelity. He had sired just one bastard child, Roger of Clarendon (by Edith de Willesford), before his marriage to Joan. After that marriage he remained entirely faithful to his wife, and she to him. The Prince called Joan 'my dearest and truest sweetheart' and on a number of occasions they were seen happily holding hands together, lost in a world of their own.

The Prince's sister Isabella would have understood. Ten years earlier, in 1351, when she was nineteen, Edward III had announced her marriage to Bérard d'Albret, son of the king's chief lieutenant in Gascony. There were good political reasons for the match, Edward speaking of his desire 'to kindle in the lord of Albret and his descendants a closer attachment to our ruling house and to bind them more intimately to us'. Five ships gathered in the Thames to transport her to Bordeaux. The bride's trousseau included robes of cloth of gold and Indian silk, embroidered in silver and gold. But perhaps remembering her sister Joan's ill-fated trip three years earlier, or not wishing to marry beneath her rank, at the water's edge 'our very dear eldest daughter' changed her mind and returned home. The king was not offended by Isabella's waywardness, and continued to shower her with gifts. The chronicler Ranulph Higden stated forthrightly that 'only for love did she wish to be betrothed'. And, as we will see, Isabella would in due course marry for love.

In the summer of 1361 the Black Prince ordered his tailor to make new clothes for himself, Joan and her daughters. No expense was to be spared: the material to be bought included blue and green cloth, russet, taffeta, ermine, gold ribbon and fur. He also paid out more than £3,000 for jewels to adorn these outfits, including nearly 9,000 pearls. A beautiful red wedding dress was made for his bride in cloth of gold (threads of gold woven on a web of silk), decorated with birds; Joan reciprocated by commissioning a lavish wedding bed of red velvet, emblazoned with the Prince's ostrich feathers – in silver – and leopards' heads, again in gold.

There was hope for the future, but trepidation too. Medieval society was fascinated by prophecies and portents, although they could be twisted and distorted to suit all manner of purposes. In a prophecy written shortly after Edward III's accession, the king was likened to a boar, the animal that had represented King Arthur himself. He would be renowned for his 'fierceness and nobility'. 'Spain would tremble,' the prophecy said, and Edward did indeed defeat the Castilian fleet off Winchelsea in 1350. The boar would 'sharpen his teeth on the gates of Paris'; the king's army had reached the suburbs of the French capital in 1360. But the king after Edward III was foretold to be a lamb. There would be a civil war, and the lamb would lose the greater part of his kingdom to 'a hideous wolf'. It was hard to imagine the Black Prince as a lamb. To some Englishmen, this suggested that he would not inherit. There would be some catastrophe, and he would die before his father. His successor – whoever he might be – would be the lamb.

Jean Froissart visited Berkhamsted shortly after the Black Prince's marriage. Seated on a bench in the hall, he overheard Sir Bartholomew Burghersh saying to one of Joan's ladies-in-waiting that 'there was a book called *The Brut* [the twelfth-century *Roman de Brut*], which many say contains the Prophecies of Merlin. According to its contents the Prince will never inherit the crown of England.' But a rival set of predictions sprang up, dating from the early 1360s; the so-called Bridlington Prophecies of John Erghome, in which the Prince not only succeeded to the throne but renewed the war with France and conquered the whole of Scotland as well. Erghome, a canon at the Augustinian priory of Bridlington, had no truck with lambs: he recast the Prince as a fighting cockerel, destined to reclaim the inheritance of his father. 'The kingdom of France will go over to the cockerel,' Erghome intoned, 'who will be called King Edward, like his father.'

Putting such divinations to one side, the new couple celebrated Christmas together at Berkhamsted Castle, where they were joined by the king and queen. In honour of the occasion, the Prince decided on the spur of the moment to deck out his servants in fresh liveries for the New Year, instructing his receiver in London, Peter Lacy, 'to arrange somehow or other to send to Berkhamsted enough cloth for the making of it all'. The order was given on 28 December, so one can only hope that Lacy was paid good overtime rates. Joan brought considerable landed wealth of her own to the marriage and also a taste for luxury and extravagance to match her husband's. Early in 1362 the Prince paid £200 for a single set of jewelled buttons for his wife and a further £200 on two rubies, four brooches and a ring with four diamonds.

†

In Gascony, Sir John Chandos, acting as Edward III's lieutenant in the region, was supervising the surrender of the towns and lands conceded at Brétigny to the English regime. The task called on much of the tact and diplomacy that Chandos was famed for. The Rouergue (in the eastern part of an expanded Aquitaine), made clear that 'it was reluctant to become English'; Chandos wisely appointed a Gascon noble as seneschal (steward) to appease local discontent. The town of Rodez demanded that it retain its right of appeal to the king of France; at Cahors, in Quercy, the city representatives wept and lamented that they had been abandoned to strangers. The Atlantic port of La Rochelle put up the strongest resistance to the change-over. In the end, they reluctantly conceded that 'they would obey the English, but remain French in their hearts'.

On 19 July 1362 preparations were far enough advanced for King Edward to formally invest his son and heir as prince of Aquitaine in a ceremony at Westminster Abbey, attended by the most important noblemen and clergy of the realm. The Prince, in full armour, knelt and did homage to his father. The grant recorded Edward's gratitude for his son's victory at Poitiers — the principality was to be his reward:

> We, intending by liberal recompense to honour you, who lately, in the parts of Gascony, where the storms of war did rage, for our sake did not refuse the summer dust and sweat of campaign, and the labour of battle, and under the name and title of lieutenant supported the burden of our cares... convey to you the principality, lands and province of Aquitaine.

The Black Prince began to make preparations for the voyage to Gascony. His and his wife's taste for luxury dictated one of his first actions, on 1 September 1362: arranging for a goldsmith to accompany them to Bordeaux, where he was to be provided with a house and living expenses, in order to 'serve the prince and princess before all others in all matters concerning his craft, for reasonable payment'. Two embroiderers were also engaged, on similar terms.

However, it was not all about outward show. That summer, the Prince had also purchased three psalters from the estate of

Humphrey de Bohun, earl of Hereford. These were devotional
works containing the Book of Psalms, a liturgical calendar and a
litany of the saints. They were not works for display in the chapel.
They were practical and designed for personal use.

The largest of the psalters was attractively decorated. The first
letter of each psalm had been enlarged and illuminated, one showing Humphrey de Bohun himself, in the arms of his guardian angel.
And the margins of the work abounded in images: minstrels, pet
animals, a peasant sowing seeds and a friar praying: drawing the
reader's attention to passages of value. On one of the pages, three
marginal portraits stood out from the rest, adorning a large initial
'D' (of 'Domine'). The first two depicted a seated ruler of France
(probably the last Capetian, Charles IV) handing a sword to a king
of England, mounted on a lion (Edward III). The third showed King
John II, holding his sword out hilt first, in a gesture of surrender at
Poitiers.

It is unclear whether the Black Prince commissioned these
decorations, as a mark of ownership, or whether de Bohun's inclus-
ion of them attracted his interest. But their applicability could not
have been more striking. They drew the reader's attention to the
beginning of Psalm 101. In it, David — about to take charge of the
kingdom of Israel — made a solemn vow to God that he would
conduct himself carefully and conscientiously, make his court a
model of good government, maintain virtue and piety and above
all justice and order. He would use his power to chastise evil-doers
and to reward those who did well. Through this devotional text,
we glimpse the Prince in a different guise, reflecting upon the position of responsibility bestowed upon him. As the Chandos Herald
said: 'Loyalty, noble deeds, valour and goodness guided him, for he
wished all his life to maintain justice and right.'

That autumn the Prince and his wife left London for Cornwall,
staying at the great castle of Restormel. Their plans to sail for the
duchy were delayed and preparations were only completed in the
summer of 1363. The Prince aimed to recruit a substantial retinue

to accompany him to his new French principality, consisting of 60 knights, 250 men-at-arms and 320 archers. Many of these soldiers were from Cheshire, while others enlisted from the duchy of Cornwall.

The Prince's new enterprise caught the popular imagination, and men wanted to join him on the strength of it. John Jodrell, a younger son of a Cheshire family, had served on the Prince's first great raid of 1355 and signed up for the Poitiers campaign the following year. He shared in the spoils of battle, winning a silver salt-cellar belonging to King John, and when the Prince crossed to Gascony in 1363 Jodrell travelled with him and left England for good, settling in Poitou and building up properties and rents in service to the English cause in the duchy.

In 1363 the Prince granted annuities to many of those willing to accompany him to Aquitaine. As he built up his military retinue once more, he turned a blind eye to previous crimes and misdemeanours. The Cheshire knight Robert Mascy received a pardon for abducting the daughter of John Snelson, 'because he is in our service'. And the humblest of his soldiers were not forgotten. Roger Swetenham, John Eton and Roger Page, enlisted archers, were promised grants of money, land and minor offices in Gascony. Military service was a point of access to the Prince's largesse and men pleaded for grants or pardons for crimes on the basis of it.

On 9 June the Prince and princess — accompanied by the earl of Warwick and a considerable retinue — finally set sail from Plymouth. They landed at Lormont, near Bordeaux, on 29 June. From the outset, the Black Prince understood the power of personal lordship, and he was always willing to show himself to his subjects. He held a series of ceremonies, beginning at Bordeaux and then criss-crossing the whole of Aquitaine.

On 9 July 1363, in the cathedral of Saint-André, the Mayor of Bordeaux, surrounded by civic dignitaries and local lords, read out the Prince's letters of commission. Then homage was paid to the new ruler. Each lord came and knelt before the Prince, without belt or cap, to take the oath of fealty for all his lands and goods, and, kissing the Bible, promised to do all that a liege vassal should for his 'true lord.' To this the Black Prince responded by kissing his vassal on the forehead and receiving his homage, 'saving the rights of our Lord the King'. The first to step forward was the powerful Arnaud Amanieu, Lord of Albret, followed by nineteen other Gascon nobles. Nearly a week later, the Prince was again at the cathedral, to receive the homage of the mayor and representatives from all the local towns.

The ceremonies continued. At the beginning of August the Prince left the Gascon capital and set out on a progress through his new domain, visiting Bergerac, where the bishop of Sarlat, Austence de Sainte-Colombe, did homage to him. From 10 to 15 August he was at Périgueux, where a deputation from Quercy and the Rouergue came to meet him. Three days later he was at Angoulême; the castle there would become one of his favourite residences. On 23 August he reached Cognac, which later became his administrative headquarters, and then he continued into the Saintonge. In September and October he was at Poitiers.

The Prince was accompanied by his wife, and she created a stir of her own. Joan of Kent set a new fashion in Gascon society, and many women followed her style of tight-fitting dresses, low-cut necklines, precious stones and pearls in the hair and lavish use of silk and ermine. It was deliberately daring, modelled on the *bonnes amies* of the Free Companies of Languedoc, beautiful female companions who wore rich and appealing clothes and also exhibited a 'scurrilous wantonness'. Joan had the class and style to pull this off, for she instinctively knew how to be provocative without crossing a line, to win attention without compromising the values of her social class.

However, it was all too much for one rather staid aristocrat. Rival Breton delegations had arrived at Poitiers in November 1363, one representing the party of Charles of Blois, the other of John de Montfort. After much delay, they were to put their seals to a truce agreed between the two sides (first brokered on 24 July at Landes d'Evran), which would suspend hostilities in the War of the Breton Succession until the following March, and they brought their wives with them. (The agreement was authenticated in front of the Prince on 26 November.) When one of these lords, Jean de Beaumanoir, heading the faction of Charles of Blois, was teased about his wife's 'overly sober' dress sense, he replied indignantly:

> I do not want my wife abandoning the clothes of honest women and adopting the fashions of the mistresses of the Free Companies, for it is they who have introduced this taste for luxurious trimmings and low-cut bodices. As for copying these creatures, I am disgusted by all those who follow such a bad example – particularly the Princess of Wales.

In December the Prince and his entourage left for Agen, intending to spend Christmas there. The winter of 1363–4 was the coldest in living memory, and one of the longest. The Seine was frozen over from Christmas to February; the Rhine from January to March; carts were driven across the Meuse and, further south, even across the Rhône. In Languedoc, a horse plodded up to an inn at Carcassonne with its rider frozen dead in the saddle; fortresses were suddenly stripped of half their defences as moats solidified and brigands advanced over the ice. Wine froze so hard in its pots that it had to be broken and sold in chunks, to be melted over a fire. Seeing the bishop of Sarlat shivering uncontrollably at a banquet, the Black Prince sat down next to him and wrapped him in his own cloak. 'Take it,' he said to the bishop, 'it is a gift.'

On 12 January 1364, Gaston Fébus, count of Foix, arrived at Agen to do homage, but only for some of his lands. The count's oddly assorted territories illustrated both the confusions of feudal geography and the opportunities it offered for political intrigue and opportunism. Fébus owed homage to the king of France for the county of Foix and its dependencies, to the king of Aragon for his fiefs in Roussillon and Castillon, and to the prince of Aquitaine for Marsan and Gabardan. The homage of the vicomté of Béarn was a

matter of contention. Fébus asked that this lordship be excluded —
and for the moment the matter was allowed to drop.

At a feast held in his honour, Fébus regaled his audience with
tales of the Prussian crusade, the rescue of the dauphin's family at
Meaux and his subsequent exploits in Norway and Sweden, where
he had gone reindeer hunting. But Fébus had also fought a battle at
Launac (north-west of Toulouse) on 5 December 1362, where he had
defeated the forces of the count of Armagnac in the long-running
feud between the two men. Armagnac and his leading followers,
including the lord of Albret, were captured and held for ransom.
Albret was required to pay 100,000 florins (around £15,000) for his
release. Armagnac was still negotiating his freedom — his ransom
was set at 300,000 florins.

The ransom Fébus had demanded for Armagnac was very
high — it was clearly intended to bankrupt the count. Joan of Kent,
who was well aware that her husband wanted to bind Armagnac
more firmly to his cause, decided that she would try to reduce the
ransom sum. To that end — and with the Prince's full approval —
she began flirting with Fébus. Jean Froissart, who was present at the
banquet, allows us to glimpse what followed.

Joan began by complimenting their guest on his chivalry
towards damsels in distress. Then she asked for a favour for herself.
Fébus, courteous but cautious, asked what this favour might be.
When Armagnac's name was mentioned he stiffened and said the
ransom terms could not be altered. Joan leaned right across the table
and asked for a reduction nonetheless. Fébus glanced at the Prince
and saw him smiling. Suddenly, the tension broke: the redoubtable
huntsman had been cornered and Fébus burst out laughing. Ten
thousand florins were taken off the ransom. When the reduction
reached 60,000 florins Joan and her husband exchanged glances.
Then the Black Prince addressed the assembly, praised Fébus's
generosity and announced that, in the matter of the ransom,
a truce was being called — he did, after all, deserve some reward
for his victory.

'The feasts, the honours, the processions, the stays, the comings and goings,' Froissart wrote. 'In the beginning all loved and honoured the Prince as their lord, and said that his kingdom was the greatest in the world.' This was more than just a charm offensive on the part of the Prince. At a time when the ritual and etiquette of the princely court was growing in importance, people wanted to be touched by something uplifting. After the horror of war and pestilence, there was a yearning for beauty and splendour. The Black Prince was able to make the ordinary visitor to his court feel special. By February 1364 the Prince had received the homage of 1,047 named individuals and towns within Aquitaine.

'Every day, there were more than eighty knights at his table, and four times as many squires,' the Chandos Herald recalled. 'They jousted and held revels at Angoulême and Bordeaux. All the nobles were there, joyful and happy, generous and honourable – and all his subjects loved him well, because he did so much good for them.' Another chronicler wrote that 'the lords of Gascony were received right joyously, and the Prince acquitted himself so nobly amongst them that every man was well content.' It was a recurring comment: 'The Prince lovingly received them, as he could right well do... There was no ruler in his time that could show more honour than he.' He had the dignified, warm friendliness of a man of proven courage and undisputed rank. And then there was his renowned largesse, the bestowal of money and other gifts. As for the entertainment his subjects received at his court, Jean Froissart was moved to write: 'The state of the Prince and Princess was so great that in all of Christendom there was none like it.'

At these great feasts mutton and veal would be served, venison, goose and rabbit, suckling pig, lampreys and oysters. Enormous tapestries were brought out and displayed: richly embroidered lengths of cloth that covered all the walls of the banqueting chamber, eight pieces for the sides and an ornate composition to hang behind the Prince. The tapestries were of many colours, but the Prince's favourite was black with silver ostrich plumes. Nearly all of them were decorated with a design of swans with women's heads.

There were matters of policy to address, and also matters of state. The Black Prince issued new coins in his own name – a source of profit and prestige but also a commitment to an environment where trade could flourish. In 1364 a large new gold coin was struck, the *pavillon,* showing the Prince standing under a Gothic canopy, wearing a crown of roses, carrying a sword in his right hand and with two leopards at his feet. Two ostrich feathers were placed on either side and the reverse of the coin displayed a cross with fleur-de-lys and leopards and a motto, from Psalm 28: 'The Lord is my strength and shield and my heart hath trusted in him.' The Prince did not degrade the metal content of the coinage and he discussed with the Gascon towns 'what type of money and what value people wanted'. But his investigation of his financial rights and fresh sources of income would continue unabated.

The Black Prince consulted regularly with his subjects. The town of Millau in Rouergue sent delegates to the Prince, at Poitiers, to swear homage to him in September 1363, and subsequently they kept in touch with him about all matters of importance. The surviving municipal accounts open a window on the Prince's dealings with the town. In January 1364 Millau sent two representatives to him to discuss the new coinage. Then, in October, the Black Prince was told about depredations committed by mercenary soldiers living off the land and the town asked for a remission from the new tax being levied – the *fouage,* or hearth tax. The Black Prince, in turn, kept in close touch with Millau through his officers, the constable of Aquitaine, Sir John Chandos and the seneschal of the Rouergue, Sir Thomas Wettenhall.

At the beginning of 1365, Joan gave birth to a son, named Edward after his father and grandfather. The anonymous chronicler of Canterbury recorded: 'On 27 January, the first-born son of the Prince of Aquitaine was born at the castle of Angoulême – an occasion for great joy there.' Joan herself wrote to the mayor of London on 4 February: 'Dear and well-beloved, for as much as we know that you earnestly desire to hear good tidings of us and our estate, be pleased to know that on Monday last [27 January] we were safely delivered of a son, for which God be thanked in all his might.'

Celebration of a birth normally took place after the 'churching' (the religious ritual of purification) of the mother, which lasted forty days, but the Black Prince's joy was so great, and his plans so splendid, that in addition a great tournament was held on its three-month anniversary, on 27 April. The event was on a scale not seen before: 154 lords and 706 knights were invited, and there were 18,000 horses to be stabled, all at the Prince's expense. The tourneys, jousting and other entertainments lasted for ten days – the cost of the candles alone was over £400.

On 27 June 1365 the Black Prince wrote to his seneschal of the Agenais about the conditions of lawlessness that prevailed in some parts of Aquitaine. He told him that he wished to stop the injustices that arose from feuding and 'restore peace and proper observance of the law within his lands'. In pursuit of that aim, he had heard the appeal of the townspeople of Agen, claiming that Arnaud de Durfort, lord of Clermont, had occupied lands rightfully belonging to them. The Prince was retaining Durfort in his service and the Gascon nobleman had already conducted a number of diplomatic missions on his behalf. But a full investigation was carried out, and at its conclusion the disputed properties were restored to Agen.

The Prince's commitment to justice and fairness in his governance of Aquitaine was also apparent in the case of the seizure of the castle of Juliac by Louis de Malval, seneschal of the Limousin. The Black Prince intervened on behalf of the castle's occupant, Étienne de Montroux, and ordered Malval to relinquish the fortress. Likewise, when the Benedictine abbey of Saint-Maixent, 15 miles (25km) north-east of Niort, petitioned him over mistreatment by his officers, the Prince commanded his seneschal, Sir William Felton, to thoroughly investigate the matter. The complaint was found to be justified and proper restitution made to the abbey. When reports reached him that the aged Louis, vicomte of Thouars, was no longer capable of holding office, the Prince instructed Felton to pay the vicomte a visit and find out how he was. Sir William reported back that the vicomte was still mentally alert but physically frail. The Black Prince's response was to observe — with a mixture of humour and compassion — that the vicomte probably needed help with the military responsibilities of his post. He therefore kept him in office and appointed his son Aymery as his deputy, to assist him in the running of the castle.

When the Prince met with the three estates, the representative body of Aquitaine, at Périgueux in September 1365 he used it as an opportunity to raise money but also to redress grievances through direct contact with his subjects. He established a dialogue with them, showing himself flexible and willing to listen to what they had to say. And when they complained about lawlessness or intimidation in his lands, he acted on it.

The inhabitants of the region around Mareuil, 25 miles (40km) south-east of Angoulême, reported that the castle there had fallen into the hands of brigands, who were robbing merchants and plundering the countryside. The Prince told Sir William Felton to take some troops and clear them out. But he also looked for a long-term solution, confiscating the castle and lordship from its owner, Jean de Rougemont, who had failed to protect the local population, and instead granting it to Amaury, lord of Craon, on condition that he upheld the peace. The citizens of Mareuil recalled with gratitude that in the time of the Prince and his seneschal, 'there was no one, however powerful, who dared disobey them'.

Such actions won the Prince genuine respect within Aquitaine. And there was more good news for the royal family back in England, where on 27 July 1365 the Black Prince's sister Isabella married the French knight Enguerrand de Coucy (one of the hostages for the Brétigny agreement) at Windsor Castle. Edward III granted her a dowry worth £4,000 a year and gave Coucy his freedom.

In the words of the Chandos Herald: 'The Prince reigned in Gascony in joy, in peace and in pleasure, for all the barons came to do him homage – and as a man, they held him in great esteem, as a good lord, loyal and wise.' The truth was not quite so simple, for clouds were beginning to gather on the horizon.

†

France had a new ruler. With his ransom in arrears and one of his sons, Louis, duke of Anjou (held as hostage for the repayment), absconding, John II felt his honour had been compromised and voluntarily returned to captivity. He was back in London in January 1364, but in March he fell ill, and died a month later. He was succeeded by his eldest son, who became Charles V. The physically weak and sickly dauphin would prove to be a stronger and more effective ruler than his father; he immediately began pressing the English over the renunciation clause outstanding from Brétigny. A delegation was sent to the Black Prince in November 1364, but all he was able to do was refer the matter back to his father.

Until the treaty of Brétigny was fully confirmed the principality of Aquitaine remained vulnerable. It was supposed to be financially self-supporting, but the Prince's extravagant spending was putting that arrangement under strain. And Gaston Fébus still refused to do homage for Béarn. He sent a succession of excuses in letters that were full of bonhomie, complimenting Sir John Chandos on his hunting dogs or recommending one of the composers at his court. However, his failure to fulfil his obligation as the Prince's vassal was even raised in a meeting of the Gascon general assembly, the estates.

The Black Prince, anticipating trouble, had investigated his legal rights thoroughly. He requested that a detailed search be carried out in the records of the English treasury. On 10 May 1365 his father informed him that 'he had undertaken a full examination of all the letters and memoranda', and on the basis of this 'Count Gaston is obliged to render homage to us for Béarn'. On 8 August 1365 the Prince wrote Fébus a sharp letter:

First you requested a safe-conduct from us, so that 200 of your household men could accompany you. When this was drawn up, you complained that you had injured your leg. One of our servants then visited you. He is a doctor – and he has told us that you are fit enough to travel. We expect you to come before the end of the month, without further delay.

Fébus, however, still refused to appear.

And then there was the count of Armagnac, who had secured his release in the spring of 1365. Armagnac expressed his gratitude for the Black Prince's help in the payment of his ransom, but was then antagonized by the Prince's seneschal in the Rouergue. Sir John Chandos had wisely appointed the Gascon, Amanieu du Fossat, to this sensitive position. The Prince had confirmed Chandos's appointment, and du Fossat had conducted matters with a light touch, preferring the path of negotiation to confrontation. But when a dispute broke out between the seneschal and the town of Agen, in November 1364, the Prince had replaced him with Sir Thomas Wettenhall. This proved to be a serious mistake, for the vigorous and energetic Sir Thomas, a tough Cheshire soldier, had the political sensitivity of a Rottweiler; even Pope Urban V petitioned the Prince complaining of his exactions. Wettenhall put up his master's coat of arms in stone at the gates of Rodez – the entry point to Armagnac's lordship – and plastered it all over the town. Armagnac was incensed.

Armagnac came to perform homage to the Prince on 2 April 1365, but refused to do so until Wettenhall removed the offending coat of arms; the homage was postponed until 12 July. The count complained that the coat of arms still had not been removed and added that his homage was now conditional on a full inquiry into his rights in the Rouergue. The Prince lost his temper: 'By God's cap, Armagnac,' he roared, 'I shall bake you such a pie that you will be unable to break the crust.' The terrified clerks of Bordeaux cathedral recorded this oath verbatim. When Charles V heard about this incident, he commiserated with Armagnac in a letter of 21 July. He expressed his high regard for the count, and his wish to always hear his news, before concluding: 'I hope that, over time, you will be able to come more fully into our service.' In the short term, matters with Armagnac were smoothed over and the act of homage completed. But the Prince's violent outburst was not forgotten.

chapter eight

THE SPANISH
ADVENTURE

Now I have a fine story to tell. And pity, love and justice are all part of it, as you will hear… King Pedro was advised to appeal to Edward III's son, the Prince of Aquitaine – a worthy man, bold, and with such a force of men-at-arms at his side no living man could do him wrong unless God willed it. If this Prince was agreeable to help [his enterprise] Spain would surely be once more restored to him… So Pedro wrote and sealed a letter at once, begging the Prince, for God's sake, out of love, friendship, alliance and ties of blood and justice, a noble, valiant and honourable champion, to listen to his plea and assist his righteous cause.

This was how the Chandos Herald, a witness to these events, opened his account of the Spanish adventure. The Black Prince met Pedro of Castile outside Bayonne, in the far south of Gascony, on 1 August 1366. Pedro was tall, well-built, blue-eyed and fair-haired, with strongly etched features and great vitality. He came with his queen and three daughters in two merchant galleys. He had been flung out of his realm by his bastard brother Enrique, had lost most of his treasure in the process and arrived in Gascony with only a small entourage and a few personal possessions. Despondent and bitter, he said that he had been betrayed by those who should have been loyal to him and that he had suffered a terrible injustice. Pedro asked the Prince to have pity on him and his family and help him recover his realm.

Pedro was thirty-two years old. He had been on the throne since the age of sixteen, succeeding his father Alfonso XI, a great warrior-king who had died when his army was struck by the plague during the siege of Gibraltar in 1350. He was the sole offspring of a loveless royal marriage between Alfonso and his queen, Maria of Portugal, whom the Castilian monarch subsequently shunned in favour of his mistress, Leonore de Guzman, who produced a whole brood of children. These brothers and sisters of the half-blood were showered with honours, love and affection; Pedro grew up in isolation from the royal court, and his own childhood was troubled and often dangerous.

Pedro harboured a deep resentment towards his father for the way he had flung him aside and indulged his half-brothers, favouring his bastard offspring over the legitimate line of succession. That resentment became all-consuming. His terrible rivalry with Enrique, the head of that family, who was rewarded by Alfonso with the aristocratic title of count of Trastamara, would dominate his life and his reign. On succeeding to the throne, he rejected his father's legacy and turned away from his policies, replacing them with their mirror opposites. He was almost pathologically suspicious, sensing treachery and betrayal everywhere.

To some extent this was understandable. The first six years of his rule were dominated by faction-fighting and intrigue, and it was only from 1356 that Pedro was able to stamp his authority on Castile. The Iberian Peninsula in the fourteenth century consisted of five kingdoms: Navarre, Portugal, Castile, Aragon and the Muslim emirate of Granada. Pedro rejected Alfonso's dream of forging a crusading coalition of the Spanish Christian states and conquering the Muslim south. Instead, he came to an agreement with Granada, and began a long war with neighbouring Aragon, inspired in part by the actions of Peter IV, ruler of that country, in sheltering his hated half-brother Enrique.

More surprisingly, Pedro also contemplated making an alliance with England. England and Castile had drawn closer together in

the last years of his father's rule. The visit of Henry of Grosmont
to the country in 1343 had left a strong and positive impression.
Grosmont had been on a diplomatic mission and, after it had
been concluded, he chose to stay on to participate in the siege of
Algeciras, alongside Alfonso's warriors and members of his chivalric fraternity, the Order of the Sash. A momentum was starting
to build — and if the Black Prince's sister Joan had safely reached
Castile on her ill-fated voyage in the summer of 1348, Pedro would
have become his brother-in-law.

In keeping with his turning his back on his father's approach,
when Pedro came to the throne he at first rejected this policy,
turning instead towards France, and marrying the French king's
niece, Blanche of Bourbon. But as the decade advanced, he began
to view England in a more positive light. From Edward III's point of
view, an alliance with Castile was enormously attractive. It was the
largest and most powerful state in the Iberian Peninsula, and it had
a very strong navy. Indeed, the long sea battle off Winchelsea in 1350
had been fought against a combined Genoese and Castilian fleet.
The English king wanted to take these ships out of the equation,
and he knew that a treaty with Castile would buttress English-held
Gascony against the ambitions of France.

In the late 1350s negotiations between the two countries proceeded apace and the Black Prince was fully involved. On 22 June
1362, shortly before the Prince was granted Aquitaine, an Anglo-
Castilian alliance was formally signed at St Paul's Cathedral in
London. For Pedro, the agreement represented a counterweight to
French support for his enemy, Peter of Aragon, and his rival for the
Castilian throne, Enrique of Trastamara. In return for English support, he was prepared to jettison the alliance with France. When the
treaty was completed the Prince had copies made for his records.

The document contained a crucial clause specifying that English
troops could be used against a French invader within Castile. This
showed the limitations of the treaty of Brétigny, whose final confirmation depended on fulfilling the renunciation clause, whereby

Edward III disbanded all remaining English garrisons in Brittany and Normandy. In the interim, England and France avoided direct hostilities, but jockeyed for political influence, first in Brittany and then in Castile. And a considerable number of their soldiers, largely drawn from the Free Companies, would be involved in both theatres of war, notably at Auray in Brittany on 29 September 1364.

This was war by proxy, for the duchy of Brittany was facing a succession dispute and civil war between rival factions, those of Charles of Blois and John de Montfort. Charles V of France supported Charles of Blois's candidacy while Edward III and the Black Prince favoured de Montfort's. At Brétigny, France and England paid lip-service to the idea of a peaceful and fair resolution of the dispute; in reality, both sides were looking to gain a foothold within the duchy. Auray was an emphatic victory for de Montfort in which his rival, Charles of Blois, was killed and the Breton succession dispute ended in his favour.

English troops helped to create John de Monfort duke of Brittany. At Auray, his army was commanded by Sir John Chandos and Sir Hugh Calveley. Chandos, a close friend and companion of the Prince and constable of Gascony, was also garrison commander at Saint-Sauveur-le-Vicomte in the Cotentin and carried considerable authority with the Free Companies in that region. His second in command, Calveley, was one of them. A tough, resourceful Cheshireman, Calveley was a veteran of the Breton wars, had participated in the famous Combat of the Thirty in 1351, and five years later was captain of a contingent of English archers at Poitiers. A large man of great personal strength and courage, he was an able fighter who commanded considerable loyalty from his men. After Brétigny he operated as a soldier of fortune on his own account, with a company of devoted English and Breton followers.

The Black Prince capitalized on the victory at Auray. De Montfort had stayed at his court and become a friend. The two men signed a treaty of mutual co-operation on 7 September 1365 and the agreement was cemented by a marriage alliance on 22 March 1366 between the new Breton duke and the Prince's stepdaughter, Joan Holland. When there was personal rapport, the Prince found it easy to create useful diplomatic alliances.

Now Spain was to be the new battleground, with both England and France jockeying for influence in Castile, Charles V favouring Enrique's claim (he had assisted Enrique's invasion of Castile in the spring of 1366) and Edward III supporting the rights of Pedro. Enrique was living in exile in neighbouring Aragon, with the support of that country's ruler, Peter IV. But Charles brought the Free Companies behind Enrique's cause, paying their wages and providing them with a redoubtable leader, Bertrand du Guesclin; their intervention proved decisive. Pedro was unable to counter these tough mercenaries, and fled in disarray, first to Portugal and then to Gascony, where he sought the protection of the Black Prince.

Under the terms of the Anglo-Castilian treaty, agreed four years earlier, Pedro of Castile was entitled to ask for English help if threatened by invasion. The offer of assistance was made with the expectation that Pedro would remain on the throne, with a regular Castilian army under his command and the resources of the royal treasury at his disposal. Edward III and the Black Prince would then provide him with reinforcements drawn from the English captains of the Free Companies and their own regular troops. These would be paid for by the Castilian king.

However, the invasion of Enrique of Trastamara had been too fast and too effective for Pedro to organize a coherent defence. He had arrived in Gascony with only a handful of retainers and few personal possessions, lacking soldiers of his own or the means to pay them. If he was to be restored to the throne, England would have to mobilize an entire army to help him regain it, and meet the costs of its recruitment on a credit arrangement with Pedro. There would be enormous risks in such an undertaking: English casualties on campaign and in battle would be far higher, while the recovery of the money would be dependent on defeating Enrique, and on Pedro of Castile then honouring his debts.

The Black Prince would bear the brunt of these risks, for an invasion of Castile would have to be organized from Gascony. The Prince would need to raise a force from his own personal retinue, those English administrators and soldiers serving in the principality of Aquitaine, Gascon lords and their retainers and captains of the Free Companies. This would be the core of his army, with further troops brought over from England to reinforce it. Initially, the Prince would have to meet its costs from Aquitaine's treasury and his own coffers, and these fiscal burdens would be substantial.

Alongside these burdens, the military operation would pose difficult diplomatic challenges. The army would need to cross the Pyrenees through the pass of Roncesvalles, which was under the control of Charles of Navarre. So Navarre would need to be brought into any treaty with Pedro of Castile, and his own support secured. This would involve further financial inducements, which would again have to be met by the Prince in the first instance. And the entire Castilian venture would thereby become dependent on Charles of Navarre, a notoriously slippery political operator, keeping his word.

The chronicler Jean Froissart was in Gascony at the time. He believed that the Black Prince immediately rushed to help Pedro, as if he saw himself as a hero fulfilling a chivalric quest, and sought the assent of his father merely as an afterthought. Froissart related how the Prince, 'of noble and gallant disposition, highly regarded throughout the world and much loved by his soldiers', took pity on the unfortunate exiled king and felt bound to assist Pedro because of the treaty of friendship between their two realms. The Prince was at the height of his martial power and the enterprise had apparently caught his imagination. As the chronicler observed: 'He had come to believe that if he decided to put Pedro back on the throne, there was no one alive who could stop him.'

Froissart revealed that many of the Prince's council were opposed to his helping Pedro. They argued that the principality of Aquitaine was at peace, and there was much benefit in being content with what one had rather than embarking upon a risky intervention in Spain. Moreover, Pedro was unstable and cruel, a vindictive tyrant who had brought the judgement of God upon him for his wicked actions. The Prince overrode such objections, declaring to his advisers:

I will tell you the reasons that convince me to offer him assistance. I do not think it either decent or proper that a bastard should possess a kingdom as an inheritance, nor drive out of his realm his own brother, heir to the country by lawful marriage, and no king, or king's son, ought ever to allow it, as it is prejudicial to all notions of royal dignity. And in addition to this, my lord and father and Pedro of Castile have for a number of years been allies, bound together by treaty, by which we are obliged to aid and assist him should he require it.

Froissart continued:

This was the explanation that the Prince offered for his action, that he had felt compelled to reach out to the king of Castile in his distress — and he made this clear to his council. And after this declaration, no one could make him change his mind in the slightest, but instead his determination [to follow this course] grew stronger every day.

For the chronicler, the Prince's greatness had turned to grandiosity, and he had lost touch with reality. He enlarged on this:

When it was publicly known that the intention of the Prince was to put Pedro back on the throne, it was a matter of great wonder to many, and a considerable talking point. Some said that pity and justice had moved him to help Pedro recover his inheritance, for it was highly unbecoming for a bastard to hold a kingdom, or bear the name of a king. But others said that the Prince was making this expedition through pride and presumption, and that he was jealous of the prestige that Bertrand du

Guesclin had gained in helping to put Enrique [of Trastamara] on the throne. And thus were many knights and squires divided in their opinions.

Froissart was there at the time and his testimony carries real conviction as a result. His account was enormously influential, and modern histories have largely followed his view.

As the campaign had such powerful and far-reaching consequences for the Prince and the region that he governed, it marked a pivotal point in his story. Froissart was relaying what became, and would remain, the English government's official position, in which Edward III recognized Pedro's rightful claim and fulfilled the terms of his treaty with him. However, the chronicler almost certainly had informants within the Prince's council and was able to speak to others at the Gascon court. And from these conversations, he made a judgement on the Prince's motivation – one that was highly critical.

Nevertheless, Froissart's assessment needs to be treated with caution. For despite the insinuations of the chronicler, the Prince did not make an immediate response to the Castilian king. Indeed, the time span covered by Froissart, from the arrival of Pedro in Gascony on 1 August 1366 to the treaty drawn up between him and the Prince on 23 September, was around seven weeks. To understand what really happened in that crucial period, we need to look more closely at Pedro's character and the course of the negotiations between the two men.

†

Pedro would become known to posterity as 'the Cruel', although the epithet has to be placed firmly in the context of Spanish power politics. Pedro's great rival Peter IV of Aragon could be harsh and even sadistic. He forced the rebel leaders of Valencia to drink the molten metal of the bell they had rung to summon their assemblies, and subsequently Peter described their punishment as 'a just thing', and 'well-deserved', and almost boasted about its ingenuity. A pitiless gaoler, he incarcerated his own nephew, James IV, pretender to the annexed kingdom of Majorca, in an iron cage, and described in meticulous detail the refinements of his imprisonment and measures taken to prevent his escape. But although the ruler of Aragon was subject to outbursts of occasional violence, his decisions were seldom dictated by rage, but were taken after deliberation with his councillors and for sound political reasons.

Peter IV's kingship had its more attractive features. He was well read, a poet and orator, a linguist and lover of ceremony, and an impassioned student of history and chivalry. He was generally well liked by his subjects and concerned to protect their interests. Pedro of Castile, in contrast, was unstable and vindictive. One ghastly example was Pedro's murder of his half-brother Fadrique (Enrique of Trastamara's twin) – a crazed act that undermined his own interests. During the opening years of Pedro's reign, Fadrique had been a leading member of the aristocratic opposition. However, at the beginning of 1356 he deserted his former allies, including his brother Enrique, and made his peace with the king.

The Castilian monarch had gained a most useful ally – a man who could considerably strengthen his cause. And in May 1358 Fadrique rode into Seville in triumph, having just won the town of Jumilla from the Aragonese. Suspecting nothing, he accepted Pedro's invitation to dine with him in the Alcázar. Pedro welcomed Fadrique with the utmost affability, then he ordered his guards to lock the doors behind him and chased his terrified guest through the royal apartments, hacking and bludgeoning him to death. After the killing, he ordered a banquet to be served in the same room as the dismembered corpse, which remained on the floor throughout the entire meal.

Gutier de Toledo was another victim of the Castilian king's paranoia and rage. He was a loyal servant of Pedro, his chief military adviser, captain of the royal bodyguard and a skilled soldier and diplomat. He had fought for his master in the Aragonese war, in which he ably defended Castile's eastern frontier. Then Pedro suddenly took it into his head – on unlikely rumour and hearsay – that Gutier was in league with the enemy. Without giving him the benefit of the doubt, or even a chance to explain himself, he lured his minister into a trap and ordered him to be killed. Shortly before his execution, Gutier de Toledo wrote a remarkably prescient letter to the king:

> My lord, I kiss your hand and take leave of you. I now jour-
> ney before an even greater lord than yourself. Since the day
> you were born I have served you loyally. Nevertheless, you have
> ordered me to be killed... Now, close to the moment of death, I
> give you my final counsel. If you do not put aside the dagger, if
> you do not stop committing such murders, then you will surely
> lose your realm and put your person in the gravest jeopardy.

Pedro of Castile's treatment of his wife, Blanche of Bourbon, was atrocious. When she travelled to Valladolid for their marriage, Pedro first kept her waiting there for several months before joining her for a hurried ceremony, and then immediately abandoned her for his mistress, Maria de Padilla. The unfortunate Blanche was first kept in close captivity, then subjected to solitary confinement and finally murdered, most likely at Pedro's instigation. And although the king's responsibility could not be proved (and he protested his innocence most vigorously, through his ambassadors, before the treaty with England in 1362), his probable involvement encouraged his enemies to spread ever more lurid stories about his behaviour, in which he consorted with a bevy of Jewish and Moorish mistresses.

Politics is all about perception. The Castilian king had bursts of lucidity and reasoned statecraft, during which he built up his navy, introduced military reforms and established a sound com-mercial policy. He had good relations with a number of Castilian towns. But he progressively lost the support of his aristocracy and the church, and his rival, Enrique, was quick to capitalize on this.

Without the support of the nobility, a medieval king could not fight successfully. As Pedro retreated before his opponent, the only troops remaining to him were the cavalry sent by his ally, Sultan Muhammed V of Granada.

It was Pedro's alliance with Muslim Granada and his enjoyment of Moorish culture (he modelled the Alcázar of Seville on the architecture of the Nasrid fortress complex, the Alhambra) that aroused the deepest suspicion throughout Europe. When he refused to abide by papal mediation and continued his war against Peter IV, he was excommunicated by Innocent VI in 1357. Cast out from the church, Pedro seemed to descend yet further into brutality. In June 1364 he sent a force of Moorish light cavalry to the frontier town of Murcia, instructing his subjects to join with it, cross the border and wreak havoc on the enemy: 'Go with them, and do such a good job that there is nothing left to destroy, and wage the cruellest war you can, cutting off the heads of everyone you capture, so that there will be no man of Aragon taken who is not immediately killed.'

Pedro made it plain that if anyone failed to carry out his blood-thirsty instructions they would themselves be in the gravest danger, adding the chilling postscript 'be assured that if you do not do this, your own heads will be sent to me'. The king's orders were disturbing, almost deranged. Over the course of time, royal documents abandoned the formula 'on pain of my displeasure' for the more florid 'if you fail, your head will be returned to me'. Such events gave the Castilian king a terrible reputation at home and abroad, and made the reservations of the Black Prince's advisers, recalled by Froissart, only too understandable:

> Pedro, king of Castile, is a man of exceptional cruelty and evil disposition. His realm has suffered a multitude of grievances at his hands and many valiant men have been beheaded and murdered without justice or reason. It is because of these wicked actions, which he ordered or consented to, that he has lost his kingdom.

> In addition to this, he is the enemy of the church and has
> been excommunicated by our Holy Father [the pope]. He has
> long been considered a tyrant... It is also commonly reported,
> and believed in his own kingdom, and even by his own attend-
> ants, that he murdered the young lady, his wife... All that he
> has subsequently suffered is the chastisement of God, who
> has ordered his punishment as an example to all the kings
> and princes of this earth, that they should never commit such
> wickedness.

Amid this catalogue of horrors, one recent action stood out. On
his flight from Spain in the summer of 1366 Pedro ordered the
murder of the archbishop of Santiago, Suero Gómez, within his
own cathedral. Santiago de Compostela housed the shrine of
St James the Great, the final destination of Europe's most famous
pilgrimage route. As the chronicler Pedro de Ayala wrote: 'It is a
very evil and ugly thing to kill the archbishop of Santiago, whose
cathedral is home to the patron saint and defender of Spain, within
his own church, which everyone in the world comes to honour
and visit.'

On returning to Castile, and claiming the kingdom in May 1366,
Enrique enjoyed a propaganda field day against his opponent, lam-
basting him as:

> An evil tyrant and enemy of God and the Holy Mother
> Church – always increasing in malice and cruelty – destroy-
> ing churches, enriching the Moors and Jews, and empowering
> them to weaken the Catholic Faith, who has committed such
> terrible excesses that we had to remove him and liberate our
> kingdom from his subjugation, so that God should be served
> and the standing of the Holy Church and Holy Faith properly
> augmented.

According to Froissart, Pope Urban V not only confirmed the
sentence of excommunication against Pedro, but sanctioned his

deposition, legitimizing Enrique and allowing him to lawfully claim the throne.

The Black Prince's difficult negotiations with his Castilian guest would show that he had considerable doubts about the original treaty and that in the intervening years his misgivings had grown. The Prince was a deeply pious man, adhering to a moral code, whose word was his bond. In terms of personal honour, European chivalry, and respect for the church, one can only imagine that Pedro was the last person he wanted to be associated with.

The Prince strongly adhered to the crusading ideal; Pedro had cultivated an alliance with Muslim Granada. The Prince treated his captured prisoners in exemplary fashion; the Castilian king ordered those taken prisoner to be killed on the spot and had no respect for chivalric convention. The Prince revered the pilgrimage site of St James of Compostela (his registers were full of grants enabling members of his household to visit it); Pedro had murdered its archbishop within the consecrated grounds of the cathedral. The Prince was well aware what was at stake: his reputation and standing within the Christian world. The account of the anonymous chronicler of Canterbury hinted at the Black Prince's lack of enthusiasm for putting Pedro back on the throne:

> The Prince was approached by Pedro, who claimed to be rightful king of Spain, passionately argued his case and appealed for assistance. The Prince listened – but his only response was that he would give an answer to these matters when and where it was convenient to do so.

The chronicler of *The Brut* emphasized that the Prince initially refused to give Pedro his support: 'He long delayed over this, only saying that he needed to take advice on the matter and consult with his father and the king's council.' The chronicler added that the Prince did not want to help Pedro 'because such an action would be disrespectful to the Pope and to the Christian Church'.

The Catalan nobleman Bernat de Cabrara, count of Odona, had

commanded a company of troops in Pedro's service earlier that summer and now joined the Castilian king at Bordeaux. The Black Prince welcomed him, and Odona was invited to take part in the deliberations of his council. The count reported on one meeting, held on 17 August. It was attended, among others, by the Prince, Pedro, Charles of Navarre, the count of Armagnac, the lord of Albret and Jean de Grailly. Odona noted, in surprise, that a decision still had not been reached about whether to assist Pedro. Negotiations had, however, taken place between Gaston Fébus, count of Foix, and the Prince. Odona commented that: 'These meetings seem more about securing reconciliation between Fébus and the Prince of Aquitaine than any agreement in favour of the king of Castile.'

The following day Odona had this to say: 'We are unsure what the outcome will be in the negotiations between the Prince and the count of Foix. These two great men have much to resolve between themselves.' He noted Pedro's increasing anxiety during this wait-ing game: 'He had hoped that the Prince would warmly welcome him and pledge his aid. Now he is growing so desperate that he will promise him anything.' The anonymous chronicler of Canterbury believed that Pedro was even considering making the Prince heir to his kingdom, if only he would offer his assistance.

Instead, the Black Prince chose to send a delegation to his father, headed by his chamberlain, Sir Nigel Loring. He knew that Edward III wanted to uphold the Anglo-Castilian treaty; the Prince, however, did not. The discussions dragged on for several weeks, in an atmosphere of growing tension. The well-informed monk of Westminster Abbey, John of Reading, provided consider-able detail on what followed, probably drawn from conversations with Loring himself or one of his entourage. John of Reading was a perceptive and sometimes acerbic observer of political affairs and contemporary mores. He had high moral standards and expected those involved in public life to live up to them. He strongly disap-proved of unnecessary ceremony and ostentation, whether on the tournament field or in the latest fashions of dress and costume,

and if the Black Prince had become lost in a world of appearances —
pandering to vanity and pride — as Froissart had suggested, this
chronicler would have immediately noticed it. But John of Reading
held an entirely positive opinion of the Prince: he praised him for
his deeply held religious conviction and for being a liberal benefactor of the church. He saw him as a man who followed wise counsel
rather than disregarding it.

John of Reading had first met the Black Prince in the summer
of 1355, when he was praying in Westminster Abbey before his expedition to Gascony, and was impressed by his spiritual devotion. He
lauded the Prince for his enthusiastic welcome of Peter of Cyprus's
ambassadors in May 1362, seeking support for a crusade against the
Ottoman Turks (they had been entertained at his new palace of
Kennington throughout their stay), and the generous reception
offered to Peter, in Aquitaine, two years later. John of Reading saw
the Prince as a leader capable of leading a crusade himself, as did
the so-called prophecies of John of Bridlington. John of Reading
believed, in the aftermath of Brétigny, that the Prince was a warrior
capable of rejuvenating the crusading movement. To see his tal-
ents misused in support of a military ally of Muslim Granada was
almost too painful for the chronicler to bear.

Well aware of Pedro of Castile's abysmal treatment of his wife,
John of Reading commended the Prince for honouring his marriage vows, as 'a true Christian should'. And — with the Spanish
negotiations in the forefront of his mind — he acclaimed him for
preferring a path of moral integrity to one of political pragmatism.
The chronicler knew that the Black Prince and his father were at
loggerheads and applauded the Prince's unwillingness to assist
Pedro. He believed that it was the honourable position to take,
in contrast to Edward III, who was prepared for reasons of state
to overlook the Castilian king's terrible deeds. John of Reading
was convinced that the English monarch had already decided to
restore Pedro to the throne; he now intended to impose that view
on his son.

The chronicler was correct. Edward III and the Black Prince had forged a partnership in which martial prowess and religious observance marched hand in hand. Father and son worshipped together before embarking upon campaigns, and offered their victories to God. The Order of the Garter was founded as a spiritual fraternity as well as a chivalric body of knights. Sincerity of belief led to success on the battlefield. And when that success had faltered, during the Rheims campaign and the terrible events of Black Monday, father and son had listened to the will of God and concluded peace. But now the English king had changed.

In the 1360s Edward III had paraded his family's glory through sumptuous court festivities, prestigious building programmes at Windsor and Westminster, and fresh titles, power and influence for his sons. Lionel of Antwerp was created duke of Clarence and given the governorship of Ireland. John of Gaunt, who had inherited the duchy of Lancaster through his marriage to Grosmont's daughter Blanche, was given lordships in the north of England and along the border with Scotland. Edmund of Langley was created earl of Cambridge and a marriage alliance was sought for him in Flanders. Edward of Woodstock had become prince of Aquitaine. There was only one thing missing: another great military victory. By winning one, the Black Prince would cement the Anglo-Castilian alliance and trumpet the prestige of Edward III's dynasty all over Europe. And the English monarch would not relinquish that prospect.

Jean Froissart was right to sense grandiosity, but it came from the king, not his son. The Prince put his chamberlain, Sir Nigel Loring, at the head of his delegation because of Loring's diplomatic skill, strength of character and integrity. However, Edward III would brook no opposition. It became a desperate rearguard action, one worthy of Count Roland himself. There was no time to relay messages from Westminster to Bordeaux and back, so the approach had been discussed by the Black Prince and his chamberlain before Loring sailed for England. Both men agreed that the Prince's loyalty to his father overrode his strong disapproval of what he was being asked to undertake. But first he would extract a substantial concession from the king.

The Black Prince would oversee the details of the treaty between himself, Pedro and Charles of Navarre. And he insisted that Pedro be required to swear a solemn oath 'to amend his life and government on his return to Castile, especially with regard to the church'. The Prince informed his father that if this was not done, he would not lead the expedition. He reserved the right to make the conditions of the oath public. Edward III agreed.

Pedro duly agreed to the conditions imposed by the Prince, and these demands were circulated in England and Gascony. Should Pedro be restored to the throne, he solemnly accepted the following:

> That he would maintain the rights, belief and faith of the Holy Church, protect her ministers and defend them against her enemies.
> That he would restore all goods and possessions wrongly confiscated from the Holy Church.
> That he would drive and put out all Saracens [Muslims] from his kingdom with all his strength and power.
> And that he would take a Christian woman as his wife, and never go into another woman's bed.
> And these things he would truly keep and maintain throughout his lifetime.
> On these conditions the Prince has agreed to support him.

The oath revealed the Black Prince's dislike and disapproval of a man he now had to risk his life for. He cannot have had much hope that Pedro would honour these promises, but he sought to deflect criticism of his association with the Castilian king and hoped to make his peace with God.

After twelve days of tense discussion at Libourne, 25 miles (40 km) north-east of Bordeaux, a treaty was finalized on 23 September 1366. It was estimated that the campaign would last a total of six months, and that the expenses of the Prince and those forces directly under his command would be 250,000 florins. The cost of the retinues of the Gascon lords was assessed at another 300,000 florins, totalling 550,000 in all (around £82,500).

If he recovered the throne, Pedro would take responsibility for payment on 10 January 1367, and reimburse the Black Prince for the sums owed over a two-year period. The Prince would have the right to all prisoners taken in battle and also would be granted territories in Vizcaya, on Spain's northern coast, on the Bay of Biscay, as a reward for his efforts. Charles of Navarre would receive further lands as the price for his support. Pedro promised that all Englishmen visiting Castile as pilgrims would be exempted from taxation.

The sums agreed at Libourne were estimates; a full statement of account would be presented to Pedro once the expedition was concluded. If the amounts grew substantially larger, greater strain would be placed on the Prince's resources and the chances of the Castilian king making a full repayment would diminish.

The treaty suggested a timetable for the campaign, in which the decisive action would take place in the late autumn. The army would muster by 10 October 1366 and cross the Pyrenees by the end of the month. The aim was to bring Enrique to battle soon afterwards, and provoke a general uprising in Pedro's favour. By early January 1367 it was hoped that the Castilian king would be back on the throne, some of the troops would then stand down and the remainder help secure his realm. The entire expedition would have returned to Gascony by the beginning of April. As with many a military operation before and since, both the financial estimate and the timescale upon which it was based were to prove unduly optimistic.

†

The decision to move in Pedro's favour generated a surge of energy. The waiting was over and the great enterprise was about to begin.

'The Prince returned to Bordeaux and got his men ready', the Chandos Herald related:

> He sent for many a noble and valiant knight from all over his lands, leaving out neither great nor small; nor did Sir John Chandos stay idle, because he went to fetch the men of the Great Company [the Free Companies], some fourteen [military] formations of them... And the Prince gathered gold and silver to pay his soldiers. Then the armourers at Bordeaux forged swords and daggers, coats of mail, helmets, short swords, axes and gauntlets – in such a number that it would have done for thirty kings.

These men were now gathering at a war camp near Dax, 90 miles (145 km) south of Bordeaux. And, as on the Prince's earlier campaigns, they came for a variety of reasons. For the Huntingdonshire knight Sir William Moigne, rewarded for his gallantry at Poitiers with an annuity of 100 marks (£66 13s 4d), it was loyalty: he had joined the Prince's household and crossed with him to Gascony in 1363, and would stand by his master in peace and war. In contrast, the Yorkshireman Sir John Saville had fought with a variety of aristocratic captains. He was highly regarded within the military community and knew many of his fellow fighters well; when two soldiers were charged with murder in Brittany in 1357, Saville spoke on their behalf and secured their pardons. He was recruited by the Prince's marshal, Henry of Berkhamsted, because of his toughness and reliability in a crisis.

Sir William Elmwood came for profit. A soldier of fortune, he had joined Bertrand du Guesclin's army for pay and helped to put Enrique of Trastamara on the throne; when offered a larger cash incentive by Sir John Chandos, Elmwood was quite happy to change sides and fight to remove him. For Sir John Godard, the motivation was adventure. It was the twenty-one-year-old's first campaign; the mission to restore the Castilian king had caught his imagination. Godard had a restless spirit: he would subsequently go on crusade in Prussia, visit the Holy Land and then Venice, from where he ventured 'beyond the Great Sea' in the company of the duke of Duras.

And then there were the Gascons, led by Jean de Grailly and Arnaud Amanieu, lord of Albret. Albret had already visited Castile in the spring of 1366, when he astutely advised King Pedro of the best way to neutralize the Free Companies: give them more money to return home again. Unfortunately, the Castilian king did not heed his counsel. Albret, a keen supporter of the campaign, had exceeded the Prince's expectations by recruiting a substantial force of over a thousand men. And the Prince's brother, John of Gaunt, was expected from England with more than 800 archers.

Charles V's brother, Louis, duke of Anjou, the French king's lieutenant in Languedoc, sent a stream of anxious messages to Peter IV of Aragon: 'The Prince is gathering a large number of troops – and it is clear that he will now lead the invasion in person... It will not be long before his army is on the move... If we cannot hold the mountain passes against him, he will completely destroy Enrique.' A Valois chronicler wrote of the assembling warriors: 'They were tough and courageous... it was the strongest and best ordered army that had been seen in a long time.'

All seemed to be falling into place. Gaston Fébus's castle of Orthez stood 25 miles (40 km) south-east of Dax. For two years there had been a stand-off between the Black Prince and Fébus over rendering homage for Béarn, which even the efforts of the papal mediator, Geoffrey, archbishop of Toulouse, had failed to resolve. The Prince now reached an accommodation with the mercurial count of Foix: he would no longer press Fébus to render homage for the contested lordship, but in return, the count would allow the Prince's army to march through his lands on its way to the Pyrenees. The two men's friendship was renewed. The Prince's 6,000-strong army now awaited John of Gaunt's archers. Once they arrived, it would march on Spain.

The Black Prince was keen to bring more bowmen into his army. Enrique's forces contained a substantial number of cavalry – the *jinetes* — mounted troops equipped with javelin, sword and shield who were lightly armoured and whose horses wore no protective armour at all. The Prince knew that the Spanish had no experience of the longbow's devastating power in a pitched battle. And his brother was recruiting hundreds of them from his northern estates.

But time was of the essence. Gaunt had planned to cross to Bordeaux on 20 October. Unfortunately, he was delayed in England by an aggressive lawsuit brought against him by Edward, Lord Despenser. For John of Reading, this was only the latest in a series of bad omens and portents that had followed the decision to support Pedro. 'Falling stars were seen in many parts of the country,' the chronicler reported, 'which burnt the hair and clothing of those they fell upon.'

The Prince's soldiers started to grow restless. 'They were at Dax for much of the winter,' the Chandos Herald recalled, 'suffering real hardship as they waited for those from far away to gather.' Gaunt was only able to set sail on 22 December, two months later than he had intended. He did not want to risk a long voyage from England to Bordeaux in winter, so he disembarked at Pointe St-Mathieu in Brittany and then marched south. It was a sensible decision, but more time was being lost.

The costs of the enterprise were mounting up. To help with the expense, the Black Prince melted down his personal plate and sold his jewels and precious stones. He attempted to reduce the size of some of the army's retinues, and argued with the Gascon lord of Albret in the process. Profiting from the delay, Enrique opened negotiations with Charles of Navarre, offering him a substantial reward if he switched sides. At the beginning of January 1367, Charles agreed to break the treaty agreed at Libourne and oppose the passage of the Prince's army through the Pyrenees. The pass of Roncesvalles would now be held against him. Peter IV of Aragon wrote triumphantly: 'The treaty that the king of Navarre has made with Enrique of Castile will make it impossible for the Prince of Wales to enter Spain. He will have to abandon his expedition.'

According to the Chandos Herald, the Prince's pregnant wife, Joan of Kent was overcome by anxiety:

> She had bitter grief at heart, and then she reproached the goddess of love who had brought her to such heights, for she had the most powerful prince in the world, without equal in valour, and yet she was terrified of losing him — for all around her said that never had anyone staked so much on such a perilous venture...
>
> The Prince comforted her as best he could, and said to her: 'Good lady, do not weep or be dismayed, for God has the power to do all. We shall meet again in circumstances full of joy, with all our friends around us, for my heart tells me so.'
>
> Very sweetly did they embrace, kiss and make their farewell. The princess sorrowed so much that, being then big with child, she through grief went into labour — and delivered a very fair son, who was called Richard. Great rejoicing was had by all — and the Prince was right glad at heart. All said with one voice: behold — a right fair beginning.

Richard was born on 6 January 1367. Shortly afterwards, the Black Prince rode to Dax, the mustering point of his army, and a week later John of Gaunt was finally able to join him. The Prince ordered Sir Hugh Calveley, who was in Spain with his freebooting troops, to march north and threaten to lay waste Charles of Navarre's lands; Calveley was only too happy to oblige. Navarre then rushed to Dax, apologized fulsomely for the 'misunderstanding', and explained that he had only been bluffing Enrique. The mountain pass of Roncesvalles was open once more.

At the beginning of February 1367, the Anglo-Gascon army assembled at the small town of Saint-Jean-Pied-de-Port, in the foothills of the Pyrenees. It was the start of the pilgrimage route to Santiago de Compostela, and from the twelfth-century pilgrim guides and itineraries had been produced in manuscript form, evoking the beauty of the mountain passes — 'a place where you can almost touch the sky' — and warning of their dangers. The guides advised that the crossing of the Pyrenees should never be undertaken in winter.

The Prince's soldiers looked up at the mountains, sometimes shrouded in mist and cloud, a rocky fastness of imposing grandeur. Here, in the pass of Roncesvalles, the *chansons de geste* sung of Count Roland's tragic stand against the might of the Saracen army. They would pass the site of his last, terrible battle and see the monastery believed to house his remains. They would make their own perilous journey, and some would not survive it. All felt the sense of destiny. History was about to be made. 'We thought of Hannibal crossing the Alps', Walter of Peterborough said simply.

The 17-mile (27-km) crossing had to be made in the nine available hours of daylight. Saint-Jean-Pied-de-Port was 590 ft (180 metres) above sea level. South of the town gate the road wound its way uphill. After 3 miles (5 km) it climbed steeply; after 7 miles (11 km), it was no longer a road but a track. The army would have to climb more than 4,000 ft (1,220 metres) in full military equipment, carrying their supplies as best they could. As they ascended the mountain pass, the weather could change in minutes, from sunshine to snow, sleet, hail and mist. If men and horses lost their footing on the narrow track, they would fall and die.

The Black Prince and his advisers split up their army; they would make the ascent in three formations, on separate days. On 14 February the Prince's vanguard crossed the Pyrenees, under the command of John of Gaunt and Sir John Chandos. Then the weather deteriorated, and the main body of the army waited a further five days. On 19 February the Black Prince decided that they would cross the following day regardless of the conditions. That evening Pedro wrote to the assembly of the town of Murcia from Saint-Jean-Pied-de-Port, announcing his imminent return to Castile, to suppress the rebellion of Enrique of Trastamara. The following day the Prince and Pedro marched towards the pass of Roncesvalles. The troops had to contend with ice, snow and bone-chilling cold. The Chandos Herald recalled it vividly:

Never was there such a difficult passage, for you could see men
and horses stumbling on the mountain side because they were
so hard pressed. No one stopped for his companion, not even a
father for his son, for there was such great cold, snow and frost
there, that everyone was afraid. But by God's mercy the crossing was made.

The main body of the army reached Pamplona, the capital of the
kingdom of Navarre, on 23 February. The rearguard, under Jean,
count of Armagnac, arrived shortly afterwards, and several days
were spent resting the troops. And then a letter to the Prince arrived
from Enrique of Trastamara, expressing his 'great wonder' at the
invasion and insisting he had never done the Prince any harm.
He then made the argument his opponent was most afraid of. 'It
does not seem to us that you have been properly informed how
our adversary [Pedro] governed this kingdom in the past,' Enrique
began ominously. 'He killed his own queen, Blanche of Bourbon,
his legitimate wife... and he usurped all the rights of the Pope and
his prelates, so that God in judgement gave sentence against him,
that his right to the kingdom be null and void.'

The Prince had attempted to restore a measure of religious
dignity to his enterprise, insisting in the treaty of Libourne that
when a crusade was launched by Castile against Muslim Granada,
he would have the right to command the vanguard of the army.
On 20 February 1367 his accounts recorded a loan to Pedro, so that
both men could make an offering to the collegiate church at Roncesvalles. However, the Prince had now learned that the masters
of three crusading orders, Calatrava, Santiago and St John, would
be lining up in Enrique's army, alongside members of the Order of
the Sash, the body of knights that had inspired the founding of the
Order of the Garter.

Enrique ended his letter by emphasizing his own chivalric credentials, and challenged the Black Prince to battle. He asked his
adversary to name the place where he would enter Castile, so that

their armies could meet in combat there. The Prince did not reply. But his sureness of touch began to desert him.

He sent out a strong reconnaissance party under Sir Thomas Felton to gather information on Enrique's movements. Felton and the 500 men under his command rode south-west through Navarre, crossed the River Ebro and entered Castile at the town of Logrono. They moved forward to the village of Navarrete and set up a 'listening-post' within 20 miles (32 km) of the Castilian army.

Charles of Navarre had promised both sides that he would serve in their respective armies 'with his body' — in person, with his retainers, but he had no intention of honouring either commitment. On 11 March Charles arranged his mock capture by a Frenchman on Enrique's side, Olivier de Mauny, a partisan of du Guesclin, while he was out hunting. He was then kept in safety in a castle in Aragon until after the battle, when he managed to 'escape'. It was an astonishing piece of absurdist theatre, giving the ghost of an impression that he was still fighting for the Prince but making Charles a laughing-stock throughout Europe. But in view of the uncertain situation, the Black Prince resolved to leave Navarre as quickly as possible.

However, he did not follow in Felton's footsteps. Instead, he swung west towards the town of Salvatierra, intending to enter Castile from a different direction, taking the road from Vitoria to Burgos. It is hard to fathom the reason for this. The pilgrim road to Santiago diverged at Pamplona, and the Prince may have been using an itinerary for the northern route. Indeed, on cursory examination it appeared the quickest way forward: the distance from Pamplona to Vitoria was 50 miles (80 km), 5 miles (8 km) shorter than the approach through Logrono. However, the terrain was far worse.

The Prince recalled Sir Thomas Felton's reconnaissance force and pushed on. But his soldiers now found themselves on increasingly poor roads, traversing a barren landscape. The men had to pass through the desolate Alavese mountains; the weather was bad, the going slow and difficult underfoot and there were few provisions to be had. 'We went through the pass of Arruazu, a narrow little place, where the army suffered much hardship', the Chandos Herald said glumly. 'There was little found to supply the army.' When the exhausted troops reached Salvatierra, six days of rest was needed and all advantage of surprise lost. Most unusually, the Prince had not properly reconnoitred his route.

By the time the Prince's army reached Vitoria, Enrique's Castilian troops and Bretons and Frenchmen under Bertrand du Guesclin and the marshal d'Audrehem were blocking his passage south. Enrique was entrenched in the mountain stronghold of Zaldiaran, 3 miles (5 km) south of Vitoria, a near-impregnable position, and held the pass at Puebla, barring the road to Burgos. Enrique and his brother Tello were content to follow the advice of du Guesclin and Charles V, to wear down the Prince's army, denying it supplies rather than risking open battle.

'There was never worse weather', the Chandos Herald reported, as the Anglo-Gascon forces encamped in the open fields south of Vitoria. 'Conditions were vile, with incessant wind and rain. Many of the troops had neither bread or wine, and the men and their horses were suffering terribly.' The campaign was coming apart at the seams. 'They will be forced to leave Castile for want of food', the French predicted, 'or die of hunger.'

On the Poitiers campaign the Prince had maintained regular watch over his war camp, visiting outposts, urging vigilance and encouraging his men. These careful precautions were absent at Vitoria. From their vantage point at Zaldiaran, d'Audrehem and du Guesclin noticed that the English were spread out all over the plain and sentry duty was lax. They resolved to exploit this by launching a surprise night attack. Two mounted forces were organized, one under Enrique's brother Tello, the other under d'Audrehem. This was an ideal mission for the Castilian light cavalry, and Enrique and Tello had been schooled in bold raiding tactics. Shortly before dawn on 25 March the horsemen swept down on the Prince's unsuspecting soldiers.

The Anglo-Gascon army was caught totally by surprise. Tello overran the war camp of Sir Hugh Calveley. Many of his soldiers were killed in their beds and the baggage train plundered. Then Tello charged towards the vanguard. English troops were panicking, but the situation was saved by the quick thinking of John of Gaunt, who rallied his forces and drew them up in battle formation. The Prince and Sir John Chandos then came to his aid and Tello was beaten off.

Meanwhile, the marshal d'Audrehem had smashed through the encampment of Sir Thomas Felton, at Aríñez, 4 miles (6 km) south-west of Vitoria. The Prince's army was too widely dispersed. A force of 400 English men-at-arms and archers under Sir Thomas's kinsman, Sir William Felton, drew themselves up on a hillock, north of the village, and beat off assault after assault. 'He was lion-hearted', the Chandos Herald said of the commander, 'and cared not two cherries for death.'

The French and Spaniards closed in for the kill, with Sir William Felton and his men still clinging onto their position. The Chandos Herald paid them tribute: 'The enemy launched many attacks, hurling javelins, spears and lances. But the brave band proved their worth that day, and time after time they pushed them back.' However, the bowmen were running out of arrows, the men-at-arms were exhausted and no assistance was forthcoming from the main army. Eventually Sir William and his fighters were overwhelmed by sheer numbers. Felton and the majority of his soldiers were slain where they stood; a few of the captains were taken prisoner. Their courage lived on in local folklore: even today the place is known as *Inglesmendi*, 'the hill of the English'.

The Black Prince had been given an unpleasant shock. He was strongly moved by Sir William Felton's heroism. 'The Prince was very sad at this,' the Chandos Herald said:

He had thought the whole enemy army had come down from the plain, and did not want to break up his forces. If it had not been for this, he would have gone to the help of his other men, *as he should have done* [author's italics].

It was a rare moment of criticism from the Prince's biographer.

Sir William Felton an experienced soldier and administrator, and former seneschal of Poitou and the Limousin had been a man with the toughness and moral authority to tackle the excesses of the Free Companies. In common with his master, he adhered to a strict understanding of chivalric protocol. In the summer of 1363 he was holding Bertrand du Guesclin his prisoner (as hostage for a truce provisionally agreed at Landes d'Evran). Du Guesclin went out riding with Felton's son, and, seeing his supervision overly relaxed, the wily Breton simply galloped off. In a letter of 24 November 1363 Felton courteously but firmly charged du Guesclin with dishonourable conduct – he had given his word he would not try to escape. In a response of 9 December du Guesclin disagreed, pointing out that if Felton failed to watch over him properly he was entitled to make a bid for freedom. The case went before the Paris Parlement, sitting as a court of honour, the following February; it found in du Guesclin's favour.

There was a pattern of inflexibility in Felton's behaviour, whether in Poitou or at Aríñez, that left him vulnerable to exploitation by a less gentlemanly opponent. It might be regarded as lacking in chivalry to attack one's opponent at night, but if there was a failure to maintain proper sentry duty, such an assault could happen nonetheless. Edward III's Weardale campaign of 1327 had revealed that danger, when Sir William Douglas caught the English war camp unawares; forty years on, history had repeated itself. On this occasion the Prince should have taken better care of his soldiers.

The death of Sir William Felton was the turning point of the campaign, however, shaking the Black Prince out of his lethargy. He had struggled to motivate himself as a champion of Pedro's cause, but now he would fight out of respect for the memory of Felton and his brave comrades. His generalship took on the drive and purpose it had hitherto lacked. Meanwhile, Enrique and Tello became over-confident: they had badly shaken the Anglo-Gascon army at Aríñez, and now they believed they could disregard the warnings of Charles V and du Guesclin, bring the Prince and his warriors to battle and roundly defeat them.

The Chandos Herald described Enrique haranguing his soldiers: 'Welcome my lords, you have done well', he told them. 'All the rest [of the Black Prince's army] will go the same way.' The marshal d'Audrehem chided him. 'Sire, what are you saying? You have not yet defeated most of the enemy. And if you meet them in battle, I fear you will find them good soldiers.' But Enrique's blood was up. He was fighting for his honour and his lands and he resolved on battle nonetheless.

The Prince now broke up his camp at Vitoria and retreated back into Navarre. He marched south, crossing the River Ebro at Logrono – the original route taken by Sir Thomas Felton several weeks ago. Food was short and conditions harsh, but the army was moving with a new sense of determination. On 1 April the men reached Navarrete. Enrique's forces occupied the town of Nájera, 12 miles (19 km) to the west, blocking the passage over the River Najerilla. The Prince had originally felt unable to meet Enrique's challenge of 28 February, but now he responded in deliberately insulting terms, addressing him as 'the count of Trastamara who at present styles himself king of Castile' and calling upon him to renounce the throne: 'You must know, in your heart, that it is not right for a bastard to become king by disinheriting the lawful heir.'

The Prince was goading Enrique to fight, and on 2 April his opponent rose to the challenge, offering him an equally offensive salutation, 'Edward, Prince of Wales, calling yourself the eldest son of the king of England and Prince of Aquitaine'. He then left his defensive position at Nájera, crossed the bridge over the Najerilla, and lined his army up on the open plain a mile to the east. Pedro de Ayala was with Enrique's army, carrying the banner of the Order of the Sash, and he said of his commander's decision: 'Enrique had a very great heart, and was a forceful man, and now said that he was determined to give battle on this flat plain, which would not give either side an unfair advantage.'

Enrique's perception of warfare was based on the *cavalgada*, fast-moving mounted raids, striking deep into enemy territory (which bore similarities to the *chevauchée*). He was naturally aggressive: his sole experience of battle had been a cavalry engagement at Araviano in September 1359 in which he and Tello had routed a larger force of Castilian horsemen. He had some good troops in his army, particularly in the vanguard, where du Guesclin and d'Audrehem were joined by members of the Order of the Sash. He held the numerical advantage – John of Malvern believed his force was twice the size of its opponent, perhaps 12,000 to the Prince's 6,000 – and was confident of victory.

Enrique drew up his army in battle formation. Behind du Guesclin's dismounted soldiers, he took command of the Castilian centre, made up of infantry and missile-bearing troops. On its wings were two cavalry divisions, commanded by his brother Tello and the Aragonese nobleman the count of Denia. He expected the Black Prince's army to approach along the road to Nájera from the west, allowing him to use the full breadth of the plain to first charge down his opponent's archers and then get his cavalry round the back of the Anglo-Gascon men-at-arms. But the Prince had no intention of letting him do this.

An hour before dawn on 3 April the Anglo-Gascon army was on the move. Undertaking a flanking manoeuvre, it left the road to Nájera and took the hillside track towards the village of Huércanos, shielded by a low ridge that rose to the north-west of the plain. 'Our men left the direct route and took a road to the right,' the Chandos Herald remembered, 'crossing a line of hills and descending into the valley below, all on horseback, nobly arrayed and in such good order that it was marvellous to behold.'

At dawn the soldiers dismounted, and readied themselves beneath the crest of the hill. They were now only 400 yards (360 metres) or so from the left flank of Enrique's army. They would appear not from the east but from the north, and within minutes of their advance would be within extreme bow range of the Castilian forces, retaining the advantage of higher ground and the protection of the River Yalde, a tributary of the Najerilla. Enrique's troops would have to turn and redeploy to meet them.

Walter of Peterborough recorded the Prince's defiant words to John of Gaunt: 'We must be mindful of our martial heritage – and that prowess stands above all other things in life… Let us be ruled by an ardent spirit. If we are to die, let our manner of dying do us credit.' Gaunt would command the vanguard alongside Sir John Chandos. The Prince promoted Chandos to knight banneret, giving him the honour of unfurling the great silk banner that would signal the attack. They would plunge into the reformed battle line of du Guesclin and d'Audrehem. The Prince then spoke frankly to his assembled men-at-arms and archers:

> You well know that we are overtaken by famine, by lack of victuals – and you will see before us enemies who have plenty of provisions: bread, wine and salted fish. Let us take it from them, with a rain of arrows and blows of our lances and swords.

The Prince intended to attack immediately after sunrise. He would engage Enrique's vanguard as quickly as possible, and the Castilian commander would fling his cavalry forward. But the enemy would be surprised and their mounted charges poorly co-ordinated. And the Prince's bowmen would be waiting. Their massed volleys would strike the lightly armoured *jinetes* hard; they would then switch to barbed arrows and take down the horses. With the cavalry in disarray, Enrique would push up his infantry and missile-bearing troops, who would be the bowmen's next target. With the Castilian centre out of position, the Prince would commit his own division to break du Guesclin's and d'Audrehem's contingent. The Prince thought of Sir William Felton and his brave companions: this would be for them. He had kept his rearguard mounted. As the

Castilians pushed back he would unleash his own horsemen on Enrique's men, intending to push them back to the River Najerilla and annihilate them. From the ashes of a lacklustre campaign had sprung extraordinary power and resolve. 'If you meet them in battle, I fear you will find them good soldiers,' the marshal d'Audrehem had warned. Enrique and Tello were about to find out. The Prince's army was united in one single, deadly purpose – to utterly destroy its foe.

At first light Enrique readied his soldiers and sent out his scouts to report on the progress of the enemy. They returned in bewilderment: the Prince's forces could not be found. And then there was sudden cacophony of sound, trumpets blowing, the war cries of 'Guienne and St George!' The entire Anglo-Gascon army was coming over the ridge only a few hundred yards to Enrique's left. There were hurried shouts and commands as du Guesclin and d'Audrehem swung their division round to meet them. For the first time in the campaign, the Castilian commander felt a sudden surge of fear. The vanguards crashed into each other. Tello's cavalry swung into action, but within minutes it was torn to pieces. The count of Denia's horsemen fared little better. 'English archers shot thicker than snow falling in winter-time', the Chandos Herald recalled. 'They wounded horses and men and the Spanish cavalry, no longer able to endure this, turned and fled.'

Enrique brought round his infantry and ordered his missile-bearing troops to attack the bowmen. 'The Castilians had slings', Froissart said, 'from which they could throw stones with such force as to break helmets and skulls. They unleashed a volley. But the English archers shot back at them sharply and continuously.' The slingers turned back, and the lightly armoured infantry followed them, unable to hold its ground as the volleys rained down. The Black Prince brought up his own men against du Guesclin's soldiers. The whole Castilian army began to break up and flee. Then a trumpet blast released the Prince's mounted rearguard. Enrique's men were surrendering in droves, and more were cut down on the wide plain. The bridge over the Najerilla became a death trap: 'There you might see knights leap into the fast-flowing water in sheer terror and drown, one on top of another,' the Chandos Herald recalled. 'It was said that the river turned red, from the blood of men and horses.' Walter of Peterborough also described the rout in graphic terms: 'The mob of Spaniards blindly fled, the skirmishers, the foot soldiers, all put to flight, as savage destruction rained down upon them.'

According to John of Malvern, 3,000 of the enemy were captured and more than 7,000 killed, in battle or in flight, with many drowning in the river. English casualties were slight. John, Lord Ferrers of Chartley, who died fighting in the vanguard, was the most notable. 'Few amongst our host were killed... through the help of God himself', said John of Malvern. 'At the end of the fight,' Walter of Peterborough added, 'I looked upon a mass of Spanish nobles struck down and killed.' Henry of Knighton summarized the day: 'It was the greatest battle to have taken place in our times.' Two days later, the Black Prince wrote to his wife:

My dearest and truest sweetheart and beloved companion, as to news, you will want to know that we were encamped in the fields near Navarrete on the second of April, and there we learned that the Bastard of Spain [Enrique of Trastamara] and all his army were encamped two leagues from us on the river at Nájera. The next day, very early in the morning, we moved off towards him, and sent our scouts to reconnoitre his position, who reported to us that he had drawn up his troops in a good place, and was waiting for us.

So we put ourselves in battle order, and did so well – by the will and grace of God – that the Bastard and all his men were defeated, thanks be to our Lord, and of those who fought us between five and six thousand of them were killed... and there were up to two thousand noble prisoners – amongst them Don Tello, the Bastard's brother, the count of Denia, Bertrand du

Guesclin, the marshal d'Audrehem, the masters of Santiago and Saint John and many others, whose names we do not know; and as for the Bastard himself, we do not know at present if he was taken, [was left for] dead or escaped.

And after the said battle we lodged that evening in the Bastard's own tents, and we were more comfortable there than we have been for four or five days, and we stayed there all the next day. On the Monday, that is the day when this is being written, we moved off and took the road towards Burgos; and so we shall continue our journey successfully, with God's help.

You will be glad to know, dearest companion, that we, our brother Lancaster [John of Gaunt] and all the nobles of our army are well, thank God, except only Sir John Ferrers, who did much fighting.

Edward III had the great victory he wanted, and the English propaganda machine went into overdrive. An anonymous Latin poem, known as the 'Gloria', sang the Black Prince's praises: 'Yet again the Prince shone forth: his enemies scattered, dead or lying bleeding on the field. He is Samson-like in war.' For the author of the 'Gloria', Nájera demonstrated England's might within Europe:

Our Prince grows great, his power increases, his courage flourishes, his prowess in war makes all his enemies afraid... England rejoices, Gascony sings, France sorrows, Iberia is reinforced... let the harp sound in praise of his renown.

Nájera should have been the Black Prince's supreme triumph. But he soon learned that Enrique had escaped, first to Aragon and then to Languedoc, to be sheltered by Louis, duke of Anjou, brother of the French king. His warhorse was recovered and sent to Edward III as a gift, but with the Castilian alive and safe, and once more under the protection of Charles V, the present did not mean a great deal.

The aftermath of the victory was further soured by a violent quarrel between the Black Prince and Pedro. Pedro had agreed that he would not execute any of his captured subjects 'until they had been legally judged', but he murdered several high-born Castilian prisoners. A particularly flagrant incident involved the nobleman Inigo de Orozco, who had remained loyal to Pedro until the mass defections of 1366. Shortly after his capture by a Gascon soldier, Orozco had the misfortune to encounter his former master, who, in a fit of rage, stabbed him to death. Robbed of a substantial ransom, the Gascon complained bitterly to the Prince, who publicly rebuked Pedro for his conduct. When the Castilian king offered to pay for the captives, the Prince retorted that he would never surrender prisoners to be butchered. Pedro de Ayala caught the moment:

> These lords who have come with me, in my service, fight for honour and the rewards of this world, not for killing captives in cold blood. Even if you offered me a thousand times more than each prisoner is worth, I would never surrender one of them because I would be handing them over to you to be killed.

At Burgos on 2 May 1367 the Black Prince presented Pedro with the full accounts of the campaign and the sums owed to him. These had now risen to the massive total of 2,720,000 gold florins (over £408,000), nearly five times the amount provisionally agreed in the treaty of September 1366. Distrust between the two men was now so great that hundreds of English soldiers manned the city's gates and surrounded the cathedral where the treaty was signed. On 6 May Pedro accepted liability for this colossal debt. How much of it would be paid remained to be seen. The Prince had planned to keep his army in Castile until the first instalment of the money was collected. But an outbreak of dysentery struck, and in August he and his army marched back across the Pyrenees to Gascony. The Prince's Spanish adventure had come to an end.

chapter nine

FORTUNE'S WHEEL

E arly in 1368, not long after his return to Aquitaine, a preacher
delivered a sermon to the Black Prince at Périgueux. Aymeric
de Peyrac, abbot of Moissac, described the event:

> In the time of Pope Urban V, Edward Prince of Aquitaine, who
> ruled the principality tranquilly, firmly and peacefully, held a
> solemn council at Périgueux, at which 22 bishops were present.
> And a sermon was preached by Austence, bishop of Sarlat, a
> great and famous theologian, discreet in spiritual and temporal
> affairs and richly endowed with worldly wealth. This bishop, in
> his sermon, compared the same Prince, in certain things, to the
> Son of God.
>
> The bishop of Sarlat told me that the Prince did not accept
> gratefully what he said in praise of him, according to what a
> friend of his told him. During a private conversation the latter
> said to the Prince: 'What did you think of the bishop's sermon
> today?' He replied that the bishop was doubtless eloquent
> and wise, and far-sighted, but that he must have been joking,
> because no one should be praised in such a fashion, least of all a
> great Prince, who might suddenly be brought low by a stroke of
> ill-fortune, so that his earlier deeds would be forgotten, brought
> to nothing and utterly confounded.

Medieval society was fascinated by the image of Fortune's Wheel.
When an individual had achieved great success, and reached the
zenith of their good fortune, the wheel might suddenly turn,

flinging those at its highest point to the ground. Where there was great opulence, and a love of earthly pleasure, the fall would be all the harder. This was the mutability of providence: when renown was at its apogee, all might suddenly be taken away. Personal destiny could be fickle and the vagaries of reputation hard to predict. And God punished those puffed up with worldly pride, those who longed for fame too much, by humbling them.

The episode described by Aymeric de Peyrac appears to be authentic. And the Prince's uneasiness was striking. Walter of Peterborough wrote a long verse poem on the Spanish campaign for the Black Prince's brother, John of Gaunt. Walter was in the business of seeking out wealthy and influential patrons who would reward him handsomely for his work, and in return, he would glorify their name. Gaunt, who loved pomp and splendour, was entirely happy with this arrangement. But Walter of Peterborough remarked ruefully that he had composed an earlier opus, on the Battle of Poitiers, entitled *Theotecon* (*Son of God*), in which he exalted Edward III's eldest son. He had hoped to receive generous payment from the victor. However, the Prince wanted nothing to do with it.

The Black Prince had been worried during the Nájera campaign that others might believe he was motivated by 'vainglory', the excessive love of a good reputation. That they would think he was marching into battle like a Caesar of old, to add fresh laurels to his victory garland. This was the risk inherent in personal lordship and the cult of chivalry – of becoming lost in a world of appearances, overly valuing one's standing among one's peers. In a sense, it was an insoluble dilemma, because appearance and reputation were vital attributes of a great military leader. The commander needed to be mindful of their importance but also aware of their consequences: overweening pride and a love of sycophancy.

This was where the inner world of the knight came into play, the religious regimen described so well by Geoffrey de Charny in his book on chivalry. 'In one brief moment, one may fall and lose everything,' de Charny had warned, 'if God does not grant us the wisdom and good judgement to know how to keep it safe... Above all else, safeguard your honour.' It provided a necessary balance, guarding against the vices of greed and vanity. It was a counterweight to the adrenalin rush of battle and the intoxication of comradeship and victory. Henry of Grosmont understood this well in his *Book of Holy Medicine,* emphasizing how the warrior always had to be on his guard against earthly sensation and pleasure, the weak points in his 'inner castle' that the devil would try to assail.

'We wish that all the jewels we have remaining be sold, and the money spent on alms,' Humphrey de Bohun wrote in his will of 15 October 1361, 'for we have had too great a delight in looking at them.' Among the devotional works the Prince had purchased from de Bohun's estate, the largest psalter contained the text of Robert Grosseteste's *Treatise on Confession,* a personal guide for the layperson that examined the seven principal vices and provided a prayer designed to bring the user's sins to mind. In this sense, it was similar to Henry of Grosmont's book, which was undertaken as a penitential exercise. 'God has bestowed upon us riches and honour in this world', de Bohun remarked, 'but at the last these are only vain glory.'

The Prince was engaged on an inner, spiritual campaign, one that ran alongside his outer, chivalric journey, and it was a campaign that had its own struggles and challenges. Love of vainglory was an accusation picked up by Jean Froissart at the outset of the Spanish expedition. It was probably made by Arnaud Amanieu, lord of Albret, a Gascon nobleman once loyal to the Prince, who subsequently quarrelled with him. Albret was well informed: he had met Pedro of Castile in Spain, was a member of the Prince's council and in the army that crossed the Pyrenees the following year and put Pedro back on the throne. Albret was an important source for Froissart, and a man not afraid to speak his mind.

As we have already heard, the lord of Albret may well have relayed to Froissart a view held by many of the council, that Pedro was too much of a liability to become involved with, that he was cruel, unstable and not to be trusted. When the Black Prince eventually repeated the order of his father, that they must help him nevertheless, Albret came to the conclusion that an overarching desire for honour and fame was driving the decision. In his reply to Enrique of Trastamara, made shortly before the battle at Nájera, the Black Prince perhaps unwisely said that he was in no way influenced by vainglory. In his riposte, Enrique latched onto that point, and said that vainglory was exactly what the Prince was motivated by.

These precepts were well known in the medieval world and had been discussed in detail by the great thirteenth-century theologian St Thomas Aquinas. According to Aquinas, vainglory was one of the gravest of vices, and a mortal sin, that led to boasting, obstinacy and a love of one's own opinions. The contrary virtue, magnanimity, involved living a good and honourable life, without concern for public fame. And these were not just remote religious or philosophical issues, they were well understood by the fighting man.

The experienced soldier Sir Thomas Gray had fought in the Prince's retinue in the Rheims campaign of 1359–60. Not long after this, he wrote an extended passage on how war could be justified. In it, he emphasized how God had prevented Moses from entering the Promised Land because of his vainglory. The lesson Gray drew from this was that rulers ought always to give God the credit for their victories, and remember that it was their subjects and their soldiers who made their success in war possible. Their well-being was all-important. Gray concluded by saying that the gift of command was not given to a monarch lightly, and that his responsibility was not ultimately to inflict destruction and devastation, but to govern virtuously, in accordance with a moral code.

It was in an atmosphere of financial strain and uncertainty in the spring of 1368 that Albret flung the accusation of vainglory in the Black Prince's face. In fact, the Prince well understood the need for humility in times of success. He had dedicated the Battle of Poitiers to God and to Saint Thomas à Becket, on the eve of whose feast of translation he began his campaign. He had asked that English bishops commemorate the victory by encouraging reverence for the cult of the Trinity, a cult that was Saint Thomas's particular object of devotion and had become his own.

Before setting sail for Gascony in 1363, the Black Prince had endowed a chantry chapel at Canterbury Cathedral, as penance for marrying Joan of Kent within the prohibited degree of blood relationship. Among its roof bosses were emblems of trailing foliage and vines, depicting the hedgerow that had protected his army at Poitiers. And in one striking image, Samson was shown slaying a lion with his bare hands. In the Biblical account, Samson was given supernatural power by God to combat his enemies and perform heroic feats of arms. The Prince clearly believed that God had also given him superhuman strength in battle and had watched over his soldiers – and that the outcome was miraculous. God, and God alone, should be thanked for it.

†

Now was a time of reckoning. At the beginning of September 1367 the Black Prince met with his general auditor, Richard Filongley, who had drawn up a list showing the estimated income and outgoings for the principality of Aquitaine. Filongley had once described himself as the Prince's 'poor clerk', possibly a reference to his actual salary but more probably an acknowledgement of his increasing workload. Pedro of Castile's failure to honour his promises had left the Black Prince on the verge of bankruptcy. Edward III was determined to see the principality financially self-sufficient, and, after pushing through the Spanish campaign over his son's strong reservations, it was the Prince who was now left to foot the bill.

And that bill was substantial. To set against the enormous cost of recruiting his army and paying its war wages, he had only the sums realized from the sale of Pedro's jewellery and the initial instalments of the ransoms of Bertrand du Guesclin, the marshal d'Audrehem and the count of Denia. These amounted to some 60,000 Gascon pounds (about £12,000), a tiny fraction of the amount needed. Most of the Prince's army was still unpaid. There was no financial reserve within the Gascon treasury, and there was no question of a subsidy from the English exchequer. Jean Froissart wrote:

> You have heard before of the expedition which the Prince made into Spain, and how he left it, discontented with the conduct of King Pedro, and returned to Aquitaine. When he arrived at Bordeaux, he was followed by all the men-at-arms... But at the time of their return, the Prince had not been able to collect sufficient money for them as speedily as he had wished, for it was terrible to see how much this campaign had impoverished and drained him.

The Prince's generosity to his followers and his grand hospitality had turned from a strength to a weakness. The only resource left to him was taxation. 'The Prince was advised by some of his council to lay a tax on the land of Aquitaine,' Froissart continued:

> The establishments of the Prince and Princess were so grand, that no ruler in Christendom maintained greater magnificence. The barons of Gascony, Poitou, the Saintonge and Rouergue, who had the right of remonstrating, as well as delegates from the principal towns of Aquitaine, were summoned to a council to discuss this matter. The chancellor of Aquitaine, in the presence of the Prince, explained fully the nature of this tax, in what manner it was to be levied, and that the prince had no intention of continuing it longer than for five years, or until the large debt caused by the Spanish expedition was paid.

The solution eventually proposed by the Prince's council was to introduce a permanent property tax, the *fouage,* to run for five years. The Black Prince had levied this tax before, but only on a one-off basis. Since its notional yield was only around £5,400 a year and the Prince needed to pay the continuing cost of his household and maintaining his court, he would remain under considerable financial pressure well after it was approved. According to Jean Froissart, the scheme was devised by John Harewell, the chancellor of Aquitaine and bishop of Bath and Wells. The proposals were brought before the estates of Aquitaine in January 1368 and, after considerable discussion, were approved with some modifications. A minority of noblemen opposed the tax and did not attend; the *fouage* was passed in their absence. Froissart again:

> The deputies from Poitou, Saintonge, the Limousin and the Rouergue were agreeable to this imposition, provided the Prince would keep his coin to the same standard for seven years, but it was refused by some of those from the upper parts of Gascony, led by the count of Armagnac and the lord Albret... saying that when they were under the vassalage of the king of France, they were not oppressed by any such tax or subsidy and that they would never submit to such oppression as long as they could defend themselves.

The estates had assembled in Angoulême on 18 January 1368 to hear the Black Prince's proposals and their deliberations lasted just over a week. The Prince wanted to impose the tax, and was direct and honest about why it was needed and how long it would last. He used the same approach that he had adopted at Chester some fifteen years earlier, bargaining with local representatives rather than imposing a levy on Aquitaine by force. The rate was reduced to ten *sous* (Gascon shillings) a hearth and important concessions were made by confirming municipal liberties, fixing the value of coinage and introducing judicial and financial reform. The Prince then wrote to all his subjects in the principality on 26 January, explaining what had been agreed.

He also began a scheme of public works, building a lighthouse, the Tour de Cordouan, on the mouth of the Gironde estuary: a polygonal beacon tower, topped by a platform, where a fire was kept burning to warn ships away from the rocks. A small chapel or hermitage, dedicated to the Virgin Mary, was constructed next to

it. He also undertook a river-clearing programme along the navigable portions of the Lot and Garonne. On 8 July the Prince's officials
reported that these projects were well under way. He embarked
upon extensive consultation with Gaillac, Moissac, Montauban,
Rabastens and other towns situated on the rivers Garonne and
Tarn, to improve the regulation of the wine trade, measures that
were passed two days later, on 10 July 1368. This was visible lordship,
producing a real financial return for the mercantile community.

However, the Prince was far more politically vulnerable in
Aquitaine than he had been in Cheshire. Jean, count of Armagnac,
was antagonized by these proceedings and refused to allow the
fouage to be collected on his lands. He almost immediately emerged
as the chief of the dissidents. Armagnac was under financial pressure himself. In the 1350s, unlike many of the Gascon nobility, he
had fought on the losing side in the war with France and had little
opportunity to gain booty or ransoms, instead incurring large
debts. His capture by the count of Foix at the battle of Launac in
1362 resulted in his imprisonment for three years and a ransom of
about 300,000 florins (about £45,000). The Prince (and princess) had
secured a reduction in the sum, and loaned him some of money to
pay it, but Armagnac was still forced to sell lands, pledge jewellery
and borrow heavily to secure his release. By his own account, he
was owed more than 200,000 florins (about £30,000) in war wages for
the Nájera campaign.

The root of Armagnac's animosity went back to the Prince's
expedition of 1355, where he had been thoroughly humiliated, and
the uneasy negotiations over the count's homage ten years later,
which began at Angoulême in April 1365, and were deferred to
Bordeaux in early July. When Armagnac continued to complain
about the incursions of the Black Prince's officials, he was told that
'secret meetings and inquiries' had taken place with the assistance
of the count's tenants, and that proceedings against his exactions
would begin shortly in Aquitaine's courts. The Prince would stay
the legal action if Armagnac dropped his own objections. The

count rendered homage, but it did not augur well for their future relationship.

The Prince had tried to accommodate Armagnac, bringing him on to his great council and giving him command of the rearguard on the Spanish expedition, but he neither liked nor trusted him. When the count ousted a minor nobleman of the Rouergue, Guy de Sévérac, from the castle and lordship of Peyrelade, 10 miles (15 km) north-east of Millau, the Prince took Sévérac's side in the dispute and placed him under his personal protection. On his return from Spain, on 17 September 1367, he ordered his officials to restore Peyrelade to Sévérac. This decision, which placed a concern for justice above political pragmatism, was an underlying reason for Armagnac's defection to the ranks of the dissidents.

The count of Armagnac was largely an outsider in Gascon politics, but he was connected by marriage to the lords of Albret and the counts of Périgord, and the grievances of all three men would pose a significant challenge to the Prince's authority. Money was at the root of Arnaud Amanieu d'Albret's difficulties, as it was for Armagnac. He had also been captured by the count of Foix at Launac, and assessed for a ransom of 100,000 florins (about £15,000) and the last instalment of this sum had only been paid in 1367. In addition, he had to contribute to the ransoms of two younger brothers and a cousin who had been captured with him.

During the 1350s he and his family had been among the most successful military entrepreneurs of the south-west of France, drawing large profits from the operations of garrisons and companies. These profits had been much reduced after the peace of Brétigny. At a banquet, Jean Froissart overheard Albret saying that he had never had so much money as in the days when every passing merchant was at his mercy. The Spanish campaign might have repaired Albret's fortunes, but instead he had lost money and gained nothing. On his return to Gascony, he quarrelled with the Black Prince over the amount owed to him for the recruitment and maintenance of his retinue.

Jean Froissart believed that the lord of Albret was originally impressed by the Prince's lordship but that the two men subsequently fell out in the aftermath of Nájera. Albret and Armagnac were sensitive to their waning influence in the enlarged principality of Aquitaine, where power had to be shared with the Prince's English advisers and captains, men such as his successive chancellors John Streatley and John Harewell and his seneschal, Sir Thomas Felton. Times were changing.

Albret was a dangerous opponent. His lands were concentrated in the lower reaches of the Dordogne, close to Bordeaux, and his family alliances spread over much of the region. His grandfather had fought for Edward I, but against Edward II. His father had opposed Edward III and then changed sides and supported him. In July 1363, at Bordeaux cathedral, he had been the first baron of Aquitaine to do homage to the Prince and was initially attracted to his lordship, bringing a substantial retinue to the Spanish expedition of 1367. But he was essentially a freebooter in outlook, fond of money and willing to sell his support to whoever was willing to offer him most. And when Charles V was prepared to grant him financial rewards to change sides, Albret negotiated long and hard to extract the maximum profit from the French king.

A Valois chronicler summed up the situation as follows: 'When the Prince of Wales wished to levy a subsidy from the Gascons, a number of the lords opposed it – and this put the Prince at loggerheads with his subjects.' In reality, the picture was more complex than the complaints of Armagnac and Albret suggested. The cadet line of the Albrets stayed loyal to the Prince and he retained a good relationship with the head of this branch of the family, Bérard, lord of Vayres and Rion. Charles V attempted to win Bérard to his cause, but his overtures were rebuffed.

Archambaud, count of Périgord, was an impulsive young aristocrat who had recently inherited his county from his father. He had also fought with the Black Prince in Spain and accumulated debts. He wanted to build up his estate, and had made a large number of claims to properties in his locality, some of which Sir John Chandos had accepted in principle before the Prince's arrival in the duchy. But the Black Prince distrusted Périgord's ambition, and when, in early 1368, Archambaud raised a small army and attacked one of his local rivals, the lord of Mussidan (who was a personal friend of the Prince), he was arrested and briefly imprisoned, a humiliation that rankled with him for many years afterwards.

However, Archambaud hesitated before finally defecting to the French king, and only did so in March 1369. The town of Périgueux, in the heart of his lordship, did not follow him. Instead, it called an emergency meeting of its assembly and declared its loyalty to the Black Prince. The Prince's open style of government, his consultation over taxation and granting of privileges in return, was popular with the townspeople. Périgueux had raised money for the expedition of 1367 and followed its progress with considerable interest, sending a stream of messengers into Spain, 'to get news of our lord the Prince and his men'.

Gascon power politics, with its strong passions and violent feuding, would have challenged any ruler. The Black Prince normally had a flair for resolving such tensions: he made adroit gifts and loans, flattered men with his friendship and the life of his court. But his capacity to charm diminished after the Nájera campaign. His natural generosity was stifled by his financial circumstances and the changes in his manner would, over time, be aggravated by illness. Unike many in his army, there is no evidence that he had contracted dysentery in the summer heat of 1367, nor that he returned home with a complication from this. It was in the autumn of 1368 that he begun to suffer from a debilitating sickness that worsened the following year. He experienced increasing periods of lethargy, during which he was sometimes bedridden. The Prince's declining health, together with his resentment and frustration as the fruits of the battle of Nájera vanished before his eyes, affected his temper and his judgement.

The religious works that he had purchased before his departure for Aquitaine offered a painful reminder of the frailty of the human condition. Humphrey de Bohun had held the most important military post in the realm, the constableship of England, but a mysterious, incapacitating illness had forced him to surrender his office (in 1338), renounce all martial activity and to turn to a life of pious reflection. He shared with the Black Prince a veneration for the cult of the Trinity, and spoke warmly in his will of his confessor, William Monkland and the illuminator of his psalters, John Tey. But he had withdrawn from the world, wishing to be buried privately and without display. Now the Prince, in his struggle with his own health, was fighting his inner demons alongside his political opponents.

To some extent, the Prince became intolerant of opposition even before the onset of his illness. When the count of Armagnac sent two of his knights to him, in January 1368, to plead for an exemption to the *fouage*, he might have treated it as an opening bid in a bargaining process. Instead, he saw it as an insult to his authority. His answer to Armagnac was that he would have the count's money, whether he objected or not, or destroy his family's power in Aquitaine. The Prince not only kept the intransigent Sir Thomas Wettenhall as his seneschal in the Rouergue, but had him bring reinforcements from England.

He became, on occasion, unnecessarily angry, and some Gascon noblemen who attended his court complained that they were stiffly, even coldly received. When the lord of Albret raised the issue of money due for his participation in the Spanish campaign, there was a dispute over the sum owed. Albret recalled that the Prince broke eye contact, and talked across him to his advisers, using English rather than French. 'The Sire d'Albret is a great lord indeed if he thinks he can break the ordinances of my council,' he said menacingly. Albret, unsurprisingly, disliked being threatened in such a manner. These tensions came at a dangerous time, for the Prince was now facing a most formidable adversary.

†

King Charles V of France was thirty years old in 1368. Pale, thin and serious in demeanour, with piercing eyes and narrow lips, he was a man who always kept his feelings under careful control. He kept his thoughts to himself and was subtle in his grasp of politics and secretive in his application of it. He had recovered from the severe headaches and other maladies that had afflicted his regency and gained confidence, strength and belief in his ability to rule in his own right.

The king's biographer, Christine de Pizan, described a man of zealous piety, who made the sign of the cross as soon as he awoke and spoke his first words of the day to God in his prayers. When dressed, he was brought his breviary and recited the canonical hours with his chaplain, and celebrated high Mass in his chapel at eight in the morning with 'melodious song'. Then he held audience for 'all manner of people, rich and poor, ladies and damsels'. On fixed days he presided over matters of state at the council. He lived with 'majestic regularity', conscious that the dignity of the crown must be maintained by solemn order.

After the midday meal, Charles would listen to minstrels playing sweetly, 'to rejoice the spirit', and then for two hours received ambassadors, princes and knights; there was often such a crowd in his great hall that 'one could hardly turn around.' He listened to news from other countries, signed letters and documents, assigned duties and received gifts. After an hour's rest, he spent time with the queen and his children – a son and heir was born in 1368 and afterwards a second son and two daughters – visited his gardens at Beauté-sur-Marne in summer, read and studied in winter, talked with his intimates until supper, and after the evening's entertainment, retired. He fasted one day a week and read the Bible through each year.

Charles possessed to the full the Valois passion for acquisition and luxury. In 1368 he was reconstructing the Château of Vincennes as a summer palace, and he would soon build or acquire three more. He employed the famous chef Guillaume Tirel, nicknamed

'Taillevent', who wrote a cookery book, *Le Viandier*, detailing the preparation of the heavy, spiced dishes, soups and stews fashionable at the time and who served up roasted swan and peacocks resting on ornate surrounds of spun sugar and painted pastry. Charles collected precious objects and gem-studded reliquaries that housed – it was believed – a piece of Moses's rod, part of the crown of thorns and a fragment of the True Cross. At his death he owned forty-seven gold crowns and sixty-three sets of chapel furnishings.

Charles was a man of inquiring mind, interested in cause and effect and in philosophy, science and literature. He created one of the great libraries of his age, which he installed in the Falconry Tower of the Louvre, where he maintained a second residence. The library's rooms were panelled in carved and decorated cypress wood. Its stained-glass windows were screened by iron wire. A silver lamp was kept burning so that the king could read at any time. Smaller libraries were also installed at Saint-Germain-en-Laye and Vincennes, where the king's most precious books were kept.

He was concerned not only with knowledge, but also with its dissemination. He ordered Nicolas Oresme, a 'councillor of scientific mind', to write a treatise, *On the Origin, Nature and Law of Money*, that explained the theory of stable currency in simple language, and commissioned translations into French of Livy, Aristotle and Augustine, 'for the public utility of the realm and of all Christendom'. It was such far-sighted statecraft that earned him the epithet 'the Wise'. His library was eclectic, containing works of the Church Fathers, Arab scientific books in French translation, a collection of works on astrology and astronomy, forty-seven Arthurian romances, contemporary poetry and satire: in all, over 1,000 volumes. When Charles was reproached for spending too much time with books, he answered: 'As long as knowledge is honoured in this country, so long it will prosper.'

In his *Coronation Book*, a manuscript recording the rituals and protocols of his kingly office, Charles showed a strong interest in the dignity and power of the House of Valois. The book also revealed his ambitions for the duchy of Aquitaine. Within it were recorded drafts of an oath of allegiance Gascon nobles might use if they switched sides and rendered homage to the French crown rather than the Black Prince. Henry of Grosmont had once dismissively referred to Charles V as 'a lawyer rather than a ruler'. But it was this legal acumen – an ability to analyse forensically the strengths and weaknesses of his opponent's position – that was emerging as a major threat to the Prince.

By 1368 Charles had succeeded in containing the plotting of Charles of Navarre and had effectively reduced the disruption caused by the Free Companies. The military strength of his realm was growing. In his library, Charles owned ten copies of Vegetius's treatise on warfare, and he encouraged his noblemen to study the Roman way of military thinking, and to apply its general precepts – to imitate the strengths of the enemy and ruthlessly seek out his weaknesses. And seeing all too clearly the financial vulnerability of the Black Prince's regime, he had accumulated a contingency fiscal reserve, in coin, at the Louvre and Vincennes. It amounted to 400,000 francs.

Cultivating his relations with prominent Gascon nobles, the French king now seized his opportunity. On 4 May 1368, Arnaud Amanieu d'Albret was married to Charles V's sister-in-law, Margaret of Bourbon, in the chapel of the king's private residence at the Hôtel Saint-Pol in Paris. Charles had arranged the marriage and contributed generously to the bride's dowry. Among the guests was Jean, count of Armagnac. Charles had been in regular correspondence with the count in the months preceding the event, and this now bore fruit. While he was in Paris, Armagnac lodged an appeal against the *fouage*, addressing it to the king of France 'in his capacity as the sovereign lord of the duchy of Aquitaine'.

'The lords of Armagnac, Albret and Périgord went to France and laid their complaints before the French king,' Froissart wrote:

They spoke of the wrongs the Prince was about to do them. They placed themselves under the jurisdiction of the king of France and recognized him as their sovereign lord. King Charles, who was desirous to not yet openly infringe the peace between the king of England and him, dissembled his joy at these words.

Edward III's failure to fulfil the outstanding renunciation clause of the Treaty of Brétigny allowed this legal loophole, which Charles V now exploited with purposeful efficiency. On 30 June 1368 he entered into a secret agreement with Armagnac, Albret and Archambaud, count of Périgord. He promised to defend them by force of arms if the Prince ever attacked their dominions. They, in turn, pledged to fight for Charles in a war to recover Aquitaine for the French crown. Charles V then granted the count of Armagnac an enormous pension of 100,000 francs (around £20,000) a year and made further grants of lands to all three noblemen.

The French king had bided his time and struck where the Prince was most vulnerable. 'Thus duplicity and treason began to govern those who ought to have loved him', the Chandos Herald wrote sadly. 'And those whom he held as friends now became his enemies.' The Black Prince understood the implications of the count of Armagnac's appeal as soon as he heard that Charles V intended to receive it. Throughout August 1368 his agents were busy recruiting men-at-arms and archers from his lands in Cheshire and North Wales, and nearly 800 of these mustered in September. He knew that Louis, duke of Anjou, Charles V's brother and military lieutenant, had already committed himself – in a private treaty – to resuming war against England and that the appeal to the Parlement would be the pretext for a resumption of hostilities. And that time was not far off.

However, a clear appreciation of this danger was lacking in London, where Edward III and his ministers observed the developing crisis in paralyzed disbelief. The English king's gift for quick, instinctive decision-making had faded. Instead of making his own judgement of the situation, Edward sent an embassy to Paris to find out what was happening. Charles V, who had no desire to bring things prematurely to a head, simply put off meeting with it. And, quite remarkably, Edward III allowed Albret to appeal over the Prince's head to the king's council in England. Albret took full opportunity to summarize his grievances and paint the Black Prince in the worst possible light.

In the meantime, the English government stuck to its flawed policy that Aquitaine must pay for its own defence, although it well knew that the treasury in Bordeaux was exhausted. Charles V continued his charm offensive on the most prominent towns and noblemen within the principality, writing to invite them to join the appeal process against the *fouage*, and promising generous grants, favours and protection from the Prince's revenge.

The noblemen of the principality weighed their options carefully. Archambaud of Périgord had begun negotiations with Charles V, but hesitated over openly showing his hand. Some who decided to join this process had genuine grievances. 'You must be well aware of the losses which I have suffered at the hands of the Prince's officers', one wrote, 'who have disinherited me of my castle.' Others succumbed to bribery. But many retained their respect for the Black Prince and stayed loyal.

Guichard d'Angle was one of the chief noblemen of Poitou. He had fought for John II at Poitiers and had then transferred his allegiance to the Prince in 1363, becoming marshal of Aquitaine. He was an obvious target for Charles V, but despite the king's efforts Guichard refused French blandishments to change sides once more. The Gascon lord Hélie de Pommiers, whose family held land near La Réole, responded to these overtures by making clear that the Prince's lordship was still far preferable to Charles's. The Black Prince had won these men's allegiance through the power of his charisma and martial prowess, and they were not willing to abandon him when he was suffering and ill. There was still hope.

Prompt support from England was now vital. By October 1368,

while Edward III and his ministers dithered, Louis, duke of Anjou, was raising a substantial body of troops. The duke was headstrong and energetic, and ready to challenge the Black Prince's authority. When Enrique of Trastamara fled from Spain in the aftermath of Nájera, Louis had offered him his support. They met at Aigues-Mortes in Languedoc and drew up a 'treaty of friendship and alliance'. It committed both parties to restore Enrique to the throne of Castile and make war on the English. And the two men began waging a powerful propaganda war against Edward III, the Black Prince and his brother, John of Gaunt.

Their treaty accused the English king and his sons of being 'oppressors of men, like Nimrod', invading France 'out of presumptuous pride' and committing a catalogue of crimes so unthinkable they would not be believed even in a work of fiction. In this extraordinary attack the Black Prince — the victor of Nájera — was singled out for particular denunciation. He was the Biblical Nimrod, a man of colossal strength, a giant and great hunter — but also had become a symbol of overweening arrogance, a man who would be condemned to Hell. The Prince was described as a 'son of Satan' — and in the vivid tapestry later commissioned by the duke for his castle at Angers (in 1373) he appeared, alongside his father and brothers, John of Gaunt and Edmund of Langley, as a horse with a human head, a demonic creature accompanying a swarm of locusts, surging out of a cloud of black smoke.

Amid all this, the Prince's illness took a drastic turn for the worse. By 18 November 1368 he was confined to his bed, with a leading physician of Bordeaux, Pierre de Manhi, in regular attendance. Jean, count of Armagnac, was already in rebellion against the Black Prince. The deterioration in the Prince's health now encouraged Arnaud, lord of Albret, to publicly follow suit and at last openly declare the transfer of his allegiance to the French king. 'When the head is sick, all the limbs will suffer', an official in the Gascon administration wrote to a friend that winter. According to one chronicler, the Prince's symptoms were psychological as well as physical: he took to his bed suffering from 'a great melancholy and affliction of the heart'. He remained incapacitated for several months, unable to control events or to follow their ramifications. Sir John Chandos, the Prince's ablest general and wisest adviser, was urgently recalled from Normandy to take charge. Froissart describes what happened next:

> Upon this, the king of France, to be better informed, and to preserve the rights of his crown, ordered all papers relative to the last peace to be brought to his council chamber, where they were read several times, so that the different points and articles might be fully examined. The king was strongly advised by those present to draw up an appeal and sent it to Aquitaine. And so it was done, summoning the Prince to appear before the Parlement of Paris.

On 23 November, two French emissaries arrived at Bordeaux with the French king's demand that he attend the supreme law court on 1 May 1369, to answer the case made against him. 'When the Prince heard this letter read, he was more surprised than ever before,' Froissart related. 'He eyed the Frenchmen for a while, and then shook his head.' According to the Chandos Herald, when the Prince heard its terms, he lifted himself up and declared:

> 'Lords, by my faith, it seems to me that the French think that I am dead; but if God gives me comfort, and I can rise from this bed, I will do them great harm even now, because God knows that they lack a good case and they will have real cause to complain of me.' And then he wrote back to the king of France, in stern and frank tone, that he would gladly come at his bidding, in the company of his soldiers, to keep him [Charles] from mischief.

Froissart also remembered the Prince's defiance: 'If God would but give me life and health, I would gladly answer this summons and go to Paris, but with a helmet on my head and an army at my back.'

At this time of impending crisis, the Black Prince needed the strong support of his father more than ever. However, Edward III was now fifty-six years old. His drive and vigour were slackening, and his own health was weakening – one yearly medical bill alone came to £54, more than the annual income of an English knight. He retained a court of appeal for his Gascon subjects, although his son had asked him to abandon it as it drew out disputes and undermined his authority. Edward had not come to a decision on this issue, and now Lord Albret's grievances were being aired in London, where they were captured by the Anonimalle chronicler. Albret depicted an increasingly despotic Prince, losing the hearts and minds of his subjects:

> In 1367 [on his return from Spain] the Prince of England contin-
> ued to live in Gascony at enormous cost, spending outrageously.
> He imposed huge levies on the land because of his lack of gold
> and silver. So great was this imposition on his liege people that
> they could not bear the cost. Every house with a hearth in it, big
> or small, had to pay him money. This intolerable burden was
> called the *fouage*.
>
> He was so haughty and carried himself like such a great
> man that he deferred to no one – and he would let various great
> lords of the country, who came to speak with him, wait four
> or five days before he would deign to talk to them. Moreover,
> when they came into his presence, he would keep them kneel-
> ing, shifting from knee to knee, for a quarter of a day before he
> told them to stand up. This was the reason why several of those
> lords rose against him, as well as because of the huge levy.

This was a harsh verdict. European courts of the day abounded in splendour and magnificence was normally regarded as a virtue in a medieval ruler. 'Be generous in your giving,' Geoffrey de Charny had written. In the summer of 1368, the Prince's brother, Lionel, duke of Clarence, had journeyed to Italy to marry Violante Visconti. The bride's father, Gian Galeazzo, duke of Pavia, paid Edward III a dowry so extensive that it took two years to negotiate and offered expenses of 10,000 florins (£1,500) a month for five months for the bridegroom and his retinue. The stupendous outdoor wedding banquet consisted of thirty courses of meat and fish, and lavish gift-giving of costly coats of mail, plumed and crested helmets, greyhounds in velvet collars and falcons wearing silver bells. The poet Petrarch was an honoured guest at the high table; Froissart and Chaucer were also in attendance. It was said that the leftover food was enough to feed 1,000 men. The round of festivities contin-ued over the summer months, and when Lionel died suddenly of fever on 7 October some wondered whether it was the cumulative result of chronic indigestion.

This was the spirit of the times. The accounts of Richard Filong-ley showed that the Black Prince allocated more than 30,000 Gascon pounds a year for his household — a substantial but not exorbi-tant sum, in keeping with the example set by his own father (the demands of Edward III's own court had, by 1365, risen to nearly £25,000 sterling). And the Prince's costs included payments made to his war retinue.

The Prince shared his wealth with those around him. He had always struggled to stay ahead of his spending – that was the danger inherent in his chivalric lifestyle. But overall, the documentary evidence of the Black Prince's administration does not bear out Albret's charges. Far from being arrogant and distant, the Prince took time and trouble over relatively small matters, ensuring, shortly after his return from Spain, that the Dominican convent of Bagnères, 15 miles (24 km) south of Tarbes, was rebuilt within the safety of the town walls to better protect it from freebooting troops. When Bérard d'Albret, from the cadet branch of the family, wanted to claim the lordship of Puynormand in the Gironde (which was in the gift of Edward III) the Prince helped him draft the petition, had his letter translated from Gascon to French and ensured it was put before the English council.

The Prince was doing his best in difficult circumstances and in the wake of the black propaganda devised by Louis, duke of Anjou, and Enrique of Trastamara, these fresh accusations – now circulating within the court and council of Edward III – were particularly painful to hear. On 7 December, the Prince, stung by the personal attacks on him, wrote to his father:

Most respected lord, I commend myself to your highness as best and as humbly as I can, asking for your blessing.

May it please your highness to know that I have received your letters and the certificate that the lord Albret sent to Paris, for which I thank you, so that I can clear my name... What I reported to you, I did as a son should do to his father, truly and loyally and in no other way – and I will maintain and prove it in all ways that a knight should or that it may please your lordship to so command.

And, my most respected lord, without wishing to displease your highness, I am amazed that anyone in your kingdom, whoever he may be, should wish to give credence to reports from anyone, messenger or otherwise, which do me dishonour and discredit my standing; for I will never repeat anything to you which will not be found to be true and which I will not maintain, with the help and grace of God, against any other subject or vassal of your realm.

And do not be displeased that I have written so forwardly about this, because it affects me and my honour and standing so closely it seems to me, my lord, that I must do so, because I would be very aggrieved to be found in such default towards your highness, and I pray that God may keep me from it.

And besides, I have heard that some people there have believed the excuses of the lord of Albret too easily – but they are not true... I ask you, most honoured lord, for the sake of such little power I have to serve you, to take these matters entirely to heart... for I will always be ready to carry out your orders as best I can.

Most respected father, may the blessed Trinity guard and maintain your highness and give you glorious victory over our enemies.

Beneath the letter's formal courtesy, the Prince's anger was all too obvious. He was a man of honour – and these reproaches and insinuations were the antithesis of everything he stood for. He was mortified to find that they were now being given credence by members of his father's government, as if they carried serious weight. At a time of grave difficulty, he deserved the king's fullest support – and his trust.

The letter was delivered by Sir John Chandos, and Chandos, on the Prince's instructions, enlarged on its content, making three pointed requests to King Edward: that he surrender his right of appeal from the Gascon courts, settle Brétigny's outstanding renunciation clause and, if war was to break out, provide Aquitaine with proper financial and military assistance.

The new year of 1369 began with a real sense of threat. On 19 January the town of Millau affirmed its loyalty to the Prince but warned him that Louis, duke of Anjou, was gathering troops in the region and appealing to men to change allegiance and join France. Edward III, shaken by his son's communication, dispatched Guillaume Hamon, one of his best surgeons, to Bordeaux on 10 February and set about recruiting an army to sail to Gascony in the spring, led by the earls of Cambridge (the Black Prince's brother, Edmund of Langley) and Pembroke. Such measures were desperately needed. War had not formally broken out, but French soldiers were on the move everywhere.

The medieval soldier instinctively sensed times of peril and danger, and his conscience awoke at the prospect of captivity or death. The Prince's companion Jean de Grailly felt the menace facing all his fighting comrades. He drew up his will on 6 March 1369, leaving the exceptional sum of 40,000 crowns (around £6,000) in pious donations, enough for 50,000 Masses to be said for his soul, eighteen chaplaincies to be founded, innumerable lamps lit and prayers recited.

Early in 1369, the bedridden Prince warned all his subjects in Aquitane that Jean count of Armagnac was in open revolt, having broken 'the most solemn oaths of loyalty sworn to us', and that he and his accomplices now intended 'through sheer malice' to destroy the peace.

'Since Christmas, the news has all been bad', a member of the Black Prince's household wrote:

> The Prince is ill, our men shut up in their castles and the danger from the enemy is all around us. More money and men are desperately needed. If they do not arrive soon, the French may deal such a blow to our principality that we shall not be able to recover.

chapter ten

LIMOGES

In June 1369 war between England and France broke out once more. Charles V cited a legal justification for this, the non-appearance of the Black Prince at the Parlement of Paris a month earlier. Charles's brother, Louis, duke of Anjou, then urged the French king's subjects to make 'as great a war as possible on the English'. In response, Edward III once more revived his claim to both kingdoms. On 19 June, the Prince was instructed to proclaim Edward's intention of regaining France by conquest throughout the principality of Aquitaine.

Charles V had been careful, if not scrupulous, in the way that he had renewed hostilities. In a letter of 28 February 1369 to Jean, count of Armagnac, the French king instructed the count not to begin military operations against the Black Prince until he authorized them. Charles outlined his thinking:

> You are the principal appellant against the Prince, and he is now your enemy. We have seen the threatening letters he has sent to you, and your response, which you then circulated amongst the nobles and townspeople of Gascony. It is vital that we proceed in this matter step by step. If the Prince wages war against you, you will be entitled to our aid and support. Until that time, we must continue along a proper judicial path.

The French king was clear and authoritative. He told Armagnac that he had dispatched similar orders, urging restraint, to Louis, duke of Anjou. Charles V added: 'If you go against our wishes, and start the fight prematurely, we will be seriously displeased.' Charles knew that the English position in eastern Aquitaine – the regions of Quercy and the Rouergue, where Armagnac's lordship carried considerable authority – was highly vulnerable, and that Armagnac's son, also called Jean, had already raised a small army to enter those territories. The Prince did not have enough troops to properly defend this part of his principality. It was all a question of timing. 'We well understand that soon you will be able to bring down overwhelming force against him,' the French king concluded with quiet satisfaction.

Charles V had much to be satisfied about. Within a month of his letter to Armagnac his foreign policy had reaped further handsome dividends, when Castile was recovered by Enrique of Trastamara. Enrique had once more invaded the country, linked up with the forces of Bertrand du Guesclin and surprised and defeated the troops of Pedro I at Montiel, near Toledo. Pedro shut himself up in the castle there and offered du Guesclin a large bribe to allow him to escape. Du Guesclin took the money and handed him over to Enrique; on the night of 23 March 1369 Pedro was murdered by Enrique and his retainers. The Spanish adventure, undertaken by the Black Prince at such great cost in men and money, had come to its strategically disastrous conclusion, with a sworn enemy of England and an ally of France back on the throne. The Anglo-Castilian alliance of 1362 had failed and the consequences for the beleaguered principality of Aquitaine would be serious.

Charles V's persistent diplomacy and far-sighted strategy in Spain had paid off. But there was, perhaps, an inevitability to the ultimate failure of the Prince's campaign in that country. It had been a mistake on his part not to bolster Pedro's regime earlier, in the spring of 1366, but Enrique's first invasion had caught every-one by surprise. It has been said that Pedro was untrustworthy and that he had no intention of honouring the treaty he made with the Prince at Libourne on 23 September 1366. But once it became clear that Enrique had escaped, in the aftermath of Nájera, and could count on French support in his efforts to regain Castile, it was entirely in Pedro's interests to honour the financial terms agreed. The balance of evidence shows he genuinely wanted to meet that commitment.

The turning point was the Black Prince's renegotiation of the treaty at Burgos on 6 May 1367, which massively increased the sums demanded and gave Pedro less time to pay them. The new treaty was effectively imposed on the Castilian king by force and led to a breakdown in relations between Pedro and the Prince. The two men fell out over a chivalric issue, the proper treatment of prisoners of war. This was a matter upon which the Black Prince would not compromise. Strict adherence to chivalric principle could be a weakness as well as a strength in the complex world of power politics, as Charles V understood. The great army that his opponent had assembled had appeared for a time invincible – but it had wasted away in a dysentery outbreak in the Spanish summer heat, leaving the Prince to return to Gascony empty-handed.

Negotiations were then opened between the Black Prince, Peter IV of Aragon and Charles of Navarre. At one stage, they envisioned partitioning Castile between themselves, but this grandiose scheme came to nothing. There were simply not the men or resources available to make it a realistic proposition, Navarre could not be trusted anyway, and the Gascon treasury was burdened with debt. By the spring of 1369 the Black Prince was in no position to make any further intervention in Spain: all his efforts were directed towards clinging on to what he already held in Aquitaine.

Enrique of Trastamara had proved a redoubtable adversary, who pursued his objective of winning back the Castilian throne with a single-minded determination. But the help that he received from the Breton captain Bertrand du Guesclin was all-important. Flat-nosed, swarthy and well built, du Guesclin was a natural soldier. The poet Cuvelier, who composed a rhyming *chanson* of the warrior's life, laughingly recalled: 'There was none so ugly from Rennes to Dinan.' Born into a minor noble family, and largely neglected by his parents, du Guesclin showed an early aptitude for fighting, organizing his friends into rival bands and staging mock tournaments. He grew to manhood at the time of the Breton War of Succession, becoming skilled in the tactics of ambush and ruse, spies and subterfuge. Intrepid and unscrupulous, he quickly made a name for himself, attracting the patronage of a host of French aristocrats: Charles of Blois, Marshal Arnoul d'Audrehem and Philip of Burgundy.

In 1357 he successfully defended Rennes in a long siege against Henry of Grosmont. This brought him to the notice of the dauphin Charles, who (with King John in captivity in England) gave him his first royal commission, the captaincy of Pontorson. On the dauphin's accession as Charles V, du Guesclin won him an important victory, at Cocherel in Normandy, on 16 May 1364, defeating an Anglo-Navarrese army led by Jean de Grailly, Captal de Buch. The battle marked the end of Charles of Navarre's ability to menace Paris and gained du Guesclin King Charles's long-standing gratitude and respect. The two men began to work together to counter the power of the English.

Their partnership was not damaged by the defeat at Auray in Brittany later that year, when the army of Charles of Blois — with du Guesclin one of its leading captains — was firmly defeated by Sir John Chandos. Charles V assisted du Guesclin with his ransom, and the following year both devised a plan to lead many of the Free Companies from France. They enlisted papal support, promising to take these men on crusade against Muslim Granada. But the two men had a very different intention. Once in Spain, they would instead join with Enrique of Trastamara in Aragon, and attack Pedro of Castile.

It was du Guesclin who had devised this clever ploy and it was kept completely secret. The diversion of a crusade was a serious matter, but Charles V and du Guesclin saw a way of justifying it. They decided to argue that Pedro was an excommunicant, in military alliance with Granada (which was supplying him with troops), and that removing him from power was the necessary prerequisite for launching military actions further south. Du Guesclin and Charles V knew that Pope Urban would be considerably relieved that the Free Companies had left the vicinity of Avignon, whatever their final destination. The stratagem worked in the longer term when Enrique, with French help, regained the Castilian throne two years after his defeat at Nájera.

Such cunning was entirely alien to the Black Prince, who, in 1365, had sent a series of messengers to Avignon to ascertain what was happening over the proposed 'crusade'. Charles V had founded a college of astrology at the University of Paris, which he equipped with a library and instruments; Bertrand du Guesclin consulted an astrologer on all his campaigns and his wife, Tiphaine, was said to possess occult powers. Yet in matters of war both were eminently practical in outlook: they understood the world of chivalry, but for them it was results that mattered. And those results were not built on chivalric prowess but on financial solvency and tough professionalism.

Neither Charles nor his Breton captain believed in fighting campaigns on credit. When du Guesclin brought the Free Companies into Spain in 1365, he did not do so not on the promise of future payment but only when the money had actually been delivered to his war chest. Bertrand would spend a further year fighting in Castile with Enrique, shoring up the new regime. His courage, skill and tireless energy would make him a formidable opponent once he returned to France.

The Black Prince had never grasped the value of financial prudence and in the summer of 1369 he was desperately short of money and manpower. He placed his administrative headquarters at Cognac, and deputed the experienced soldier and administrator Sir Thomas Felton to run his affairs in Bordeaux. He raised forces from castle garrisons, the retinues of Gascon and Poitevin lords who had remained loyal and captains of the Free Companies. An army arrived under John Hastings, earl of Pembroke, and the Prince's brother Edmund of Langley, earl of Cambridge. These commanders took the war to the enemy in the north, besieging the duke of Anjou's fortress of La Roche-sur-Yon, some 50 miles (80km) north-west of La Rochelle. A second force was expected under John of Gaunt, and this army was required to oppose the incursions of the count of Armagnac in the Rouergue. However, Edward III decided to divert it to Calais instead. It was a decision that would considerably damage the Prince's chances of defending Aquitaine.

Charles V had appointed Armagnac his captain-general and governor in the Rouergue and granted him a yearly pension of 100,000 francs (around £20,000) 'to better make war upon our enemies'. The count had over 300 men in his own military retinue and was able to put a total of more than 1,000 troops into the field. More forces were being brought into Quercy and the Rouergue by the duke of Anjou. Rodez returned to Armagnac's allegiance and the badges of the Black Prince were knocked from the city gates. With no Anglo-Gascon army in the region more towns followed suit. Raiding parties were not enough. The Prince desperately needed reinforcements to stop wholesale defections to the French.

King Edward and his government had to consider the bigger picture and balance the needs of their footholds in northern France against those of the principality of Aquitaine in the south. The loss of possessions in Ponthieu in the late spring raised fears that Calais might be in danger. Ponthieu was Edward III's ancestral estate, where he had first challenged the French king and won his resounding victory at Crécy. It had great sentimental importance for him. However, this was not a time for sentiment but clear-headed thinking. Calais was well defended by an able commander, the earl of Hereford, and when the English Parliament was nervously summoned on 3 June there was no French army north of the Loire to threaten it. Reinforcements should have been sent to shore up Hereford's garrison — but not Gaunt and his entire 3,000-strong army.

Edward III was toying with the idea of crossing to Calais in person and sallying forth to challenge the French king to battle.

Edward was in poor health and the notion was hardly realistic, but Gaunt was ordered to wait for the king's arrival nonetheless. On 15 August Queen Philippa died and Edward now chose not to cross the Channel at all. Gaunt undertook some inconclusive raiding in Picardy and in September a second army, commanded by the redoubtable earl of Warwick, was also sent to join him. However, it was unclear what this large force was supposed to do.

Warwick was a highly regarded fighter, earl marshal, founder member of the Order of the Garter and hero of Crécy and Poitiers. He had fought with the Black Prince in both these battles, accompanied him to Gascony in 1355 and again in 1363, and knew Aquitaine well. His presence would have made a huge difference in the principality. Chroniclers applauded the resolve of this tough veteran, the Anonimalle chronicler noting with delight that when the earl appeared outside Calais French forces fled in terror. But his troops were largely consigned to garrison duties, while John of Gaunt led an inconclusive raid into eastern Normandy. Thomas Walsingham criticized the lack of direction behind this campaign; it would have been far better if Warwick and his two-thousand-strong army had been employed supporting the Prince in Aquitaine.

Charles V's correspondence with the count of Armagnac showed a monarch who had grown into his office, displaying drive, purpose and consistency in pursuit of his ambitions. Edward III's letters to one of his captains, Sir John Kyriel, in the summer of 1369, revealed something rather different. On 7 August the English king wrote to Kyriel, informing him that he planned to cross the Channel and instructing him to join his army in two weeks' time. Edward told Kyriel that he had decided to respond personally to the French threat, 'which greatly affects our royal dignity'. On 13 August Kyriel received a second letter, countermanding the earlier order, as the king 'had now learned for certain that the enemy intended to invade'. No invasion was in fact to materialize.

On 14 August Kyriel received two royal letters in the same day. In the first, Edward said that he had decided to cross the Channel after all, but had postponed his army's date of assembly to the beginning of September, when Kyriel was once again told to join him. Another arrived in the afternoon, with completely different instructions for the bemused captain: he was to proceed to Sandwich immediately because enemy galleys were planning an attack there. When Kyriel arrived at the port no French ships could be seen.

On 18 August Kyriel received his fifth royal letter in eleven days. He was now to cross the Channel at once, as battle with the French was expected the following week. No clash actually occurred, but Kyriel and his followers did find large supplies of wine and beer left by the retreating enemy soldiers. At the end of this rush of contradictory commands, they were probably badly needed.

Charles V was no warrior, but he had emerged as a strong and effective ruler; Edward III had been a great warrior, but was now lacking clarity and direction in his kingship. Buffeted by rumours and poor military intelligence, he had lost sight of the broader strategic picture and was largely ignoring the needs of Aquitaine. Within the principality, hunger for military action was still very much in evidence. The French were shaken when the earl of Pembroke captured La Roche-sur-Yon and launched a raid along the Loire, even more so when English captains struck into the Bourbonnais, burst into a poorly defended castle at Belleperche, 12 miles (19 km) north-west of Moulins, and captured Isabella of Valois, duchess of Bourbon, Charles V's mother-in-law. But a field army was also needed in eastern Aquitaine, led by a commander of standing – John of Gaunt or the earl of Warwick – to stem the tide of defections to the French. King Edward could and should have provided it.

The Prince was engaged in a propaganda battle alongside the military one. Those renouncing their allegiance to his cause and joining the party of Charles V were only too keen to blacken his name. Alongside the complaints of the chief appellants, and the slurs of Enrique of Trastamara, came fresh accusations from Louis, vicomte of Rochechouart. A nobleman of the Limousin,

Rochechouart had rendered homage to the Black Prince on 13 September 1363 and subsequently had been appointed a member of his governing council. Uncomfortable at this close association, the vicomte alleged that at the beginning of June 1369, the Prince, 'already suspecting his loyalty', had summoned him to Angoulême, 'and there put him in harsh prison, where he was for a long time in danger of his life'.

Rochechouart added the heart-rending detail that he was only released on the entreaties of his desperate family. However, documentary evidence showed that Rochechouart was already in Paris on 23 June 1369: his 'long and harsh imprisonment' had been a fabrication. His further claim that he had left his estates in the hands of a certain Thibault du Pont, a minor Breton captain, who had then 'made great and damaging war against the Prince', was both self-serving and absurd.

It was a case of 'damned if you do, damned if you don't'. Jean Froissart had already accused the Prince of naivety in releasing Bertrand du Guesclin, his prisoner at Nájera, against the advice of his council. Froissart portrayed this as an impulsive and careless chivalric gesture; in reality, the ransom treaty – for the considerable sum of 100,000 Spanish gold crowns (around £20,000) – was agreed between the Prince, his advisers and du Guesclin over a month of hard negotiations in December 1367. Du Guesclin – no chivalric paragon – respected his opponent's sense of fairness, and refused to campaign against him in France until the sum was fully paid off.

†

In the late summer of 1369 the Black Prince began to lose some of the sturdiest of his companions. Sir James Audley died of sickness in the aftermath of the siege of La Roche-sur-Yon at the end of August. Sir Thomas Wettenhall was killed in an ambush later in September. The citizens of Millau – still holding out for the

English – paid for his funeral and held a memorial Mass for the fallen captain. And in the same month the Prince heard news from England that his mother, Queen Philippa, had died after a long illness. 'Thus every kind of mischance arose', wrote the Chandos Herald, 'and one after another they fell upon the noble Prince, who lay ill in bed. But despite all this, he kept his faith in God, saying: "If I could rise from here, I would take good vengeance."'

The Black Prince made preparations for the new campaigning season as best he could. He sent out instructions to his captains and rewarded his loyal followers. On 23 October Jean de Grailly was granted land and rents in Cognac. On 14 November John Harpenden, his seneschal in the Saintonge, was ordered to inspect and repair those fortifications still in English hands. Later that month, Edward III's council attempted to recall the Prince's chancellor, John Harewell, bishop of Bath and Wells. The Prince refused to let him go, saying that 'he would be unable to carry on without him'.

Harewell had been one of the principal architects of the *fouage,* and the issue behind this tug-of-war was the levying of the tax, which some of the English king's ministers – unduly influenced by the lord of Albret's appeal – strongly criticized. In the financial crisis of the early 1340s King Edward had insisted on his right to levy war taxation without consultation with Parliament. In contrast, the Black Prince and Harewell had fully consulted the estates of Aquitaine and amended the *fouage* as a result.

The year of 1370 began in terrible fashion. At the end of December, Sir John Chandos, the Prince's most experienced captain in Aquitaine, set up an ambush on the bridge at Lussac, spanning the River Vienne in Poitou. Chandos knew that a French raiding party would be passing along the old Roman road from Limoges to Poitiers. When they reached that bridge, the enemy found their passage blocked by a hand-picked body of knights. As they engaged with this force, Chandos brought up more troops behind them. This clever move should have led to a resounding victory. The chronicler Jean Froissart took up the story:

Chandos, who was a strong and bold knight, and calm and measured in all his undertakings, ordered that his banner be borne before him, surrounded by a picked body of his men. He was dressed in a great robe, richly emblazoned with his coat of arms, on front and back – so that he appeared resolved in some adventurous undertaking – and in this state, with sword in hand, he advanced on foot towards the enemy.

Chandos called out a challenge to his opponents: 'I am John Chandos – look at me well, for, if God pleases, we will now put to the test your great deeds of arms that are so renowned.' The knight dismounted, and was advancing upon the French on foot. Froissart continued: 'That morning there had been a strong frost, which had made the ground slippery, and as he strode forward he got his legs caught up in his robe, which was particularly long, and stumbled.'

Sensing an opportunity, one of the French knights rode hard at Sir John and thrust his lance straight at his face. Chandos, conscious of the power of visual display on the battlefield, had wanted to encourage his men and see their responses. He had been so caught up in the drama of the moment that he had neglected to pull down the visor of his helmet. The blow struck him between the nose, eye and forehead – and in falling forward he impaled himself on the lance tip. 'He rolled over twice, in great agony, like one who has been given his death-wound. Indeed, after receiving the blow, he never uttered another word.' His enraged companions fought to defend their fallen chief. One stood over Chandos's body, determined to prevent the French from hauling him off, and dealt such powerful sword blows to those around him that none dared approach. Another pursued Sir John's assailant, overtaking him and striking him with such force that his lance ran through the Frenchman's armour and pierced his thighs.

This small-scale skirmish ended when reinforcements rushed to join the English force and carried off their mortally injured leader. Even the French were saddened, for Chandos was widely

respected by friend and foe alike. One of the opposing captains, Jean
du Mesnil, later referred to the engagement in simple and moving
terms, not by place or location, but as 'the misfortune of Chandos'.
Chandos's tragic and unfortunate death recalled the strictures of
the twelfth-century cleric, Bernard of Clairvaux, when he derided
the vanity of the warrior class:

> What then, O knights, is this monstrous error, this overwhelm-
> ing urge, which bids you to fight with such pomp? You cover
> your horses with silk, adorn your armour with plumes and
> paint up your shields and saddles. You garnish your spurs with
> gold, silver and precious stones and then, in all this glory, you
> fearlessly march to your ruin... Do you think the swords of
> your enemy will be deflected by embroidery or fine silks? You
> wear such long and full tunics – you will simply trip yourselves
> up on them.

But on that bitterly cold morning, rallying his troops after a difficult night march, Chandos was not lost in a realm of overblown
pomp. Fearing the tide of war was turning against the English, he
had tried – through gesture and display – to give heart to his men.
Chandos embodied the very spirit of chivalry. He had unfurled his
banner with martial pride on the field of Nájera. A soldier, administrator and counsellor famed for his courteous speech, in his way
with words, his courage and prudence in matters of war and peace,
he was Oliver to the Prince's Roland. But Chandos's own particular
chanson was drawing to its end. He was now in such pain that he was
unable to utter a sound, and he died the following day, on 1 January
1370. 'And thus the noble knight Sir John Chandos passed away, may
God have mercy on his soul. For in a hundred years there would
not be found a more courteous knight or one fuller of noble virtues.' When the news was carried to the Black Prince and his court,
all were grief-stricken. The sense of ill-omen was palpable.

In the aftermath of Chandos's death, the Prince, always pious,
became increasingly scrupulous in his relations with the church, as

if he was trying to deflect some form of divine punishment being visited on him and his circle of warriors. On 15 January 1370 he wrote from Angoulême to the abbey of Sainte-Croix in Bordeaux. Under the terms of his feudal overlordship he had inherited property and goods belonging to a minor Gascon nobleman, Arnaud de Campania, who had died without heirs. But upon inspecting these possessions, it became clear that some of it was stolen church property. Mortified that he might become associated with this sin, the sick Prince made strenuous inquiries to find out where these ecclesiastical items had come from, and once successful, informed the abbey that he was returning them without further delay.

In Paris, Charles V called a council of war to consider how to strike a decisive blow against the English. For his Gascon allies there was little attraction in piecemeal actions: they had joined him on the promise of increased privileges and full restoration of their estates. If they did not soon receive them, they could possibly defect back to the other side. It was common knowledge that the Prince was lying sick at Angoulême. The French council decided on a bold move, to strike hard at his position and if possible, capture him.

A plan was quickly devised. Louis, duke of Anjou, would advance through the Agenais and Périgord; another of the king's brothers, John, duke of Berry, would push forward in a south-westerly direction, through the Limousin. In support of this, Charles V now ordered Bertrand du Guesclin to return from Spain to join Anjou's forces. But du Guesclin would not return to France until the summer of 1370, when the residue of his ransom was settled by the French king.

The Black Prince was making plans of his own. A disastrous attempt to relieve the siege of Belleperche in March 1370 had shown that his brother Edmund of Langley, earl of Cambridge, was unfit for military command. On 13 March, struggling with the weight of responsibility, he delegated powers in Poitou to local noblemen he still trusted, 'his good and loyal friends' Guillaume lord of Parthenay, Louis vicomte of Châtellerault and Guichard d'Angle, who would be governors of the region on his behalf. Edward III was now distracted by a fresh attempt to ally with Charles of Navarre in Normandy. The Prince warned his father that Navarre was not to be trusted, and the policy would only fritter away precious resources. Edward persisted with his efforts. John of Gaunt would sail to Bordeaux that summer and reinforce the Prince's position, but his army consisted of fewer than 1,000 men.

It was now clear to the Prince that there would be no easy recovery from his illness. He asked that Gaunt be given the full powers of king's lieutenant, to be able to grant military safe-conducts, to knight members of his army 'and all other such things, in agreement with the Prince, whether he is present or absent'. In practice, he envisaged Gaunt taking the field on his behalf. He was concerned that those who remained loyal to his cause, and had lost lands and possessions by doing so, be properly rewarded with estates confiscated from those who had deserted to the French. And on 1 July 1370, after discussions with his brother and his father, the Prince determined on a new way of waging war, one of clemency and persuasion rather than threat and intimidation. The details were set out on the Gascon Rolls, which formed part of the administrative records of the principality:

> For the comfort and support of Edward of Woodstock, Prince of Aquitaine and Wales, and the inhabitants of his principality, it has been decided that he should be able to admit and receive into the king's peace and grace those who have left the Prince's obedience, whether through the persuasion of the king's enemies or of their own free will, who now wish to return to his allegiance, pardoning their crimes, even the most serious, and restoring their privileges. While it is sometimes justifiable to punish such actions through the exercise of royal authority, it is also, on occasions, right to temper such a policy with leniency.

Any change or renunciation of allegiance threw up complex ethical dilemmas, where idealism and notions of honour often conflicted with material self-interest. The Gascon nobleman Renaud de Pons, lord of Ribérac, changed sides four times between 1369 and 1370, only finally throwing in his lot with the French after the Prince had left Aquitaine. When he did so his wife, Marguerite de Périgord, refused to join him, and stayed loyal to the English cause.

A nobleman of the Rouergue, Guy de Sévérac, who had benefited from the Prince's patronage and judicial protection, struggled over renouncing his oath to him. On 3 December 1368 Charles V heard that Sévérac was unsure about committing himself to the French cause and wrote to him explaining his position. 'It has come to our knowledge', Charles said, 'that you have received copies of the appeals made before the court of our Parlement by certain lords of Gascony, which you believe are against the tenor of the treaty made between our late father, God preserve his soul, and the king of England.' The French king then explained that the appeal was permissible because the renunciation clauses of the treaty of Brétigny had been delayed and not properly put into effect by the English. Guy de Sévérac still hesitated, but in the summer of 1369 Charles V bribed him to join the French side, granting him a host of lands and offices.

On 4 November 1369 Sévérac — recently appointed captain and governor of Compeyre in the Rouergue — was still uneasy and the French king sought to reassure him. Charles wrote:

> My good lord, we know well the considerable efforts and great diligence you have shown on our behalf, and think it is no bad thing to have such affection for our realm of France and to keep it in your heart. We believe that these events have come to pass through the help of Our Lord, and we are sure that He will keep you in his protection.

But Sévérac remained unconvinced and, early the following year — overcome by remorse for abandoning the Black Prince — he sought an audience with Pope Urban V and begged for a full remission of his sins. On 21 February 1370 he was granted a confessor and the right to receive an absolution, 'as he has promised to amend his conduct, and repair the oaths he has broken [to the Prince]'. Sévérac's course of action was roundly mocked by Jean, count of Armagnac.

Under the laws of war, a medieval ruler was entitled to punish most severely those towns and communities that had first accepted his allegiance and then renounced it. But the Prince chose not to follow this path. He was aware that the lack of an army in the eastern part of his principality had left many with little option but to go over to the French. The count of Armagnac and other lords were able to raise forces of several thousand, while his own harassed officials could muster forces of little more than a hundred or so.

The Prince had also begun to reflect more deeply on the renewal of the war, and on the events that had led up to it. He feared that his own illness and the broader reverses suffered in Aquitaine were a sign that God no longer favoured the English cause, and that divine approval had been lost through the sin of supporting Pedro of Castile. And he was mindful that his own influence was waning. His new policy, offering forgiveness to others rather than punishment, was a gesture of contrition.

The French were readying themselves for a summer offensive. They set off in July 1370 and scored a succession of small victories. By late August the duke of Anjou was at Périgueux, 55 miles (88 km) south-east of Angoulême, where he was reinforced by du Guesclin and the Breton mercenaries he had brought back from Spain; the duke of Berry was at Limoges, the same distance to the east. The Prince was at Cognac, which he had chosen as a rallying point for all his available forces. And then he learned of the surrender of Limoges.

Limoges was a city of about 15,000 inhabitants. It was divided into two distinct parts. The cité, composed of the cathedral, the bishop's palace and houses of the canons, some small churches and fairly humble dwellings, was controlled by the bishop. Further up the hill was the newer part of the town, known as the château, dominated by the castle and abbey, around which a prosperous mercantile community had developed, specializing in enamel work and ceramics. Most of the population of Limoges lived in the new town.

The Black Prince was on good terms with the entire city. He had spent a month there in May 1364 and on 24 November 1365 he had ratified and amplified its privileges. He kept in regular touch with its citizens. Indeed, his last communication with some of its traders was on 10 August 1370, when he instructed his seneschal, Richard Abberbury, to allow them to acquire smallholdings within the *cité* without having to pay tax.

✝

The Prince's opponent in the region, John, duke of Berry, younger brother of King Charles V, was a sensual, pleasure-loving aesthete, and a supreme accumulator of manuscripts and other works of art. Berry had gathered around him an extraordinary collection of precious stones, musical instruments, antique cameos, hunting dogs and exotic animals, including a leopard, a camel and a monkey. As an architectural patron, he built or renovated seventeen châteaux. His favourite, at Mehun-sur-Yèvre, 10 miles (16 km) north-west of Bourges, was described by Froissart as 'one of the most beautiful houses in the world'. He commissioned densely woven tapestries, depicting the nine worthies or heroes, and lavishly decorated with his coats of arms. He loved jewellery, devised individual names for his favourite rubies and once interrupted an encounter with the papal legate to attend a meeting with his favourite diamond merchant. He had a connoisseur's eye for fine table decorations: his inventories of possessions record a bluish-white vase, the first example of Chinese porcelain known to have entered Europe. Above all, he commissioned exquisite books of hours.

Berry's *Très Riches Heures,* designed by the Limbourg brothers, has provided us with some of the most enduring images of medieval life. This magnificent liturgical work was the first western manuscript to depict shadow; its composition had a richness and depth that allowed its scenes to step out of the page. The January mini-ature depicted the duke himself, resplendent in a gold-threaded gown trimmed with fur, surrounded by his attendants, typically engaged in a festival of gift-giving. Berry was lost in a world of artistic delight, and the inscribed prayer scroll at the head of his magnificent tomb caught the anguish of finally having to relin-quish the beauty and richness of his collection: 'Contemplate what nobility, what abundance, what glories were present before me. Once I had these things. Now they are passing away.'

The Black Prince had encountered Berry once before, during the Poitiers campaign of 1356, when – as count of Poitiers – the teen-ager had been entrusted with the defence of French lands south of the Loire. He had been prepared on that occasion to meet his opponent in battle, but John had slipped away to join his father. Six years later the duchy of Berry was settled upon him, a wealthy fiefdom that allowed him to indulge his taste for luxury to the full. In the intervening years it become all too clear that Berry preferred the touch of gold and gems, many small enough to fit in the palm of his hand, to the grip of the sword hilt.

In the summer of 1369 Charles V had appointed his brother 'lieutenant-general for the making of war'. For once, the French king's innate sense of realism seems to have deserted him. Berry's household accounts show that over the next three years he only left the security of the French capital or his provincial estates on three occasions. Two of these were visits to the papal court at Avignon; the third would be his brief foray into the Limousin in August 1370. The duke enjoyed gazing at tapestries depicting the battles of classical antiquity; the harsh realities of medieval warfare were delegated to others.

This so-called 'lieutenant-general' preferred secret negotiation to military activity, and bribery to feats of arms. Berry's accounts recorded regular payments to his agents for embarking on missions of undercover diplomacy within the duchy of Aquitaine, plotting the surrender of towns by means of generous gifts to their leading officers. The duke prepared his expedition to Limoges with care, for he did not wish to be troubled with the inconvenience of actually having to fight. He sent a trusted servant, the soldier Louis de Malval, lord of Châtelus, ahead of him with a force of 200 mounted men, to ensure that the area surrounding Limoges had gone over to the French.

Louis de Malval had fought in the army of John II at Poitiers, but after the treaty of Brétigny rendered homage to the Black Prince and served with him in Spain. On the resumption of hostilities he changed sides once more and entered the service of the duke of Berry, who sent him on a number of missions into the Limousin. Another servant, the Poitevin baron Renaud de Montléon, was then dispatched to Limoges to conduct secret negotiations with its bishop, Jean de Cros. By 15 August these had been successfully concluded and both men were handsomely rewarded. Berry's intended route was free of English troops and Cros had promised to surrender the *cité* once the duke arrived outside its gates. The art connoisseur now moved quickly, travelling the 125 miles (200 km) from Bourges to Limoges in under a week. On the evening of 21 August the duke established himself in the Dominican convent in the city's suburbs.

The following day found Berry in an exultant mood. Sound military strategy dictated keeping his movements secret for as long as possible, to retain the advantage of surprise. But the duke was revelling in the moment, as if he was handling one of his beloved illuminated manuscripts. Believing the Black Prince to be too ill to respond, he sent of a letter of challenge to him, summoning him to come to the relief of Limoges. Not satisfied with this, he dispatched another, demanding that the Prince appear, if he had the courage to do so. The day was devoted to a feast of self-satisfied gloating. By the end of 22 August the ducal account book recorded that he had sent no fewer than five different messages to his sick opponent.

Two days later, Berry's euphoria had evaporated. It was now clear that the largest part of Limoges, the prosperous and well-defended *château*, which included the castle and wealthy merchants' quarters, was staying loyal to the English. The duke had hoped that a real soldier, Bertrand du Guesclin, would appear and through his presence overawe it into submission, but on 24 August the ducal accounts noted sadly that du Guesclin was still in the Périgord. More worryingly, news had reached Berry that a fresh English army under John of Gaunt had landed at Bordeaux and was now marching to reinforce the Prince. And the bishop Jean de Cros was struggling even to surrender the *cité*.

On 24 August a draft treaty of surrender between the duke of Berry and the bishop of Limoges was abandoned when not enough citizens were found to put their name to it. Facing considerable opposition from the cathedral chapter and the townspeople of the *cité*, Cros resorted to the desperate expedient of claiming to have found out that the Prince had passed away, 'that it was confirmed that he was dead – and he had been put under his shroud'.

While the inhabitants were digesting this entirely fictitious report, Berry ordered a small garrison to enter the *cité*, commanded by one of his captains, Jean de Villemur. Villemur was a skilful soldier who had been given a commission by the duke to 'wage war on the frontiers of the Limousin' on 23 February 1370 and was granted the town and lordship of Blanc-sur-Creuse by a grateful Charles V the same day. But the contingent under his command was small and his master showed no further interest in Limoges, leaving as abruptly as he had arrived.

The Prince was deeply angered by Jean de Cros's defection. The bishop had been a friend and had stood as godparent to his eldest child. Froissart gave a chilling description of his reaction:

> When intelligence was brought to the Prince that the city of Limoges had become French he fell into a violent passion... He swore by the soul of his father, which he had never perjured, that he would have it back again, that he would not attend to anything until he had done this and that he would make the inhabitants pay dearly for their treachery.

However, Froissart's account was almost certainly fanciful. The Prince had decided on a policy of clemency towards those towns that had transferred their allegiance to the French, most of Limoges had stayed loyal and was still holding out for him and the remainder had been tricked into admitting the duke of Berry's troops by a subterfuge.

John of Gaunt took command of the relief force. It consisted of knights who had crossed from England and Poitevins such as Guichard d'Angle, who would later become a tutor to the Prince's son Richard, and Perceval de Coulonges (the former chamberlain of King Peter of Cyprus and, according to Froissart, 'a most skilful and daring knight', who had won fame for his part in the capture of Alexandria in 1365). After the death of King Peter in 1369 Coulonges had returned to France, and refusing the blandishments of Charles V, had enlisted in the Prince's service. There were Gascons who had remained loyal to the English cause – Raymond of Montaut, lord of Mussidan and Jean de Grailly, Captal de Buch – and men of the Free Companies under Eustace d'Aubrecicourt. It was an impressive army, some four thousand strong.

The Prince, grateful for its loyalty, rewarded those who had responded to his summons as best he could. The lord of Mussidan received extensive lands in Poitou and the Périgord. Another Gascon nobleman, the lord of Rauzan, was granted 500 Gascon pounds (£100 sterling). And when the Prince received the taunts of the duke of Berry, he resolved – stung by the insult to his honour – to join his followers on one last campaign. 'So all these men of war went forth in good ordinance', a chronicler wrote, 'and took to the open countryside, and their opponents trembled before them. The Prince was so ill that he could not ride, but was carried in a litter.'

Even when sick, the Black Prince could inspire fear in his enemies. Much alarmed, the bishop of Limoges begged John, duke of Berry, to return. Berry, however, simply speeded his progress in the opposite direction. The relief force under John of Gaunt arrived outside Limoges on 14 September; the troops immediately entered the *château*, and Gaunt took charge of the siege operations around the *cité*. When its inhabitants realized the Prince was still alive, and that they had been tricked by their bishop, they resolved to hand the *cité* back to him and opened communication with the besiegers.

On 18 September a mine was successfully dug under a portion of the walls. John of Gaunt fought in hand-to-hand combat with a French knight and was so impressed by his courage that he halted proceedings to inquire of his name. It was Jean de Villemur, the garrison commander. Gaunt complimented him on his bravery and informed him that he had been fighting against a royal duke. Villemur smiled, and said that 'he was only a poor knight' and that he doubted he would receive such honours over the course of his fighting career. The words were more prophetic than he realized. After this chivalric interlude, a general assault was prepared for the following day. It was the anniversary of the Prince's victory at Poitiers.

Information on what followed is drawn from a lawsuit between two merchants of Limoges held before the Paris Parlement more than thirty years later, on 10 July 1404. The testimony concerned the rival claimants' suitability to hold royal office. The deposition referred to the appellant's father, Jacques Bayard, a furrier within the city, and other members of his guild, who with a body 'of other poor people' had conspired to admit the Black Prince's soldiers into Limoges on that fateful day.

On the morning of 19 September the besiegers collapsed the mine, bringing down a section of the wall, and launched an all-out attack. The garrison beat off the first assault. With most of the French struggling to hold the breach in their defences, Jacques Bayard and his followers rushed the main gate, planted the banner of England and France above it, and flung it open. The Black Prince's troops poured into the city.

The reaction of the garrison was to turn on the citizens of Limoges. Bayard's head was hacked off, his band of supporters slain, and the French then fired the inhabitants' houses and retreated to the square in front of the bishop's palace. The Prince's men, witnessing what was happening, chased after them, refusing to take any prisoners. Seeing the desperate courage of Villemur and his remaining fighters, as they made their last stand, John of Gaunt and the Prince – viewing proceedings from his stretcher – then relented, and allowed the remainder to be taken captive and ransomed. The Black Prince turned on the terrified bishop, Jean de Cros, and told him that he deserved to be executed. But he was spared as well.

The Prince was proud of his last short campaign. On 22 September, still encamped within the city, he wrote a letter to Gaston Fébus, count of Foix, informing him of the successful recovery of the place, and that 200 French knights and men-at-arms had been taken prisoner. The Chandos Herald gave the complete garrison strength as 300 men and the chronicler of the abbey of Saint-Martial of Limoges said that there were around 300 fatalities in total, so it seemed that about 100 enemy soldiers and 200 civilians were killed. These figures would later become important.

The Prince gave the right to administer the *cité* to the cathedral chapter, making clear that he did not blame either its clergy or the citizens for the treachery of Jean de Cros. The grant ran as follows:

> Edward, son of the king of France and England, and Prince of Aquitaine and Wales... to the cathedral chapter of Limoges.
>
> ...
>
> Understanding that as a result of the treason of their bishop, the clergy and inhabitants of the *cité* suffered grievous losses to their bodies and possessions, and endured much hardship... we do not wish to see them further punished as accomplices in this crime, when the fault lay clearly with the bishop and they had nothing to do with it.
>
> ...
>
> We therefore declare them pardoned and quit of all charges of rebellion, treason or forfeiture and any penalties in criminal or civil proceedings, and revoke and annul any inquiries or

processes into their conduct, fully restoring their good name and right to administer their church and those areas under its jurisdiction peacefully and without obstruction.

It had been a supreme effort, but the Prince was happy to have been in the company of his soldiers one last time. He may have hoped that, by concluding matters with a display of justice and clemency towards his subjects, the cycle of divine punishment for wrongdoing would be broken. But devastating news awaited him when he returned: his elder son Edward had died of the plague at Angoulême on 29 September. He was just five years old.

The Prince now resolved to leave Aquitaine. He made Florimond, lord of Lesparre – a Gascon nobleman who had distinguished himself on the Limoges campaign – governor of Gascony, and rewarded his brother, John of Gaunt, with the lordship of Bergerac, passing his remaining military authority over to him on 11 October. Gaunt, aware of the perilous state of Aquitaine's finances, only agreed to occupy this post until the following summer.

For Charles V the Prince's recovery of Limoges was a shock. It showed up the military ineptitude of his brother, the duke of Berry, and the killing of the townspeople was a particular embarrassment at a time when the French king was trying to win people over to his cause. At Montauban, the captain Ratier de Belfort had been introducing a range of arbitrary punishments against those citizens linked to the English regime – even expelling some of the inhabitants from the town – and Charles had instructed his brother, Louis, duke of Anjou, to bring these excesses to an end. At Limoges, the garrison commander Jean de Villemur was held responsible for the deaths of civilians. Villemur had conducted himself with distinction during the siege and his courage had been praised by the Valois chroniclers. But on his release from captivity, Charles, angered by what had happened, revoked all his land grants. In 1375 he would petition the French crown, complaining that he was living in abject poverty, but he would never receive another command.

Charles now made a far-sighted decision. On 2 October he appointed Bertrand du Guesclin constable of France, the supreme military position within the realm. As the Prince was passing over the baton of command, du Guesclin was taking up his own, and he immediately demonstrated his mettle.

An English army of over 4,000 men under Sir Robert Knolles had been recruited that summer to support Charles of Navarre in fomenting an uprising against Charles V in Normandy. However, Navarre — a most unreliable ally — was now in a much weaker position within France and once again had second thoughts about risking open rebellion. Knolles's army, originally intended for Normandy, disembarked at Calais instead, in August 1370, with no clear instructions as to what to do next. Once more, reinforcements that could have bolstered Aquitaine were being frittered away, to no useful purpose.

Knolles awaited further orders from Edward III. When these did not materialize, he eventually launched a meandering raid through the Île-de-France and then plundered French lands north of the Loire. In the course of his campaign, he quarrelled with a number of his aristocratic captains, and by November his army had encamped in Maine, divided among itself and with little achieved for its efforts. Bertrand du Guesclin, sensing an opportunity, began to raise a force at Caen in Normandy to oppose it.

At the end of November Sir Robert Knolles took part of his army into Brittany for the winter. The remainder — under Walter Lord FitzWalter — refused to join him and stayed in Maine. Du Guesclin now struck. He left Caen on 1 December and in a series of forced marches covered the 100 miles (160 km) to Le Mans in a staggering two days. Learning that FitzWalter's troops were at Pontvallain, 20 miles (32 km) south of the city, he then undertook a further night march and attacked at dawn on 4 December. The surprised English soldiers were routed.

Pontvallain was a remarkable victory. And yet, in contrast to the Black Prince, du Guesclin did not win his reputation through

great campaigns and set-piece battles. He was a formidable opponent because of his mastery of innumerable small-scale sorties and
sieges. He did the spade-work of war, eliminating isolated enemy
garrisons, bolstering local defences and galvanizing his subordinates. He was blessed with immense physical powers of endurance
and, as the Black Prince succumbed to illness and disability, the
contrast between the two leaders became all the more marked.
The Prince was bedridden and confined to a litter; du Guesclin,
inured to the hardships of camp life, pushed himself and his men
to ever greater extremes.

Bertrand du Guesclin was not a man of large armies, show
and apparel. Sometimes he led a force of several thousand men,
but more frequently he drew upon a group of just a few hundred.
For what he lacked in numbers he made up for in speed and sheer
toughness: a lightning march to a military trouble spot was the
signature of his operations. He would confer with local leaders and
create a strategy with them, all the while lifting their spirits and
self-belief. Then he would rush off to another crisis point.

Du Guesclin, the new constable of France, understood the conventions of chivalry. Yet his outlook, unlike that of the Prince,
was not fundamentally shaped by it. A humble man from humble
stock, who jested that it would be the ordinary folk, the spinners
and weavers of France, who would find the money – however small
each individual contribution – to release him from captivity, he
surrounded himself by like-minded companions. These were not
great nobles or aristocrats but experienced soldiers, many of them
Bretons, that he had known from his days fighting in Spain, or
the Breton civil war, where he forged his martial reputation. This
seasoned war captain's skill and energy would shape the future
direction of the war.

Towards the end of 1370, Renaud de Montléon, one of the French
garrison at Limoges, secured his freedom. Montléon, a highly
regarded servant of the duke of Berry, had negotiated the surrender
of the *cité* and subsequently served in Jean de Villemur's 300-strong

retinue. Montléon now complained that the Black Prince had forced him to sell his lordship of Touffou 'under threat of death', and then imposed an excessively high ransom upon him. These charges were unwarranted. It was normal for an aristocratic captive to sell property to secure his freedom – and the sum agreed, 3,650 *livres tournois* (around £730) was entirely reasonable for a man of Montléon's standing. These manufactured grievances could be taken with a pinch of salt, but far worse was to follow.

At the end of the year, Jean de Cros was released. The man who had betrayed the Black Prince's trust now made his way to the papal court at Avignon. The new pope, Gregory XI, was the brother of one of Limoges's French defenders, the captain Roger de Beaufort, and Cros's reports of the Prince's high-handed behaviour during the siege, and the 'cruel excesses' of his soldiers, found a sympathetic audience. Cros was referring to the order not to take prisoners, which was given during the storming of the *cité* and then rescinded. But the chronicler Jean Froissart now became interested in the matter. He sensed that a far more sensational story lay waiting to be told.

Froissart had left English employ after the death of Queen Philippa and subsequently secured the patronage of the French aristocrat Guy de Châtillon, count of Blois, becoming the count's chaplain. Hearing of the destruction of much of the *cité* of Limoges, he began to weave his own account together, based on eddies of fact, supposition and rumour, drawing upon the Prince's illness, his anger and frustration, the death of civilians and the literary tradition of the fallen hero. Froissart's great gift was his empathy with those he met and talked to, and his ability to weave their reminiscences into a striking narrative of his age. But the chronicler's love of a good story also led him to invent passages of his history – to simply make things up.

When Jean Froissart had described the Black Prince and the captive King John progressing to London in the spring of 1357, in the aftermath of Poitiers, he could have easily found out their exact

route, from Plymouth to London. Instead, he had them landing at
Sandwich, possibly because he knew the town, and could therefore
describe it more vividly. On the Prince's voyage to Gascony in 1363 the
chronicler was simply cavalier: he had him disembark at La Rochelle
rather than Bordeaux, and misdated his arrival by several months.

Froissart does not seem to have ever visited Limoges. He was
unaware that the city was divided into two parts, the *cité* and
the *château*, and that the larger of these, the *château*, had remained
loyal to the Prince in the summer of 1370. His view of events was
highly coloured by the hostile testimony of Arnaud, lord of Albret,
who had described the Prince as increasingly arrogant and self-
important, prone to bouts of anger and frustration as his illness
worsened. Froissart jumped to the conclusion that Limoges had
become the victim of the Prince's vengeful rage, and wove a story
around it according to which the Black Prince's soldiers ran amok,
killing the inhabitants of Limoges indiscriminately:

> You should have seen these pillagers, bent on doing mischief,
> marauding through the town, slaying men, women and chil-
> dren according to their orders. It was a most melancholy
> business: all ranks, ages and sexes cast themselves on their knees
> before the Prince, begging for mercy; but he was so inflamed
> with passion and hatred that he listened to none, and all were
> put to the sword, wherever they could be found.

Froissart went on:

> There was not that day in the city of Limoges any heart so
> hardened, or any that had some sense of religion, who did not
> deeply bewail the unfortunate events passing before their eyes.
> Upwards of three thousand men, women and children were put
> to death. God have mercy on their souls — for they were truly
> martyrs.

And so the courage of Jacques Bayard and his fellow citizens — who
had raised the banner of England and France above the gates of

Limoges and let the besiegers into the city, and paid the price for it — was turned on its head, and the Prince's strong wish for clemency traduced. It would become the greatest slur on his reputation: through Froissart's compelling passage, the legend of a 'Black Prince' stained by evil was born. (Further analysis of Froissart's account of this episode may be found in the Appendix.)

†

On 5 November 1370 Edward III formally revoked the *fouage*, stating that the fiscal exactions imposed by his son had alienated his Gascon subjects. The imposition of the *fouage* had rankled with the king from the moment that he received the appeal of Jean, count of Armagnac, in February 1368. The following month he had even — briefly — considered recalling the Prince from Aquitaine. Armagnac, a skilled diplomat, had cleverly framed his petition to sow doubt in the mind of the king. Edward's anger subsided but now the issue had erupted again.

It is hard to see what this belated measure was supposed to achieve. The complaints of the appellants — the count of Armagnac and the lord of Albret — were repeated as if established fact, alongside the charge that the Prince had failed to treat Armagnac in a fair and honourable fashion, the king adding that 'this matter has displeased us greatly and has been the cause of all that has followed'. This hurtful letter, in which King Edward or his ministers appeared to be championing the cause of Armagnac and Albret at the Prince's expense, was — a year and a half after the renewal of war, with most of the tax no longer being collected anyway — manifestly unjust.

Almost a month later, on 2 December 1370, Edward III finally came to an agreement with Charles of Navarre. Navarre claimed that he would support the English war effort in return for grants of land and money. Some of these territories were in Poitou and the Limousin and for the treaty to come into effect, the Black Prince needed to set his seal to it. In different circumstances, it might have been a routine measure, with the Prince respecting the wishes of his father. But relations between Edward and his son were now at their lowest ebb. Strikingly, the Prince refused to agree, and months of diplomatic effort came to naught. His response was blunt and to the point. He informed the king 'that for great and mighty reasons which moved him to do so, he would neither assent nor agree to the said treaty, in order to retain his honour and estate'. In other words, he no longer wished to be associated with any endeavour that damaged his own personal reputation and standing.

The Prince clearly distrusted Charles of Navarre, who had reneged on his agreements during the Spanish expedition of 1367, and felt an abiding anger towards his father, who had insisted that he support Pedro of Castile in the first place. In response to King Edward's cancellation of the *fouage*, he expressed that anger openly. Assailed by illness and the threats of his enemies, he was determined to uphold his chivalric principles and would no longer compromise on them.

The Prince asked John of Gaunt to make the arrangements for the funeral of his son, Edward, at Bordeaux. It was too painful for him to attend. In early January 1371, accompanied by his wife, his surviving son Richard and members of his household, he sailed for England. The joy which he had felt when this son was born, nearly six years earlier, had turned to despair.

chapter eleven

A DWINDLING FLAME

The days of lordship in Aquitaine were over. The Prince arrived back in Plymouth in late January 1371; the sea voyage had exhausted him and he spent several weeks recuperating. This was to become the rhythm of what remained of his life: bursts of activity followed by long periods of exhaustion and pain. And during these times of convalescence, and attempts to recover from his illness, the Prince sought the help of spiritual advisers and friends. The most prominent of these was Thomas de la Mare, abbot of St Albans.

De la Mare was a remarkable man. A resolute administrator, he visited all the churches under his jurisdiction and established procedures for resolving disciplinary problems within these religious communities. He began a programme of rebuilding at St Albans and also increased the abbey's landed income, frequently engaging in litigation with local landowners as he augmented its properties. He was an uncompromisingly determined advocate: his dispute with one tenant, John Chiltern of Langley, continued through the courts for almost thirty years and he even fought protracted legal actions with Edward III's officials and the Black Prince's brother, John of Gaunt. De la Mare's perseverance prompted Thomas Walsingham, a chronicler at St Albans, to liken him to the Roman general Julius Caesar.

The abbot was a patron of manuscript illuminators and architects and encouraged education and scholarship among his monks. He taught the liturgy and music, and introduced a rigorous

curriculum of studies. In theological knowledge, Thomas Walsingham remarked, 'He surpassed the sum of all England's learned
clergy'. De la Mare encouraged the ablest of his community to attend
university; for the remainder, he commissioned a large number of
books for the monastic library. He raised the profile of the shrine of
St Alban, inaugurating a lavish procession on the martyr's feast day
and building extensive new accommodation for visitors.

Thomas de la Mare was also a prominent public figure, a
spokesman for the Benedictine order in England, a reformer of university education and the monastic life who, according to Thomas
Walsingham, was highly regarded by Edward III and even invited to
sit on the royal council. He was a distinguished theologian who had
already won the admiration of the Black Prince, who intervened on
several occasions to protect de la Mare and the interests of St Albans
and sent the abbot frequent gifts of silver plate and wine.

The two men's friendship deepened on the Prince's return to
England as a result of Thomas de la Mare's own struggle with serious illness. De la Mare had become gravely ill in 1349, at the height
of the Black Death, in which more than fifty monks of St Albans
died after drinking infected water. He attributed his recovery to the
miraculous intervention of St Alban. His life in the following two
decades was extraordinarily active but he was struck down again
in a fresh wave of the pestilence, in 1369, and never fully regained
his health. De la Mare dealt with his illness by following a strict
spiritual regimen, abstaining from meat and rich food, observing
frequent nightly vigils, during which he often recited the psalter
alone while other monks slept, and continuing his studies in devotional literature and scripture. According to Thomas Walsingham,
the Prince was inspired by the abbot's fortitude in adversity, and
grew to love de la Mare 'as a brother' — and through the example of
his asceticism, was encouraged to follow a similar path.

The Black Prince and Joan of Kent became generous patrons of
St Albans and joined a confraternity there — a lay order devoted
to a religious or charitable cause — along with members of the

Prince's entourage. The Prince's son, Richard, would later write to
the pope recalling his father's 'special affection for the monastery'.
That respect extended to the Prince's household: his chamberlain,
Nigel Loring, was a generous benefactor, assisting in the building
of a new abbey cloister and his confessor, Robert Walsham, gifted
St Albans 400 marks (£266 13s 4d). Through this close association,
Thomas Walsingham gained an insight into the Prince's illness and
the suffering it caused.

Walsingham was able to describe in detail some of the symptoms
of the Prince's illness – including frequent discharges of blood that
left him weakened and sometimes in a state of semi-consciousness –
and the consternation of his household servants, who feared that
their master was on the point of death. It was highly unlikely that
the Prince could have survived chronic amoebic dysentery, which
according to both Walsingham and the chronicler Henry Knighton
was prevalent on the Nájera campaign, for a further nine years.
Many alternatives have been suggested, ranging from prostate disease to rectal cancer. But there can be no sure diagnosis.

In medieval medicine and theology, a flux of the blood or haem-
orrhoidal bleeding was often seen as a form of divine punishment.
The Prince may have come to believe that through his assisting of
an excommunicant – Pedro of Castile – to recover his throne, he
had committed a grievous sin and he was now being punished for
it. If so, he sought God's absolution and forgiveness by adopting a
regimen of penitence and confession.

It took time to put a spiritual routine in place. In the interim, in
the spring of 1371, the Prince journeyed from Plymouth to Windsor
to meet with his father. They had last seen each other some eight
years earlier and much had happened in the interval. It was not an
easy reunion. Edward III had forced the Spanish expedition on his
son, failed to provide any financial assistance in that campaign's
aftermath and then, in allowing appeals from disaffected Gascon
noblemen and cancelling the *fouage*, had undermined the Prince's
authority in the region. King Edward and his son had grown apart

and it was only too evident that the king's own health and judgement had deteriorated alarmingly.

The parliament that opened on 24 February 1371 was highly critical of Edward III's government, the level of war taxation and the forced loans imposed on the country to pay for military expeditions to France. The House of Commons demanded royal ministers be dismissed, adding bluntly that the next time the king wanted to raise money for a campaign he should do so out of his own coffers. In discussions with his father, the Prince suggested that if a national levy was imposed, the English clergy should contribute a fair share of it. The Prince had faced exactly the same problem in Gascony three years earlier, where some form of tax had been equally necessary, a fact not properly grasped by Edward at that time. This was the shadow that hung over the conversation between father and son.

At the time of their meeting, it became clear to the Black Prince that his father was completely under the influence of his young mistress, Alice Perrers. Perrers had been a lady-in-waiting to Queen Philippa and was only a teenager when the king had initiated their relationship. The well-informed chronicler John of Reading praised the Prince's faithfulness to his wife as proper conduct in a Christian marriage, contrasting his behaviour with that of Pedro of Castile, who had abandoned his wife for the charms of his mistress. But John of Reading may also have heard rumours of Edward III's infatuation with Perrers. Unsavoury rumours abounded: that she was the daughter of a humble London plasterer and was using witchcraft and an array of magical potions to captivate the hapless monarch. Many of these emanated from the abbey that the Prince was now attached to.

Alice Perrers was intelligent and resourceful and, while it was not uncommon for kings to take mistresses, her influence over Edward and royal policy making was striking. She controlled access to the king, guided his thinking and intervened in matters of state. Above all, she sought to further her own interests and those of the clique who had gathered around her. And in matters of the law she was a formidable adversary.

Perrers waged a bitter property dispute with St Albans over a contested Essex manor, using all her influence in the royal courts to secure a favourable verdict. The response of the monastic community was virulent. 'That unspeakable whore', Thomas Walsingham fulminated, 'is responsible – alongside her cronies – for all the manifold injustices present in the land.' Walsingham was putting his own spin on events. Perrers was in fact the daughter of a Hertfordshire knight and there is some evidence that she was either betrothed or married to another man, William of Windsor. But she would also have a son by Edward III, and by 1371 her emotional hold over the king was total. It seemed a sad reflection of the state of the realm, and Perrers's manipulation of the aged monarch aroused alarm and envy among the governing elite and sorrow and contempt among the king's subjects. Edward brought expensive gifts for his lover, including a pearl-encrusted brooch with the inscriptions 'Think of me' and 'Never apart'. A chronicler wrote of Edward III at this time:

> For as in his beginning, all things were joyful and liking to him and to all the people, and in his middle age he passed all men in high joy, worship and blessedness, right so as when he drew into old age, drawn downward through lechery and other sins, little by little all those joyful and blessed things, good fortune and prosperity, decreased and misshaped, and unfortunate things and unprofitable harms with much evil, began to spring.

As the elderly Edward was driven to foolishness by his young lover, losing his remaining vigour and becoming a laughing-stock to his subjects and enemies, John Gower wrote: 'No king will ever be feared if he gives up his shield and wages battle in bed.' Thomas Walsingham and his fellows at St Albans believed Perrers's control over the king was achieved by the use of magic and sorcery. Over time, this also became the view of the Prince.

An aura of disapproval and derision surrounded the once illustrious king, but it did not spread to his eldest son. Crippled by illness, often forced to take to his bed, 'where he had scant cheer', as the Chandos Herald glumly recounted, the suffering warrior retained the respect of the nation. Thomas Walsingham spoke of him as 'the hope of all Englishmen'; for the Anonimalle chronicler he was 'the comfort of the realm'. Although he was largely incapacitated, his earlier deeds retained a hold in the popular imagination: he remained the young man who had won his spurs at Crécy, the courageous commander at Poitiers. 'It was sad to see the victor of so many battles now so enfeebled', Walsingham commented. But people were reluctant to let his martial image go.

This was seen in the response of the City of London, which made a remarkable and quite spontaneous gesture. Remembering the Black Prince's sacrifices for the Nájera campaign four years earlier, when he had melted down his own gold and silver plate to pay for his soldiers' wages, the capital's ruling council voted at the end of January 1371 that 'there should be levied on all men of the wards a fifteenth and half a fifteenth for two presents to be made to Edward Prince of Wales and to the Princess his consort at their return to England from Gascony'.

The council bought a magnificent set of gold and silver vessels to replace those the Prince had lost. The new items included eighteen pots, nine basins, six ewers, thirty-six hanaps (drinking vessels with handles), twenty chargers and sixty saltcellars – and the cost was nearly £700. Three leading London goldsmiths provided more than 270 items in all. The gift was promised to the Prince when he reached London on 19 April 1371 – to be welcomed by mayor, citizens and a band of minstrels – and was delivered later that year. The Prince was ill again and his wife wrote the letter of thanks: 'Dear and well-beloved, we thank you for the great gifts that you, of your own free will, ordained for us, with all our heart… May God have you in his keeping.'

The Prince's public appearances were now sporadic. At the

beginning of May 1371 he was well enough to be able to meet with the Convocation of Canterbury at the Savoy Palace in London, to discuss the church's financial contributions to the continuing war in France. The effort seems to have weakened him, and he then returned to his castle of Berkhamsted to rest. In the meantime, his brother John of Gaunt was struggling to maintain the situation in Gascony, as more and more towns and castles defected to the French. In the autumn of 1371, desperately short of funds, he returned to England. Charles V now began to stir up trouble in Scotland. There were also rumours that a French naval force was assembling in the Seine, preparing to raid the English coast.

Edward III's own health suffered a further setback when, in the late summer of 1371, he suffered a mild stroke, which incapacitated him for several months and may have caused partial paralysis of his face. He briefly appeared in public later that autumn, but medications were now regularly prescribed for him. It was John of Gaunt who was becoming the most energetic member of his ruling house.

The Black Prince remained loyal to his family. His relations with his father were correct but distant – communication was largely by messenger and they now rarely met in person. The Prince respected John of Gaunt for the support he had given him in Gascony, and – in public at least – kept up a show of solidarity. He demonstrated this early in 1372, when he was once more strong enough to engage in a round of public ceremonies in London.

The Spanish alliance was now being revived. Blanche of Lancaster had died four years earlier, and on 9 February John of Gaunt arrived in the capital with his new bride, Constanza, daughter of Pedro of Castile. It had been a deeply flawed cause to fight for, one that had left its mark on the Prince and England's fortunes as a whole. To justify it, Edward III's government had stressed Pedro's legitimacy. The same argument did not apply to his daughters, for they were not the offspring of his ill-fated queen, Blanche of Bourbon, but a royal mistress, Maria de Padilla. In 1363, King Pedro had claimed before the Castilian Cortes that he had secretly married Maria before the match with Blanche was arranged, but few believed him.

In subsequent negotiations with Peter IV of Aragon, the Prince showed himself one of the doubters. He made it clear to the Aragonese that, for him at least, Pedro's daughters did not represent a viable line of succession: the only solution was for Pedro to marry again and produce legitimate heirs. These concerns were shared in a round of private diplomacy. Four years later, the Prince decided to put his moral scruples aside and make a display of common cause with his brother. For this reason, he met with John of Gaunt and his entourage. The Anonimalle Chronicle related:

> The Prince of England [the Black Prince], accompanied by several lords and knights, the mayor of London and a great number of the commons, well dressed and nobly mounted, conducted Constanza of Castile through London in a great and solemn procession. In Cheapside were assembled many gentlemen with their wives and daughters to look at the beautiful young lady. The procession passed in good order along to the Savoy.

With Edward III a shadow of his former self there were few other candidates for power. The king's second son, Lionel, duke of Clarence, had died in October 1368. His fourth, Edmund of Langley, showed little appetite for hard work, preferring instead to indulge in recreation and the hunt; his fifth, Thomas of Woodstock, just seventeen years old, had little practical political experience. With the Black Prince ill, it was his third son, John of Gaunt, who possessed the ambition and determination to take up the mantle of royal authority.

John of Gaunt now saw an opportunity to proclaim his eminence on the European stage and assumed the title of king of Castile in the right of his wife. It was a bold gesture, but with England on the defensive in Gascony and struggling to retain its outposts in northern France, it belonged more to the realm of fantasy than reality. Enrique of Trastamara was securely on the Castilian throne and very much intended to stay there. Confident of his position, and the strength of his alliance with France, he took the war to the English.

In the summer of 1372, John Hastings, earl of Pembroke, was appointed king's lieutenant in Gascony. Pembroke was a young and vigorous commander and he sailed for Bordeaux with troops and sufficient money to pay 3,000 soldiers for a year. However, Enrique of Trastamara – only too willing to help the French – sent a strong Castilian fleet to intercept him. On 23 June the two naval forces engaged off La Rochelle. The Castilian ships were light, manoeuvrable and had the advantage of the wind behind them. They struck hard, sailing up close to the English vessels, spraying oil on their decks and igniting it by shooting flaming arrows. In the ensuing battle all the English ships were sunk or captured and Pembroke was taken prisoner. The chronicler of St Mary's Abbey, York, commented sadly: 'It was the greatest loss ever sustained by our nation at sea.'

Edward III's government clung to the notion that Enrique had no right to be on the throne, continuing – after this debacle – to describe the Castilian ruler as 'the Bastard calling himself king' and repeating the comforting but illusory mantra that John of Gaunt 'was lawful heir to the kingdom'. It carried on building its castles in Spain, arranging another marriage in which the Prince's brother, Edmund of Langley, wedded Pedro's younger daughter Isabella. This was a policy that pandered to Gaunt's ambition but played into the hands of the French.

In return, Enrique showed himself unwilling to respect chivalric convention where the English were concerned. Pembroke and his fighting captains were held prisoner 'bound together by chains round their necks, like dogs on their leads'. The earl was then taken to the grim fortress of Curiel, above the River Duero, where he was kept in appalling conditions which broke his health. Pembroke's leadership was sorely missed. A general attack by Charles V's forces on Poitou followed his incarceration; after several weeks of successful campaigning, Charles's constable Bertrand du Guesclin entered Poitiers on 7 August.

The aged Edward III gathered ships and men at Sandwich a fortnight later in an attempt to reinforce the port of La Rochelle. He summoned the great lords of the kingdom. John of Gaunt brought in a substantial retinue from his estates; the Prince insisted on leaving his sickbed to join the expedition. Despite his personal appearance, it was all in vain. The English naval expedition sailed on 30 August but was immediately confronted with fierce, adverse winds. It took more than a week for it to get beyond Winchelsea, and the scattered ships, unable to make further progress, were eventually forced to give up, allowing themselves to be blown back into English ports. La Rochelle surrendered on 7 September and other towns in Poitou and the Saintonge shortly afterwards. The Black Prince's last Poitevin supporters gathered in the stronghold of Thouars on 18 September and appealed for help. But the relief army was unable to reach them and was disbanded in early October.

It was a time of disillusion and loss. Jean de Grailly, Captal de Buch, one of the Prince's closest companions and most loyal supporters, was captured by the French at Soubise in late August. He was overcome, fighting bravely, in a night-time assault. Charles V, well aware of his military skill, refused to allow him to be ransomed; de Grailly languished in prison, succumbed to illness and died four years later. The Chandos Herald mournfully compiled a list of notable captains killed or captured in the defence of Gascony. The Prince formally surrendered the principality of Aquitaine to his father on 5 November 1372.

Edward III requested that the Black Prince attend the ceremony of surrender in person, 'knowing that he loves the king and his honour, and his own... and that he would not wish business so difficult be treated without the Prince's advice or counsel.' But his son did not come. At a ceremony in the White Chamber at Westminster, Sir Guy Bryan, one of his officials, acted as his spokesperson. Bryan explained that the costs of the principality exceeded its revenues, emphasizing that the Prince had written to the king on numerous occasions explaining this:

> And the said Prince himself came to England and explained to the king and his council the aforesaid reasons and other later ones, and for these notable reasons the Prince surrendered the principality back to the king... together with the charters and other deeds in connection with the granting of the principality.

The underlying cause of this breach between father and son, hinted at in the formal surrender, was the Nájera campaign and its aftermath, in which the Prince had been expected to meet sums owed for the expedition entirely from Gascon revenues. The accounts of the Prince's auditor, Richard Filongley, were pointedly presented to the king. They showed that the debts accruing from the ill-advised foray into Spain were larger than the entire income drawn from Aquitaine over the seven-year period that the Prince had governed it. When Parliament met that month, men complained: 'Twenty years ago, our kingdom's navy was so powerful that all countries called our King "the Lord of the Sea"... And now it is so diminished, that there hardly remains enough to defend the country.'

A last effort was made. In the summer of 1373 a new expedition was sent out under John of Gaunt. He marched from Calais on 4 August, ravaging the territory of the French crown, but he could not force Charles V to fight. He struck deep into the heart of the country, down to Troyes, into the Auvergne and on to Bordeaux. Summer turned to autumn and autumn into winter. Bitter weather came to the aid of the French, who followed on the flanks and rear of Gaunt's army, pouncing on stragglers but never accepting battle. 'Let them go,' said Charles. 'Though a storm and tempest rage together over a land, they disperse of themselves. So it will be with the English.'

Charles's prediction proved correct. Food ran short – even the bread supplies were exhausted – horses succumbed to malnourishment, waggons were jettisoned. When John of Gaunt and his army limped into the Gascon capital in December, 300 of his knights were on foot. They had lost their mounts and, unable to march under the weight of their armour, had thrown it into rivers and ravines to prevent the French getting it. Of the long baggage train filled with booty, two thirds had been abandoned along the way.

A generation earlier, a wide-ranging *chevauchée* that marched some 550 miles (885 km), laying waste to the land from Calais to Bordeaux, would have been praised by English chroniclers. Now the opportunities for plunder were reduced and far less damage was inflicted on the French rural economy. Charles V was protecting his subjects more effectively and du Guesclin harrying the enemy. The expedition had cost over £80,000 and there was precious little to show for it. The English war effort was running out of ideas.

Edward III was also fast losing what was left of his grip on government and his kingdom. In May 1374 he let his mistress Alice Perrers lead a procession from the Tower to the jousting ground at Smithfield attired as the 'Lady of the Sun… accompanied by many lords and ladies', where she presided over a seven-day tournament. Edward III purchased fine cloth of gold for her costume. Shocked observers noticed that she was wearing the late queen's jewellery, which the besotted monarch had given to her. The king made a brief appearance at the tournament, attired in new armour. But it was an awful parody of the martial prowess that had illuminated so much of Edward's reign.

On 25 September 1374 the Prince's officials in Flint convened a judicial session to identify supporters of Owain Lawgoch. Thirty-seven Welshmen were named. Lawgoch was a professional soldier and a descendant of the House of Llywelyn, whom Charles V was sheltering and encouraging to claim the principality of Wales. The Anonimalle chronicler described him as 'a great enemy of England'. His invasion efforts had got no further than an attack on the island of Guernsey in May 1372, but he was an able war captain (who had helped defeat and capture Jean de Grailly at Soubise the following August) and, with the Black Prince disabled by sickness, the English government was nervous.

Charles V had played the cards in his hand with consummate skill, but at times even this arch manipulator was taken aback by the strength of residual loyalty to the Black Prince. In a grant of properties in the vicinity of La Rochelle, formerly held by Raymond, vicomte of Fronsac, the king noted in bewilderment that Poitou and the Saintonge had been reconquered and Fronsac's wife (Jeanne de la Marche) and daughter had returned to French allegiance, and yet 'he still insisted that he was in the service of the Prince of Wales'.

By the autumn of 1374 the great principality of Aquitaine had shrunk to little more than the hinterlands of Bordeaux and Bayonne. In the following year, fighting shifted to Normandy and Brittany, but was brought to a temporary halt by a year's truce, sealed on 27 June 1375 at Bruges by John of Gaunt and the French king's brothers, the dukes of Anjou and Berry.

A chivalrous knight was expected to make careful preparation for his death. The warrior-hero of the thirteenth century, William Marshal, was applauded by contemporaries for doing so, and the Black Prince was now putting his own affairs in order. A file of petitions addressed to him survives for the year 1375. Most of the matters were dealt with by his council, but some were referred to the Prince himself. Some requests were from former soldiers, recalling war service undertaken in northern France, Gascony and in Spain. By now their leader had been reduced to near total passivity.

Parliament met on 28 April 1376. Its members were seething with resentment at corruption at home and defeat abroad. They demanded a thorough investigation of the king's council, prosecution of ministers found guilty of misconduct or fraud and the removal of the king's mistress, Alice Perrers. Neither Edward, who was ill at Eltham, nor his eldest son, who was virtually bedridden, was able to attend.

The Anonimalle chronicler believed the Prince was in sympathy with many of the demands for reform made in the so-called 'Good Parliament'. 'He was at one with the Commons in counselling and ordering the affairs and estate of the kingdom, and correcting all that had been done in extortionate fashion.' Thomas Walsingham concurred: 'The common people [in this parliament] had the advice and support of the Prince.'

There may have been truth in these sentiments. 'He always comforted the good and loyal people of the realm', said the chronicler of St Mary's Abbey, York, 'begging them to be obedient to his father, to govern responsibly and to maintain the good laws and customs of the kingdom – and to put no faith in evildoers.' But the Prince had no wish to openly undermine the position of his father, or his brother John of Gaunt. It was the dominion of the king's mistress, Alice Perrers, and her clique of favourites, that rankled with him.

The Black Prince's frustration, anger and fear for the future would find expression in a legal attack on Perrers and the witchcraft that he believed was being used to manipulate the king. It was a symbolic act, for on a larger stage the Prince feared that God no longer favoured the English and was punishing the realm for its sins. His view was shared by the monastic community of St Albans, which hated and feared Perrers and was convinced that she was dabbling in the black arts. Its abbot, Thomas de la Mare, wanted to see her brought before an ecclesiastical court.

The Prince, unable to take action himself, chose one of his most loyal servants, the Berkshire knight Sir John Kentwood, a veteran of Poitiers and Nájera and his steward in the duchy of Cornwall, to strike back. During the Parliamentary session Kentwood arrested the Dominican friar whose magical gifts Alice Perrers was believed to have used to ensnare the king. On 18 May the friar was hauled up before the House of Lords and interrogated. He revealed that he had made wax effigies of the king and Alice and recited incantations, and also confessed to making enchanted rings for Perrers, so that she could give them to Edward as a gift. When worn, they would strengthen his infatuation with her and cause him to lose awareness of all other responsibilities. A judgement was reached – the king was a victim of necromancy.

This startling process, almost certainly initiated by the Prince, was now supported by others. Thomas Brinton, bishop of Roches-ter, even delivered a sermon in which he denounced Edward III for allowing Alice to hold the keys of kingdom. It led to Perrers being banished from the royal council, the court and from the king's own person.

The Black Prince had little appetite for further intervention. Thomas Walsingham remembered how Sir Richard Sturry, a knight of the king's chamber, who had also been barred from court, appealed to the Prince for help. The reply was brusque: 'God is just – and he will reward you according to your merits. Do not trouble me any longer.' Early in June 1376 the Prince's con-dition worsened visibly. He was dying, not as a warrior of wounds or in the heat of battle, nor as a king anointed and full of years, but wasted by disease, his tale incomplete, neither young nor old, in a land that had once acclaimed his prowess but was now bedevilled by faction-fighting and self-doubt, divided within itself.

The Black Prince was approaching his forty-sixth birthday, and illness held him firmly within its grasp. 'It was a grievous malady', the Anonimalle Chronicle recounted, 'that left him languishing in his bed.' Thomas Walsingham added: 'For more than five years he had been visited by a great and incommodious disease of his body… which made him so feeble that on occasions his servants sometimes mistook him for dead.'

At six years old he had been created the first duke in English history; at sixteen he had won fame by his bravery at Crécy; at twenty-six he had astounded Europe by capturing King John of France at Poitiers; at thirty-six he had sealed his supremacy as a military leader with the victory at Nájera. Now scarcely able to move, he retired to his manor of Kennington. The king, freed from the influence of Alice Perrers, visited the Prince there on 1 June and ensured he was carried to the royal palace of Westminster later the same day. Edward wanted to be close to his son, who was not expected to live long. This moving act of reconciliation did much to lessen the estrangement between them.

On Saturday 7 June the Black Prince had his clerks draw up his will 'in our chamber within the palace of our redoubtable lord and father the king at Westminster'. The Prince began: 'First, we bequeath our soul to God our Creator and to the Holy Blessed Trinity, to the Glorious Virgin Mary and to all the Saints.'

To the cathedral of Canterbury, where he directed that his body be buried, he gave his breviary and missal and tapestry of ostrich plumes. To the religious brethren of the House of the Bonhommes at Ashridge, near his castle of Berkhamsted, he left a great altar of silver and gold, encrusted with rubies, sapphires and pearls and inlaid with a fragment of the True Cross. To his son Richard he gave tapestries, fine clothes and 'our great bed with the embroidered angels'; a fine hanging of red worsted, woven with eagles and griffins was left to 'our consort the Princess'.

He was humble before God, but proud of his achievements before men. He instructed that his tomb should be set 10 ft (3 metres) from the altar in the chapel of Our Lady of the Undercroft. It was to be made:

Of good masonry, in marble. And we desire that around the tomb shall be twelve latten escutcheons [coats of arms], each a foot wide, six with our arms entire and the other six of ostrich plumes, and on each... shall be written *houmont*... an image in copper-gilt relief in memory of us, all armed in steel for battle... with our leopard-helm placed above it.

Around the tomb would be engraved an epitaph, 'As thou art, once the world saw me; as I am, so thou in time shall be.'

The Prince detailed the manner in which 'our body shall be led through the town of Canterbury unto the Priory':

It is my wish that two warhorses, covered with trappings of my coat of arms, ridden by two men, bearing my own armour and equipment, proceed before my body... carrying all my banner, badges and insignia.

He put his name and seal to the will and ordered the doors of his room to be opened and members of his household brought in. The Anonimalle chronicler recalled the Prince asking everyone present to care for the kingdom, its laws and customs. Thomas Walsingham gave a more intimate account: 'Sirs', the Prince said, 'pardon me, for by my faith you have loyally served me yet I cannot of myself give each of you his reward – but God, by his most Holy name, will give you it in Holy Heaven.'

A repentant King Edward was to honour all those debts that the Black Prince could not meet. There were ninety-four of them, totalling £2,972 – of which thirty-two grants were made and confirmed on the Prince's deathbed. And there was a special act of redress, as the king later stated:

> Many of our loyal subjects of Cheshire have sustained much in the way of damage, oppression and loss in the forest of the Wirral. Our son had the greatest desire to further their peace and alleviate their condition – and at the very end of his life he made a strong recommendation to us in these terms. We therefore grant that the said place be disafforested [freed from the burden of forest dues and taxation] for ever.

Despite this act of redress to the long-suffering inhabitants of Cheshire, the Prince's primary loyalty was to his fighting soldiers. One of these men was the Hampshire knight Sir John Sandys, who had first entered the Prince's service on the Nájera campaign; on 27 January 1367, he was granted a substantial annuity of £50 shortly before the army crossed the Pyrenees. He remained in the Prince's company, first in Spain and then in France. On his return to England he was charged, in November 1375, with the abduction of the recently widowed Joan Bridges from Romsey Abbey, where she had been staying. His arrest was ordered, inquiries were made regarding the goods in his possession (which, when brought to London the following January, were found to have been worth over £120 and to have belonged to Joan's previous husband) and one of the

Prince's squires had to be sent to Chester to bring the lady back to the capital for examination by the king's council. It was then found that Sandys had already forcibly married her.

These were hardly the actions of a chivalrous knight. But on 8 April 1376 a much-relieved Sandys was granted, on the Prince's intercession, a royal pardon for all homicides, rapes and felonies for which he stood indicted. He was obliged to pay the king a fine of £1,000 for his misdeeds, but the sum was assigned to the Prince, who on his deathbed expressed a wish for it to be pardoned in full. It was through this opportunistic marriage that Sandys became a landowner of substance. He subsequently resumed his military career, putting to sea in the autumn of 1377 in the company of the Prince's youngest brother, Thomas of Woodstock, in an action against the Castilian fleet and later becoming constable of Southampton castle. What his new wife thought of it all is not recorded.

However, the Prince had larger concerns on his mind. Walsingham continued his account of the Prince's farewell, recalling that he said to those around him: 'I commend my son to you, who is young and small, and beg you to serve him as loyally as you have served me.' This thought dominated his last moments – his fear for the future of his nine-year-old son, Richard.

> He called the king and the duke of Lancaster [John of Gaunt] his brother, he commended them to his wife and son, whom he greatly loved, and begged that each should help them. Each swore it on the Holy Book, and freely promised to aid his child and maintain him in his right.

The Chandos Herald wrote:

> Never, so God help me, was there such sore pain beheld as at his departing. The lovely and noble Princess felt such grief that one's heart was nigh breaking. The lamentation and sorrowing would have touched any man of this world.

The Prince was fading fast. The following day was Sunday, 8 June 1376:

> The feast of the Holy Trinity... about 3 of the clock [in the afternoon]... he began to faint and lose his strength, so that scarce any breath remained in him, whereupon the Bishop of Bangor, who was present, came unto him and said: 'Now, without doubt, death is at hand... therefore I counsel you, my lord, to now forgive those who have offended you.'
>
> The Prince managed to say 'I will', but could not make any other intelligible sound... The Bishop, taking the sprinkler, cast holy water on the four corners of the chamber where he lay... Suddenly the Prince, with joined hands and eyes lifted up to Heaven, said: 'I give thee thanks, O God, for all Thy benefits, and with all the pain of my soul I humbly beseech Thy mercy, to give me remission of sins which I have wickedly committed against Thee; and of all mortal men whom willingly or ignorantly I have offended, with all my heart I desire forgiveness.' And when he had spoken these words, he passed away.

'He was the flower of the world's chivalry,' Jean Froissart said, 'the most fortunate in great feats of arms and the most accomplished in brave deeds.'

The poet John Gower hailed him as an exemplar of knighthood:

> He was never discomfited in a fight, dreading neither the strokes of battle nor the straits of the campaign. He was a wellspring of courage. His name will never be erased from the face of the earth, for his feats of arms surpass even those of Hector.

This was the highest praise in the medieval pantheon – and others echoed it. 'His fortunes in war were those of Hector himself,' John of Malvern emphasized. 'He was another Hector,' said Thomas Walsingham, 'and in his lifetime the English feared no onslaught.'

These plaudits were intended for public consumption, but the surgeon John Arderne, who had tended to a number of the Prince's soldiers, paid a more personal tribute in a medical treatise, brought out later in 1376. In an annotation to the manuscript, Arderne spontaneously commented: 'In this year the strenuous and warlike Prince departed to God. He died on Trinity Sunday, during the Great Parliament, and may God protect him, for he was the very flower of chivalry, without peer in this world.'

In the aftermath of the Prince's death his father left the capital and departed for the royal manor of Havering, where he remained in the quiet seclusion of mourning until early July. On 29 September 1376 the Prince's funeral was held at Canterbury Cathedral. The burial was conducted 'most worshipfully', with all due respect and honour. Thomas Brinton, bishop of Rochester, preached the sermon. He spoke of the 'great sorrow' felt by the entire nation and continued:

> Any prince should excel his subjects in power, wisdom and goodness, just as the image of the Holy Trinity represents these, the Father being the power, the Son wisdom and the Holy Spirit goodness. But this lord prince had all three qualities in the highest degree.

England's fortunes in war had faded, and Brinton was moved to single out the Prince's virtues to show up a prevailing moral decay within England's warrior class:

> His power appeared in his glorious victories, for which he is to be greatly commended... Above all, for his victory at Poitiers, where there was such a force of men with the French king that ten of his armed knights, defending their own land, faced one Englishman; yet God favoured the just cause, and the French army was wonderfully scattered and their king taken... And again, because of his deeds in Spain.

Then Brinton made a larger point. With the present reverses in France very much in mind, he declared it was part of a knight's duty to help his king in time of war, and that his rank was a sign of honour and a mark of responsibility that needed to be lived up to. 'A true knight', the bishop continued 'must be ready to fight hard when the king requires it of him; he must never desert, nor must he refuse to fight for the common good; and above all, he must fight fearlessly.'

Brinton no doubt recalled a famous axiom of Geoffrey de Charny, author of the book of chivalry and bearer of the *Oriflamme* banner at Poitiers, who fought to the death defending his king: 'Who does most is worth most.' The bishop evoked, through the example of the Prince, an era that seemed to be passing:

> His wisdom appeared in his habit of speaking prudently and his manner of acting, because he did not merely talk like the lords of today but was a doer of deeds, so that he never began a great work without bringing it to a praiseworthy end... His goodness came principally from three things. Where the lords of this world usually oppress and afflict their tenants, this lord always cared for them, comforting them in many ways. Where other lords are usually ungrateful to those who serve with them and labour with them in wars, this lord was so open-handed to his servants that he made them rich and himself poor. And where earthly lords are not usually devout before God, not caring, except for form's sake, whether they hear mass or divine service, this lord was so devout in the service of the Lord that his like has never been seen in such times.

This was an idealized portrait. The Prince did not always care for his tenants, as his actions in the Wirral, which he came to regret, clearly showed. And the pardon of Sir John Sandys placed loyalty to a fellow soldier over the proper exercise of justice. Already a mythology was being created. But there was real truth in it, nonetheless. For the most powerful tribute would come from the Prince's opponents. Jean Froissart told how Charles V and his court put aside all accusations and complaints and paid him the most solemn reverence in a Mass held at the Sainte-Chapelle in Paris. No other English war leader would ever be accorded such a tribute. The French author of the *Chronique des Quatre Premiers Valois* added:

> This Prince was one of the greatest and best knights ever seen. In his time he was renowned the world over and won the respect of all. His passing left the English in a state of profound grief and shock. On hearing of his death, the king of France – notwithstanding the fact that the Prince was his enemy – held the most solemn memorial service for him.

The French were right. 'Thus died the hope of the English,' Thomas Walsingham wrote:

> For while he lived they feared no invasion of the enemy, no onslaught of battle. Nor, in his presence, did they do badly or desert the battlefield. He never attacked a people he did not conquer; he never besieged a city he did not take.

For a moment, the entire chivalric world froze in time. Friend and foe honoured the departed Prince and mourned the passing of an age.

EPILOGUE

The ailing Edward III did not long outlive the Black Prince. He died on 21 June 1377 and the Prince's own son Richard was crowned king little more than three weeks later, on 16 July. The early years of his reign were dominated by fears that Richard's uncle, John of Gaunt, might take the throne. Gaunt was not appointed regent and government was instead conducted by a council until Richard came of age. The realm was struggling under an increasingly heavy burden of taxation, levied to fund the largely unsuccessful war with France, and a growing distrust of royal government. In the summer of 1381 the country erupted into open revolt.

The uprising was sparked by a poll tax levied across the kingdom, and was fuelled by the tensions between peasants and landowners — one of the consequences of the Black Death and subsequent returns of the plague. Rebellions started in Kent and Essex in late May, and by June had spread to London and other parts of the kingdom.

On 12 June a large band of peasants had gathered at Blackheath under their leader Wat Tyler. They burned down John of Gaunt's Savoy Palace, killed the archbishop of Canterbury, Simon Sudbury, who was Richard II's chancellor, and his treasurer, Robert Hales. The fourteen-year-old king, sheltering in the Tower of London with his remaining councillors, agreed that his government did not have the strength to disperse the rebels. The only option was to negotiate.

Three days later, the king went to meet the rebels at Smithfield. He listened to their demands, and was responsive to their grievances. However, an altercation broke out between the leader of the revolt, Wat Tyler, and some of the royal retinue, in which the mayor of London pulled Tyler down from his horse and killed him. When the mass of peasants realized what had happened they prepared to kill all of the royal entourage. Showing enormous courage and presence of mind, the young Richard rode out in front of them, saying 'I am your captain — follow me!' and led the mob away. The king granted them all pardons and allowed them to return to their homes. But once the crisis had passed, brutal royal sanctions were imposed after the initial appearance of clemency and the pardons were revoked. In the following weeks the whole uprising was put down.

For a brief but extraordinary moment, the young Richard II had demonstrated a true likeness to his father, in sheer bravery. However, that remarkable occasion was not to be repeated. As he grew into manhood, Richard became fascinated by the trappings of kingship and court ritual. He was a generous patron of the arts. But unlike his father or grandfather, he did not understand how to translate such display into real power and authority.

Richard's mother, Joan of Kent, died on 7 August 1385. She had remained a popular figure, but her beauty had waned and at the end of her life, afflicted by dropsy, she was scarcely able to move from her favourite residence of Wallingford in Oxfordshire. In the years after the rebellion Richard married Anne of Bohemia, daughter of the Holy Roman Emperor Charles IV, and chose the men who were to be his councillors. He mixed with a group of young, ambitious aristocrats, intensely jealous of the power and ambition of John of Gaunt. It created an atmosphere of rancour and suspicion at court.

Richard negotiated a treaty with France, bringing the conflict begun by Edward III to a temporary end. The war was now unpopular, and accusations of corruption and incompetence against royal ministers were commonplace. The status of the soldier in late medieval society had declined. Unlike his father and grandfather, Richard showed no interest in martial activities. But he was unable to bind the English nobility together in a common cause. Intensely loyal to his favourites, the king could be petulant and vindictive against those he felt threatened by. An open revolt against his authority, from a group called the Appellants, led to a reduction of his power, but the king was to strike back against his opponents in the last years of his rule.

Jean Froissart, 'filled with a strong desire to return to England', visited the court of Richard II at Eltham in July 1395 and presented a copy of his verse romance *Méliador* to the English king. Richard was delighted by the gift. He admired the manuscript's rich binding, browsed through its pages and read passages aloud in fluent French. Then he gave the book to a member of his household, to place in his private chambers. The chronicler was impressed by the magnificence of Richard's court but sensed the tensions eddying around it.

Froissart's intuition was on this occasion correct. The king's increasingly tyrannical behaviour provoked a political crisis that led to his deposition, four years later, in 1399. He was replaced on the throne by John of Gaunt's eldest son, Henry of Bolingbroke, who became Henry IV. Richard was imprisoned at Pontefract castle, and almost certainly murdered there on the new king's orders. It was a tragic end for the lineage of the Black Prince.

†

The Prince's standing contrasted with the sad decline in England's fortunes that followed his death, but was well deserved in its own right. The 'blackening' of his reputation, in part through the insinuations of Jean Froissart, can now be righted. He was not hungry for glory and heedless of its consequences in his campaign in Spain in 1367. He did not senselessly alienate the majority of the Gascon nobility in that expedition's aftermath and, as sickness took hold, his increasing anger and frustration did not lead to a massacre of civilians at Limoges in September 1370.

He was a Prince who never became king – and his relationship with his father, and the obedience and loyalty it demanded, would be both a blessing and a curse. But in his prime, the Black Prince created a world of heroic enchantment for those around him, one that did not simply depend on personal charm and bravery. He won over the tough and independent-minded, both in Cheshire and in Gascony, not so much by living a chivalric life as by fully embodying it.

The Prince's conduct was by no means flawless. His expenditure always outstripped his income, and even in the aftermath of his great victory at Poitiers, his habitual generosity left him out of pocket, despite his haul of prisoners. 'This lord was so open-handed to his servants that he made them rich and himself poor,' Bishop Thomas Brinton had remarked in his funeral oration. The Prince's hero, Jean of Luxembourg, king of Bohemia, had also been praised for his near-reckless largesse – but it was a double-edged compliment. The poem *Wynnere and Wastoure* toyed with the themes of profligate spending and miserly saving, with wealth 'hoarded in chests, so the sun cannot see it'. But saving did not have to be miserly. Charles V's coffers certainly saw the light of day: they funded the war in Aquitaine that would break the power of the principality.

The Prince upheld chivalric principles of good lordship, and clearly believed in them, yet he turned a blind eye to the serious misdemeanours of some of his soldiers. And he could let his emotions overrule his better judgement. His failure, as prince of Aquitaine, to strike up a better relationship with Jean, count of Armagnac, cost him dearly. But the Prince's faults have to be placed in the context of his times. In an era blighted by plague and violence, he gave people something uplifting, sometimes through a mere couple of words, a comment or a gesture.

The Gascon nobleman Arnaut de Preissac fought in the Black Prince's bodyguard at Poitiers. At the end of the battle the Prince thanked him for his courage, noticing that because he had been fully occupied defending his person, Preissac had 'not been able to take any prisoners, and obtain their ransoms'. In contrast, Arnaut's brother, Bertran, was one of six Gascons who had captured the French marshal Arnoul d'Audrehem. When the Prince found this out he granted Arnaut an annuity of 200 gold crowns a year as recompense.

From a modern viewpoint, we often distrust such gestures, seeing them as showy and impulsive, and being no match for calculated statecraft. Yet in the world of chivalry they carried enormous power. As the Black Prince lay dying, early in June 1376, the French re-opened the war (after the one-year truce negotiated by John of Gaunt) and launched a concerted attack on the remains of English-held Gascony. Preissac's stalwart defence of the strategically important castle of Mortagne-sur-Gironde kept them at bay, an act of valour that earned him elevation to the Order of the Garter early in Richard II's reign. Arnaut held the castle out of respect and admiration for the Prince, and Gascony was saved as a result.

The Black Prince did not shun the hard work of government. On 15 July 1365 he reinstated a series of privileges to the region of Quercy, in eastern Aquitaine, which were first made by the French king, Philip IV, at the beginning of the fourteenth century. This should have been a routine procedure, reciting the original Latin document and then adding a confirmation. But the Prince, after inspecting it carefully, inserted several sentences of his own. He referred to the passages in the first grant by line number, and where they seemed ambiguous, he clarified them. He made complicated matters simple.

The Black Prince lived a life in service to *houmont*, 'high courage'. At Poitiers he believed himself blessed by an almost supernatural strength, and was fascinated by stories of others who had experienced something similar, whether it was the Biblical Samson, whose image adorned the roof bosses of his chantry at Canterbury Cathedral, or a monk at Moissac who was reputed to be able to bring a cantering horse to a stop with his outstretched arms and twist a lance out of shape with his bare hands. The abbey chronicler, Aymeric de Peyrac, recalled that the Prince delighted in hearing about his exploits.

For the medieval knight, the highest form of courage was to scorn death rather than fear it. The Prince's leadership at Poitiers and Nájera caught that truth. He would live and die a warrior. His funeral achievements, which were to be placed above his tomb, included his shield, helmet, ceremonial cap and magnificent leopard crest. Their arrangement was anticipated in a striking wax seal attached to a grant to Canterbury Cathedral on 1 September 1362, which showed in fine detail the achievements in an almost identical position.

This memorial motif was created fourteen years before the Prince's death. It suggests that at the height of his worldly success, recently married and soon to sail for Aquitaine, the Prince was already planning to be buried at Canterbury Cathedral and thinking about the accoutrements for his funeral. He did not flinch from death but embraced it — and that gave his martial valour exceptional force.

He chose Canterbury because he believed that the intercession of St Thomas à Becket had saved himself and his army at Poitiers, allowing them to face their terror and despair and overcome it. When Bishop Brinton spoke in wonder of the mass of soldiers around the French king, so many that 'ten of his armed knights faced one Englishman — and yet God favoured the just cause', he was almost certainly drawing upon the Black Prince's own recollections. The Prince fully inhabited the inner world of the knight, a world of piety and devotion, and that formed the wellspring of his prowess on the battlefield. These were the virtues that Geoffrey de Charny extolled in his book of chivalry. 'Be humble towards your friends, proud and bold towards your foes, merciful to those who need assistance and a cruel avenger against your enemies.' The Black Prince brought these qualities to life. As we gaze upon his tomb, we rightly pay tribute to a hero of his times.

APPENDIX

Black Propaganda and the Sack of Limoges

In the Middle Ages, a chivalric hero was charismatic and generous, and able to win others to his cause; but he could also be the target of rumour, insinuation and slander. At the beginning of Edward III's reign, the king was accused of the murder of his brother, John of Eltham, in 1336, and the seduction and rape of Catherine Grandison, the wife of his closest friend and martial companion William, earl of Salisbury, while William was abroad on royal service in 1342. In both cases, the charges were made by one chronicler (John of Fordun and Jean le Bel respectively). Historians have assessed them in the light of other chronicle accounts and documentary evidence, and found both reports to be extremely unlikely. In the case of John of Eltham, the cause of his death (at Perth on 13 September) is unclear – it may have been of fever – but the king was very close to his brother and grief-stricken at his loss. And the rumour concerning the countess of Salisbury was almost certainly devised by Jean le Bel in an attempt to blacken Edward's reputation.

For the Prince's so-called sack of Limoges on 19 September 1370 we are again largely reliant on one chronicler, Jean Froissart. Froissart's account is echoed in a much briefer comment by Thomas Walsingham, who spoke of the Prince's anger, adding that, after the city was captured 'he almost totally destroyed it, and killed all those he found there, a few only being spared their lives and taken prisoner'. But elsewhere Walsingham described Limoges as one of the military operations the Prince was most proud of, saying – in terms of his illness – that 'it was sad to see the victor of Poitiers, Nájera and Limoges in such an enfeebled state'. The Chandos Herald only remarked that 'everyone there was either killed or taken', a comment more likely referring to those bearing arms rather than the civilian population as a whole. The local chronicler of the abbey of Saint-Martial said that 'they pillaged the city and then set it on fire', but gave the figure of those dead as 300, not 3,000.

To these responses we can add the comments of Christine de Pizan, the contemporary biographer of Charles V, who did not mention any massacre of civilians, and simply put the siege of Limoges in the context of military actions in the summer of 1370, stressing the relative failure of the planned offensive, and that a new war strategy was adopted by Bertrand du Guesclin soon after he became constable of France. She gave the number of those killed and taken prisoner as 400. The full range of source material, including archaeological evidence, confirms that the part of Limoges known as the *cité* was badly damaged in the siege of 1370, and many houses burned to the ground. But on the sequence of events that led up to this, Froissart's account is not supported by the full range of chronicle evidence, and it is contradicted by the documentary sources.

1. On 1 July 1370 the Black Prince, in discussions with John of Gaunt and the king, rejected a policy of punishment towards those towns that had gone over to Charles V and now wished to return to English allegiance. The Prince made clear he preferred a path of clemency. This decision, recorded on the Gascon Rolls (TNA, C61/94/40; translated by the Gascon Rolls project), also gave John of Gaunt overall authority in the conduct of military operations; any decision on the fate of Limoges's civilians would have to be agreed by both men.

2. The majority of Limoges stayed loyal to the Prince. The *château* district refused to surrender to John, duke of Berry, and the *cité*

only did so when the bishop, Jean de Cros, announced that the Prince was dead. A surrender document of 24 August 1370 was left in draft form when not enough citizens put their name to it (AD de la Haute-Vienne, AA13). Most importantly, letters of the Prince himself, granting the cathedral chapter the right to administer the *cité*, stated that he did not blame the clergy or the local population for the treason of their bishop (AD de la Haute-Vienne, G8). On the authorization of the Prince, the chapter took possession of the *cité* on 3 February 1371.

3. On the massacre itself, surviving documentary evidence points in a different direction. The depositions of a case before the Paris Parlement on 10 July 1404 involved two merchants of Limoges (Bizé versus Bayard, Archives Nationales, X2a/14, ff.193-194), in which Bizé responded to Bayard's claim that his family had always supported the French crown. Bayard said that his father had been a 'notable man' within Limoges, and had assisted in the surrender of the *cité* to Charles V in 1370, for which the king had rewarded him with offices and lands. Bizé's lawyer contradicted this by detailing the actions of Bayard's father, along with many others within the *cité*, during the Black Prince's siege. To drive his point home, Bizé was keen to give additional detail, referring to the raising of the banner of England and France above the city gate, clearly as a signal to the Anglo-Gascon army. Bizé suggested that members of the French garrison killed Limoges's civilians when they opened the gates to the Prince on 19 September 1370. Here is a section of Bizé's testimony:

> Le contraire est vrai, car le père dudit Bayard estoit pouvre homs et pelletier, et par le père du Bizé et non par ledit pelletier fit obeissance au Roy; mais, qui plus est, le père Bayard et se compaigna d'autres pelletiers, print et emporta la banière des Englois à la porte de Limoges, et s'il eust esté prins par le connestable de la garnison, il lui eust fait couper la teste.

(On the contrary, Bayard's father was only a poor man, a furrier, and it was Bizé's father, not this furrier, who demonstrated his loyalty to the king. Moreover, Bayard's father, accompanied by other furriers, took and carried the banner of the English to the gate of Limoges, where he was captured by the captain of the garrison, who then beheaded him.)

4. The general context is all-important. The Prince had already been the victim of hostile propaganda on the resumption of war in 1369, and the accusations made against him seem entirely unfounded. He was aware that this would be his last campaign and in terms of his reputation and standing before God, his actions at Limoges would colour how he would be seen and judged. A letter recently discovered in the Spanish archives by Guilhem Pépin, in which the Prince wrote to Gaston Fébus, count of Foix, from Limoges on 22 September 1370, revealed his evident pride in regaining the city, spoke of high-ranking captives, including Jean de Cros and Roger de Beaufort, and added that he took 200 knights and men-at-arms prisoner. No civilian deaths were mentioned. It appeared that Charles V held the French garrison commander Jean de Villemur responsible for the deaths of civilians and punished him for it. Although Villemur defended Limoges bravely (and he was praised for it by Froissart and the author of the *Chronique des Quatre Premiers Valois*) Charles V revoked his grant of the town and castle of Blanc-sur-Creuse and offered him no further military command. Villemur died in poverty on 13 May 1375, when the guardianship of his two young children was given to his uncle (Archives Nationales, JJ100/292, 819; X1a/24, f6). It would be extremely odd for the French king to hold a solemn memorial Mass, when news of the Prince's death reached Paris, for an opponent who had recently massacred some 3,000 French citizens. On balance, I think it is time to dismiss this slur by Froissart, as we have done with the earlier accusations against Edward III.

NOTES

prologue

I am most grateful to Sarah Turner, Canterbury Cathedral Collections Manager, and Karen Brayshaw, the Librarian, for allowing me to inspect the Prince's funeral achievements. Useful information on the tunic is provided in Janet Arnold, 'The jupon or coat-armour of the Black Prince in Canterbury Cathedral', *Church Monuments*, 8 (1993); also Stella Newton, *Fashion in the Age of the Black Prince*. The references to the Cathedral Archives (henceforth CCA) are CCA/DCc/ChAnt/C/145 (foundation of the chantry in honour of the Holy Trinity); DCc/ChAnt/N/37 (letter of 17 February 1359). On Moissac, see Régis de la Haye (ed.), *Chronique des Abbés de Moissac*. The Prince held a high reputation throughout the remainder of the Hundred Years War: Christopher Allmand, 'Edward, the Black Prince', *History Today*, 26 (1976). For the historiography in general, see Barbara Gribling, 'The Black Prince: hero or villain?' *BBC History Magazine* (January 2013), and her forthcoming book: *The Black Prince in Georgian and Victorian England: Negotiating the Medieval Past*. Examples of more recent academic criticism, some of it harsh, include Scott Waugh's 1991 *England in the Reign of Edward III*, where the Prince's rule over Aquitaine was 'marked by bickering and ineptitude' and Mark Ormrod's *The Reign of Edward III* (2000), according to which the Black Prince showed 'a complete misunderstanding of local [Gascon] traditions', and eagerly seized upon the Nájera campaign 'to escape the boredom of administration'; while his sack of Limoges 'destroyed any last vestiges of English sympathy' and 'brought about the collapse of English rule in southern France.'

chapter one

To understand the sense of triumph in the early part of Edward III's reign, we have to recognize the political chaos and military humiliation prevalent before it. The general narrative has been drawn from Roy Haines,

King Edward II; Seymour Phillips, *Edward II*; Kathryn Warner, *Edward II: the Unconventional King* and *Isabella of France: the Rebel Queen*; Mark Ormrod, *Edward III* and Ian Mortimer, *The Greatest Traitor* and *The Perfect King*. In addition, the following articles were helpful: Claire Valence, 'The deposition and abdication of Edward II', *English Historical Review* [henceforth *EHR*], 113 (1998); Caroline Shenton, 'Edward III and the coup of 1330', in *The Age of Edward III*. For the emotional significance of the birth of Prince Edward (the future Edward III) see the comments in the *Vita Edwardi Secundi*, ed. Denholm-Young: 'a handsome and long looked-for son... it much lessened the grief which had afflicted the king on Piers Gaveston's death'.

On Bannockburn, the classic account is Geoffrey Barrow, *Robert Bruce*; a useful recent one is David Cornell, *Bannockburn*. The painful correspondence between Edward II and his son is from James Halliwell (ed.), *Letters of the Kings of England*, vol. 1, pp. 25–9. Isabella's denunciation of her husband's relationship with Hugh Despenser is relayed in the *Vita Edwardi Secundi*. Material on Philippa of Hainault is from Juliet Vale, 'Philippa, queen of England, consort of Edward III', *The Oxford Dictionary of National Biography* [henceforth *Oxford* DNB]. The description of her is found in Francis Hingeston-Randolph (ed.), *The Register of Walter de Stapledon*. For the fighting in Gascony, Pierre Chaplais (ed.), *The War of Saint-Sardos*. On Edward III's humiliation against the Scots in 1327, Ranald Nicholson, *Edward III and the Scots: The Formative Years of a Military Career* and Clifford Rogers, *War Cruel and Sharp*. For the likely effect this had on the king, Rogers, 'Edward III and the dialectics of strategy', *Transactions of the Royal Historical Society*, 4 (1994). The exact circumstances of Edward II's death remain difficult to reconstruct: Paul Doherty, *Isabella and the Strange Death of Edward II*; Ian Mortimer, 'The death of Edward II in Berkeley Castle', *EHR*, 120 (2005). For a recent overview of the debate, Andy King, 'The death of Edward II revisited', in James Bothwell and Gwilym Dodd (eds), *Fourteenth Century England, Volume 9*. On the vital role of William Montagu in the Nottingham coup, and his friendship with Edward III: Mark Ormrod, 'William Montagu, first earl of Salisbury (1301–1344), soldier and magnate', in *Oxford DNB*. For Edward III's triumph at Halidon Hill in 1333, Nicholson, *Formative Years*; Matthew Strickland and Robert Hardy, *The Great Warbow*.

chapter two

For chivalry and the court, I have used Richard Barber, *Reign of Chivalry*; Maurice Keen, *Chivalry*; and the essays in John Scattergood and James Sherborne (eds), *English Court Culture in the Later Middle Ages*. For the Prince's upbringing, the two pioneering studies by Margaret Sharp, 'The central administration system of Edward, the Black Prince', in Thomas Tout, *Chapters in the*

Administrative History of Medieval England and 'The administrative chancery of the Black Prince before 1362', in *Essays in Medieval History presented to Thomas Frederick Tout* alongside Richard Barber, *Edward Prince of Wales*, were particularly helpful. A number of household accounts survive for the Prince's childhood and adolescence: The National Archives [henceforth TNA], E387/25 and E388/12 cover the period 1336-8; E389/6, 13 and 15, that of 1340-44. For Henry of Grosmont and *Le Livre de Seyntz Medicines (The Book of Holy Medicine)* see Margaret Labarge, 'Henry of Lancaster and *Le Livre de Seyntz Medicines*', *Florilegium*, 2 (1980); Kenneth Fowler, *King's Lieutenant*. On campaigning in Scotland, Rogers, *War Cruel and Sharp* and for the death of John of Eltham, Tom James, 'John of Eltham: history and story', in *Fourteenth Century Studies*, II; Scott Waugh, 'John earl of Cornwall (1316–1336)', in *Oxford DNB*. For the letters between the Prince and Edward III, Clifford Rogers (ed.), *The Wars of Edward III*. On the broader political crisis of 1340–2: Ormrod, *Edward III*.

Not everyone was won over by Edward III's show and magnificence; similar criticisms would later be made of the Black Prince. Here Andy King, 'A helm with a crest of gold: the Order of Chivalry in Thomas Gray's *Scalacronica*', in *Fourteenth Century Studies*, I, has been particularly helpful. But such pomp could be deceptive. For King Edward's toughness, the high standards he set for himself and his aristocracy, sometimes unrealistically so, see the valuable article of Richard Partington, 'The nature of noble service to Edward III', in *Political Society in Later Medieval England*. This relentless royal ambition impacted strongly upon others, and would play out in Edward's relationship with his eldest son. For gift-giving to the young Prince and leading aristocrats, as a way of forging brotherhood-in-arms: Thom Richardson, 'Armour in England, 1325–99', *Journal of Medieval History*, 37 (2011). Background detail on the Burghersh family is found in Anthony Verduyn, 'Burghersh, Bartholomew, the elder', second Lord Burghersh (d.1355), magnate and adminsistrator', in *Oxford DNB*.

For the Battle of Sluys and siege of Tournai there are two important articles by Kelly DeVries, 'God, leadership, the Flemings and archery: contemporary perspectives of victory and defeat at the battle of Sluys, 1340', *American Neptune*, 55 (1995) and 'Contemporary views of Edward III's failure at the siege of Tournai', *Nottingham Medieval Studies*, 39 (1995). On King Edward's borrowing, and the collapse of the Peruzzi and Bardi banks: Edmund Fryde, 'Financial resources of Edward III in the Netherlands, 1337-40', *Revue Belge de Philologie et d'Histoire*, 45 (1967) and Edwin Hunt, 'A new look at the dealings of the Bardi and Peruzzi with Edward III', *Journal of Economic History*, 50 (1990). The Windsor tournament of 1344 is surveyed in Julian Munby, Richard Barber and Richard Brown, *Edward III's Round Table at Windsor*. The Prince's household account for 1344–5 is BL, Harley Ms 4304. An important study of the Black Prince's evolving retinue is made in David Green, 'The household and military retinue of Edward the Black Prince', University of Nottingham Ph.D. thesis (1998), his subsequent *The Black Prince* and a number of articles (which will be referred to in later Notes).

chapter three

Bartholomew Burghersh's letters, reporting the progress of the Prince's vanguard, are given in Richard Barber, *Life and Campaigns of the Black Prince*. The pioneering narratives of the Crécy campaign by Jules Viard, *La Campagne de Juillet–Août 1346*, and Alfred Burne, *Crécy War*, have now been supplemented by a series of important studies, including Andrew Ayton and Philip Preston, *The Battle of Crécy, 1346*; Jonathan Sumption, *Trial By Battle*; Rogers, *War Cruel and Sharp* and most recently, Michael Livingston and Kelly DeVries, *Crécy: A Casebook*. The source material for the chapter is drawn from Barber, *Life and Campaigns* ; Rogers, *Wars of Edward III* and Livingston and DeVries, *Crécy*. The Kervyn de Lettenhove edition of Jean Froissart has been used whenever possible; for Jean de Venette there is now Colette Beaune's recent (2011) edition.

There are problems ascertaining the exact location of two of the Prince's battles, Crécy and Poitiers; only the site of Nájera can be identified with full confidence. A number of alternatives have been suggested for Crécy, the most recent by Livingston and DeVries, but at present the balance of evidence suggests the traditional site is most likely correct. As Gordon Corrigan stated in his *Military History of the Hundred Years War*: 'The best argument is that if Edward III wanted a battle... there was simply nowhere else within a day's march that offered anything like the advantage of the Crécy position.' I am grateful to Gordon Corrigan and Sir Philip Preston for discussing this issue with me. For the inner world of the knight, see Richard Kaeuper (ed.), *The Book of Chivalry of Geoffroi de Charny*. On logistics, see Michael Prestwich, *Armies and Warfare in the Middle Ages* and Yuval Harari, 'Inter-frontal co-operation in the fourteenth century and Edward III's 1346 campaign', *War in History*, 6 (1999). On the campaign in Normandy, and the chronicle sources, Henri Prentout, *La prise de Caen par Edouard III*, is still useful. For the intensity of the fighting around the Prince, Livingston and DeVries, *Crécy*; the reward to Danyers, 'for the recovering of our banner' is from the Black Prince's Registers (henceforth BPR), I, 45. The frst volume contains letters issued under the Prince's privy seal between July 1346 and January 1348. The three others consist of warrants issued between February 1351 and November 1365, one dealing with Cheshire, one with Cornwall and one with the Prince's other lands in England and Wales and matters of his household.

The quotation from Thomas Bradwardine's address to Edward III and his captains is from Gilles Teulié and Laurence Lux-Sterritt (eds), *War Sermons*. On Arderne, and his remarks on the ostrich feathers, D'Arcy Power (ed.), *John Arderne: Treatises of Fistula*. However, the Black Prince's use of the two mottoes 'Ich dene' and 'Houmont' ('I serve' and 'High courage') only occurred in Aquitaine in July 1363, as part of a cipher written in the Prince's own hand, and does not seem linked to Crécy: Sharp, 'Edward, the Black Prince.' The Prince's revealing comment on his 'exploit', in a letter to Sir Thomas Ferrers, justice of Chester, of 12 September 1346, is found in TNA, E36/144, fo. 12. The opening section is merely glossed in BPR, I, 14, as 'with the help of God the Prince has prospered in his present expedition'; in doing so, the power of the Black Prince's observation is largely lost.

chapter four

For the onset of the Black Death: Barbara Tuchman, *A Distant Mirror*; Benedict Gummer, *The Scourging Angel*; Philip Ziegler, *The Black Death*, Colin Platt, *King Death* and Rosemary Horrox (ed.), *The Black Death*. On the military activities: Susan Rose, *Calais: An English Town in France*; Craig Lambert, 'Edward III's siege of Calais: a reappraisal', *Journal of Medieval History*, 37 (2011). For the Prince's illness: BPR, I, 51; Jan Willems (ed.), *En Letterkunde en de Geschiedenis des Vaderlands*. His rapid, almost miraculous, recovery further reinforced his sense of religious conviction. In his will, of 23 August 1348, Archbishop John Stratford left the Prince 'a fine missal' and a resurrection scene, fashioned in silver (Roy Haines, *Archbishop Stratford*). On the upsurge of piety and prayers for the souls of the dead, see a perceptive piece by Nigel Saul, 'The Lovekyns and the Lovekyn chapel at Kingston-upon-Thames', *Surrey Archaeological Collections*, 96 (2011). For the defence of Calais, see Yuval Harari, *Special Operations in the Age of Chivalry*; for the sea battle at Winchelsea, Graham Cushway, *Edward III and the War at Sea*. On Joan of Kent: Karl Wentersdorf, 'The clandestine marriages of the Fair Maid of Kent', *Journal of Medieval History*, 5 (1979). The views of Margaret Galway, 'Joan of Kent and the Order of the Garter', *University of Birmingham Historical Journal*, I (1947), have now been substantially modified (see the comments of Barber, *The Black Prince*). And Richard Barber, *Edward III and the Triumph of England*; Mortimer, *Perfect King* and Jonathan Sumption, 'Sir Walter Mauny (c. 1310–1372), soldier and founder of the London Charterhouse', *Oxford DNB*, have been particularly helpful.

The full list of founder knights is drawn from a fifteenth-century copy of the Garter statutes (given in full in Barber, *Edward III*), although, as Richard Barber notes, there are some inconsistencies (in regard to the election dates of the earls of Northampton, Suffolk and Sir Walter Mauny) when this source is compared to the incomplete but near-contemporary list of founders provided by Geoffrey le Baker. On the Prince's estate management: John Hatcher, *The Rural Economy in the Duchy of Cornwall*; David Evans, 'Some notes on the history of the Principality of Wales in the time of the Black Prince (1343–1376)', *Transactions of the Honourable Society of Cymmrodorion* (1925-26); David Pratt, 'The lead mining community at Minera in the fourteenth century', *Transactions of the Denbighshire Historical Society*, 11 (1962); Paul Booth, *The Financial Administration of the Lordship and County of Chester* and 'Taxation and public order: Cheshire in 1353', *Northern History*, 12 (1976). Booth provides a more positive context for the Prince's visit than the insinuation of coercion and profiteering found in Henry Knighton's Chronicle, written some forty years after the event. On Wingfield's ruthless efficiency, Mark Bailey, 'Sir John de Wingfield and the foundation of Wingfield College', in Peter Bloore and Edward Martin (eds), *Wingfield College and its Patrons*. In the aftermath of the Black Death, once a measure of recovery had occurred, the Prince's lands in England and Wales brought in an annual income of around £8,600.

The modernized version of *Wynnere and Wastoure* is from Victoria Flood, '*Wynnere and Wastoure* and the influence of political prophecy', *Chaucer Review*, 45 (2015). Its performance at Chester Castle in August 1353 is suggested by Thorlac Turville-Petre, '*Wynnere and Wastoure*: When and Where?' in L. A. J. R. Houwen and Alasdair MacDonald (eds), *Loyal Letters*. For the invitation to attend the banquet: *BPR*, 3, 112; the red hangings and vestments decorated with eagles (the 'noblest bird', a motif often found in the Prince's gifts to his warrior companions) are noted by Juliet Vale, 'Image and identity in the Order of the Garter' in Nigel Saul (ed.), *St George's Chapel, Windsor, in the Fourteenth Century*. John Scattergood, 'Wynnere and Wastoure and the mid-fourteenth century economy' in Thomas Dunne (ed.), *The Writer as Witness: Literature as Historical Evidence*, summarised that 'none of this evidence is entirely conclusive... but taken as a whole, the case for dating the poem to 1353 is a strong one'. For the tournaments of 1353/4 and the visit to Cornwall: Richard Barber, *Edward, Prince of Wales and Aquitaine*. The improvements to Berkhamsted Castle are from John W. Cobb, *History and Antiquities of Berkhamsted*.

chapter five

I am grateful to the Duchy of Cornwall Record Office for permission to use John Henxteworth's Day Book. The major survey of this campaign is H. J. Hewitt, *Black Prince's Expedition*. On the general background: Pierre Capra, 'Le siège d'Aiguillon en juin 1354', *Revue de l'Agenais*, 2 (1962) and Jonathan Sumption, *Trial by Fire*. On the campaign preparations: *BPR*, 4, 157-168; Mollie Madden, 'The indenture between Edward III and the Black Prince for the prince's expedition to Gascony, 10 July 1355', *Journal of Medieval Military History*, 12 (2014) . For the Black Prince's arrival in Bordeaux: Guilhem Pépin, 'La collégiale Saint-Seurin de Bordeaux aux treizième et quatorzième siècles et son élaboration d'une idéologie du duché d'Aquitaine anglo-gascon', *Le Moyen Âge*, 118 (2011). For Jean de Grailly: Malcolm Vale, 'Jean III de Grailly [known as Captal de Buch] d. 1377, soldier', in *Oxford DNB*. On the Prince's residence in Bordeaux: Archives Départementales [henceforth AD] de la Gironde, G238, and Pierre Capra, 'Le séjour du Prince Noir à l'archevêché de Bordeaux', *Revue Historique de Bordeaux et de la Gironde*, 7 (1958). For the earl of Warwick: Anthony Tuck, 'Thomas Beauchamp, eleventh earl of Warwick, soldier and magnate', *Oxford DNB*. Details on Robert Neville and Robert Marney are from: *House of Commons, 1388–1422*; Adam Mottram and Richard Mascy in Philip Morgan, *War and Society in Medieval Cheshire*.

A useful comparison with the system of recruitment employed by Henry of Grosmont a decade earlier is provided in Nicholas Gribit, *Henry of Lancaster's Expedition to Aquitaine, 1345–46*. And excellent on the logistics is Mollie Madden, 'The Black Prince at war: the anatomy of a chevauchée', University of Minnesota Ph.D. (2014). For Jean, count of Armagnac, Bertrand Darmaillacq's 'Le Prince Noir contre le comte d'Armagnac: l'expédition de 1355', *Revue de Gascogne*, 14 (1914), can now be supplemented by Dominique Barrois's important 2004 University of Lille doctorate, 'Jean, premier comte d'Armagnac'. The key chronicle sources for the campaign itself are drawn from Barber, *Life and Campaigns* and Rogers, *Wars of Edward III*. Geoffrey le Baker is particularly valuable, as he incorporates a day-by-day account from one of the soldiers who took part. A new edition of his chronicle is David Preest and Richard Barber (eds), *Chronicle of Geoffrey le Baker of Swinbrook*. The Prince's own version of events, set out in a letter to the bishop of Winchester on 25 December 1355, and the comments of his business manager Sir John Wingfield, are from Barber, *Life and Campaigns*.

On the crossing of the Garonne near Portet, the identification by Peter Hoskins, *In the Steps of the Black Prince,* is confirmed by Archives Municipales de Montpellier, AA9. Payments to local guides are from the Henxteworth Day Book. On the growing French panic and attempted defence measures: Archives Municipales de Nîmes, LL1; Henri Bousquet, *Comptes de Rodez (1350– 1358)*. For increasing criticism of Armagnac's passivity, Barrois, 'Jean, premier comte d'Armagnac'. On the meeting with the count of Foix: Henxteworth Day Book; *Chronicle of Geoffrey le Baker;* Pierre Tucoo-Chala, *Gaston Fébus et Le Prince Noir.*

For the broader evaluation of the campaign, a welcome reappraisal of later French mythology surrounding the 'Black' Prince is found in Jacqueline

Caille, 'Nouveaux regards sur l'attaque du Prince Noir contre Narbonne en Novembre 1355', *Bulletin de la Société d'Études Scientifiques de l'Aude*, 109 (2009): some of the destruction blamed (in later, popular tradition) on the English army was in fact the result of seventeenth-century demolition work. However, the fourteenth-century trail of devastation was real enough: Sean McGlynn, '"Sheer terror" and the Black Prince's grand chevauchée of 1355', in *The Hundred Years War (Part III): Further Considerations*. The inquiry of Thibault de Barbazan, seneschal of Carcassonne, is in Henri Roucou, 'Bernard de Bonne, seigneur de Graulhet', *Bulletin de la Société d'Histoire de Graulhet*, 35 (2014). Significantly, Barbazan did not criticize the Prince, but those who had failed to maintain the region's defences. The Black Prince's pass, to 'one of our archers' – William Jodrell – to take Christmas leave is found in Margaret Sharp, 'A Jodrell deed and the seals of the Black Prince', *Bulletin of the John Rylands Library*, 7 (1922). For John Stretton and Richard Mascy, see Philip Morgan, *War and Society in Late Medieval Cheshire*. Sir John Wingfield's letter to the bishop of Winchester on 23 December 1355 (Barber, *Life and Campaigns*) reveals the cold economic calculation that underpinned the campaign. French documentary sources cited by Henri Mullot, 'Nouvelles recherches sur l'itinéraire du Prince Noir à travers les pays de l'Aude', *Annales du Midi*, 21 (1909), show that estate accounts and records were deliberately seized by the Prince's officials in order to substantiate the scale of the destruction. The 'loyal friends' quotation is from Clifford Rogers, 'The Black Prince in Gascony and France (1355-57), according to Ms78 of Corpus Christi College, Oxford', *Journal of Medieval Military History*, 43 (2009).

chapter six

For the Black Prince's spiritual regimen: Joseph Parry (ed.), *Register of John de Trillek* (for the letter to the bishop of Hereford on 25 June 1356); Preest and Barber (eds), *Chronicle of Geoffrey le Baker;* and also see the payments made by the Prince on 7 September 1355, just before he set sail for Gascony, 'for painting and repairing a breviary' (a book containing all the liturgical texts of the Office that he would be able to carry with him): BPR, 4, 167. There are many valuable studies on the Poitiers campaign: Hewitt, *Black Prince's Expedition*; David Green, *Battle of Poitiers*; David Nicolle, *Poitiers, 1356*; Peter Hoskins, *In the Footsteps of the Black Prince* and Christian Teutsch, *Victory at Poitiers*, alongside important general surveys in Rogers, *War Cruel and Sharp* and Sumption, *Trial By Fire*. Source material is drawn from Barber, *Life and Campaigns* and Rogers, *Wars of Edward III*.

On 3 July 1356 the archiepiscopal accounts recorded 'tous ses cavaliers et son monde quittent Bordeaux' to join the Prince's mustering-point (AD de la Gironde, G238). However Jean, count of Armagnac's, invasion of Gascony

(Bibliothèque Nationale, Collection Doat, and Barrois's 2004 thesis) substantially changed matters. For the Prince's difficult negotiations at Bergerac, the petitions of the town of Mézin, requesting payment for damage suffered when the count of Armagnac besieged it, and confirmation of its privileges: TNA, SC8/211/1051 and 1054.

For the broader context: Ormrod, *Edward III* and Fowler, *King's Lieutenant*. I have benefited from the following *Oxford DNB* articles: Mark Ormrod, 'Robert Ufford, first earl of Suffolk (1298–1369), soldier and diplomat'; Michael C. E. Jones, 'Sir James Audley (*c.* 1318–1369), soldier'; John Leland, 'William Montagu, second earl of Salisbury'. On the route taken by the Prince's army, the itinerary given in Frank Haydon (ed.), *Eulogium Historiarum* has been supplemented by Peter Hoskins's valuable study *In the Footsteps of the Black Prince*. The Prince has been criticized for 'wasting time' at Romorantin: René Crozet, *Le Siège de Romorantin*, provides a useful re-evaluation, stressing – from chronicle evidence – that the military action significantly lifted the morale of the army. On Poitiers itself, Barber, *Edward III* and Strickland and Hardy, *Great Warbow* are also useful.

The similarity of tactics at Limalonges (on this occasion enacted by the French) and Poitiers is striking. The earlier engagement is only mentioned in one source: Auguste and Émile Molinier (eds), *Chronique Normande*. Émile Molinier was struck by the presence of Jean de Grailly at both battles and also by the role of the freebooting Poitevin Amanieu lord of Pommiers (Pommiers-Moulons, in Poitou-Charente), whom the English recruited for the Poitiers campaign because of his exceptional military skill. The *Chronique Normande* credited him with turning the tables on the French at Limalonges (in 1349) and praised his tactical ability when he defeated Marshal d'Audrehem at Corrèze in the Limousin four years later (an action fought at a time of supposed peace between England and France). The *Chronique* singled him out as one of the Black Prince's chief advisers at Poitiers. The archivist Paul Guérin said: 'By September 1356 he had propelled himself to the front rank of the Prince's captains': Guérin, *Recueil des documents concernant le Poitou, 1334–48* (the comments are made in a footnote on the start of Pommiers' career in 1345, pp. 412–13).

On the remarkable co-ordination between Jean de Grailly's picked force and the Prince's main army, and the use of signals, see Guilhem Pépin's general but important article 'Les cris de guerre "Guyenne!" et "St Georges!"', *Le Moyen Âge*, 112 (2006) and Robert Jones, *Bloodied Banners*. Andrew Ayton, 'War and the English gentry under Edward III', *History Today*, 42 (1992), rightly stresses that the annuity of £400, granted to Sir James Audley by the Prince in the battle's aftermath, was 'an exceptional act of generosity'. Audley's courage in leading the final charge against the French was a turning point, and he nearly paid for it with his life.

The vexed question of rights to prisoners is well surveyed in Françoise Bériac-Lainé and Chris Given-Wilson, *Les Prisonniers de la Bataille de Poitiers*. For the battle's aftermath, see Archives Municipales de Montpellier, AA9; Françoise Autrand, 'La deconfiture: la Bataille de Poitiers', in *Guerre et Société*, which cites the count of Armagnac's moving letter. For the Black Prince humorously putting the lands of the cardinal of Périgord under English protection, in a grant made at Bordeaux on 20 October 1356: AD des Pyrénées-Atlantiques, E746.

The Prince's letter to Reginald Bryan, the bishop of Worcester also on 20 October 1356, made clear his veneration for the Feast of the Translation of St Thomas à Becket (on 7 July), on the eve of which, he informed the bishop, his army had begun its march and his wish that credit for the victory be given to God and that saint (also see his undated letter, circa October 1356, to the prior of Winchester): Charles Lyttelton, 'A letter from the Black Prince to the bishop of Worcester', *Archaeologia*, 1 (1779); Arthur Goodman (ed.), *Chartulary of Winchester Cathedral*. Both Froissart and the anonymous chronicler of Canterbury describe the Prince offering at the shrine of Becket on his return to England in gratitude for his success. The strong link, in the Prince's own mind, between his most famous military triumph and the cult of Thomas à Becket at Canterbury offers the most likely explanation for his decision to be buried in that cathedral, 'where the body of that true martyr my lord Thomas rests' (from the will of the Black Prince, printed and translated in full by Arthur Stanley, in his *Historical Memorials of Canterbury*) as close as possible to the saint. The iconography of the Prince's chantry chapel at Canterbury, and its strong links with the battle, are discussed in William Scott Robertson, 'The chantries of the Black Prince', *Archaeologia Cantiana*, 13 (1880). The images found there, of Samson subduing the lion, and the vines and foliage (evoking the hedgerows protecting the Anglo-Gascon army), echo Geoffrey le Baker's account, and his description of the 'wild courage' shown by the Prince: 'hewing at the French with his sharp sword... teaching the enemy what the true fury of war meant'.

Some of the Black Prince's soldiers reached Bordeaux on 2 October 1356 (AD de la Gironde, G238). The Prince made his own formal entry into the city three days later: a contemporary report of Poitiers and its aftermath in Charles Higounet and Arlette Higounet-Nadal (eds), *Le Grand Cartulaire de l'Abbaye de la Sauve-Majeure*. This source (which has not to my knowledge been used in accounts of the battle) stated the victory was 'fultus potentia baronum Vasconie' — 'brought about by the might of the Gascon lords'.

It listed numbers of the enemy killed, captured and those believed to have fled – and gave one of the earliest battle names ('in loco vocato Beuvoyr' – 'at a place called Beuvoyr': the present-day village of Beauvoir, 3 miles (4.5 km) south-east of Poitiers and just under a mile (1.5km) north-west of Nouaillé-Maupertius. Patrice Barnabé, 'Guerre et mortalité au début de la guerre de cent ands: l'exemple des combattants gascons (1337-1367)', *Annales du Midi*, 113 (2001), identified twenty-three Gascon nobles present at the battle. For a grant from the Black Prince to the abbey: British Library (henceforth BL), Add. Ch. 66316. The Prince and John II set sail from Bordeaux on 19 April 1357: AD de la Gironde, G238; for their arrival in England and reception on reaching London: Given-Wilson and Scott-Stokes (eds), *Chronicle of the Anonymous of Canterbury*.

chapter seven

For the Black Prince's grandmother, Isabella, see Edward Bond, 'Notices of the last days of Isabella, queen of Edward II, drawn from an account of the expenses of her household', *Archaeologia*, 35 (1854); also Michael Bennett, 'Isabella of France, Anglo-French diplomacy and cultural exchange in the late 1350s', in James Bothwell (ed.), *The Age of Edward III*. On the French king, Neil Murphy, *The Captivity of John II*. The Prince's indebtedness after Poitiers is from references in Paul Booth, *The Financial Administration of the County of Chester* and Paul Booth and Anthony Carr (eds), *The Account of John de Burnham, 1361–62* and for the result of it, P. Hill and J. Heery (eds),*The Cheshire Forest Eyre Roll*, Lancashire and Cheshire Record Society, 151 (2015). On Kennington, Graham Dawson, 'The Black Prince's palace of Kennington, Surrey', *British Archaeological Reports*, 26 (1976); for Vale Royal, John Brownbill (ed.), *Ledger Book of Vale Royal Abbey*. For the general narrative: Barber, *Edward, the Black Prince* and Green, *Black Prince*.

On the chaos in France, Tuchman, *A Distant Mirror;* on the Jacquerie, Justine Firnhaber-Baker, 'Soldiers, villagers and politics: military violence and the Jacquerie of 1358', in Guilhem Pépin, Françoise Lainé and Frédéric Boutoulle (eds), *Routiers et Mercenaires*. On the Free Companies, or *Routiers*, many of the essays in the same volume, including Armand Jamme, 'Routiers et distinction sociale: Bernard de la Salle, l'Angleterre et le Pape', and Guilhem Pépin, 'Les routiers gascons, basques, agenais et périgourdins du parti anglais'. Amanieu lord of Pommiers rose to prominence as a freebooting captain in the Saintonge in the 1340s. Recruited by the English at Poitiers, he was then bought back by the French, who – overlooking his earlier career – offered him a generous annual pension of 1,500 *livres tournois*, a clear sign of his role in the battle's outcome: Guérin, *Recueil des documents*. For the Rheims campaign, Rogers, *War Cruel and Sharp*; Thomas Gray's account is in Rogers, *Wars of Edward III*. On the siege itself, Henri Moranville, 'Le siège de Reims, 1359–1360', *Bibliothèque de l'École des Chartes*, 56 (1895). Mobberley's death from 'the sickness' is in Morgan, *War and Society*. For Brétigny: John Le Patourel, 'The treaty of Brétigny, 1360', in *Transactions of the Royal Historical Society*, 10 (1960).

The Black Prince's marriage to Joan of Kent allowed the creation of a glittering court in Aquitaine. The match was controversial (see the comments in Given-Wilson and Scott-Stokes (eds), *Chronicle of the Anonymous of Canterbury*); Joan was another big spender, and the couple's ostentatious display would make the Prince a target of criticism in his later years in Gascony. But such show and finery was expected at any major European court (on this see Malcolm Vale, *Princely Court*) and his beautiful and astute wife was a considerable asset on the chivalric stage. A positive reappraisal of Joan is provided in Penny Lawne's recent biography, *Joan of Kent*. For the Prince's expenditure on his wife: BPR, 4 401–3, 427, 475–6; Green, *Black Prince*. The comparison with his sister, Isabella, is from James Gillespie, 'Isabella, countess of Bedford (1332–1379)', *Oxford DNB*.

For prophecy and the Prince: Lesley Coote, *Prophecy*; Ian Mortimer, *Fears of Henry IV*. The marginal images of the kings of France and England and John II at Poitiers are found at BL, Egerton Ms. 3277, f. 68v. On the purchase of the psalters: BPR, 4, 476; Jeremy Catto, 'The prayers of the Bohuns', in Peter Coss and Christopher Tyerman (eds), *Soldiers, Nobles and Gentlemen;* Lucy Sandler, *Illuminators and Patrons in Fourteenth Century England: The Psalter and Hours of Humphrey de Bohun;* Lynda Dennison, 'British Library, Egerton Ms. 3277: a fourteenth-century psalter-hours and the question of the Bohun family ownership', in Richard Eales and Shaun Tyas (eds), *Family and Dynasty in Late Medieval England*.

On the preparations in Aquitaine before the Prince's arrival, and the role of Sir John Chandos as king's lieutenant there: Robert Favreau, 'Comptes de la sénéchaussée de Saintonge (1360–1362)', *Bibliothèque de l'École des Chartes*, 117 (1959) and 'La cession de la Rochelle à l'Angleterre', in Robert Bautier (ed.), *La 'France Anglaise';* Max Aussel, 'Conditions dans lesquelles Cahors accepte la domination anglaise, Janvier 1362', *Bulletin de la Société des Études du Lot*, 119 (1998).

Details on the Prince's progress in Gascony, and the acts of homage, are from Delpit, *Documents Français*. Valuable background on the Prince's administration, showing his co-operation with the Gascon nobility, is found in Pierre Capra's (1972) Paris thesis, 'L'administration anglo-gasconne au temps de la lieutenance du Prince Noir, 1354–62', and in his 'Les bases sociales du pouvoir anglo-gascon au milieu du quatorzième siècle', *Le Moyen Âge*, 81 (1975). See also Eleanor Lodge, *Gascony under English Rule* and Margaret Wade Labarge,

Gascony: England's First Colony. I owe the reference to the bishop of Sarlat and the Prince's gift of his cloak to Guilhem Pépin. The background to the Prince's meeting with Fébus at Agen, and particularly the negotiations over the ransoms of Armagnac and Albret (both captured at Launac) which the Black Prince was seeking to moderate, are found in the Bibliothèque Nationale, Collection Doat.

Joan of Kent's letter announcing the birth of her son is from Corporation of London Archives, Letter Book G, f. 168. Her 'corsets, cut back at the sides, bordered in ermine' and 'silk belts, woven in gold and silver, and adorned with precious stones' certainly created a stir in Gascon society: Mila de Cabarieu, 'Documents historiques sur le Tarn-et-Garonne', *Bulletin Archéologique et Historique de Tarn-et-Garonne*, 14 (1886). For the reaction of Jean de Beaumanoir: Michael C. E. Jones, *Letters and Orders of du Guesclin* (who correctly dates Landes d'Evran and provides the content for the Poitiers agreement); David Green, *Edward the Black Prince: Power in Medieval Europe.*

For the extraordinary expenditure on the tournament in Edward of Angoulême's honour, see: Antonia Gransden, 'A fourteenth-century chronicle from the Grey Friars at Lynn', *English Historical Review*, 72 (1957). The three account books of Richard Filongley (TNA, E177/1, 9 and 10) and that of Bernard Brocas, receiver of Aquitaine 1363–4 (TNA, E177/3) only offer a partial picture of the Prince's financial administration. The Black Prince's coinage is surveyed in Pierre Capra, 'L'histoire monétaire de l'Aquitaine anglo-gasconne au temps du Prince Noir', *Bulletin de la Société Archéologique de Bordeaux*, 64 (1968) and Jean-Paul Casse, 'La monnaie du Prince Noir', in Jacques de Cauna (ed.), *L'Aquitaine au Temps du Prince Noir.* On the search for revenue, and the Prince's personal interest in the collection of it: Adrien Blanchet, 'L'atelier monétaire du Prince Noir à Limoges en 1365 et 1366', *Revue Numismatique*, 54 (1898).

A comparison with the rule of the Black Prince's brother, Lionel duke of Clarence, in Ireland is provided by David Green, 'Lordship and principality: colonial policy in Ireland and Aquitaine in the 1360s', *Journal of British Studies*, 47 (2008). But unlike the Prince, Clarence never developed any empathy with his Irish subjects. The Prince's letters to the seneschal of the Agenais, of 2 February and 27 June 1365, concerning the dispute between Arnaud de Durfort and the town of Agen and Louis de Malval's seizure of the castle of Juliac, are from AD de Lot-et-Garonne (Agen), FF 144. His declaration that he 'wished to restore peace and proper observance of the law to his lands' echoed the statement made to the community of Cheshire twelve years earlier.

On the abbey of Saint-Maixent, Louis vicomte of Thouars and Mareuil: Bibliothèque Municipale de Poitiers, Collection Dom Fonteneau; Louis de la Boutière (ed.), *Cartulaire de l'Abbaye d'Orbestier;* Archives Nationales, X1a 1472,

18 February 1380, stating retrospectively that in the time of the Prince and Felton 'il n'y avoit nul, tant fut grand, qui osait les désobéir'. For the inquiries about the lordship of Béarn: TNA, C61/78/39 and Pierre Tucoo-Chala, *Gaston Fébus et la Vicomté de Béarn*; the Black Prince's letter to Fébus is AD des Pyrénées-Atlantiques, E409. The Prince's replacement of Amanieu du Fossat, lord of Madaillan as seneschal of the Rouergue by Sir Thomas Wettenhall (by 4 December 1364) proved to be a serious mistake: William Bliss and Jessie Twemlow (eds), *Calendar of Papal Registers, vol.4*, 17–18, 20, 22. On the count of Armagnac's homage: Bibliothèque Nationale, Collection Doat; the Black Prince's oath – and the pie – is from AD des Pyrénées-Atlantiques, E251, cited in Guilhem Pépin, 'Towards a new assessment of the Black Prince's principality of Aquitaine: a study of the last years (1369-72)', *Nottingham Medieval Studies*, 50 (2006).

chapter eight

The long-standing view of Peter Russell, *English Intervention in Spain*, on the Nájera campaign, that the Black Prince 'allowed his own ambitions... to take precedence over English strategy' has been challenged by Clara Estow, *Pedro the Cruel*, remarking that Russell judged the Prince's actions 'against unfair standards'; it deserves a full reappraisal. On Auray, Strickland and Hardy, *Warbow;* on the Black Prince's friendship with John de Montfort, who succeeded to the duchy of Brittany in 1365, and Montfort's subsequent marriage to the Prince's stepdaughter: Michael C. E. Jones, *Ducal Brittany.* For the character of Pedro: Benjamin Taggie, 'Pedro I of Castile (1350–69): a Mediterranean prince captured in a chivalric paradigm', *Mediterranean Review*, 4 (2011). Bretton Rodriguez, 'Pedro López de Ayala and the poltics of rewriting the past', *Journal of Iberian Studies,* 7 (2015). Froissart described the Prince's enthusiasm for the campaign, but the weight of evidence does not support this portrayal. A very different version of events is provided by John of Reading, and the anonymous chronicler of Canterbury (for a new edition of this source: Christopher Given-Wilson and Charity Scott-Stokes (eds), *Chronicle of the Anonymous of Canterbury*) and also by *The Brut*. In the eighteenth century Thomas Rymer transcribed some of the articles of the treaty of Libourne in his *Foedera*, but others were omitted. The oath that the Prince insisted Pedro swear (a key feature in the accounts of John of Reading and *The Brut*) was partially damaged and Rymer did not include it. But its existence substantiates John of Reading's testimony (TNA, E30/1255). The letters of the count of Odona also show the Prince's reservations over assisting Pedro: Mahine Béhrouzi, 'Le procès fait à Bernat de Cabrara (1364–1372)', University of Bordeaux doctoral thesis, 2014.

On Froissart and the preparations for the campaign: Peter Ainsworth, 'Collationnement, montage et jeu parti: le début de la campagne espagnole du Prince Noir (1366–67) dans les chroniques de Jean Froissart', *Le Moyen Âge*, 100 (1994). For Elmwood, Godard, Moigne and Saville: *House of Commons, 1388–1422*. There was a sense of awe as the Prince's army gathered, and here the account of the *Chronique des Quatre Premiers Valois* is supported by that of Pedro de Albornoz, archbishop of Seville (cited in Moisant, *Le Prince Noir en Aquitaine*). But the longer John of Gaunt's reinforcements were delayed, the greater was the risk of Charles of Navarre plotting with Enrique and Charles V (TNA, C61/79; Archivo Generalo de Navarra, Comptos Cajón, 21). For the crusading context: Timothy Guard, *Chivalry, Kingship and Crusade*; for the Prince's reception of Peter of Cyprus's ambassadors: *BPR*, IV, 428. Pedro's grant to the Prince of the right to fight in the vanguard of 'the army against the Infidels' is found in TNA, E30/237; the loan of 5,000 florins on 20 February 1367 so that he could make an offering alongside the Prince at the monastery of Roncesvalles is in TNA, E30/231.

Excellent narratives of the campaign are provided in Peter Russell, *English Intervention in Spain* and Kenneth Fowler, *Medieval Mercenaries*. For Felton, see Richard Barber, 'Sir William Felton the younger, soldier and administrator', *Oxford DNB*. On the battle itself: Strickland and Hardy, *The Great Warbow*; Andrew Villalon, 'Spanish involvement in the Hundred Years War and the battle of Nájera', in *The Hundred Years War: A Wider Focus*. The eye-witness accounts on the English side are the Chandos Herald and Walter of Peterborough, in his *Victoria Belli in Hispania (The Victorious War in Spain)*, who provides detail on the rituals employed by the Prince before the encounter; on the Castilian side, Pedro López de Ayala (*Crónica del rey don Pedro y del rey don Enrique*). On the letters of challenge between the Prince and Enrique see Roland Delachenal, *Histoire de Charles V*, vol. 5. The Black Prince's letter to Joan of Kent is discussed in Eugène Déprez, 'La bataille de Nájera (3 avril 1367): le communiqué du Prince Noir', *Revue Historique*, 136 (1921). For the aftermath: Donald Kagay and Andrew Villalon, 'Poetry in celebration of the battle of Nájera (1367)', *Journal of Medieval Military History*, 11 (2013); David Carlson, 'The English literature of Nájera from battlefield dispatch to the poets', in *John Gower in England and Iberia*.

The ransoms of the principal captives were not, as Froissart suggested, decided on a whim; the sums agreed for the Marshal d'Audrehem and Bertrand du Guesclin were fixed after much careful negotiation: Bibliothèque Nationale, Pièces Originales (d'Audrehem), 18–30; Jones, *Du Guesclin*. The military achievement was real, as was the sense of comradeship it evoked: When John, lord Bourchier, returned from the battle, the duke of Brittany wrote to him, praising 'the exploits of our fellow lords and brothers': Michael C. E. Jones, 'The fortunes of war: the military career of John, second lord Bourchier (d. 1400)', *Essex Archaeology and History*, 26 (1995). The battle report given in Archives Municipales de Montpellier, AA9, showed that the news of the Prince's victory was received with real concern in France. But in political terms, the campaign would prove to be a disaster.

chapter nine

The lofty praise of the Prince is found in *Chronique des Abbés de Moissac*; the source is discussed in Barber, *Black Prince*. But the abbot himself provided a sober and positive appraisal of the Prince's rule, commending his political wisdom and the tranquillity he brought to Aquitaine. For the Black Prince seeking spiritual solace: Melville Bigelow, 'The Bohun wills', in *American Historical Review*, I (1896); Jeremy Catto, 'The prayers of the Bohuns', in *Soldiers, Nobles and Gentlemen*. A major re-assessment of the levying of the *fouage* is provided in Guilhem Pépin, '*The Parlament of Anglo-Gascon Aquitaine: the Three Estates of Aquitaine* (Guyenne)', *Nottingham Medieval Studies*, 52 (2008). Jonathan Sumption, *Divided Houses*, provides a perceptive overview, that has been particularly helpful. For the lighthouse, TNA, C61/112/104 and Gustave Labat, *Documents sur la Tour de Cordouan*; the river-clearing programme is AD du Lot (Cahors), EDT/042/DD 34 and 35. Measures to improve the wine trade are found in de la Haye, *Archives de Moissac*.

The Prince's anger and frustration were used by his opponents as a justification for switching allegiance, not always convincingly. Jacques de Surgères, lord of Flocellière, claimed to Charles V that the Black Prince 'had conceived a great hatred [of him]' ('il eust prins en haine') and wrongfully deprived him of lands in Poitou. As the archivist Paul Gaul Guérin pointed out, 'that hatred did not seem to impede a highly successful career under the Prince' – and Surgères remained loyal to the very end, only surrendering to the French at Thouars on 30 November 1372. (Archives Nationales, JJ118/123; Guérin, *Recueil des documents concernant le Poitou*).

On Charles V's growing confidence: Françoise Autrand, *Charles V: Le Sage*; Craig Taylor, *Chivalry and Ideals of Knighthood in France*. On the judicial appeals to the French king: Edouard Perroy, 'Edouard III d'Angleterre at les seigneurs Gascons en 1368', *Annales du Midi*, 61 (1948); Delachenal, *Charles V*, vol. 5. Perroy was struck by the fact that Charles V encouraged first Armagnac and then Albret to appeal to Edward III's higher court at Westminster in the midst of his own negotiations with the appellants. (Albret had formally lodged his appeal with Charles on 8 September 1368; he then appealed to Edward a week later, on 15 September.) Perroy believed that the French king did this in a bid to undermine relations between Edward III and the Prince.

Material on the dispute between Jean count of Armagnac and Guy de Sévérac over the castle and lordship of Peyrelade, and the Prince's role in it, is from Bibliothèque Nationale, Collection Doat. For Albret: Gabriel Loirette, 'Arnaud Amanieu, sire d'Albret, et l'appel des seigneurs Gascons en 1368', in *Mélanges d'Histoire Offert à Charles Bémont*. On Périgueux's loyalty to the Prince: Ariette Higounet-Nadel, *Les Comptes de la Taille de Périgueux au Quatorzième Siècle*. On Pommiers: Françoise Beriac and Eric Ruault, 'Guillaume-Sanche, Elie de Pommiers et leurs frères', *Cahiers de Recherches Médiévales*, I (1996). (This was a different family from that of Amanieu, lord of Pommiers who fought with the Prince at Poitiers, who was from Pommiers-Moulons in Poitou-Charente; instead, their holdings were in the region of La Réole.) The treaty of Aigues-Mortes (13 August 1367) between Enrique of Trastamara and Louis duke of Anjou is printed in Roland Delachenal, *Histoire de Charles V*, vol. 5. I owe the translation to Paul Booth. The duke of Anjou's Apocalypse tapestry is described in Liliane Delwasse, *La tenture de l'Apocalypse d'Angers*. For the Prince's recruitment of additional soldiers from England in the autumn of 1368: David Green, 'The later retinue of Edward the Black Prince', *Nottingham Medieval Studies*, 44 (2000).

On the Prince's worsening illness, see AD de la Gironde, G239 (payments to the doctor Pierre de Manhi, a leading surgeon of Bordeaux, on 18 November and again on 10 December 1368); Ernst Wickersheimer, *Dictionnaire Biographique des Médecins*. These references support the view of the Chandos Herald that it was only after the serious deterioration in the Prince's health (evident in the documentary sources only in November 1368, well over a year after the conclusion of the Spanish campaign and the army's return to Gascony) 'that his enemies agreed to begin the war anew'. The Anonimalle chronicler and the Chandos Herald described it as a 'wasting sickness'. Those who contracted amoebic dysentery in Spain in the summer of 1367 did not last long, as the chronicler Henry Knighton remarked: 'So many English perished there of the bloody flux that scarcely one in five returned.' When Henry V contracted it, during the siege of Meaux in the summer of 1422, he was dead within two months. Dysentery may have been a secondary symptom of an underlying disease. Two sources say that the Black Prince was afflicted by it: Haydon (ed.), *Eulogium Historiarum*, which places its onset early in 1369, and Thomas Walsingham, who says that the Prince suffered from it sporadically 'in the last five years of his life', that is after his return to England in 1371.

The archives of the house of Armagnac show that Charles V sent his summons to the Black Prince to attend the Paris Parlement as soon as he learned of the seriousness of his illness. The messengers arrived in Bordeaux (from Toulouse) on 23 November 1368 (not in late January 1369, as Froissart claimed): Barrois, thesis cit. These records also show that the emissaries were not imprisoned and left to die, on the Prince's orders (as the chronicler also insinuated). Instead, both were released within the year. Bernard Palot had returned to Toulouse by November 1369; Jean de Chaponval was exchanged for the English knight Thomas Banaster (captured by the French in the summer of 1369) at around the same time.

For Harewell, Roy Haines, 'John Harewell, administrator and bishop of Bath and Wells'; *Oxford DNB;* for the Prince's comment 'that he cannot do without him': TNA, C61/81/54 (28 November 1368). A counter to the hostile portrait of the Prince's rule in Aquitaine in the Anonimalle Chronicle is provided by David Trotter, 'Le Prince Noir et les Dominicains de Bagnères-de-Bigorre', *Annales du Midi,* 114 (2002). For Bérard d'Albret: TNA, C61/79/99 and AD des Pyrénées-Atlantiques, E203. The Prince's letter to his father is from Perroy, 'Les seigneurs Gascons en 1368', translated in Barber, *Black Prince.* The establishment of a superior court in Gascony to hear appeals only took place, belatedly, in 1370. For the continuing loyalty of Millau: Archives Municipales de Millau, CC (1368-9). For the dispatch of the royal surgeon Guillaume Hamon to the Black Prince on 10 February 1369 see Simon Harris and Anne Curry, 'The surgeon prior and the Prince', on www.gasconrolls.org/fr/blog. On the general mood of pessimism in Aquitaine: Dominica Legge (ed.), *Anglo-Norman Letters*; Morgan, *War and Society.*

chapter ten

The failure of the Prince's diplomacy with Aragon is described by Donald Kagay: 'The unstable bond between Castile and Aragon in the late fourteenth century', in *The Emergence of Léon-Castile.* Rochechouart's complaint is from Archives Nationales, JJ 100/137. On Pons: Jules Chavanon, 'Renaud de Pons, vicomte de Turenne et de Carlat, seigneur de Ribérac', *Archives Historiques de la Saintonge,* 31 (1902). The story of Guy de Sévérac is drawn from the Bibliothèque Nationale, Collection Doat and Étienne Cabrol, *Annales de Villefranche.* On the rearguard action in eastern Aquitaine: Philip Morgan, 'Cheshire and the defence of the principality of Aquitaine', *Transactions of the Historic Society of Lancashire and Cheshire,* 128 (1978); Pépin, 'The last years (1369-72)'. The Prince's letter to the abbey of Sainte-Croix concerning the restoration of its stolen property is in AD de la Gironde, H377. For his delegation of power in Poitou in March 1370, Bibiothèque Municipale de Poitiers, Collection Dom Fonteneau.

Edward III's preoccupation with northern France is ably demonstrated by James Sherborne, 'John of Gaunt, Edward III's retinue and the French campaign of 1369', in *War, Politics and Culture in Fourteenth Century England.* Robert Jones,

Bloodied Banners: Martial Display on the Medieval Battlefield, is particularly good on the death of Sir John Chandos. For Limoges: Alfred Leroux, *Le Sac de Limoges* and the recent appraisal by Catherine Faure-Delhoume, 'Le Sac de la Cité de Limoges par le Prince Noir en 1370', in *Le Limousin: Pays et Identités*. A comparison can be made with Ratier de Belfort, who broke his allegiance to the Prince for reasons of personal interest, surrendered Montauban to the French, and then persecuted the many members of the town council who opposed this course of action (some were flung into jail, others expelled from the town): Emmanuel Moureau, 'Ratier de Belfort, capitaine quercinois durant la guerre de cent ans', in *Vivre et Mourir en Temps de Guerre*. Louis de Malval's reason for returning to French allegiance was probably the Black Prince's confiscation of his castle of Juliac (unlawfully seized from Étienne de Montroux): AD de Lot-et-Garonne, FF 144. The Prince's restoration of Juliac to Montroux incensed Malval, who then appealed to Edward III's council at Westminster. For Renaud de Montléon: Archives Nationales JJ103/6; KK251. Information on Perceval de Coulonges is drawn from Peter Edbury, 'The crusading policy of Peter I of Cyprus', in Peter Holt (ed.), *The Eastern Mediterranean Lands in the Period of the Crusades*. Coulonges continued to resist Charles V up to the surrender at Thouars on 30 November 1372.

The incomplete *procès-verbal* between Jean Le Cros, bishop of Limoges and John, duke of Berry — revealing the lack of support for Cros's decision to surrender within the *cité* — is AD de la Haute-Vienne, AA13. The duke of Berry's goading the Black Prince is from his account book: Archives Nationales, KK 251. For Berry's artistic patronage: Françoise Lehoux, *Jean de France, Duc de Berri*. The case in the Paris Parlement, which revealed how a group of Limoges's citizens opened the town gate to the English army, and were subsequently slain by the French garrison, is Archives Nationales, X2a 14, ff. 193-194. Guilhem Pépin's discovery of the Black Prince's letter to Gaston Fébus, written at Limoges on 22 September 1370, is discussed in *BBC History Magazine* (July 2014).

The Prince subsequently remitted government of the *cité* to the cathedral chapter, making clear that neither they nor the inhabitants were blamed for the treason of their bishop: AD de la Haute-Vienne, G8. His personal interest in the matter was shown in a further letter instructing his seneschal in the Limousin, Sir Richard Abberbury, 'to command all sergeants to fully execute our warrant, without disturbance or obstruction': Bonaventure de Saint-Amable, *Histoire du Limousin*. Abberbury was one of the Prince's most trusted officials: for his career see Simon Walker, 'Sir Richard Abberbury and his kinsmen', *Nottingham Medieval Studies*, 34 (1990).

Bertrand du Guesclin's continuing military rise is chronicled in Ambroise Ledru, 'La bataille de Pontvallain, 4 décembre 1370', in *La Province du Maine*,

2 (1894), 14 (1907) and Richard Vernier, *Flower of Chivalry*. For insights into du Guesclin's skill, far wider than the specific campaign covered: Michael C. E. Jones, 'Bertrand du Guesclin, the truce of Bourges and campaigns in Périgord (1376)', in *Soldiers, Nobles and Gentlemen*. A cogent examination of Jean Froissart's reliability is offered by Richard Barber, 'Jean Froissart and Edward, the Black Prince', in *Froissart: Historian*. The Wigmore Chronicle, found in *English Historical Literature in the Fourteenth Century*, has now been edited by Paul Remfrey, *The Wigmore Chronicle, 1066–1377;* it placed Edward of Angoulême's death 'around the feast of St Michael', that is, 29 September 1370.

The full text of Edward III's letters revoking the *fouage* is from Gabriel de Lurbe, *Chronique Bourdeloise*. For the king's earlier anger about the tax: *Calendar of Patent Rolls, 1367–70*, entry of 23 March 1368 (the Prince 'being about to return to England from the parts of Aquitaine at the king's order'). The Black Prince's refusal to consent to the draft treaty with Navarre is set out in Denis-François Secousse, *L'Histoire de Charles, roi de Navarre*. Eleanor Lodge, *Gascony under English Rule*, was right to describe the king's action as 'intending to inflict humiliation upon his son'. In such circumstances, the Prince's response was hardly surprising.

chapter eleven

For England's deteoriorating fortunes abroad, see: Sumption, *Divided Houses*. The increasingly fraught atmosphere at home is caught well in Ormrod, *Edward III*. For Gaunt's growing influence: Anthony Goodman, *John of Gaunt*; David Nicolle, *John of Gaunt's Raid in France, 1373*. The Black Prince's close association with the abbey of St Albans is from: James Clark, *Monastic Revival at St Albans* and 'Thomas de la Mare, abbot of St Albans', *Oxford DNB*; Green, *Black Prince*. An important new (2011) edition of Walsingham is provided by John Taylor, Wendy Childs and Leslie Watkiss, *St Alban's Chrincle, 1394–1422*. Two very useful articles are: David Green, 'Masculinity and medicine: Thomas Walsingham and the death of the Black Prince', *Journal of Medieval History*, 35 (2009); Paul Booth, 'The last week in the life of Edward, the Black Prince', in *Contact and Exchange in Later Medieval Europe*.

On Owain Lawgoch: Anthony Carr, 'Owen of Wales', *Oxford DNB*; Adam Chapman, *Welsh Soldiers*. For Raymond, vicomte of Fronsac: Archives Nationales, JJ104/343. Petitions to the Prince in the last year of his life are found in TNA, SC8/333. As Gwilym Dodd points out, in 'Kingship, parliament and the court: the emergence of the "high style" in petitions to the English crown, c. 1350–1400', *English Historical Review*, 129 (2014), the forms of address, including 'high majesty' and 'benign grace' are less the result of arrogance and aloofness (of the kind portrayed by the Anonimalle chronicler) and more to do with changes in courtly etiquette.

The worsening political situation is surveyed in Holmes, *The Good Parliament*. For Kentwood and Sandys: *House of Commons, 1388–1422*. The Prince's patronage of the House of the Bonhommes is discussed in Henry Chettle, 'The Bonhommes of Ashridge and Edington', *Downside Review*, 62 (1944). On the Black Prince's death, funeral and commemoration: Arthur Stanley, *Historical Memorials of Canterbury*; John Harvey, *The Black Prince and his Age*; David Carlson, *John Gower: Poetry and Propaganda*; Mary Devlin (ed.), *The Sermons of Thomas Brinton*; Diana Tyson, 'The epitaph of the Black Prince', *Medium Aevum*, 46 (1977). For Arderne: Peter Murray Jones, 'Four Middle English translations of John of Arderne', in Alastair Minnis (ed.), *Latin and Vernacular*.

epilogue

The sad story of the son who could never match up to his father is well told in Nigel Saul, *Richard II* and Mortimer, *The Fears of Henry IV*. For Richard II and anti-war sentiment: Nigel Saul, 'A farewell to arms? Criticism of warfare in late fourteenth-century England', *Fourteenth Century England*, II. The seal depicting the helm, cap of maintenance and crest, above the shield, is attached to CCA/DCc/ChAnt/F/49 (the Prince's grant of the manor of Vauxhall to Canterbury Cathedral, 1 September 1362). I am grateful to Sarah Turner for drawing it to my attention. The Prince's grant to Quercy is from Sotheby's Medieval and Renaissance Catalogue (8 December 2015). Also noteworthy is the record of John Delves's visit to the Prince in Aquitaine over the winter of 1363–4 (TNA, E1647): it lists points on which members of his English council wish to get his instructions or learn of his opinions. For Arnaut de Preissac: Guilhem Pépin, 'Les Soudans de Preissac ou de la Trau', *Les Cahiers du Bazadais*, 54 (2014); for Moissac: *Chronique des Abbés*. De Preissac was not alone. In 1376 Raymond, lord of Mussidan had continued to 'serve the Prince well and loyally and at his own expense'. Mussidan had lost most of his lands and goods but did not renounce his allegiance: TNA, SC8/262/13069.

appendix

On the charges against Edward III the two key articles are Tom James, 'John of Eltham: history and story', in *Fourteenth Century England*, 2 (2002) and Antonia Gransden, 'The alleged rape by Edward III of the countess of Salisbury', *English Historical Review*, 87 (1972). On Froissart's reliability see Richard Barber, 'Jean Froissart and Edward, the Black Prince', in *Froissart: Historian*. The key archive material for Limoges, as already indicated, is from TNA, C61/94/40, AD de la Haute-Vienne, AA13 and G8 and Archives Nationales, X2a/14, ff. 193–4.

BIBLIOGRAPHY

Ainsworth, Peter, *Jean Froissart and the Fabric of History: Truth, Myth and Fiction in the Chroniques* (Oxford, 1990)

Allmand, Christopher, *Society at War: The Experience of England and France in the Hundred Years War* (Edinburgh, 1973)

The Hundred Years War (Cambridge, 1988)

The De Re Militari of Vegetius: the Reception, Transmission and Legacy of a Roman Text in the Middle Ages (Cambridge, 2011)

Ambühl, Rémy, *Prisoners of War in the Hundred Years War: Ransom Culture in the Late Middle Ages* (Cambridge, 2013)

Armitage-Smith, Sydney, *John of Gaunt* (London, 1904)

Artières, Jules (ed.), *Documents sur la Ville de Millau* (Millau, 1930)

Asbridge, Thomas, *The Greatest Knight: The Remarkable Life of William Marshal* (London, 2014)

Autrand, Françoise, *Charles V le Sage* (Paris, 1994)

Ayton, Andrew, *Knights and Warhorses: Military Service and the English Aristocracy under Edward III* (Woodbridge, 1994)

Ayton, Andrew and Preston, Philip, *The Battle of Crécy, 1346* (Woodbridge, 2005)

Barber, Richard, *Edward, Prince of Wales and Aquitaine* (Woodbridge, 1978)

The Life and Campaigns of the Black Prince (Woodbridge, 1979)

The Reign of Chivalry (Woodbridge, 1980)

Edward III and the Triumph of England (London, 2013)

Barckhausen, Henri (ed.), *Livre de Coutumes* (Bordeaux, 1890)

Barnie, John, *War in Medieval Society: Social Values and the Hundred Years War* (Ithaca, New York, 1974)

Barrow, George, *Robert Bruce and the Community of the Realm in Scotland* (London, 1965)

Bautier, Robert (ed.), *La 'France Anglaise' au Moyen Âge* (Paris, 1988)

Beaune, Colette (ed.), *Chronique dite de Jean de Venette* (Paris, 2011)

Bell, Adrian, *War and the Soldier in the Fourteenth Century* (Woodbridge, 2004)

Bell, Adrian and Curry, Anne (eds), *The Soldier Experience in the Fourteenth Century* (Woodbridge, 2011)

Bennett, Michael, *Community, Class and Careerism: Cheshire and Lancashire Society in the Age of Sir Gawain and the Green Knight* (Cambridge, 1983)

Bennett, Nicholas (ed.), *The Registers of Henry Burghersh, 1320–1342* (Lincoln, 1999–2011, 3 vols)

Bériac-Lainé, Françoise and Given-Wilson, Christopher, *Les Prisonniers de la Bataille de Poitiers* (Paris, 2002)

Bicknell, Alexander, *History of Edward the Black Prince* (London, 1777)

Binski, Paul, *Westminster Abbey and the Plantagenets: Kingship and the Representation of Power, 1200–1400* (New Haven, 1995)

   Medieval Death: Ritual and Representation (London, 1996)

   Gothic Wonder: Art, Artifice and the Decorated Style, 1290–1350 (New Haven, 2014)

Birdhall, Jean and Newhall, Richard (eds), *The Chronicle of Jean de Venette* (New York, 1953)

Blanchard-Dignac, Denis, *Le Captal de Buch: Jean de Grailly 1331–1376* (Bordeaux, 2011)

Bliss, William and Twemlow, Jessie (eds), *Calendar of Entries in the Papal Registers, vol. 4* (London, 1902)

Bloore, Peter and Martin, Edward, *Wingfield College and its Patrons: Piety and Pedigree in Medieval Suffolk* (Woodbridge, 2015)

Booth, Paul, *The Financial Administration of the Lordship and County of Chester, 1272–1377* (Manchester, 1981)

Booth, Paul and Carr, Antony, *Account of Master John of Burnham, Chamberlain of Chester, 1361–62* (Stroud, 1991)

Bothwell, James (ed.), *The Age of Edward III* (Woodbridge, 2001)

Bothwell, James, and Dodd, Gwilym (eds), *Fourteenth Century England, Volume 9* (Woodbridge, 2016)

Bousquet, Henri (ed.), *Comptes Consulaires de la Cité et du Bourg de Rodez* (Rodez, 1943)

Boutruche, Robert, *La Crise d'une Société: Seigneurs et Paysans du Bordelais pendant la Guerre de Cent Ans* (Paris, 1963)

Bradbury, Jim, *The Medieval Siege* (Woodbridge, 1992)

Brereton, Geoffrey, *Jean Froissart: Chronicles* (London, 1978)

Brie, Friedrich (ed.), *The Brut or the Chronicles of England* (London, 1906)

Broome, Dorothy, *The Ransom of John II, King of France, 1360–1370* (London, 1926)

Brownbill, John (ed.), *The Ledger Book of Vale Royal Abbey* (Manchester, 1914)

Burne, Alfred, *The Crécy War* (London, 1955)

Cabrol, Étienne, *Annales de Villefranche-de-Rouergue* (Villefranche, 1860)

Carlson, David, *John Gower: Poetry and Propaganda in Fourteenth-Century England* (Woodbridge, 2012)

Cazelles, Raymond, *Société politique, noblesse et couronne sous Jean le Bon et Charles V* (Paris, 1982)

Chaplais, Pierre (ed.), *The War of Saint Sardos* (London, 1954)

Chapman, Adam, *Welsh Soldiers in the Later Middle Ages, 1282–1422* (Woodbridge, 2015)

Charrière, Ernst (ed.), *Chronique de Bertrand du Guesclin par Jean Cuvelier* (Paris, 1839, 2 vols)

Chazaud, Martial-Alphonse (ed.), *Chronique du Bon Duc Loys de Bourbon* (Paris, 1876)

Clark, James, *A Monastic Renaissance at St Albans: Thomas Walsingham and his Circle, circa 1350–1440* (Oxford, 2004)

Cobb, John, *History and Antiquities of Berkhamsted* (London, 1883)

Cole, Hubert, *The Black Prince* (London, 1976)

Collins, Arthur, *The Life and Glorious Actions of Edward Prince of Wales* (London, 1741)

Collins, Hugh, *The Order of the Garter, 1348–1461: Chivalry and Politics in Late Medieval England* (Oxford, 2000)

Contamine, Philippe, *War in the Middle Ages* (New York, 1984)

Contamine, Philippe, Giry-Deloison, Charles and Keen, Maurice (eds), *Guerre et Société en France, en Angleterre et en Bourgogne* (Lille, 1991)

Cooper, Stephen, *Sir John Chandos: the Perfect Knight* (self-published, 2011)

Coote, Lesley, *Prophecy and Public Affairs in Later Medieval England* (Woodbridge, 2000)

Cornell, David, *Bannockburn: The Triumph of Robert the Bruce* (New Haven, 2014)

Corrigan, Gordon, *A Great and Glorious Adventure: A Military History of the Hundred Years War* (London, 2013)

Coss, Peter and Tyerman, Christopher, *Soldiers, Nobles and Gentlemen: Essays in Honour of Maurice Keen* (Woodbridge, 2009)

Creighton, Louise, *Life of the Black Prince* (London, 1877)

Curry, Anne and Hughes, Michael (eds), *Arms, Armies and Fortifications in the Hundred Years War* (Woodbridge, 1994)

Cushway, Graham, *Edward III and the War at Sea: the English Navy 1327–1377* (Woodbridge, 2011)

Davies, Clarice (ed.), *A History of Macclesfield* (Manchester, 1961)

Davies, Rees, *Lordship and Society in the March of Wales, 1282–1400* (Oxford, 1978)
  The Revolt of Owain Glyn Dwr (Oxford, 1995)

Dawes, Michael (ed.), *The Black Prince's Register* (London, 1930–3, 4 vols)

De Cauna, Jacques (ed.), *L'Aquitaine au temps du Prince Noir: Actes du colloque de*

Dax, 12 Décembre 2009 (Cressé, 2010)

De La Boutière, Louis, *Cartulaire de l'Abbaye d'Orbestier* (Poitiers, 1877)

Delachenal, Roland, *Histoire de Charles V* (Paris, 1909–31, 5 vols)

Delachenal, Roland (ed.), *Chronique des règnes de Jean II et de Charles V* (Paris, 1910)

De La Haye, Régis (ed.), *Chronique des Abbés de Moissac* (Moissac, 1999)
   Les Archives Brûlées de Moissac: Reconstitution du Chartrier de la Ville (Moissac, 2005)

Delpit, Jules (ed.), *Collection générale des documents français qui se trouvent en Angleterre* (Paris, 1847)

De Lurbe, Gabriel, *Chronique Bourdeloise* (Bourdeaux, 1594)

Delwasse, Liliane, *La tenture de l'Apocalypse d'Angers* (Paris, 2008)

Denifle, Henri, *La Guerre de Cent Ans et la désolation des églises, monastères et hospitaux en France* (Paris, 1902)

DeVries, Kelly, *Infantry Warfare in the Early Fourteenth Century* (Woodbridge, 1996)

Devals, Jean-Ursule, *Histoire de Montauban sous la domination anglaise* (Montauban, 1843).

Deviosse, Jean, *Jean le Bon* (Paris, 1985)

Devlin, Mary (ed.), *The Sermons of Thomas Brinton, Bishop of Rochester, 1373–1389* (London, 1954, 2 vols)

Ducluzeau, Robert, *Guichard d'Angle* (Paris, 2002)
   Le Connétable du Prince Noir: Jean Chandos (Stroud, 2004)

Dunn, Diana (ed.), *War and Society in Medieval and Early Modern Britain* (Liverpool, 2000)

Dunn-Pattison, Richard, *The Black Prince* (London, 1910)

Dunne, Thomas (ed.), *The Writer as Witness: Literature as Historical Evidence* (Cork, 1987)

Duplès-Agier, Henri (ed.), *Chroniques de Saint Martial de Limoges* (Paris, 1874)

Dupuy, Michelline, *Le Prince Noir* (Paris, 1970)

Eales, Richard, and Tyas, Shaun (eds), *Family and Dynasty in Late Medieval England* (Donington, 2003)

Edbury, Peter, *The Kingdom of Cyprus and the Crusades, 1191–1374* (Cambridge, 1991)

Emerson, Barbara, *The Black Prince* (London, 1976)

Emery, Anthony, *Seats of Power in Europe during the Hundred Years War* (Oxford, 2015)

Estow, Clara, *Pedro the Cruel of Castile* (Leiden, 1995)

Faucon, Jean-Claude (ed.), *La Chanson de Bertrand du Guesclin par Cuvelier* (Toulouse, 1990–1, 3 vols)

Favier, Jean, *La Guerre de Cent Ans* (Paris, 1980)

Favreau, Robert (ed.), *Aunis, Saintonge et Angoumois sous la domination anglaise* (Poitiers, 1999)

Firnhaber-Baker, Justine, *Violence and the State in Late Medieval Languedoc, 1215–1400* (Cambridge, 2014)

Foissac, Patrice (ed.), *Vivre et mourir en temps de guerre: Quercy et régions voisines* (Toulouse, 2013)

Fowler, Kenneth, *The King's Lieutenant: Henry of Grosmont, First Duke of Lancaster, 1310–1361* (London, 1969)

   The Age of Plantagenet and Valois (London, 1980)

   Medieval Mercenaries (Oxford, 2001)

Galbraith, Vivian (ed.), *The Anonimalle Chronicle, 1333–1381* (Manchester, 1970)

Gertz, Sunhee, *Visual Power and Fame in René d'Anjou, Geoffrey Chaucer and the Black Prince* (New York, 2010)

Getz, Faye, *Medicine in the English Middle Ages* (Princeton, 1998)

Given-Wilson, Christopher, *The Royal Household and the King's Affinity, 1360–1413* (London, 1986)

   The English Nobility in the Later Middle Ages (London, 1996)

Given-Wilson, Christopher (ed.), *The Chronicle of Adam of Usk* (Oxford, 1997)

   Fourteenth-Century England, II (Woodbridge, 2002)

Given-Wilson, Christopher and Scott-Stokes, Charity (eds), *The Chronicle of the Anonymous of Canterbury, 1346–1365* (Oxford, 2008)

Goodman, Anthony, *John of Gaunt: the Emergence of Princely Power in Fourteenth-Century Europe* (Harlow, 1992)

Goodman, Arthur (ed.), *Chartulary of Winchester Cathedral* (Winchester, 1927)

Grandcoing, Philippe and Tricart, Jean, *Le Limousin: Pays et identités* (Limoges, 2006)

Green, David, *The Black Prince* (Stroud, 2001)

   The Battle of Poitiers, 1356 (Stroud, 2006)

   Edward the Black Prince: Power in Medieval Europe (London, 2007)

   The Hundred Years War: A People's History (London, 2014)

Gribit, Nicholas, *Henry of Lancaster's Expedition to Aquitaine, 1345–46: Military Service and Professionalism in the Hundred Years War* (Woodbridge, 2016)

Gross, Guy, *Le Prince Noir en Berry: 1356* (Bourges, 2004)

Guard, Timothy, *Chivalry, Kingship and Crusade: the English Experience in the Fourteenth Century* (Woodbridge, 2013)

Guenée, Bernard, *Histoire and culture historique dans l'Occident médiéval* (Paris, 1980)

Guérin, Paul (ed.), *Recueil des documents concernant le Poitou, 1334–48; 1348–69; 1369–1376* (Poitiers, 1883–91, 3 vols)

Haines, Roy, *King Edward II: The Reign and its Aftermath* (Quebec, 2003)

Harari, Yuval, *Special Operations in the Age of Chivalry, 1100–1550* (Woodbridge, 2009)

Harriss, Gerald, *King, Parliament and Public Finance in Medieval England to 1369* (Oxford, 1975)

Harvey, John, *The Black Prince and His Age* (London, 1976)

Hatcher, John, *Rural Economy and Society in the Duchy of Cornwall, 1300–1500* (Cambridge, 1970)

The Black Death: An Intimate History of the Plague (London, 2008)

Haydon, Frank (ed.), *The Eulogium Historiarum* (Wiesbaden, 1967)

Henneman, John, *Olivier de Clisson and Political Society in France under Charles V and Charles VI* (Philadelphia, 1996)

Hewitt, Herbert, *The Black Prince's Expedition of 1355–57* (Manchester, 1958)

The Organisation of War under Edward III (Manchester, 1966)

Hicks, Eric and Moreau, Thérèse (eds), *Christine de Pizan: Le Livre des faits et bonnes moeurs du roi Charles V le Sage* (Paris, 1997)

Higounet, Charles and Higounet-Nadal, Arlette, *Le Grand Cartulaire de l'Abbaye de la Sauve-Majeure* (Bordeaux, 1996, 2 vols)

Higounet-Nadal, Arlette, *Les Comptes de la taille de Périgueux au quatorzième siècle* (Paris, 1965)

Hill, Phyllis and Heery, Jack, *The Cheshire Forest Eyre Roll* (Lancashire and Cheshire Record Society, 2015)

Hingeston-Randolph, Francis (ed.), *The Register of Walter de Stapledon, Bishop of Exeter, 1307–1326* (London, 1892)

Holmes, George, *The Good Parliament* (Oxford, 1975)

Holt, Peter (ed.), *The Eastern Mediterranean Lands in the Period of the Crusades* (Warminster, 1977)

Horrox, Rosemary (ed.), *The Black Death* (Manchester, 1994)

Hoskins, Peter, *In the Steps of the Black Prince: the Road to Poitiers, 1355–1356* (Woodbridge, 2011)

Houwen, Luuk and MacDonald, Alisdair (eds), *Loyal Letters: Studies in Alliterative Poetry* (Groningen, 1994)

Hughes, Jonathan, *The Rise of Alchemy in Fourteenth-Century England* (London, 2012)

Isaacson, R. F. (ed.), *Calendar of Patent Rolls: Edward III, 1327–1377* (London, 1901, 16 vols)

James, George, *A History of the Life of Edward the Black Prince* (London, 1839, 2 vols)

Jones, Dan, *The Plantagenets: The Kings Who Made England* (London, 2012)

Jones, Michael C. E., *Ducal Brittany, 1364–1399* (Oxford, 1970)

Letters, Orders and Musters of Bertrand du Guesclin, 1357–1380 (Woodbridge, 2004)

Jones, Robert, *Bloodied Banners: Martial Display on the Medieval Battlefield*
    (Woodbridge, 2010)

Kaeuper, Richard, *Chivalry and Violence in Medieval Europe* (Oxford, 1994)

Kaeuper, Richard and Kennedy, Elspeth (eds), *The Book of Chivalry of Geoffroi
    de Charnay* (Philadelphia, 1996)

Kagay, Donald and Snow, Joseph (eds), *Medieval Iberia: Essays on the History
    and Literature of Medieval Spain* (New York, 1997)

Keen, Maurice, *The Laws of War in the Late Middle Ages* (London, 1965)
    Chivalry (New Haven, 1984)

Kendall, Elliot, *Lordship and Literature: John Gower and the Politics of the Great
    Household* (Oxford, 2008)

Labarge, Margaret Wade, *Gascony: England's First Colony 1204–1453* (London, 1980)

Labat, Gustave, *Documents sur la ville de Royan et le Tour de Cordouan* (Bordeaux,
    1884–1901, 5 vols)

Lawne, Penny, *Joan of Kent* (Stroud, 2015)

Lefferts, Peter, *The Motet in England in the Fourteenth Century* (Lincoln, Nebraska,
    1983)

Legge, Dominica (ed.), *Anglo-Norman Letters and Petitions* (Oxford, 1941)

Lehoux, Françoise, *Jean de France, duc de Berri (1340–1416)* (Paris, 1966)

Lépicier, Jules (ed.), *Archives Historiques du département de la Gironde* (Bordeaux,
    1902)

Leroux, Alfred, *Le sac de la cité de Limoges et son relèvement, 1370–1464* (Limoges,
    1906)

Lettenhove, Kervyn de, *Chroniques de Jean Froissart* (Brussels, 1867–77, 26 vols)

Little, Andrew and Powicke, Frederick, *Essays in Medieval History Presented to
    Thomas Frederick Tout* (Manchester, 1925)

Livingston, Michael and DeVries, Kelly, *The Battle of Crécy: A Casebook*
    (Liverpool, 2015)

Lodge, Eleanor, *Gascony Under English Rule* (London, 1926)

Luce, Siméon (ed.), *Chronique des quatre premiers Valois (1327–1393)* (Paris, 1861)

Luce, Siméon and Mirot, Léon (eds) *Chroniques de Jean Froissart* (Paris,
    1869–1975, 15 vols)

Mann, Sir James, *The Funeral Achievements of Edward the Black Prince* (Beccles,
    1950)

Martin, Geoffrey (ed.), *Knighton's Chronicle, 1337–96* (Oxford, 1995)

Maxwell, Herbert (ed.), *Thomas Gray: Scalacronica* (Glasgow, 1907)

McGlynn, Sean, *By Sword and Fire: Cruelty and Atrocity in Medieval Warfare*
    (London, 2008)

McKisack, Mary, *The Fourteenth Century, 1307–1399* (Oxford, 1959)

Milner, Nicholas, *Vegetius: Epitome of Military Science* (Liverpool, 1996)

Minnis, Alastair (ed.), *Latin and Vernacular: Studies in Late Medieval Texts and Manuscripts* (Cambridge, 1989)

Minois, George, *La Bataille de Poitiers* (Paris, 2014)

Moisant, Joseph, *Le Prince Noir en Aquitaine* (Paris, 1894)

Molina, Angel-Luis (ed.), *Documentos de Pedro I, 1334–1369* (Murcia, 1978)

Molinier, Auguste and Émile (eds), *Chronique normande du quatorzième siècle* (Paris, 1882)

Molinier, Émile, *Étude sur la vie d'Arnoul d'Audrehem, maréchal de France* (Paris, 1883)

Morgan, Philip, *War and Society in Medieval Cheshire, 1277–1403* (Manchester, 1987)

Mortimer, Ian, *The Greatest Traitor: The Life of Sir Roger Mortimer* (London, 2003)
 The Perfect King: The Life of Edward III (London, 2006)
 The Fears of Henry IV (London, 2007)
 The Time Traveller's Guide to Medieval England (London, 2009)

Munby, Julian, Barber, Richard and Brown, Richard (eds), *Edward III's Round Table at Windsor: The House of the Round Table and the Windsor Festival of 1344* (Woodbridge, 2007)

Murphy, Neil, *The Captivity of John II, 1356–60: The Royal Image in Later Medieval England and France* (New York, 2016)

Myers, Alec, *English Historical Documents 1327–1485* (London, 1969)

Newton, Stella, *Fashion in the Age of the Black Prince* (Woodbridge, 1980)

Nicolas, Sir Harris and Tyrrell, Edward (eds), *A Chronicle of London from 1089 to 1483* (London, 1827)

Nicolle, David, *Poitiers 1356* (Oxford, 2004)
 The Great Chevauchée: John of Gaunt's Raid on France, 1373 (Oxford, 2011)

Nicholson, Ranald, *Edward III and the Scots: The Formative Years of a Military Career, 1327–35* (Oxford, 1965)

Oduna, German (ed.), *Pedro de Ayala: Crónica Del Rey Don Pedro y Del Rey Don Enrique* (Buenos Aires,1997, 2 vols)

Orme, Nicholas, *From Childhood to Chivalry: The Education of the English Kings and Aristocracy, 1066–1530* (London, 1984)

Ormrod, Mark, *The Reign of Edward III* (Stroud, 2000)
 Edward III (London, 2011)

Pailhès, Claudine, *Gaston Fébus* (Paris, 2007)

Palacios, Bruno Ramirez de, *Charles dit le Mauvais: Roi de Navarre* (Paris, 2015)

Palmer, John, *England, France and Christendom, 1377–1399* (London, 1972)

Palmer, John (ed.), *Froissart: Historian* (Woodbridge, 1981)

Parry, Joseph (ed.), *Register of John de Trillek, Bishop of Hereford, 1344–1361* (Hereford, 1910–12, 2 vols)

Paterson, Linda, *The World of Troubadors: Medieval Occitan Society* (Cambridge, 1993)

Pépin, Guilhem, Lainé, Françoise and Boutolle, Frédéric (eds), *Routiers et mercenaires pendant la guerre de cent ans* (Bordeaux, 2016)

Phillips, Seymour, *Edward II* (New Haven, 2010)

Platt, Colin, *King Death: The Black Death and its Aftermath in Late Medieval England* (London, 1996)

Pope, Mildred and Lodge, Eleanor, *Life of the Black Prince by the Herald of Sir John Chandos* (Oxford, 1910)

Power, D'Arcy, *John of Arderne's Treatise of Fistula in Ano: Haemorrhoids and Clysters* (London, 1910)

Preest, David and Barber, Richard, *The Chronicle of Geoffrey le Baker of Swinbrook* (Woodbridge, 2012)

Preest, David and Clark, James (eds), *The Chronica Maiora of Thomas Walsingham (1376–1422)* (Woodbridge, 2005)

Prentout, Henri, *La Prise de Caen par Edouard III, 1346* (Caen, 1904)

Prestwich, Michael, *The Three Edwards: War and State in England, 1272–1377* (London, 1980)

   Armies and Warfare in the Middle Ages: The English Experience (London, 1996)

Putnam, Bertha, *The Place in Legal History of Sir William Shareshull, Chief Justice of the King's Bench, 1350–1361* (Cambridge, 1950)

Rawcliffe, Carole, *Medicine and Society in Later Medieval England* (Stroud, 1995)

Remfry, Paul (ed.), *The Wigmore Chronicle, 1066–1377* (Malvern, 2013)

Renaud, Yves (ed.), *Bordeaux Sous Les Rois d'Angleterre* (Bordeaux, 1965)

Rogers, Clifford, *The Wars of Edward III: Sources and Interpretations* (Woodbridge, 1999)

   War Cruel and Sharp: English Strategy Under Edward III 1327–1360 (Woodbridge, 2000)

Rollason, David and Prestwich, Michael (eds), *The Battle of Neville's Cross, 1346* (Stamford, 1998)

Rose, Susan, *Calais: An English Town in France, 1347–1558* (Woodbridge, 2008)

Roskell, John, Clark, Linda and Rawcliffe, Carole (eds), *The History of Parliament: The House of Commons, 1386–1421* (Woodbridge, 1993)

Rougerie, Jacques-Marcelin (ed.), *Tableau synoptique des Archives Communales de Limoges* (Limoges, 1900)

Rouquette, Joseph, *Le Rouergue sous les Anglais* (Millau, 1887)

Ruddick, Andrea, *English Identity and Political Culture in the Fourteenth Century* (Cambridge, 2013)

Russell, Peter, *The English Intervention in Spain and Portugal in the Time of Edward III and Richard II* (Oxford, 1955)

Rymer, Thomas (ed.), *Foedera* (London, 1704–35, 20 vols)

Sáez-Hidalgo, Ana and Yeager, Robert (eds), *John Gower in England and Iberia: Manuscripts, Influences, Reception* (Woodbridge, 2014)

Saint-Amable, Bonaventure, *Histoire de St Martial et du Limousin* (Limoges, 1685)

Sandler, Lucy, *Illuminators and Patrons in Fourteenth Century England: The Psalter and Hours of Humphrey de Bohun and the Manuscripts of the Bohun Family* (Toronto, 2014)

Saul, Nigel, *Richard II* (New Haven, 1997)

  Death, Art and Memory in Medieval England: The Cobham Family and their Monuments, 1300–1500 (Oxford, 2001)

  For Honour and Fame: Chivalry in England, 1066–1500 (London, 2012)

Saul, Nigel (ed.), *Fourteenth-Century England*, I (Woodbridge, 2000); *St George's Chapel, Windsor, in the Fourteenth Century* (Woodbridge, 2005)

Savy, Nicolas, *Cahors pendant la Guerre de Cent Ans* (Cahors, 2005)

  Les villes de Quercy en guerre: La défense des villes et des bourgs du Haut-Quercy pendant la Guerre de Cent Ans (Pradines, 2009)

  Bertrucat d'Albret: Le destin d'un capitain Gascon du roi d'Angleterre pendant la Guerre de Cent Ans (Pradines, 2015)

Scattergood, John and Sherborne, James (eds), *English Court Culture in the Later Middle Ages* (London, 1983)

Secousse, Denis-François, *Mémoires pour servir à l'histoire de Charles, Roi de Navarre, dit le Mauvais* (Paris, 1758)

Sedgwick, Henry, *The Black Prince, 1330–1376: The Flower of Knighthood* (Indianapolis, 1932)

Sharpe, Reginald (ed.), *Calendar of Letter Books of London, G (1352–1374)* (London, 1905)

Skoda, Hannah, Lantschner, Patrick and Shaw, Robert (eds), *Contact and Exchange in Later Medieval Europe: Essays in Honour of Malcolm Vale* (Woodbridge, 2012)

Soar, Hugh, *The Crooked Stick: A History of the Longbow* (Yardley, Pennsylvania, 2010)

Southworth, John, *The English Medieval Minstrel* (Woodbridge, 1980)

Stanley, Arthur, *Historical Memorials of Canterbury* (London, 1868)

Stratford, Jenny, *Richard II and the English Royal Treasure* (Woodbridge, 2012)

Strickland, Matthew and Hardy, Robert, *The Great Warbow* (Stroud, 2005)

Sumption, Jonathan, *The Hundred Years War I: Trial by Battle* (London, 1990)

  The Hundred Years War II: Trial by Fire (London, 1999)

  The Hundred Years War III: Divided Houses (London, 2009)

Tait, James (ed.), *Chronica Johannis de Reading et Anonymi Cantuariensis, 1346–1367* (Manchester, 1914)

Talbot, Charles, *Medicine in Medieval England* (London, 1965)

Talbot, Charles and Hammond, Eugene, *The Medical Practitioners in Medieval England: A Biographical Register* (London, 1968)

Taylor, Craig, *Chivalry and Ideals of Knighthood in France during the Hundred Years War* (Cambridge, 2013)

Taylor, John (ed.), *The Universal Chronicle of Ranulph Higden* (Oxford, 1966)
   English Historical Literature in the Fourteenth Century (Oxford, 1987)

Taylor, John, Childs, Wendy and Watkiss, Leslie (eds), *The St Alban's Chronicle: The Chronica Maiora of Thomas Walsingham, 1394–1422* (Oxford, 2011)

Teulié, Gilles and Lux-Sterritt, Laurence (eds), *War Sermons* (Newcastle upon Tyne, 2009)

Teutsch, Christian, *Victory at Poitiers: The Black Prince and the Medieval Art of War* (Barnsley, 2010)

Thompson, Benjamin and Watts, John (eds), *Political Society in Later Medieval England: A Festschrift for Christine Carpenter* (Woodbridge, 2015)

Thompson, Edward Maunde, *Adam Murimuth Continuatio Chronicarum: Robertus de Avesbury De Gestis Mirabilibus Regis Edwardus Tertii* (London, 1889)

Timbal, Clément, *La Guerre de Cent Ans vue à travers les registres de parlement, 1337–1369* (Paris, 1961)

Todesca, James (ed.), *The Emergence of Léon-Castile, 1065–1500: Essays Presented to J. F. O'Callaghan* (New York, 2016)

Tourneur-Aumont, Jean, *La Bataille de Poitiers et la construction de la France* (Paris, 1940)

Tout, Thomas, *Chapters in the Administrative History of Medieval England*, V (Manchester, 1930)

Tricart, Jean, *Les campagnes Limousines du quatorzième au quinzième siècles* (Limoges, 1996)

Trigg, Stephanie (ed.), *Wynnere and Wastoure* (Oxford, 1990)

Tuchman, Barbara, *A Distant Mirror: The Calamitous Fourteenth Century* (New York, 1978)

Tuck, Anthony (ed.), *War, Politics and Culture in Fourteenth Century England: The Essays of James Sherborne* (Woodbridge, 1994)

Tucoo-Chala, Pierre, *Gaston Fébus et la vicomté de Béarn* (Bordeaux, 1959)
   Gaston Fébus et le Prince Noir (Bordeaux, 1985)

Turville-Petrie, Thorlac, *The Alliterative Revival of the Later Middle Ages* (Cambridge, 1977)
   England the Nation: Language, Literature and National Identity, 1290–1340 (Oxford, 1996)

Tyerman, Christopher, *England and the Crusades, 1095–1588* (Chicago, 1988)

Tyson, Diana (ed.), *Chandos Herald: La vie du Prince Noir* (Tübingen, 1975)

Vale, Juliet, *Edward III and Chivalry* (Woodbridge, 1982)

Vale, Malcolm, *War and Chivalry* (Oxford, 1981)

    The Origins of the Hundred Years War: the Angevin Legacy, 1250–1340 (Oxford, 1996)

    The Princely Court: Medieval Courts and Culture in North-West Europe, 1270–1380 (Oxford, 2001)

Vernier, Richard, *The Flower of Chivalry: Bertrand du Guesclin and the Hundred Years War* (Woodbridge, 2003)

Viard, Jules, *La campagne de Juillet–Août 1346* (Abbeville, 1926)

Viard, Jules and Déprez, Eugène (eds), *Chronique de Jean le Bel* (Paris, 1904)

Villalon, Andrew and Kagay, Donald (eds), *The Hundred Years War, Part 1: A Wider Focus* (Leiden, 2005)

    The Hundred Years War, Part 2: Different Vistas (Leiden, 2008)

    The Hundred Years War, Part 3: Further Considerations (Leiden, 2013)

Vitz, Evelyn, Regalado, Nancy and Lawrence, Marilyn (eds), *Performing Medieval Narrative* (Cambridge, 2005)

Walker, Simon, *The Lancastrian Affinity, 1361–1399* (Oxford, 1990)

Warner, Kathryn, *Edward II: The Unconventional King* (Stroud, 2015)

    Isabella of France: the Rebel Queen (Stroud, 2016)

Waugh, Scott, *England in the Reign of Edward III* (Cambridge, 1991)

Wickersheimer, Ernst, *Dictionnaire biographique des médecins en France au moyen âge* (Paris, 1979)

Wilkins, Nigel, *Music in the Age of Chaucer* (Woodbridge, 1995)

Willems, Jan (ed.), *Belgische Museum Voor de Nederduitsche Tael – En Letterkunde en de Geschiedenis des Vaderlands*, vol. 4 (Ghent, 1840)

Wood, Charles, *The Age of Chivalry: Manners and Morals, 1000–1450* (London, 1970)

Wright, Nicholas, *Knights and Peasants: the Hundred Years War in the French Countryside* (Woodbridge, 1998)

Wright, Thomas, *Political Poems and Songs Relating to English History* (London, 1859)

Wroe, Ann, *A Fool and His Money: Life in a Partitioned Town in Fourteenth Century France* (London, 1995)

Zaerr, Linda, *Performance and the Middle English Romance* (Cambridge, 2012)

Ziegler, Philip, *The Black Death* (Stroud, 1991)

ACKNOWLEDGEMENTS

It has been a pleasure to tell the story of the Black Prince, a true chivalric hero of medieval England. I wrote my thesis on the Hundred Years War at the University of Bristol with the help of James Sherborne, and will always be grateful for his many insights into fourteenth-century campaigning and his support and friendship. James's important article on John of Gaunt's 1369 expedition appeared at this time, alongside the book *Froisxsart: Historian,* which he co-edited with John Palmer. The chronicler Jean Froissart presents a challenge for every historian: at his best, he is well sourced and brings the period to life; however, he can also be unreliable and cavalier with the facts. John Palmer remarked that Froissart gave us a unique window on his age; James added that the chronicler was quite happy to make things up. Both comments are true, and it is a dilemma that inevitably affects this book. I have tried to use Froissart when I feel he is reliable, but have also challenged his narrative of the Black Prince's later military career.

I would like to thank the many people who have encouraged my work, particularly Guilhem Pépin, whose own research on the Prince's administration in Aquitaine has brought important new source material into play and provided a corrective to some of the overly critical chronicle accounts. Professor Michael C. E. Jones's grasp of fourteenth-century political life in general, and the career of Bertrand du Guesclin in particular, has considerably assisted my own work, as have the major contributions to our understanding of the warfare of that period from Professors Clifford Rogers, Matthew Strickland and Kelly DeVries, alongside Dr Philip Morgan's study of war and society in medieval Cheshire. Sir Philip Preston has been a friend and supporter, and it has always been a pleasure to guide the battlefield of Crécy with him; Professor Andrew Ayton has shared his insights into that battle and late medieval military retinues in general. Richard Eales kindly gave me material on Gaston Fébus's castle at Pau and Orthez. Professor Carole Rawcliffe has discussed the Black Prince's illness with me; to Dr Ian Mortimer I am grateful for his enthusiasm and understanding of the reign of Edward III and late medieval society as a whole.

My book draws on the scholarship of many others, and among the acknowledgements in the Notes and Bibliography I am particularly grateful to Richard Barber, whose own biography of the Prince, collection of source material, and scholarship on Edward III and chivalry, have been enormously helpful, as has the work of Dr David Green on the Prince's life, its political context and especially the functioning of his retinue. For the broader background, the magisterial survey of the Hundred Years War by Jonathan Sumption has been an essential port of call, alongside the work of Professors Kenneth Fowler, Michael Prestwich and Mark Ormrod. For the Black Prince's career in Cheshire, and a broader examination of his life and motivation, I have found the books and articles of Professor Paul Booth of considerable value. I am grateful to everyone involved with the Gascon Rolls project (www.gasconrolls. org). Work on the Prince's life is progressing all the time, and it is a pleasure to thank Peter Hoskins, for his examination of the itineraries of the campaigns of 1355 and 1356, and Mollie Madden, for her research on their logistical operation.

A medieval biography needs to tell a story, and draw upon the chronicle and documentary sources to make that narrative come alive. I would like to thank the staff at The National Archives, and the Duchy of Cornwall Record Office, for permission to use John Henxteworth's Day Book. I have felt it particularly important to bring fresh French archival material into play for the latter part of the Prince's rule over Aquitaine, and for this I am grateful to the staff at the Archives Nationales and Bibliothèque Nationale in Paris, the departmental archives at Agen, Bordeaux, Cahors, Limoges and Pau, the municipal records at Cognac, Millau and Poitiers and, for the 1367 Nájera campaign, the Spanish material in the Archivo General de Navarra at Pamplona.

I would like to thank Anthony Cheetham, Richard Milbank, Ellen Parnavelas and everyone at Head of Zeus, and my agent Charlie Viney, for their encouragement and support as this book was written.

And finally, as history is all about making a connection with the past, I would like to thank Sarah Turner, the Collections Manager at Canterbury Cathedral, and Karen Brayshaw, the Librarian, for allowing me to view the Black Prince's funeral achievements and some of the manuscripts concerning his life from the cathedral archives. And I wish them well with the Canterbury Journey project, and its new plans to present the artefacts of one of our greatest warriors to the general public.

INDEX